T5-CAJ-610

GERMAN ELECTORAL POLITICS

Oxford University Press, Amen House, London E.C.4

GLASGOW NEW YORK TORONTO MELBOURNE WELLINGTON
BOMBAY CALCUTTA MADRAS KARACHI KUALA LUMPUR
CAPE TOWN IBADAN NAIROBI ACCRA

GERMAN ELECTORAL POLITICS

A STUDY OF THE 1957 CAMPAIGN

BY

U. W. KITZINGER

RESEARCH FELLOW OF NUFFIELD COLLEGE

OXFORD
AT THE CLARENDON PRESS
1960

PRINTED IN GREAT BRITAIN

TO G. K.

PREFACE

ELECTION studies have sometimes been divided into the 'classical', based primarily on official voting results, and the 'modern', which rely on opinion polls and up-to-date psychological and sociological techniques. The present essay is in that case best classified as being of the Neanderthal variety. It seeks to continue the series of Nuffield election studies which has now been carried on for twelve years.[1] Its author is innocent of statistical method and sociological techniques, spoke to only a small number of 'men in the street', and had the assistance of a few colleagues only for a few weeks.

It would thus be as pretentious to call this a scientific study as it would be to dignify it with the dubious term of 'psephology'. It is moreover not concerned with the substance of German politics but only with the manner in which political life was carried on for a few months of crucial West German history. It is and it sets out to be no more than one observer's very personal impressions corroborated or modified by the observations of colleagues with more detailed knowledge of the campaign in certain areas of the Federal Republic.

In a very real sense this book is the result of international collaboration. I am indebted to Mr. Dunstan Curtis, then acting Secretary-General of the Council of Europe, for the leave of absence which allowed me to undertake this work. To the Warden and Fellows of Nuffield College I owe not only my election to a Research Fellowship, but an extremely happy year spent in their midst. Both the Gladstone Professor of Government and Public Administration, Mr. Max Beloff, and the Censor of St. Catherine's, Mr. Alan

[1] The following Nuffield Studies of British General Elections had been published by April 1958: R. B. McCallum and A. Readman, *The British General Election of 1945*, Oxford University Press, London, 1947; H. G. Nicholas, *The British General Election of 1950*, Macmillan, London, 1951; D. E. Butler, *The British General Election of 1951*, Macmillan, London, 1952; and D. E. Butler, *The British General Election of 1955*, Macmillan, London, 1955. For Nuffield Studies on other European elections see Roy Pryce, *The Italian Local Elections of 1956*, Chatto & Windus, London, 1957, and the series of articles on 'The French Election of 1956' published in *Political Studies*, vol. iv, Nos. 2 and 3 of June and Oct. 1956, pp. 139–75 and 250–82. (Compare also the two articles on 'Electoral Studies and Democratic Theory', based on papers read to the Nuffield College Private Conference on European Electoral Studies held in March 1957, published in *Political Studies*, vol. vi, No. 1, Feb. 1958, pp. 1–15.)

Bullock, have been generous in the time they have devoted to giving me their invaluable criticism and advice. The Ford Foundation provided the funds with which I was able to travel for over three months in Germany, and the kind hospitality extended to my family by Dr. and Mrs. P. V. Lyon of the Canadian Embassy in Bonn and Professors Georges and Ernestine Goriely of the Universities of Brussels and Saarbrücken provided me with advance bases from which to foray. I have in addition benefited from discussions with both our hosts as well as with Mr. S. L. Wahrhaftig (formerly on the staff of the U.S. High Commissioner for Germany) and with the three British and German colleagues who contribute local studies to this volume.

One of these contributors, Mr. Klaus Schütz, is a member of the Berlin Institute of Political Studies, joint author of its survey of the 1953 election,[1] and now himself a representative of Berlin in the Bundestag. He placed his knowledge of people and affairs, his experience of election studies, and his impartial advice unstintingly at my disposal during all stages of this study. Dr. Wolfgang Hirsch-Weber of the same Institute very kindly also read and commented on the typescript. To the Director of the Berlin Institute, Professor Otto Stammer, my very special thanks are due for generously making possible this close co-operation between a German and a British institution.

Miss B. Ruhm von Oppen, who observed the election in Hamburg and translated the two local studies originally drafted in German, Dr. M. M. McGowan, and several other colleagues also commented on parts of the text. My Research Assistant Dr. Reinhard Lamer of Berlin and Nuffield provided me with much general help and was responsible for the tabulation of the data for Chapter IV. Mrs. Marcus Rolfe has given me very real encouragement by her enthusiasm in the onerous task of typing the whole book and dealing with the extensive correspondence involved in attempting to check its data.

My greatest debt of all, however, is due to those 200 Germans from Kiel to Munich and from Aachen to Wolfsburg—members of the Bundestag, civil servants, party officials, advertising agents,

[1] Wolfgang Hirsch-Weber and Klaus Schütz (in co-operation with Peter Schran, Martin Virchow *et al.* and with a preface by Otto Stammer), *Wähler und Gewählte — Eine Untersuchung der Bundestagswahlen 1953* (vol. vii of the series of the Institute of Political Studies), Vahlen, Berlin and Frankfurt, 1957. For a study by the same Institute of the Berlin municipal election of 1950 see Stephanie Müncke (edited and introduced by Dr. A. R. L. Gurland), *Wahlkampf und Machtverschiebung — Geschichte und Analyse der Berliner Wahlen vom Dezember 1950* (vol. i of the series of the Institute of Political Studies), Duncker & Humblot, Berlin, 1952.

church leaders, trade unionists, and representatives of trade and professional associations—who spared me so much of their time in the thick of the election. It would be invidious to single out any of them for special mention, the more so as some of those who were of the greatest assistance do not wish to be named. But my warm thanks are due to Mr. Johannes Gross of the CDU, Mr. Fritz Heine of the SPD, and Mr. Karl-Hermann Flach of the FDP, whose doors were open to me for one visit after another.

Yet, even given all such help, one cannot write a study of this kind without encountering certain difficulties. In the arrangement of my material I have attempted to offer the reader some variety of fare rather than follow the dictates of a stricter logic. Footnotes on sources have been restricted to a minimum: ephemeral election literature unlikely to be available outside specialized archives and declarations to be found in all the major newspapers reporting on the day concerned are quoted without reference. The campaign chapters have been submitted to all the parties in question and have greatly benefited from their comments—though I have no illusions that any party would wish to identify itself with my view of its campaign. Nevertheless some errors are almost bound to have crept into the text particularly on those subjects which are surrounded by an aura of professional secrecy. Where such mistakes and inadequacies of fact and interpretation subsist the responsibility for them, needless to say, lies with myself alone.

CONTENTS

LOCAL STUDIES

LIST OF TABLES

TABULATIONS IN THE TEXT

LIST OF FIGURES

LIST OF PLATES

(*Between pp.* 112 *and* 113)

Plates I *b* and *c* by courtesy of the Federal Press and Information Office, Bonn; Plates II*a*, III *c*, *d*, and *f* by courtesy of J. H. Darchinger, Bonn; Plate IV*a* by courtesy of *Telegraf* / Bankhardt, Berlin; Plate IV*b* by courtesy of Presse Photo Aktuell, Saarbrücken; Plate IV*c* by courtesy of the Deutsche Presse Agentur, Frankfurt; other plates by courtesy of the parties concerned.

THE FEDERAL REPUBLIC OF GERMANY
0 50 100 Miles
Land capitals underlined = Mainz
DENMARK
SWEDEN
BALTIC SEA
NORTH SEA
Flensburg
SCHLESWIG-
Kiel
HOLSTEIN
HAMBURG
Buxtehude
Elbe
Oldenburg
BREMEN
Lüneburg
Heath
LOWER SAXONY
NETHERLANDS
GERMAN
DEMOCRATIC
REPUBLIC
BERLIN
Diepholz
Wolfsburg
Hanover
Braunschweig
Osnabrück
Greven
Münster
Bielefeld
NORTH-RHINE
Ahlen
Dortmund
Paderborn
Essen
Bochum
Ruhr
Göttingen
Kassel
Düsseldorf
Neviges
Remscheid
WESTPHALIA
Leipzig
Jülich
Cologne
Düren
Aachen
Bonn
Bad Godesberg
Hersfeld
Gera
BELG
Koblenz
HESSE
Wiesbaden
Frankfurt
RHINELAND-
Mainz
PALATINATE
LUX
Main
Franconia
CZECHO-
SLOVAKIA
Bamberg
St. Wendel
SAAR
Mannheim
Saarbrücken
Heidelberg
Nuremberg
Rhine
Karlsruhe
BADEN-
BAVARIA
Pforzheim
Stuttgart
WÜRTTEMBERG
Baden
Danube
Pfarrkirchen
Freising
Erding
Munich
Altötting
Upper Bavaria
Iller
FRANCE
Allensbach
Traunstein
SWITZERLAND
AUSTRIA
Berchtesgaden
M.E.P.

I

INTRODUCTION

THE history of Germany over the last hundred years has been a series of bewildering upheavals. A collection of kingdoms and principalities united only in 1871, she had become a world power by 1914. Defeated by the Allies in the first world war, she was stripped of her colonies, her frontiers were pushed back in Europe, and her most important industrial centres occupied by foreign troops. Twenty years later she was more powerful than ever: she conquered all Europe from the Black Sea and the Pyrenees to the Arctic Circle and resisted the combined war potential of the United States, the Commonwealth, and Soviet Russia. By 1945 she had collapsed for the second time: a twelfth of her population had been killed, 9 million were driven out of the territories taken over by Poland and Russia, her political system was destroyed, and her former leaders executed as criminals against humanity. Yet only twelve years later, at the time of the election which this book sets out to describe, Western Germany had achieved a political stability and a rate of economic progress that were the envy of her victorious neighbours.

Certainly she was favoured by factors beyond her control. Opposition speakers never tired of insisting that she owed this third swift rise in her fortunes to the deepening division of the world. Eighteen million Germans were forced to take a different road. Germany, like Korea, was divided by the thin deep line that separates the domains of the two great power blocks: and while thousands fled westward every week across the zonal frontier, two hostile German armies faced each other on key squares in the game of world strategy.

What then was the reaction of West Germans to the turbulent events of their recent history? For five years they had been taught to think of war as an instrument of national renewal; then for five years they fought, first victoriously and afterwards on to complete disaster; for the next five years out of their own bitter experience they embraced pacific ideals; and now they were again to be armed by the same victors who had made the permanent demilitarization of Germany one of their principal war aims and had lectured them on the wickedness of war. It was hardly surprising that after so much re-education they should turn sceptical of any great political doctrines. National Socialist idealism had placed the power and honour of nation and race high above private selfishness and material comfort; but political adventure and national exhilaration had resulted only in national and personal disaster. The capacity for corporate enthusiasm was exhausted, emotional disillusionment set in, and Germans desired above all to withdraw from world politics and retire to their private lives.

After years wasted in the service of the nation followed by the hunger and cold of the first post-war winters, the desire for personal survival was uppermost in most Germans' minds. They wanted to rebuild a civilized existence for themselves, to find a job and to 'get on'. While after 1918 a people had felt betrayed and humiliated, after 1945 national consciousness was bankrupt, families felt trapped in misfortune, and individuals devoted their energies to immediate practical problems rather than great ideological and political questions. As one of the most acute observers of the post-war Republic put it:

> For thirty-five years, half a life-span, with not a pause but that of the middle twenties, Germany had kept herself and the world breathless; the volcano had hurled out eruption after eruption. It was now burnt out, the revolutionary fire grown cold, all passion spent; and one longed for 'a little happiness'.[1]

This desire for security, this preoccupation with the material, this abandonment of ideology spread far through German society. It is a strange contrast to the German universities of earlier epochs that an institute of public opinion regarded as a not untypical answer to the question 'What two books have meant most to you?' the reply of a student: 'Mother's cookery book and father's cheque book, I think.'[2]

The cookery and cheque books, irrelevant as they had been in the first post-war years, now took on a powerful significance. The Germans 'bettered themselves' and as a result of their individual efforts so did the economy as a whole. The stimulus of immediate material necessities and the new ethic of individual work which came to replace that of collective heroism produced an intense effort from the population. The Government in which Professor Ludwig Erhard held the economic portfolio contributed a neo-liberal economic policy and an austere social policy which, in their emphasis on

[1] Fritz Rene Allemann, *Bonn is nicht Weimar*, Kiepenheuer und Witsch, Cologne and Berlin, 1956, p. 108.

[2] Quoted by Robert d'Harcourt, *L'Allemagne d'Adenauer*, Flammarion, Paris, 1958, p. 246.

immediate concrete achievements, matched the whole 'post-revolutionary mentality' of Western Germany. But two further factors were essential ingredients in the misnamed 'economic miracle': first Marshall Aid, and then the Korean export boom; both were again not unconnected with the new division of the world. The fantastic rise in the national product from the deceptively low levels of the early post-war years is sufficiently familiar to need no further discussion;[1] it is at least as remarkable that this spectacular progress was kept up thereafter and that further big strides were taken even after 1953.[2] By 1957 Western Germany had more than doubled her gross national product of 1936 and, in spite of the greatly increased population, the gross national product per head had risen to half as much again as that pre-war level. Nearly 2 million new passenger cars registered since the beginning of 1953 and 3½ million holidays in Italy during the single summer of the election may give an idea of the new standard of living of the citizens of the Federal Republic.

Such rapid progress from acute misery to a prosperity never known before naturally served to consolidate the political structure within which it took place. In 1949 the population of the three Western zones of occupation was prepared to accept the Federal Republic as a system of self-determination and to participate at least to the extent of casting their votes. But they had no particular enthusiasm for a state which covered only half the nation and which was set up by three of the victorious Allies obviously on their own conditions. The republican sentiments expressed by the new anthem 'Unity and Law and Freedom' (the third verse of *Deutschland, Deutschland über Alles*), the black, red, and gold colours of the abortive 1848 revolution and of the unsuccessful Weimar Republic, and a harmlessly octagonal federal eagle were not a symbolism calculated to arouse new national feelings.

But with time the new Republic grew some roots. Emotional exhaustion, like economic progress, was a natural ally of stable government. First-hand experience of the Soviet Union and of victorious Russian troops inside Germany cut the ground from under the feet of the West German Communist Party, and it was too soon

[1] Compare Henry C. Wallich, *Mainsprings of the German Revival*, Yale, New Haven, 1955.

[2] Between 1953 and 1957 the volume of the gross national product of Western Germany rose by 34 per cent. (as against 11 per cent. in the United Kingdom), industrial production by 46 per cent. (as against 14 per cent.), wages by 53 per cent., but prices only by 7 per cent. (as against wages by 26 per cent., prices by 16 per cent. in the United Kingdom) and personal consumption rose by a third (as against a tenth in Britain). (O.E.E.C. Statistical Bulletins, *General Statistics*, Paris, 1958, No. 4, pp. 95–96, 130–1, and 151–2.)

after the defeat for the extreme right to create an opposition to the State at the other end of the political spectrum. The Federal Republic thus formed a complete contrast to that of Weimar. The 'unconditional surrender' of the previous régime and the late foundation of the new Republic saved it from being associated in German consciousness with national defeat; they allowed it on the contrary to reap the credit for the recovery of national status and equality. Instead of post-war distress, inflation, and finally 6 million unemployed, the new Republic harvested the political benefit of full employment and surging prosperity. And instead of being forced to harbour enemies within its own fabric in the shape of strong parties opposing not simply each others' policies but the whole constitutional system as such, the new Republic and the rules of its game were accepted by all important parties and their differences were fought out within it.

The basic reasons for the smooth running of the Bonn Republic must thus be sought in fundamental psychological, economic, and external political causes. But over and above such broad essentials, the new order was shaped by two almost 'accidental' domestic factors: the provisions of the new constitution, and the crystallization of a slightly authoritarian democracy round the person of Dr. Konrad Adenauer, who imposed his individual style on West German political life. To permit an understanding of the 1957 election this sketch of West German moods must thus be supplemented by an outline of the constitutional framework within which political life took place and by a brief description of the main personalities and events which shaped the first eight years of the Second German Republic.[1]

The Basic Law

It was not until after the dialogue on German problems with Soviet Russia had clearly broken down that the Anglo-Saxon Powers, unwilling to see a political and economic vacuum in the heart of Europe, decided to grant self-government to their own zones of occupation and that the French were forced to follow suit. Local and Land institutions were by then firmly established and

[1] For other interpretations of post-war Western Germany compare: Norbert Muhlen, *The Return of Germany*, Regnery, Chicago, 1953; Alfred Grosser, *Western Germany from Defeat to Rearmament*, Allen and Unwin, London, 1955; Richard Hiscocks, *Democracy in Western Germany*, Oxford University Press, London, 1957; and Brian Connell, *Watcher on the Rhine*, Weidenfeld and Nicolson, London, 1957. An American edition of Alfred Grosser, *La Democratie de Bonn*, Armand Colin, Paris, 1958, has also been promised.

representatives of the Land Parliaments met in 1948 to elaborate the Basic Law of the Federal Republic of Germany.[1] In this provisional federation the Länder retained sole responsibility in religious and educational matters and certain powers concurrent with those of the Federation particularly in the economic and social fields. Each elects its own legislature, the Landtag, every four years and each is governed by a Land cabinet headed by a Minister-President.[2]

The head of the Federal Republic is the Federal President, elected for not more than two consecutive five-year terms; Professor Theodor Heuss of the Free Democratic Party, elected in 1949, was re-elected in 1954. The federal legislature consists of two chambers, the Bundesrat (Federal Council) as the upper, the Bundestag (Federal Diet) as the lower house. The upper house has certain veto powers over legislation and, like the lower house, cannot pass amendments to the Basic Law by less than a two-thirds majority. Since the Bundesrat is composed of representatives of the Land governments with three to five members (according to the size of the Land) voting as a block, the complexion of the Land governments can have a direct influence on federal affairs.

The lower house, the Bundestag, is elected every four years and can be dissolved only in special circumstances. It is to this house that the Federal Chancellor is responsible. But in order to avoid cabinet crises of the type known in the Weimar Republic and in the third and fourth French Republics, article 67 of the Basic Law lays down that: 'The Bundestag may express its lack of confidence in the Federal Chancellor only by electing a successor with the majority of its members and submitting a request to the Federal President for the dismissal of the Federal Chancellor.' By however small a majority he may originally have been elected, once in office a Federal Chancellor is thus in a strong position. He selects and dismisses his ministers and can allow whole Government parties to pass over to the Opposition without thereby affecting his Government—provided only that the Opposition does not become strong enough to elect a successor to himself.

[1] The amalgamation of three of the eleven original Länder into the Land Baden-Württemberg in 1953 reduced the number to nine, but the political integration of the Saar on 1 Jan. 1957 brought it up again to ten. West Berlin is not formally a part of the Federal Republic and its electorate did not go to the polls in 1957. For an account of the drafting of the Basic Law published as the present study was going to press see John Ford Golay, *The Founding of the Federal Republic of Germany*, University of Chicago Press, Chicago, 1958.

[2] In the case of the two city states of Hamburg and Bremen, the *Bürgerschaft* is the legislature, the Senate its cabinet, and the Mayor the responsible head of the Land Executive.

The First Two Bundestag Elections

The first federal election was held in August 1949. Two parties emerged from it with roughly a third of Bundestag seats each: the Christian Democratic Union (CDU) with its Bavarian sister party, the Christian Social Union (CSU) as the one, and the Social Democratic Party (SPD) as the other. Eight other parties also secured representation in the Bundestag.[1]

TABLE I

The Voting in Bundestag Elections

	1949	*1953*	*1957*
A. *The electorate and the turnout*			
1. Registered electors (million)	31·2	33·1	35·4
2. Percentage turnout	79%	86%	88%
3. Invalid (list) votes as percentage of ballot papers cast	3%	3%	4%
4. Valid (list) votes cast (million) . .	23·7	27·6	29·9
B. *Party strengths as a percentage of valid (list) votes cast*	%	%	%
1. CDU/CSU Christian Democrats: Adenauer	31	45	50
2. SPD Social Democrats: Schumacher, then Ollenhauer . . .	29	29	32
3. FDP Free Democrats: Heuss, Blücher, Dehler, then Maier . . .	12	10	8
4. KPD Communists: Reimann . .	6	2	..
5. DP German Party: Hellwege . .	4	3	3
6. BP Bavarian Party } 1957 Federalist	4	2	} 1
7. Z Centre Party } Union	3	1	
8. WAV Economic Reconstruction League	3	..	..
9. DRP German Reich Party . . .	2	1	1
10. SSW South Schleswig Voters' League	0	0	0
11. GB/BHE Refugees' Party . . .	..	5·9	4·6
12. Others (including Independents) .	6	2	1
	100	100	100

The Christian Democrats based themselves largely on the tradition of the Centre Party of the second Empire and the Weimar Republic, but its founders came from a variety of other parties as well—and some from no parties at all. They were thus well placed

[1] For the results of the first three Bundestag elections see Tables I and II, pp. 6–7. For brevity's sake the CDU and CSU are usually referred to simply as the CDU, and in this study the sister party is included in the meaning unless the reverse is explicitly stated or clearly implied.

to extend the new party's domain beyond the 'tower of isolation' within Catholicism inside which the old Centre Party had been confined. The exclusion of Middle and Eastern Germany[1] had reduced the ratio of Protestants to Catholics from two-thirds to little more than one-half, so that a Catholic party could in any case have

TABLE II

Seats won in Bundestag Elections
(excluding Berlin seats)

	1949	*1953*	*1957*
A. *Total number of seats*			
1. Constituency seats	242	242	247
2. Planned list seats	158	242	247
3. Retained excess seats*	2	3	3
4. Total	402	487	497
B. *Party strengths resulting from the election*			
1. CDU/CSU Christian Democrats	139	244	270
2. SPD Social Democrats	131	151	169
3. FDP Free Democrats	52	48	41
4. KPD Communists	15	..	..
5. DP German Party	17	15	17
6. BP Bavarian Party } 1957 Federalist	17	..	} ..
7. Z Centre Party } Union	10	2	
8. WAV Economic Reconstruction League	12	..	..
9. DRP German Reich Party	5	..	..
10. SSW South Schleswig Voters' League	1	..	..
11. GB/BHE Refugees' Party	..	27	..
12. Independents	3	..	..
	402	487	497

* See below, Chapter II, pp. 27–28.

been in a stronger position in the Federal than in the Weimar Republic. But the founders of the CDU from the very start set out to make the new organization an all-embracing Christian popular party in which Protestants too should play their full part. The founders of the CDU demanded that Liberals should abandon the notion that religion and politics could coexist unrelated to each other; that Protestants should abandon their suspicion of political Catholicism; and that former adherents of the Centre should

[1] It is West German practice to refer to what was the Russian zone of occupation and became the German Democratic Republic (DDR) as Middle Germany, reserving the term Eastern Germany for the territories beyond the Oder–Neisse line which are under Russian and Polish administration.

sacrifice the historic name and tradition for a new and wider concept. At home the party began with a programme of moderate socialism; in foreign affairs it stressed the bankruptcy of the national ideal and aimed at realizing the resolve expressed in the preamble to the Basic Law: that the German people should 'serve world peace as an equal member in a united Europe'.[1]

If the Christian Democrats had set up an essentially new party, the Social Democrats prided themselves on their old tradition. By 1948 they had reached a membership figure of 900,000 (as against the Christian Democrats' 200,000 or so) and rebuilt the strong party machine which had run the party until 1933 and whose executive had held together in exile thereafter.[2] But they were faced with serious problems. Through the division of Germany and the formation of the Socialist Unity Party in the Russian zone they had lost the domains of their former strength, above all in the industrial areas of Protestant Middle Germany: and in the West the CDU as a Christian unity party was becoming a dangerous rival. Kurt Schumacher, the SPD's brilliant party leader, was all the more determined for the party to emerge from that ghetto of a third of votes within which the SPD had been confined since 1920, and to engage in battle with the Christian Democrats for the no man's land between them.[3]

From the experience of the Weimar Republic Schumacher drew the lesson that Socialists must not be outdone in national feeling by the right. As a man who had undergone horrible suffering in the concentration camps of the National Socialist régime he could speak out against the Occupying Powers with a violence that few other responsible politicians could afford. His first stand in 1945 was an outright refusal to co-operate with the Communists. Thereafter he opposed every step that seemed to consolidate the division of Germany. He may have succeeded in stealing the nationalists' clothes: but they were not only out of fashion, but an actual encumbrance amid the realities of a divided post-war world.

Between Schumacher and the emergent leader of the Christian

[1] Compare, for example, the speech by Freiherr von Gumppenberg at the founder meeting of the Rhineland CDU on 2 Sept. 1945 reported in H. G. Wieck, *Die Entstehung der CDU und die Wiedergründung des Zentrums im Jahre 1945*, Droste, Düsseldorf, 1953.

[2] Compare Lewis J. Edinger, *German Exile Politics, the Social Democratic Executive in the Nazi Era*, University of California, Berkeley, 1956.

[3] The SPD and Communists together had polled 40 per cent. of all German votes in 1918, but in the areas now included in the Federal Republic the combined vote for both parties still lay well below that figure, the vote for the SPD below 30 per cent.

Democrats, Dr. Konrad Adenauer, there developed a deep animosity in the years before 1949 which made coalition between the two forces that had formed the mainstay of the Weimar Republic, political Catholicism and socialism, impossible even at the outset of the new Republic. In September 1949 Adenauer was elected as first Chancellor of the Federal Republic by a margin of one vote—his own.[1] He formed a government in which the Free Democrats (FDP) and the German Party (DP), which described themselves as liberal and as conservative respectively, occupied five of the thirteen cabinet seats.

The economic resurgence of Western Germany, Adenauer's policy of friendship with the West, and the process of European integration brought with them a recovery of German prestige, and Adenauer's personality impressed itself on the electorate no less than on the outside world. In the elections to the second Bundestag, held in 1953, the votes polled by the Christian Democrats rose from 7 to 12 million and made the CDU the first party in history to obtain an absolute majority in a German legislature.[2] Adenauer was triumphantly confirmed in his tenure of office for a second term.

While it eliminated several minor parties from the Bundestag, the second federal election also brought a new party into federal politics: the 'All-German Block/League of the Homeless and those Deprived of their Rights' (*Gesamtdeutscher Block—Bund der Heimatvertriebenen und Entrechteten*), commonly referred to as the BHE. Founded in 1950 in Schleswig-Holstein it had spread rapidly through the Federal Republic and achieved substantial successes in Land elections. It claimed to speak above all for the expellees from the Sudeten lands and the territories under Russian and Polish administration beyond the Oder–Neisse line and to champion their social and political demands.[3]

[1] An account of Adenauer's earlier career is given in Paul Weymar, *Konrad Adenauer, the Authorised Biography*, adapted and translated from the German by Peter de Mendelssohn, André Deutsch, London, 1957.

[2] For an account in English of the 1953 election see James K. Pollock *et al.*, *German Democracy at Work*, University of Michigan Press, Michigan, 1955. A detailed analysis is presented by Hirsch-Weber and Schütz, op. cit.

[3] After a lengthy controversy, German legislation and statistics distinguished between refugees (*Flüchtlinge*) from the territory of the Democratic Republic on the one hand, and expellees (*Vertriebene*) from the areas which lie to the east and south of the Democratic Republic. The expellees argued that they did not flee, but were expelled from their homelands, which, in the case of the *Volksdeutsche* (ethnic Germans) lay outside German territory even in 1939. To avoid the appearance of pedantry, the word 'refugees' is here also used in the technical sense of expellees, refugees from the Democratic Republic being expressly referred to as such.

By 1957 the Federal Republic contained some 9 million such refugees, and since in addition nearly 3 million people had fled to the Federal Republic from the Democratic Republic, 23 per cent. of the population consisted of refugees of both kinds. While their arrival imposed a heavy social burden on the Federal Republic, it was not an unmixed economic disadvantage, for many of the refugees were skilled, enterprising, and mobile. Politically they formed a bulwark against Communism which their past experiences led them to detest; but it was feared that they might provide a reservoir of votes for parties that would combine social radicalism with a foreign policy prepared to take large risks to win back the homes they had left behind in the East.

For this reason the occupying forces had refused to license any refugee party in the early West German elections. By 1953 Catholic refugees and former socialist refugees had largely become supporters of the established parties at least where the federal (as distinct from Land) elections were concerned. Millions of refugees had been caught up into the fast growing economy and had been absorbed into West German society. Moreover, the social legislation of the Federal Republic had by then recognized a substantial part of the claims of the uprooted, and in consequence they in turn had acquired a direct stake in the new system and no interest in internal or external instability.

The BHE thus polled only 1·6 million votes and obtained only twenty-seven seats in the second Bundestag election. Its comparative moderation was enhanced by the decision of the Chancellor to take two of its leaders into his second cabinet which thus included four parties in all. The Social Democrats—led, after Schumacher's death in 1952, by Erich Ollenhauer—were left isolated as the only Opposition party in the Bundestag, though they carried their share of executive responsibility in the new Republic by participating and in some cases leading the coalition governments of various Länder.

Adenauer's Second Term

The second Adenauer Government continued and developed the policy of the first. At home it consolidated what Erhard called a 'social market economy' of free enterprise, guided mainly through fiscal and monetary policies and tempered by social legislation. Incomes were unequal to a degree that post-war Britain would not have tolerated, and the power of industrial combinations grew rapidly in step with the pace of capital accumulation. But the bulk of the citizens of the Federal Republic saw their real incomes rise dramatically, and were content.

Into this dynamic equilibrium at home the only hotly contested issue was introduced by the exigencies of foreign affairs. Already at the time of the Korean crisis in 1950 the American military authorities had demanded twelve German divisions. Adenauer's policy of alliance with the West and his desire for European economic and political integration facilitated the acceptance of this demand by the other Western allies. The Social Democrats strenuously opposed the rearmament of a divided Germany, and the authors of the Basic Law had, by implication, banned conscription as unconstitutional. But the CDU's coalition with the Free Democrats, the German Party, and the BHE narrowly assured the two-thirds majority required to amend the Basic Law, and in 1954 the SPD's opposition to rearmament was outvoted. The attempt to build a European Defence Community suffered shipwreck in the French National Assembly, but on 5 May 1955—ten years to the day after 'unconditional surrender'—the Western powers recognized the sovereignty of the Federal Republic, made it a member of the North Atlantic Treaty Organization, and committed it to establishing new German armed forces.

It might at first sight seem normal that the German 'left' should thus oppose rearmament, the 'right' be in its favour. But at least in part this normalization of their respective positions was the result of a curious double reversal of roles. The Social Democrats had come to emphasize the national concept, while some of the business and middle-class elements more traditionally on the 'right' had come to support the surrender of national sovereignty to European institutions. When the problem of rearmament began to be posed, it had to be seen against the background of the division of Germany and the recognition that national unity could be restored only by negotiation. If the Social Democrats were opposed to rearmament, it was not merely out of a certain traditional internationalism, but even more because of their concern for the unity and integrity of the German nation. And if the traditional 'right' was in favour of rearmament, it was not merely out of anti-communist considerations but also to offer an irksome sacrifice at the shrine of that European idea which was to supersede the national concept.

Once the crucial votes had been taken and the Basic Law amended to make possible the rearmament which its authors had hoped to ban for ever, the need for a broadly based government to secure a two-thirds majority became less imperative. At the same time the disadvantages of reaching agreement in a cabinet composed of representatives of four different parties became more apparent, particularly as acute tensions developed both within the BHE and among the Free Democrats. In fact within twelve months two of the four Government parties had passed over into opposition.

The BHE split in the summer of 1955, and when the Chancellor retained the two ministers of the seceding group in his Cabinet, the rump of the party withdrew its support for the Government; most of the seceding group eventually joined the CDU.

More important politically was the split within the Free Democratic Party, though this split, too, left the existence and the personnel of the Cabinet intact. The Free Democrats claimed the heritage of German liberalism, and (very much in accordance with this tradition) emphasized the importance of national unity just as much as what would elsewhere be considered general liberal principles. Its membership had originally been drawn from the politically liberal middle-class strata of whom the Federal President was himself a representative, but in the early years of the Federal Republic economically liberal elements farther to the political 'right' joined the party and began to exercise a growing influence within it. In 1952 the Free Democrats operated with two alternative programmes, the 'Liberal Manifesto' and the 'German Programme', but the problem of German unity preoccupied the more liberal as well as the more national sections of the party.

The FDP joined the Chancellor's second cabinet, but it was not completely happy about doing so. Particularly after the amendments to the Basic Law had been passed it felt faced by the alternative of subordination to the Chancellor or opposition to him. When the CDU envisaged the 'Europeanization' of the Saar in 1954 and 1955, the Free Democrats' loyalty was strained to its limits. Their party leader Dr. Thomas Dehler (who had been Adenauer's first Minister of Justice) criticized the Chancellor heavily on the grounds that his European policy would separate the Saar permanently from Germany and that his whole foreign policy only made German reunification all the more difficult. The CDU's plans to amend the electoral law in a way which would have cut the Free Democrats' representation by about one-half[1] had a certain restraining influence on the party at first, but only increased its mounting irritation with the Chancellor.

Such was the position when in January and February 1956 a small group of Free Democrats in Düsseldorf—sometimes called the 'Young Turks'—counter-attacked against the Chancellor: they withdrew the FDP's support for the North-Rhine Westphalian

[1] See Chapter II, pp. 25–26.

Cabinet and joined a Land coalition with the Social Democrats instead. For the first time since its existence began, North-Rhine Westphalia (which contains nearly a third of the German electorate and more than a third of its industry, capital, and national income) was no longer governed by Minister-President Karl Arnold of the CDU.

But the importance of the change of government in Düsseldorf did not lie in Land politics. This was not the first time that Free Democrats had formed a Land government with Social Democrats and other parties and had left the CDU in opposition: almost every possible permutation of party coalitions had been tried at some time in one or other Land of the Federal Republic.[1] The startling new element brought into West German politics by this 'Düsseldorf revolt' was the deliberate attempt to call in Land politics to redress the balance of federal power. The change of government in Düsseldorf was designed to produce an ominous shift in the political balance in the Bundesrat, where the Chancellor lost his two-thirds majority—and the Free Democrats threatened to provoke similar changes of government in other Länder. By the time the 'Düsseldorf revolt' actually took place the CDU had abandoned its plans for electoral reform; but the Free Democrats proceeded with their gesture of defiance, and the possibility that they might, in the third

[1] At the time of the 1957 election the FDP was a pivot represented in nine of the ten Land Governments; only Bremen and the Saar had the same type of Government coalition. In the following table M stands for the Minister-President, p for participation in the Government: since the Länder are here listed for the first time, figures for their population in 1957 are also given.

	Population (million)	*CDU*	*SPD*	*FDP*	*BHE*	*German Party*	*Others*
Schleswig-Holstein	2·3	M	..	p	p	..	..
Hamburg	1·8	M	..	p	..	p	..
Lower Saxony	6·5	p	..	p	p	M	..
Bremen	0·7	M	p	p	..	..	..
North-Rhine Westphalia	15·0	..	M	p	..	..	Centre
Hesse	4·6	..	M	..	p	..	..
Rhineland-Palatinate	3·3	M	..	p	..	..	..
Baden-Württemberg	7·3	M	p	p	p	..	..
Bavaria	9·2	..	M	p	p	..	Bavarian Party
Saar	1·0	M	p	p	..	..	..
Total	51·5	7	6	9	5	2	2

Bundestag, make a similar alliance with the Social Democrats against the Christian Democrats opened up new perspectives for Germany's foreign policy as well.

This initiative of the 'Young Turks' led to bitter dissension within the FDP. Towards the end of February 1956 sixteen members of the Bundestag left the party in protest against the ambivalent leadership of Dr. Dehler, who had first advised against the change of government in Düsseldorf but then condoned it. Among these sixteen were all four Free Democratic ministers. As in the case of the two ministers of the BHE, Adenauer retained them in his cabinet; in due course they founded a separate 'Free People's Party' (*Freie Volkspartei*—FVP) of their own. The Free Democrats themselves went into opposition and the Düsseldorf group and those who thought like them increasingly gained control of the federal party machine. By the turn of the year they secured a majority within the party congress against Dehler, who was too mercurial and impulsive for their purposes. In January 1957 the former Minister-President of Baden-Württemberg, Reinhold Maier, was brought out of political semi-retirement: Maier was regarded as an old-fashioned liberal of the South-West German tradition, he was a bitter personal opponent of the Chancellor, and moreover he was thought of as a clever tactician whose leadership would help the party in the country and the 'Young Turks' within the party itself.

It is thus not altogether easy to characterize the parties of the Federal Republic in terms of the classical scale of 'right' to 'left'. In the second Bundestag the order of seating was German Party, Free Democrats, Christian Democrats, BHE, and Social Democrats. Thus at the end of the second legislative period the Free Democrats, violently in opposition to the Government, sat between the two Government parties, while the Social Democrats sitting on the left stressed national concerns more than the Christian Democrats did in the centre. If opposition to military force is traditionally regarded as a characteristic of the left it is worth noting that some of the most violent protests against the equipment of the federal forces with atomic weapons came from the more right-wing Free Democrats for much the same reasons as those which actuated the SPD. The Social Democrats, the party that insisted on the dangers of forgetting the crimes of the National Socialist era, were less ready to ally with the Christian Democrats, some of whose leaders had records of opposition to that régime, than with the Free Democrats who openly wooed the votes and did not discourage the candidatures of former National Socialists. The Free Democrats in their turn, champions of free enterprise and opponents of the welfare state, were preparing for the possibility of a coalition with the 'left' against the 'centre' and had already fired the warning shot against the Christian Democrats by their alliance with the SPD in Düsseldorf.

The year 1956 was in fact a poor one for the Chancellor and the CDU, particularly when compared with 1955. In the summer of 1955 Adenauer had flown to Moscow and secured the release of nearly 10,000 German prisoners of war still held in Russian hands. But in the autumn of 1955 he fell ill, his sure touch seemed to be failing in domestic affairs and rearmament was a far from popular measure. The evolution of events in Russia and Eastern Europe did not fit into the picture of Soviet Communism as it had been presented to the German public, and complaints became widespread that the Chancellor was too inflexible to exploit the opportunities presented by the changed situation for some step forward towards the reunification of Germany.

By August 1956 the institutes of public opinion were publishing the most discouraging results for the CDU ever known. Within twelve months the percentage of the population favourable to the Chancellor's policies had dropped from 59 to 37 per cent. and according to the poll of July 1956 only 34 per cent. of the population wanted him to remain Chancellor for another four years, while 44 per cent. thought he should hand over to someone else.[1]

Those who doubted the validity of such public opinion polls saw concrete evidence in the local government elections held in five Länder in October and November 1956. They were fought in large part on federal issues—rearmament and social policy in particular—and the Social Democrats could record startling advances. In four Länder containing well over half of the total electorate their share of the poll rose from 34 per cent. in the local elections of 1952 (and 30 per cent. in the second Bundestag election) to 41 per cent. in the local elections of 1956.[2] The results in Baden-Württemberg revealed an equally remarkable success for the Social Democrats, who suddenly appeared to be expanding well beyond their usual third of votes. The auguries taken ten months before the probable date of the Bundestag election were thus far from favourable to the CDU.

It was not until the world events of November and December of that year—above all after the Russian intervention in Hungary—that the CDU's fortunes began to rise again. The 'Geneva spirit'

[1] Elisabeth Noelle and Erich Peter Neumann, *Jahrbuch der Öffentlichen Meinung 1957*, Demoskopie, Allensbach, 1957, pp. 182–3 and 262–3. (The same institute published a forecast of the 1957 election result which was accurate to the nearest percentage point for both the CDU and the SPD.)

[2] The turnout had been 77 per cent. in 1952 and 1956, 87 per cent. in 1953.

had evaporated, and the 'cold war' seemed on the brink of turning hot. German rearmament now appeared to be a vital necessity and the Chancellor's prestige rose as that of a man who had been right after all. For the first time for months the CDU pulled ahead of the SPD in the opinion polls and thereafter it was never to fall very far behind again. The events of November 1956 thus marked a turning-point in German domestic politics also and it was really from that moment that the election campaign began.

II

THE ELECTORAL LAW

THE West German electoral law is an attempt to get the best of all possible worlds: and in a surprising measure it succeeds. It is designed to meet the chief objections levied both against single-member constituencies and against proportional representation; and it squares the circle by a system of 'personalized P.R.'.

The Evolution of the System

In the second Empire from 1871 to 1918 the members of the Reichstag were elected in single-member constituencies by absolute majorities; these absolute majorities were obtained, if necessary, in a second ballot after the elimination of all but the two candidates who had emerged at the top of the first. In the Weimar Republic, on the other hand, the Reichstag was elected by a strictly proportional system of party lists on which the voter could not alter the order of the candidates; every 60,000 votes cast for a party qualified it for a seat.

When the Parliamentary Council drew up the Basic Law of the Federal Republic in 1948–9 the Christian Democrats pleaded for a 'British' system of relative majorities in single-member constituencies, most of the other parties (notably the Social Democrats, though they did not yet know how much the 'British' system would have handicapped them) demanded proportional representation as a fairer method. The electoral system was not enshrined in the Basic Law; Article 38 laid down no more than that:

(1) Representatives to the German Bundestag are elected by the people in universal, direct, free, equal and secret elections. They are representatives of the whole people, not bound by orders and instructions and subject only to their conscience.

(2) Any person who has reached the age of 21 years is entitled to vote, and any person who has reached the age of 25 years may stand for election.

(3) Details are determined by federal law.

The Parliamentary Council also decided that it would confine itself to drafting a law for the election of the first Bundestag only; this Bundestag could then itself pass a law to govern the election of its successor.[1] The military governors—who at one stage questioned the right of the Parliamentary Council to draw up an electoral law at all—modified the draft adopted by the Parliamentary Council in several respects, partly at the request of the Ministers-President of the Länder. As finally proclaimed, the solution was one broadly foreshadowed in various Land electoral laws passed after 1945.[2] It looked complex, but it was in fact based on three very simple considerations:

Firstly, to establish a personal link between a locality and a member of the Bundestag, three-fifths of the members were to be elected by a relative majority in single-member constituencies.

Secondly, to overcome the grossly unrepresentative composition of the Bundestag which would in Western Germany have resulted from the exclusive application of such a purely 'British' system of relative majority election, the remaining seats were to be filled from party lists in such a way as to give parties an overall proportional representation (taking constituency and list members together) on each Land delegation to the Bundestag.

Thirdly, to prevent a recurrence of the profusion of splinter parties which was thought to have been one of the weaknesses of the Reichstag in the Weimar Republic, no party was to be thus proportionately represented which had not either won a constituency seat or else polled 5 per cent. of valid votes cast in the Land concerned.

The three basic principles of this system—'personalized' proportional representation with a 5 per cent. hurdle—were retained in the second electoral law, which again was an *ad hoc* law passed in great haste just before the 1953 election,[3] and in the law of 1956,

[1] For the arguments brought forward in the Parliamentary Council for and against various electoral systems see the Stenographic Reports of the 7th Sitting of 21 Oct. 1948, pp. 109–24, of the 8th Sitting of 24 Feb. 1949, pp. 125–67, and of the 11th Sitting of 10 May 1949, pp. 246–64.

[2] 'Wahlgesetz zum ersten Bundestag und zur ersten Bundesversammlung der Bundesrepublik Deutschland' of 15 June 1949 (*Bundesgesetzblatt*, pp. 21–24). The Electoral Decrees in 1949 were issued on a Land basis—for specimen see *Badisches Gesetz-und Verordnungsblatt*, 24 June 1949, pp. 231–8, and *Regierungsblatt der Regierung Württemberg-Baden*, 12 July 1949, pp. 106–18. For discussions of the first electoral law in English see Richard M. Scammon, 'Postwar Elections and Electoral Processes', in Edward H. Litchfield and associates, *Governing Post-War Germany*, Cornell University Press, Ithaca, 1953, pp. 500–33, and James K. Pollock, 'The Electoral System of the Federal Republic of Germany', in the *American Political Science Review*, 1952, pp. 1056–68. The story of its adoption is told by J. F. Golay, op. cit., pp. 138–47.

[3] 'Bundeswahlgesetz zum zweiten Bundestag und zur Bundesversammlung' of 8 July 1953 (*Bundesgesetzblatt I*, pp. 470–91), and 'Bundeswahlordnung' of 15 July 1953) *Bundesgesetzblatt I*, pp. 514–49). For an authoritative commentary see

which was the first to imply a claim to more permanent validity.[1] Both the second and the third electoral laws did, however, modify the application of these three basic principles in important respects. The second electoral law raised the number of list seats to equality with the number of constituencies. The third electoral law abandoned the assignment of a fixed number of seats to each Land and gave parties an overall proportional representation not primarily on each Land delegation to the Bundestag, but in the Bundestag taken as a whole. Thirdly, both the second and the third electoral laws each accentuated the severity of the splinter party clause: the law of 1953 demanded not 5 per cent. of votes in the Land, but 5 per cent. of all votes in the Federation (or one constituency seat anywhere in the Federation); and the third electoral law increased the number of constituency victories required (as an alternative to 5 per cent. of federal votes) from one to three constituencies.

The third Bundestag election was thus fought within essentially the following system:

Firstly, one-half of Bundestag members were elected in 247 single-member constituencies by simple relative majority vote.

Secondly, the remaining seats were filled from party lists in such a way as to give each party which surmounted the splinter party clause a total number of seats exactly (or almost exactly) proportional to the number of votes it had polled in the Federation.

Karl-Heinz Seifert, *Das Bundeswahlgesetz*, Kohlhammer, Stuttgart, and Deutscher Gemeindeverlag, Cologne, 1953. For a discussion in English see James K. Pollock, 'How the Voters Decide', and Daniel S. McHargue, 'The Voting Machinery', in James K. Pollock, op. cit.

[1] 'Bundeswahlgesetz' of 7 May 1956 (*Bundesgesetzblatt I*, pp. 383–413), and 'Bundeswahlordnung' of 16 May 1957 (*Bundesgesetzblatt I*, pp. 441–95 and 532). The report of a Commission of Inquiry set up by the Minister of the Interior to explore the theoretical aspects of electoral legislation was published as *Grundlagen eines deutschen Wahlrechts-Bericht der vom Bundesminister des Inneren eingesetzten Wahlrechtskommission*, Metzner, Frankfurt, 1955. (For an expanded version of a mathematical paper presented to this Commission see Helmut Unkelbach, *Grundlagen der Wahlsystematik*, Vandenhoek & Ruprecht, Göttingen, 1956.) The discussions of the Bundestag Committee on the subject were confidential. The main Bundestag debates will be found in the Official Records of the Second Bundestag for 6 July 1955, 94th Sitting, pp. 5317–49 and for 15 March 1956, 134th Sitting, pp. 6934–62. They should be read in conjunction with the proposals presented by the SPD (Document 1272), FDP (Document 1444), and by Abgeordneter Stücklen (Document 1494), and with the report of the Committee presented by Abgeordneter Scharnberg (Document 2206 and Annex), as well as the amendments presented from various sides (*Umdrucke* 540, 542, 543, 545, 547, and 548). For the Bundesrat debate see the Official Record of 23 March 1956, 156th Sitting, pp. 108–12. Commentaries on the law are provided in detail by Karl-Heinz Seifert, *Das Bundeswahlgesetz*, Vahlen, Berlin and Frankfurt, 1957, and, more briefly, by Hermann Feneberg, *Bundeswahlgesetz*, Jehle, Munich, 1957.

Thirdly, no party was allowed such list seats which had not either won three constituency seats or else polled 5 per cent. of valid votes cast in the Federation.

Stimmzettel

für die Bundestagswahl im Wahlkreis Nr. 69 Bonn-Stadt und Bonn-Land am 15. September 1957

Jeder Wähler hat

eine **Erststimme** für die Wahl des Wahlkreisabgeordneten	und	eine **Zweitstimme** für die Wahl nach Landeslisten

	Erststimme		
1	**Dr. Adenauer, Konrad** Bundeskanzler Rhöndorf, Zennigsweg 8 a	Christlich Demokratische Union **CDU**	◯
2	**Stelling, Heinrich** Baukaufmann Bonn, Endenicher Str. 230	Sozialdemokratische Partei Deutschlands **SPD**	◯
3	**Kühn, Walther,** Regierungspräsident a. D. Bonn, Kreuzbergweg 18	Freie Demokratische Partei **FDP**	◯
4	**Dr. Kather, Linus** Rechtsanwalt Bad Godesberg, Am Glückshaus 8	Gesamtdeutscher Block/BHE **GB/BHE**	◯
5	**Frau Kremmer, Ilse** Verw. Angestellte (Hilfsreferentin) Bonn, Renoisstraße 4	Deutsche Partei (Deutsche Partei/ Freie Volkspartei) **DP**	◯
6	**Esser, Peter** Rentner Heimerzheim, Kirchstraße 11	Föderalistische Union (Bayernpartei-Zentrum) **FU/Zentrum**	◯
7			
8	**Bieber, Erich** Metallarbeiter Bonn, Schillerstraße 16	Deutsche Reichspartei **DRP**	◯
9			

	Zweitstimme	
1	**Christlich Demokratische Union** Adenauer, Arnold, Frau Dr. Rehling, Blank, Dr. Schröder **CDU**	◯
2	**Sozialdemokratische Partei Deutschlands** Mellies, Dr. Menzel, Kinat, Frau Albertz, Kühn **SPD**	◯
3	**Freie Demokratische Partei** Weyer, Dr. Mende, Scheel, Döring, Frau Friese-Korn **FDP**	◯
4	**Gesamtdeutscher Block/BHE** Petersen, Dr. Kather, Gemein, Stegner, Frau Immisch **GB/BHE**	◯
5	**Deutsche Partei (Deutsche Partei/Freie Volkspartei)** Dr. Blücher, Dr. Preusker, Dr. Schild, Freiherr von Oer, Körner **DP**	◯
6	**Föderalistische Union (Bayernpartei/Zentrum)** Dr. Bertram, Dr. Rüther, Sudowe, Meiwes, Kreiterling **FU/Zentrum**	◯
7	**Bund der Deutschen, Partei für Einheit, Frieden und Freiheit** Elfes, Frau Arnold, Dr. Klös, Dr. Wenzel, Langenfeld **BdD**	◯
8	**Deutsche Reichspartei** Meinberg, Dr. Freiherr v. Weichs, Gebhardt, Diekelmann, Dr. von Grünberg **DRP**	◯
9	**Deutscher Mittelstand** Freybe, Löbbert, Dr. Steinkraus, van Suntum, Dr. Schmitz **Mittelstand**	◯

FS-DRUCK-BONN Fritz Scheur 25179

FIG. 1. A ballot paper, 1957.

Each voter had two votes to cast, one to choose between the candidates in his constituency, and one to choose between party lists (see Fig. 1). It remains to examine the detailed working of this electoral system and the reasons for its evolution in this particular way.[1]

The Constituencies

The first electoral law had left it to the Länder to appoint Landtag committees to determine the boundaries of constituencies and indeed the exact number of them. It had simply assigned to each Land a given number of seats (totalling 400) and ordered the Länder to have these seats filled in the approximate ratio of 60 per cent. by constituency and 40 per cent. by list election. The sum of the constituencies set up by the Länder happened to come to 242, two more than the strict ratio of 60:40 would have warranted for a Bundestag of 400;[2] but given the indivisibility by 5 of most of the numbers of seats assigned to each Land, some small discrepancy was natural. When the second and third electoral laws made the definition of constituencies a matter of federal legislation, the same 242 constituencies were maintained substantially intact.

In a sense the size of the constituency is of little importance in this system since it is, of its essence, one of proportional representation. Nevertheless a certain dissatisfaction was expressed with the very wide differences in the number of electors per constituency: thus in 1957 the constituency Oberbergischer Kreis in North Rhine–Westphalia had less than 90,000 electors, while Gelsenkirchen in the same Land had over 265,000, the federal average lying around 143,000 electors per constituency. The third electoral law therefore consciously followed the British precedent and set up a permanent Constituency Boundaries Commission to be appointed by the Federal President; it was to consist of the President of the Federal Statistical Office, a judge of the Federal Administrative Court, and five other members. Within a year of the opening of each Bundestag this Commission was to propose constituency redistributions such that the spread in the number of electors per constituency did not exceed one-third of the average number of electors either way, that Land boundaries continued to be respected and urban and rural district boundaries were respected as far as possible, but that each constituency was also to form a connected whole.[3]

[1] The reader whose interest in electoral legislation is more cursory is permitted —indeed encouraged—to spare himself the perusal of the remainder of the present chapter and to continue with Chapter III on p. 38.

[2] Cf. Table II, p. 7.

[3] The political *Kreis* is somewhat larger than a British urban or rural district, but it has seemed best to reserve the term 'county' for the much larger administrative *Regierungsbezirk*.

This last, far from being a formal flourish, was a provision of a very practical kind. The definition of constituencies in terms of administrative units had until then been relatively simple; but for that very reason there were a great number of enclaves of one constituency totally surrounded by the territory of the neighbouring or even next-but-one constituency. These lands, acquired by some local princeling through marriage or purchase centuries ago, had found their legal appurtenance preserved, like flies in amber, by the historical definition of administrative boundaries. The third electoral law left them to be reallocated by the Boundaries Commission after the 1957 election.

As from 1 January 1957 the law on the integration of the Saar into the Federal Republic added five further constituencies (and also another five list seats) bringing the total number of constituencies up to 247.[1]

The Attribution of List Seats

The first electoral law had required each voter to mark only one cross against the name of one party candidate and had treated a vote cast for a party candidate as constituting simultaneously a vote for the Land list of that candidate's party. The total votes cast for all the candidates of each party throughout the Land were thus added together and used as the basis for the distribution of list seats between the Land parties by proportional representation.

In the two subsequent electoral laws, this automatic attribution of a vote for a candidate to the candidate's party was abandoned. The voter was allowed to make that distinction between candidate and party which was one of the chief arguments used to justify the system of 'personalized' proportional representation. Each voter was given two votes to cast, one to decide between his constituency candidates, and one to decide between the party lists presented in his Land. Only the first vote counted in the constituency, only the second in the proportional calculation of party strengths.

The system of proportional representation adopted was the 'greatest average' system of d'Hondt. The numbers of votes cast for each party were divided successively by 1, by 2, by 3, and so forth, and tabulated. The resulting quotients were numbered in order of magnitude, and each party received one seat for each highest quotient it scored in the table until the number of seats available had

[1] 'Gesetz über die Eingliederung des Saarlandes' of 23 Dec. 1956, *Bundesgesetzblatt I*, pp. 1011–16, paras. 2 and 14 and appendix.

been exhausted.[1] The object of this method was to ensure proportionality under conditions where the total number of representatives to be elected, but not the total number of votes cast, was predetermined. Its incidental though not unwelcome result was slightly to favour the large as against the small parties.[2]

From the number of seats each party was to have in the Bundestag there was then deducted the number of constituency seats which the party had already secured by direct election. Only the difference was made up from the party lists. It was thus the total number of seats and not the list seats only that were divided proportionally between the parties; proportional representation was in fact superimposed on the single-member constituency system.

In the elections to the first and second Bundestag, the d'Hondt calculation was made separately for each Land. The third electoral law changed this method: list seats were allocated federally, every Land party list competing simultaneously for each Bundestag seat in turn. Although no federal party lists were allowed, Land organizations of the same federal party could before the election ask to have two or more of their Land lists combined for the purposes of the final count:

Several Land lists of the same party may be combined with one another. In the distribution of seats, combined lists are treated as a single list in relation to other lists. The seats gained by a list combination are distributed among the [component] lists in the d'Hondt proportion of their list votes'.[3]

[1] Thus if four parties, *A*, *B*, *C*, and *D*, poll 144, 120, 90, and 66 votes respectively, the table would look as follows:

	Divisor			
	1	*2*	*3*	*4*
Party *A*	144 (*1*)	72 (*4*)	48 (*7*)	36 (*10*)
Party *B*	120 (*2*)	60 (*6*)	40 (*9*)	30
Party *C*	90 (*3*)	45 (*8*)	30	22½
Party *D*	66 (*5*)	33	22	16½

The italicized figures in brackets number the quotients in order of magnitude. Seats would thus be assigned in the following order: *A*, *B*, *C*, *A*, *D*, *B*, *A*, *C*, *B*, *A*, &c., and it would simply depend on the number of seats available where the distribution would stop. Given the voting figures of the example, if seven representatives were to be elected, every completed 48 votes qualified a party for one seat; if ten were to be elected, every completed 36 votes qualified it, and so forth.

[2] In contrast to this d'Hondt method, a straight proportional system would have assigned only 3 seats to Party *A*, which had polled 34 per cent. of votes, but 2 seats to party *D* with its 16 per cent.

[3] 'Bundeswahlgesetz' of 1956, para. 7.

In 1957 the d'Hondt system of proportionality was thus used twice over: first to share out seats between rival combinations of lists, and then again to share out the seats won by each list combination between the component Land lists of the same party. All the parties—except one, by error—took full advantage of this clause: not to have done so might have left votes in one Land unused when in combination with those unused in other Länder they could have brought in another seat or more.[1]

It should be noted that the CSU, being a party with an organization distinct from that of the CDU, could not combine its Bavarian list with those of the CDU in the other Länder. Parties were, however, allowed slight variations in their labels provided they had a common federal executive and used an identical principal party designation.[2]

It may be asked why this complicated system of combined Land lists should have been used. Could not each party have submitted a single federal list? The party composition of the Bundestag would then have been just the same. (Only where different Land parties which were not really branches of the same federal party had succeeded in circumventing the electoral law would it have been different: and to prevent such abuses a federal list might certainly have been the better system.)

[1] Supposing in our previous example lists *C* and *D* combined, the table would have read:

Party *A*	144 (*2*)	72 (*5*)	48 (*8*)	36
Party *B*	120 (*3*)	60 (*6*)	40 (*9*)	30
Party *C*+*D*	156 (*1*)	78 (*4*)	52 (*7*)	39 (*10*)

The tenth seat would then have been allocated not to *A* but to *C*+*D* and the four seats thus gained by *C*+*D* distributed as follows:

Land list *C*	90 (*1*)	45 (*3*)	30	22½
Land list *D*	66 (*2*)	33 (*4*)	20	16½

In 1957 every complete 56,015 votes entitled a party to one seat, though in the distribution of seats between Land lists of the same party the FDP reached as low a quotient as 50,434.

It might be noted that, just as the d'Hondt system entailed a slight disadvantage for the smaller party, so its use at this second stage, being a handicap to the smaller Land organization within each party, resulted in a slight over-representation (by three seats) of the biggest Land—a curious phenomenon in a federal state.

[2] Thus the Federal Returning Committee allowed the Free Democrats to combine all their lists although they were labelled with the traditional title FDP/DVP (Democratic People's Party) in Baden-Württemberg, and by FDP/DPS (Democratic Party Saar) in the Saar, while the Federalist Union could call itself *FU/Zentrum* in North Rhine–Westphalia and Lower Saxony.

The formal difference between the system of combined lists and that of a single federal list consisted in this: that the allocation of seats between Land parties (and thus between individuals) was made not at the nomination stage, but after the election and by the Federal Returning Committee in the d'Hondt proportion of the votes cast for each Land party. Moreover each Land list was distinct from every other, and no candidate could stand on more than one Land list any more than he could stand in more than one constituency. (Candidates could, however, stand simultaneously for one constituency and on one list—and that not necessarily in the same Land.)

The essential political difference between a single federal list and ten Land lists lay, however, not so much in the election as in the nominating procedure. A federal list system would almost inevitably have implied giving the final monopoly power over all list nominations to one central body in each party, and it would then have been too much to expect the party leadership not to extend their say in nomination beyond the mere co-ordination of Land suggestions. The preservation of Land lists even within a federal system of proportionality thus preserved the rights of Land parties to select their own candidates regardless of advice from federal headquarters; it emphasized the special responsibility even of list members for the affairs of one part of the country and, incidentally, it also prevented the name of Adenauer from appearing at the head of the CDU list on the ballot paper of every single voter in the country.

This new list system was only adopted after a bitter conflict. Unable to secure a single member, relative majority system which would have given them the maximum advantage,[1] members of the CDU tried to obtain what was not too happily called the 'ditch' system: half the seats were to be filled by constituency election, and the other half were to be distributed in proportion to the votes cast for each party in the country—no deduction being made for any constituency seats already won.[2] With a 'ditch' drawn between the two methods of election only one-half of the Bundestag would then have reflected the proportionate strength of parties in the country; the other half would have consisted of (predominantly CDU) members elected on the straight 'British' system.[3] Certainly the

[1] Cf. Report presented by Abgeordneter Stücklen (Doc. 1494).

[2] Cf. Report presented by Abgeordneter Scharnberg on behalf of the Bundestag Committee (Doc. 2206 and Annex).

[3] Thus in 1957 the CDU with 50 per cent. of the federal poll won 194 (or 79 per cent.) of the 247 constituency seats. The system would no doubt have forced parties to ally in competing for constituency votes.

smaller parties, which could scarcely hope to win any constituency, would have found their parliamentary representation cut by about one-half. The threat to enforce some such system was held over the Free Democrats through 1954 and 1955 in order to make them more loyal partners in the Adenauer coalition, particularly over the Saar question, and it was to stop any such system being implemented that the 'Young Turks' set in motion what became known as the 'Düsseldorf revolt'. Early in 1956 a different system still was put forward and gained wide agreement: the transfer of Land votes unused in the allocation of Land list seats to a federal list from which some 10 per cent. of the Bundestag would be chosen. It was not until after much further discussion that the method finally embodied in the 1956 law was adopted.

Land Representation

The first electoral law had distributed the 400 basic seats of the first Bundestag in proportion to the population of the Länder. The second electoral law did the same, but since quite important shifts in population had occurred in the intervening four years, the relative strength of various Länder in the Bundestag had to be changed in consequence. Fortunately such a reallocation of seats did not entail taking a single seat away from any Land; for in the meantime it had been decided that the Bundestag was too small to perform its functions without undue strain on its members and to train a new generation of parliamentarians. It was for these reasons, and not in order to diminish the relative importance of the constituency as against the list members, that the number of list seats was raised to equality with that of the constituencies: and since the constituencies were left untouched and there were 242 of them the basic figure of 484 Bundestag seats resulted.

Although the federal ratio of constituency seats to list seats was now one of equality, the ratio tended naturally to be higher in Länder that had lost, lower in Länder that gained in population between the drafting of the first and the second electoral law. Most of these relative population shifts were due to the movement of refugees from the agricultural areas to the towns. Thus Schleswig-Holstein, which had divided its 23 seats of 1949 into 14 constituency and 9 list seats in 1953, had only 10 list seats as against the 14 constituencies; whereas the adjoining city state of Hamburg, which had divided its 13 seats of 1949 into 8 constituency and 5 list seats, found that in 1953 it had 9 list seats as against its 8 constituencies.

We have seen that the third electoral law departed radically from this system of fixed Land quotas of seats. Rather than charge the Constituency Boundaries Commission with the task of also revising the Land allocation of seats, it had provided for an automatic method of adjustment to be built into the system: proportional representation applied not only within, but also between Länder. For if seats were to be distributed between all Land party lists simultaneously then the number of members representing the Land was simply the sum of the number of members representing each of the Land parties.

But it should be noted that in making this provision the legislature in fact changed the basis of Land representation from relative population figures to the relative figures of valid votes cast for parties qualifying for proportional representation. Abstentions, invalid votes and votes cast for parties that failed to surmount the splinter party clause were not taken into account. Bavaria was hit hardest by this provision. In 1957 12 per cent. of its votes (as against a federal average of 7 per cent.) were cast for parties that failed to clear the splinter party hurdle. The Bavarian representatives who had voted in favour of this provision—apparently without understanding its implications—had a rude awakening thereafter. But once its working was understood, the new federal proportionality gave the big parties an additional argument against the small regional parties: unlikely to gain 5 per cent. of federal votes, such parties would defeat their own local patriotism by reducing the number of seats assigned to their Land. Hence the paradox pointed out by the CSU to prospective voters of the Bavarian Party: 'A vote for the Bavarian Party is a vote for the Prussians.' In fact in 1957 Bavaria lost 9 seats as a result of this change in the law, Lower Saxony lost another 5, while North Rhine–Westphalia gained 16 seats and four other Länder experienced minor changes in their representation.

Retained Excess Seats

The combination of the constituency plurality with the proportional system makes for no particular difficulty so long as the overall number of seats attributable to a party is greater than or equal to the number of its constituency victories: constituency seats are simply deducted from the overall total of seats attributable to the party. But what if the party has won more constituency seats than the total number of seats warranted by its share in total votes? It would be awkward to take a constituency seat away from a newly elected member and from his party after the d'Hondt calculation is completed. Each of the three electoral laws therefore allowed such an excess constituency seat (*Überhangsmandat*) to be retained, the parliamentary strength of the winning Land party, the number of seats held by members elected in the Land, and the membership of the Bundestag rising by one seat in consequence.

Two such excess seats were retained in the 1949 and 3 in the 1953 and again in the 1957 elections. All 3 excess seats retained in the 1957 election were won in Schleswig-Holstein, a Land whose electorate had diminished even further since 1953. Given its 1957 poll, Schleswig-Holstein would have been entitled to only 20 seats. But as the CDU swept each of the 14 constituencies while the other parties were entitled to 9 seats, the total number of Schleswig-Holstein members rose to 23.[1]

The Splinter Party Clause

We have seen how successive electoral laws weighted the scales with increasing severity against the small parties. Those representing national minorities were, however, always exempted from these tests. In fact this exemption has so far been applied only to the South Schleswig Voters' League recognized as the party of the Danish minority. It had won one list seat in 1949 but with 0·2 per cent. of federal votes in 1953 and 0·1 per cent. in 1957 was not big enough thereafter to take advantage of its special right to proportional representation given a Bundestag of less than 500 members. In 1957 there was talk of the formation of a Polish national minority party in the Ruhr as a successor to the banned Communist Party; if the plan was ever serious it did not succeed.

Less remarkable in some ways than the apparent severity of this clause[2] was the easy option of one or even of three constituency seats. Not merely is there a large difference between the nearly 1,500,000 votes that a 5 per cent. poll demanded and the less than 40,000 votes that could often secure a constituency victory; more important was the open door to party arrangements and alliances which this alternative qualification provided. How far large as well

[1] For a more detailed discussion of retained excess seats see the author's article on 'The West German Electoral Law' published in *Parliamentary Affairs*, Spring 1958, esp. pp. 230–3.

[2] The Lower Saxon constitution goes so far as to allow a 10 per cent. splinter party clause—perhaps an understandable provision in a Land which has seen the emergence of various groups of the extreme right, and the 1954 law regulating elections to the Bavarian Landtag excludes from the distribution of list seats (which is carried out separately in each of seven electoral areas) any party which has not polled 10 per cent. of votes in the electoral area concerned.

as small parties went in their attempts to exploit this alternative and what tortuous negotiations were set in train by the whole splinter party clause are subjects discussed in the next chapter.

The Law of Nomination

Minor and insignificant parties were, however, not only prevented from obtaining representation by the provisions of this splinter party clause, but were also handicapped and discouraged from cluttering the ballot paper by the legal provisions on the nomination of candidates. These provisions, while pursuing much the same aim as the British law of nomination, set about achieving them by a rather different method.

In the British electoral system any ten electors may nominate any eligible citizen as a candidate. Candidates stand officially without a party label simply as individuals. The only safeguard against frivolous candidatures is a deposit of £150 forfeited by candidates who do not obtain one-eighth of the votes cast. Given this ease of nomination and given the legal equality of party candidates, of party dissidents, and of non-party candidates, no particular legal regulation of the selection process is thought necessary.

Here as in so many other respects German practice differs sharply from the British. Not only the nomination but also the selection of candidates was carefully regulated by the electoral law and the electoral decree. In the first electoral law, it must be remembered, a vote cast for an individual candidate (except in the case of independents) automatically represented a vote cast for a party list: the parties were therefore given special privileges with regard to constituency as well as list candidatures. These party privileges were largely maintained in the electoral laws of 1953 and 1956.

The third electoral law distinguished three types of constituency candidate: candidates sponsored by what we may call 'established' parties, candidates sponsored by other parties, and independent candidates—'established' parties being those which had been continuously represented by at least five members in the Bundestag or in a Land legislature since the last election of the legislature concerned.

'Established' parties (in this sense) could nominate even constituency candidates simply over the signature of the Land executive of the party. Other parties were required to prove that they had a democratically elected executive, a written constitution and a written programme, and were obliged to collect the signatures of 200 electors for the nomination papers of a constituency candidate, and of one in a thousand of Land electors (up to 2,000 such signatures) for their nomination of Land lists. This requirement proved a handicap to several of the smaller parties, though to none which could possibly have cleared the splinter party hurdle.[1]

Independent candidates also required the signatures of 200 electors for their nomination in a constituency; since only parties were allowed to nominate lists an independent was not able to constitute himself into a Land list of one name. In fact independents played a wholly insignificant role in the first three Bundestag elections in spite of the absence of any deposit requirement: in 1953 only 7 out of some 1,800 constituency candidates could (even by stretching the term) be described as independent, and in 1957 the figure was 3 out of 1,700: and of these 3, 2 purported to stand for an organization of some kind, 1 for the 'Party of Good Germans', and the other for the 'German Peace Vote League'. They did not poll 10,000 votes between them.

With parties in this monopoly position in regard to Land lists and 'established' parties privileged in regard to the nomination of constituency candidates, the parties' selection of candidates naturally required public control. The third electoral law laid down the procedure for the adoption of party candidates even more explicitly than the first and second—and thereby forced some CDU and SPD Land parties to amend their statutes. Constituency candidates could be nominated only after selection by a secret ballot held either in a meeting of all members of the constituency party, or else in a selection committee elected by all such members from among their own number not more than a year before polling day. In large cities which form more than one constituency a common body could decide for all the constituencies concerned.

The electoral law gave the Land Executive of the party the right to object to any adoption and to force the adopting body to reconsider its decision: if the local selection committee in another secret ballot maintained their choice, the adoption was final. The minutes of the meeting at which the adoption took place, including the number of those attending the meeting, together with a declaration of the secrecy of the ballot and the exact results of it, formed part of the nomination papers checked by the Constituency Returning Officer.

[1] The Federalist Union, the German Community, and the Union of the Middle Class all failed to submit the required number of valid signatures in more than half the Länder. Naturally enough it was easier for these parties to collect the necessary signatures in the bigger Länder where the 2,000 signatures required represented much less than one in a thousand voters: of the eleven lists for which these three small parties obtained recognition, all but two were submitted in the four biggest Länder.

Analogous provisions applied to list candidatures: the Land Returning Officer had to be satisfied that a secret ballot of a duly constituted party body had been held to determine the Land list candidates and the order in which their names appeared on the nomination form. It was left for the parties themselves to decide whether an absolute, qualified, or simply a relative majority was to be required in these ballots.

In fact the methods used varied from Land to Land and from party to party. Some half-dozen men drew up the list of the Union of the Middle Class in the biggest Land; some 300—about a quarter of the membership—drew up the Hamburg list of the German Party. The number of members of both constituency and Land selection conferences appears most usually to have varied between 25 and 250, constituency selection conferences tending to be nearer the lower limit. How these selection conferences reached their decisions and what kinds of consideration seemed relevant in their selection of candidates forms the subject of Chapter IV below.

Absent Voters

The first electoral law had allowed voters who for urgent reasons could not vote in the polling booths at which they were registered to apply for an electoral certificate which allowed them to vote (in person) in any constituency of the same (but of no other) Land. Their vote was counted in favour of the candidate in whose constituency they happened to go to the poll. By 1953 the idea of a postal ballot had gained favour, but the electoral law was discussed so late that it seemed technically impossible to introduce a postal ballot at such short notice. The validity of the electoral certificate which allowed electors to vote at a polling booth at which they were not registered was therefore simply extended to allow them to cast their vote anywhere in the Federal Republic.

This arrangement, however illogical theoretically, was obviously a much less arbitrary and a much more satisfying one from the voter's point of view. Over 3 per cent. of the electorate made use of the electoral certificate in 1953. In several of the more attractive constituencies of the South holidaymakers and other voters with electoral certificates accounted for over 10 per cent. of the poll: in the Bavarian lake district votes cast even exceeded the number of registered electors.[1]

[1] It is worth noting that the electoral certificate thus introduced a considerable complication into the calculation of 1953 turn-out percentages on anything less than a federal level.

But there were still two major objections to the issue of such electoral certificates, whether they were confined to the Land or valid throughout the Federation. The first was the obvious one that a Hamburg businessman who wanted to vote FDP while on a September holiday in Baden-Württemberg could not be expected to know or care much about the personality (and indeed about the political views) of the local farmer bearing the corresponding DVP label; if the personal element in the election was to be taken seriously, it was worth making provision for absent electors to vote for the man who would represent them if elected.

There was, however, a further argument against the electoral certificate in its 1949 and 1953 form: it could be used to flood any particular constituency with supporters of one particular party. A well-organized party machine might have swung the result in a marginal seat by the import of certificate voters to gain either a remainder seat or else a constituency seat needed as an alternative to the 5 per cent. qualification for list seats. In 1953 the Communist Party, then not yet outlawed as unconstitutional, had attempted to organize a festival for its supporters on polling day in the constituency of Remscheid-Solingen, where the party had come to within 6,000 votes of victory in 1949. The attempt was foiled and the Communists suffered shipwreck on the 5 per cent. clause. Nevertheless other parties with regional concentrations of voters might have tried to do the same in three constituencies in 1957, so that it seemed better to abolish the mobility of electors from one constituency to another.

The 1956 law thus introduced a postal vote for voters absent from their constituency on polling day. The electoral certificate as such was, however, maintained: besides being the document which justified the postal voter's ballot paper it could also be used to vote at any polling station within the voter's home constituency—a useful service where polling stations within the same constituency might be forty or more miles apart and where the Sunday excursion is a time-hallowed family ritual. One per cent. of the electorate made use of this certificate for casting their votes in person anywhere within their own constituency, and another 5 per cent. voted by post in the 1957 election.

After the election certain objections were made against the postal ballot on constitutional grounds. Firstly it was argued that the voter might find himslf unprotected against intrusions on the secrecy of his vote, either at home or more particularly if confined to a hospital or a similar institution: and one or two concrete cases where advice had been given on voting or where there had been no guarantee of the secrecy of the poll were drawn to the attention of the Federal Returning Committee. In spite of the electoral Order, postal voting papers had often been issued for convenience where in the past an institution had been visited by a mobile polling committee; in such instances administrative decisions rather than the introduction of the postal ballot as such were to blame, and even in such cases the law at least in theory safeguarded the voter against such intrusions by making them punishable offences.

A second ground of objection was that the votes of those who had died between the dispatch of their voting papers and polling day would be included in the count. But then only a few hundred such posthumous votes were involved; and it was also argued that the law did not stipulate that the voter must have been alive on polling day itself, and that it would have been possible, if the law were to be interpreted that way, to segregate such ballot envelopes at the cost of a slight delay in the declaration of the final result. Since the postal vote allowed some 1·5 million ballot papers to be counted, many of which would never have been cast otherwise, the postal ballot would seem on balance to have greatly increased rather than reduced the democratic character of the electoral system.

The Representation of Berlin

When they approved the Basic Law of the Federal Republic the Military Governors expressly construed it

> as constituting acceptance of our previous request that, while Berlin may not be accorded voting membership in the Bundestag or Bundesrat nor be governed by the Federation, she may nevertheless designate a small number of representatives to attend the meetings of these legislative bodies.[1]

From an original figure of nine such attenders the Berlin delegation then rose to twenty-two. In January 1957 the SPD put down a motion asking that they should be directly elected and given the right to vote from October 1957 onwards. The SPD had long been in favour of a greater degree of integration of Berlin into the Federal Republic, and this particular measure would of course also have strengthened the party slightly in the third Bundestag, since it naturally polled a larger share of votes in Berlin than in the Federal Republic. But the proposal was buried in committee proceedings at the Chancellor's insistence on the grounds that it was incompatible with the Federal Republic's undertakings to the Western powers.

[1] Quoted in Litchfield and associates, op. cit., p. 577.

Electoral Machinery and Administration

In contrast to the French system, the West German electoral machinery was not controlled by the Federal Ministry of the Interior, for it was not thought wise to entrust the administration of elections to an organ of the Central Government which was under the direct control of the governing political parties. The Federal Ministry of the Interior therefore confined itself to preparing an electoral Bill for presentation to the Bundestag and to issuing the Order for the implementation of the electoral law once it was passed. The Federal Minister of the Interior then appointed a Federal Returning Officer—in the past three federal elections the President of the Federal Statistical Office—and thereafter the responsibility of his ministry was no more than the usual routine one of preserving order in the country during the election as at other times, though the minister could remove the Federal Returning Officer if necessary.

In the first two Bundestag elections the Federal Returning Officer's functions were relatively few: he had certain rights of objection against decisions by lower organs of the electoral machinery and he published the overall results of the election: in 1953 this meant in particular that he ascertained for the benefit of all Land Returning Officers which parties had secured 5 per cent. of the federal poll. In view of the very limited functions of the Federal Returning Officer no committee appeared necessary to assist him and to engage the responsibility and preserve the confidence of the political parties in the decisions he took.

In 1957, however, the electoral law had abandoned a system of Land for a system of federal proportionality. As a result no Land Returning Officer could work out in isolation which of his list candidates had been returned: results for half the Bundestag seats had to be determined in calculations carried out on the federal level. For the first time, therefore, a Federal Returning Committee was constituted by the Federal Returning Officer. It consisted of one nominee from each of the six largest parties in the Federation with a substitute for each. This Returning Committee met in public, decided by simple majority vote, and required no quorum for its decisions. Each member was pledged to act on the committee impartially; service was honorary (though expenses were refunded) and it was obligatory in the same way as jury duty, refusal without one of several specified causes being punishable by a fine.

Analogous to the Federal Returning Officer and his committee each Land and each constituency had its Land Returning Officers and Constituency Returning Officers with their committees, consisting each time of nominees of the six largest parties in the Land or constituency. Land and Constituency Returning Officers were nominated by the Land government or an authority (such as the Land Ministry of the Interior) designated by it. Land Returning Officers were either the heads of Land statistical offices or else leading officials of the Land (not Federal) Ministry of the Interior. Land Returning Committees decided appeals on the admissibility of constituency candidatures, and themselves decided on the admissibility of Land lists; Land Returning Officers transmitted list vote results to the Federal Returning Officer, and informed list candidates of their election as soon as the Federal Returning Committee had determined the result. Constituency Returning Committees accepted or rejected constituency candidatures, and decided on the results of the constituency contests.

Complaints were heard at the nomination stage that while the original purpose of establishing Land and Constituency Returning Committees had been to check on the impartiality of the Returning Officer, it in fact became the function of the Returning Officer to see that decisions were taken on the formal merits of each case and not as the by-product of coalitions of party representatives deciding in the best interests of their own parties. Questions of party labels and of whether a party was new or 'established' in the sense of the law of nomination (particularly where parties had fused) did not at first secure uniform treatment throughout the Federal Republic, though they affected the obligation on parties to collect signatures and the place number which they occupied on the ballot paper. But Constituency and Land Returning Officers had the right to appeal to the Land and Federal Returning Committees respectively against the decisions of their own committees, so that in the end a reasonable degree of uniformity was reached. In fact the machinery worked well and on the whole with satisfactory impartiality also towards the smallest parties.

Each constituency was divided into wards which were not to comprise more than 2,500 electors nor—in theory—so few that the secrecy of the poll might be violated. This last provision, however, was honoured by frequent breach rather than by observance. The desire for a speedy declaration of results led to the counting of votes in the polling station and, hence, almost inevitably to publication by ward; and the sparseness of population in many areas and the desire to save voters trouble led to the declaration of scores or even hundreds of results for less than 100 electors—in one case at any rate for only 19 electors. A random thumbing of election results in the newspapers of the Rhineland-Palatinate reveals that in the two villages of Trierscheid and Obliers every single one of the 41 and 33 electors respectively went to the poll and cast both their constituency and their list votes for the CDU ticket, while the village of Bauler contained one black sheep: all 47 electors voted, 46 of them for the CDU, but the forty-seventh cast both his votes for the SPD.[1]

The electoral register was kept by the authorities of the commune on the basis of police registrations of residence. They were not published, but open to inspection for a period before the date of poll, when appeals for and against the inclusion of names were heard. The voter was usually informed of his inclusion in the register and in all communes forming more than one ward he was individually notified of the time and place of polling.

Each polling station was supervised by a polling officer with a polling committee of three to eight members selected in theory on much the same principles as the Federal, Land, and Constituency Returning Committees. Some local parties penalized members who had been slack in their electioneering efforts by suggesting their names for the polling committees. But on the whole these committees tended to be composed of local government employees.[2] The polling stations were open to the public; the marking of ballot papers outside a strictly private booth was forbidden.

Large institutions such as hospitals could form a ward of their own: smaller institutions, monastic establishments, and prisons could be visited by a mobile polling committee (composed of a few members of the polling committee responsible for the ward in which the institution happened to be), the ballot papers being mingled with those of the ward as a whole before the count. Postal votes were treated as a distinct ward and counted by a separate polling committee.

The count was public: it began immediately at the end of polling in the polling station itself. The results were transmitted in accordance with carefully prepared forms to the Constituency Returning Officer. Supporting documents, in particular the ballot papers, were

[1] Unless, of course, one CDU voter cast his constituency vote for the SPD candidate, and the SPD voter cast his for the CDU candidate—an unlikely hypothesis.

[2] Where volunteers from other parties were not forthcoming or the local government officials in the polling station all sympathized with one party there was nothing to prevent the adherents of one party from doing all the counting in a ward by themselves. No cases of irregularity were reported during the Bundestag election, but an amusing account of how two SPD adherents set about to *corriger la fortune* in the Hamburg election two months later is given in an article published in *Die Zeit* of 20 Feb. 1958 under the title 'Stimmzettel im Küchenherd' (Ballot Papers in the Kitchen Stove).

preserved by the communal authorities and could be demanded by the Constituency or Land Returning Officer, who might revise decisions taken in the polling station such as those on the validity of particular ballot papers. During the night of the election the whole machinery worked with extreme smoothness: the sixty million list and constituency votes cast in every single polling booth in the country were added, the d'Hondt calculation completed, and the names of the 487 elected members announced within twelve hours of the close of the poll.

III

PARTY MERGERS AND ALLIANCES

WE have seen in the previous chapter that the third electoral law excluded from the distribution of list seats all parties that did not either win three constituencies outright or poll 5 per cent. of the federal vote. A dozen or so parties felt themselves threatened by this clause and the present chapter seeks to sketch the more important negotiations in which they engaged in order nevertheless to secure representation in the third Bundestag. It is a complicated story in its mixture of public, semi-public, and would-be private flirtations, refusals, arrangements, marriages, and annulments continuing until nomination day; yet this very interweaving of local and international, federal, personal, and purely arithmetical considerations illuminated German politics as a whole and forms an essential part of the story of the election.

The negotiations were followed in detail by the newspapers for some six months and provided them with ample material for editorials and cartoons. They preoccupied not merely the leaders of the smaller parties whose survival was involved, but also loomed large in the calculations of the CDU and the SPD. At the turn of the year and through the spring these two parties appeared to be very evenly balanced in public favour.[1] The search for allies thus assumed far-reaching importance. Even the very smallest parties that might somehow slip into the Bundestag under one arrangement or another might tip the scales between an Adenauer and an Ollenhauer government. Both large parties were therefore prepared to intrigue with very minor groups and with otherwise insignificant men so as to gain every ounce of extra strength they could muster for a struggle of which the outcome seemed so uncertain, and on which the whole future of German foreign and military as well as domestic and economic policy seemed to hinge.

The Subject of Negotiations

In a system of single-member constituencies like the British, there is obvious room for agreements between two parties not to fight each

[1] See Fig. 3, p. 276.

other in constituencies which can thereby be won from a third: and the only problem that remains is how to distribute the seats to be won between the partners in the alliance. In a purely proportional system such arrangements are practically useless and almost irrelevant:[1] it was not the proportional system but the limitation of it by the splinter party clause which lay at the root of the inter-party negotiations before the election.

The methods by which the small parties hoped to escape the splinter party clause were various. The amalgamation of two or more small parties might result in a total poll of 5 per cent. or in three constituency victories; a big party might stand down in favour of a smaller one in three constituencies and advise its supporters to cast their constituency vote for the candidate of the small party; or else both these methods could be combined.

The larger parties, while they were primarily concerned with gaining potential allies in the third Bundestag, also had various other objects in view. They might wish to see votes siphoned off from another big party, and thus to reduce its strength; they might wish to allow their junior partners to win a 'retained excess seat'[2] that could reinforce their own position in the Bundestag; or they might wish to oblige a small party as part of a package deal balanced by counter-favours in spheres other than those of federal politics. In practice both large and small parties tended to keep several such considerations in view simultaneously in every successive negotiation.

CDU, SPD, and FDP were for these purposes large parties: few felt that the Free Democrats were in danger of falling below the 5 per cent. mark in the election, and they themselves certainly hoped to improve on their 9 per cent. share of the poll of 1953. All the other parties were in danger of failing to be represented in the third Bundestag unless they could come to an arrangement. Three of these parties had secured election to the second Bundestag; two more had been added by the integration of the Saar; several others had been eliminated from the Bundestag in 1953 by the change in the electoral law or by a drop in their votes; and the rest were almost parties that had never been represented in Bonn at all.

The Main Small Parties Involved

The BHE was the only party to be elected to the second Bundestag without winning a single constituency seat, and it could certainly not hope to win any constituency in 1957. But it had secured almost

[1] At most they could help to win the last seat where a d'Hondt rather than a quota system of seat allocation is used. (See footnote, p. 24.)

[2] See pp. 27–28 above.

6 per cent. of the federal vote in 1953; the split in its parliamentary party had no parallel in the country; and it had maintained its 1953 poll in the intervening Landtag elections. On these grounds its leaders publicly displayed great confidence that they would again poll at least 5 per cent. of the total vote. Privately, however, they must have been far from certain that their return to Bonn could be assured without some kind of electoral alliance.

The fifth strongest party to emerge from the 1953 election had been the German Party. It had originated as a regional and largely farmers' party glorifying the Guelph past of Lower Saxony;[1] its first conceptions had been strongly federalist and it had even toyed with the idea of returning Hanover to the sovereignty of the throne of England. After the immediate post-war years the German Party came to represent a Protestant force of the conservative right. It became national in sentiment, and, though not necessarily always nationalist in tone, it appealed also to a number of former National Socialists, particularly as it expanded to the Hanseatic and other cities of the North. Finally, a third element entered into its character: as a coalition partner in Adenauer's first and second administrations it supported his foreign policies; on the federal level at any rate, it thus also came to adopt less a regional or national than a still wider 'European' loyalty.

In 1949 the German Party had polled 18 per cent. of Lower Saxon votes and easily cleared the splinter party hurdle in its original form. In 1953 it won two constituencies in the teeth of CDU opposition and secured the return of eight further constituency members through electoral alliances with its partners in the Government. In 1957 the CDU again pledged itself to conclude sufficient electoral alliances in safe constituencies to retain this faithful ally in the Bundestag. The German Party was thus the only one of the small parties which felt assured that even if it did not surpass its 3 per cent. poll of 1953, the CDU would still safeguard its survival on the federal level.

The smallest party to be elected to the second Bundestag was the almost entirely Catholic one which bore the historic name of the Centre. Catholic groups had been formed in the South German Landtage in the first half of the nineteenth century and in the National Assembly of 1848, and had adopted the name 'Centre' in the Prussian Landtag in 1858. A re-founded Centre Party was represented in the first Reichstag and thereafter it stood for the answer of Catholics to Bismarck in the *Kulturkampf*. The Centre Party provided the Weimar Republic with five Chancellors and with

[1] The Guelphs had been the royal house of Hanover until 1866.

much of its stability during the twenties, though in 1933 it voted for the Enabling Law that eased Adolf Hitler's seizure of dictatorial power.

In 1945 the chief remaining leaders of the Centre had struck out on a new course and joined in the foundation of the CDU, so that much of the wind was taken out of the sails of the party that bore the traditional name. Polling 9 per cent. of votes in North Rhine–Westphalia, the Centre still sent ten list members to the first Bundestag. In 1953 its vote fell even in North Rhine–Westphalia and it was only able to enter the second Bundestag thanks to an arrangement with the CDU: the CDU surrendered the constituency of Oberhausen to the Centre leader in return for the Centre surrendering one of its two top places on the Land list to a CDU man to square the account. In addition the Centre pledged itself to put up no list of candidates outside North Rhine–Westphalia. It is more than doubtful whether the CDU would have regarded another such arrangement as worth while in 1957 when it would have involved three constituency seats; certainly once the Centre had joined the SPD–FDP coalition in Düsseldorf, only an alliance with some other party could allow the Centre to figure on the list of the third West German legislature.

In 1949 the Bavarian Party, which was at least as particularist as the German Party of Lower Saxony, had polled more votes than either the German or the Centre Party. Licensed in 1948, the Bavarian Party was founded as a federalist 'homeland' force claiming in this case Bavaria for the Bavarians. Its formation was closely connected with a movement of protest against the export of potatoes from Bavaria to the rest of Western Germany, and its programme demanded the return of all non-Bavarian evacuees to their homes. The party stood for

> the mental and moral renewal of the Bavarian people according to the principles of truth, justice and love, an independent viable Bavarian state in the framework of a German and European community of states, a [Bavarian] State President, a Bavarian nationality law . . . the cultivation of the true Bavarian national character (*Volkstum*) and an art rooted in the Bavarian people.[1]

The demand for a State President waned after old Prince Rupprecht of Wittelsbach died and was given a State funeral (in which the Bavarian SPD took its full share[2]). But for the rest the members

[1] The original programme also demanded corporate representation of all trades and professions and the creation of a corporate chamber in Bavaria—an aim which was achieved by the establishment of the Bavarian Senate.

[2] The Bavarian SPD was not immune from particularist pride: in autumn 1957 he SPD Minister-President Hoegner called the Cabinet to his country residence

of the Bavarian Party remained a slightly anti-clerical but distinctly Catholic group which campaigned in the traditional costume of leather shorts and chamois-beard hats and appealed above all to the peasant electorate with country music bands and the blue and white lozenge flag of Bavaria.

In 1949 the Bavarian Party polled 21 per cent. of the Bavarian vote and obtained 17 Bundestag seats. But the party passed through difficult periods. Some of its members were involved in various scandals, mostly of a financial kind,[1] and the attractions of the bigger CSU were becoming too much for many, including some of those who represented the party in Bonn. Threatened by the splinter party clause of 1953 the Bavarian Party concluded a number of electoral alliances with the CSU. In the four Munich constituencies, two Bavarian Party candidates were to stand unopposed by the CSU and two CSU candidates were to be unopposed by the Bavarian Party. But by an obscure process the two Bavarian Party candidates changed their party label at the critical moment and were elected on the CSU ticket.[2] As a result the 9 per cent. of Bavarian votes cast for the Bavarian Party were wasted and the party relegated to Land politics.

The BHE, the German Party, the Centre, and the Bavarian Party had all four been represented in the Bundestag in the past. (So had the Communists, who proved the fourth strongest party in 1949; but the electorate only gave them 2 per cent. of votes in 1953 and in late 1956 the party was outlawed by the Constitutional Court and dissolved.)[3] The political integration of the Saar now brought two further parties into the picture: the Christian People's Party (*Christliche Volkspartei*—CVP) and the Democratic Party of the Saar

to debate the serious problems arising out of the erection on the Austro-German border of black, red, and gold signs reading 'Federal Republic of Germany' alongside the blue and white ones reading 'Free State of Bavaria'.

[1] Compare, for example, Document 2274 of the First Bundestag, reporting on the allegations made against certain Bundestag members by the news magazine *Der Spiegel*.

[2] Compare Documents 511 and 512 of the Second Bundestag, reporting on the appeals of the Bavarian Party against its disqualification. At the Bavarian Party Congress in July 1957 the party Chairman Professor Joseph Baumgartner read out a long list of 'traitors' (including the two members of the Bundestag involved) and expressed the hope that none of his listeners would figure on the list which he proposed to read to the next congress.

[3] The Communist Party was banned under the same Article 21 (2) of the Basic Law under which the neo-Nazi Socialist Reich Party had been dissolved in 1952: 'Parties which, by reason of their aims or the behaviour of their members, seek to impair or destroy the free democratic basic order or endanger the existence of the Federal Republic of Germany, are unconstitutional. The Federal Constitutional Court decides on the question of constitutionality.'

(*Demokratische Partei Saar*—DPS). In addition there were a host of smaller parties such as Dr. Gustav Heinemann's neutralist All-German People's Party (*Gesamtdeutsche Volkspartei*—GVP) and the avowedly nationalist German Reich Party (*Deutsche Reichspartei*—DRP). Given the new electoral law these parties could have no reasonable hope of a Bundestag seat unless they could merge with a bigger party before nominations closed.

A last effort was therefore made to change the law by an appeal to the Constitutional Court. As leader of the GVP Heinemann argued that the splinter party clause violated the equality of the vote and the freedom to form parties. As leader of the Bavarian Party Baumgartner demanded that parties whose very character confined them to one Land should be given a fair chance by a return to the 1949 system in which 5 per cent. of Land votes were considered an adequate basis for proportional representation. The Constitutional Court delivered judgement in January 1957: it found that paragraph 6 of the electoral law did not violate the Basic Law of the Republic.

The Disappearance of the Free People's Party

One party at any rate did not wait for this decision before taking cover. Fifteen of the sixteen Free Democratic members of the Bundestag who had remained loyal to the Chancellor's Government (in which indeed four of them were then ministers) had formed themselves into a new party. This Free People's Party held a party congress and took part in the local elections of the autumn of 1956. It fared so badly that it could not expect to obtain even 1 per cent. of the federal vote, and in spite of a well-financed Bonn office it failed to build up any effective organization in the country. By November rumours were spread and denied about a fusion between the Free People's Party and the German Party, in December negotiations became serious, and in January 1957 the two parties announced their amalgamation.

The agreement was very far from being an equal one. The FVP had a certain amount of money to contribute, which it had received at the time of its establishment from sources close to the CDU. It had two names which might add to the drawing power of the German Party's own public figures, those of Dr. Viktor Emmanuel Preusker, the Minister of Housing, and of Dr. Franz Blücher, Adenauer's Vice-Chancellor. Lastly it expected to be able to keep its hold on a good proportion of the former Free Democratic vote at least in Hesse and perhaps in some other areas as well. The CDU did not need any such dowries and did not think it worth while trying to find three safe seats in which CDU voters could be relied upon to vote for the Free People's Party. The FVP could thus hope for nothing more from the CDU than to be swallowed up unconditionally. The German Party did not admittedly offer such very different terms. The name was in general to be 'German Party', though it might be varied to 'German Party/Free People's Party' where this appeared to give an electoral advantage. And it was really only in Hesse that FVP members of the second Bundestag might expect to be given promising candidatures for the third.

The Free People's Party thus virtually ceased to exist less than twelve months after its foundation. It was never more than a group of party managers with a few local committees and no appreciable following among the electorate at all. It was an extreme case, but an illustration of the character of some of the parties involved in these negotiations: not parties in the popular sense but little more than small groups acting as liquidators for the political goodwill attached to traditional party labels or to the names of a few politicians. In the case of the Free People's Party the absence of a membership base combined with not particularly modest ideas of the party machinery required resulted in the dependence of the party for its very existence on large financial supporters: and when these suggested a merger with the German Party in order to save the expense of an additional party machine there was no option but to take their advice.[1]

The financial backers of the Free People's Party had in fact no further incentive to maintain two separate parties for essentially the same purpose when the two could amalgamate and adopt a new platform common to both elements. Both parties were members of the Adenauer coalition; both supported the Government's foreign and rearmament policies; both were 'anti-Marxist' in economic views. Their avowed object was to form an effective bloc to the right of the CDU: they would then be able to force the Government to take a firm line against the SPD and against those within the CDU's own ranks whom they regarded as putting up insufficient resistance against the encroachments of the welfare state. Preusker declared that the difference between conservatism and liberalism was of little relevance in a world threatened by Communism today; 'national liberalism' might be the concept to be applied to the newly formed political body.

Since the new group was one which could not ally with the SPD, such a consolidation of the forces on the moderate right into a

[1] For a description of the system of political finance in the Federal Republic see Chapter X.

parliamentary party of over thirty seats could only be welcome to the Chancellor: indeed there must have been a certain satisfaction for CDU strategists in preventing any reconciliation between the FVP and the FDP, and in marrying off to its junior partner the group which had just broken away from the FDP.

The Difficulties of the Bavarian Party

One might at first sight have expected a similar blessing from the CDU when the German Party, flushed with the success of this first operation, went on to consider an alliance with the Bavarian Party as well. Although ousted from the Bundestag in 1953, the Bavarian Party was far from extinct. In the Land elections of November 1954 it had polled 13 per cent. and remained the third strongest party in the Land. Moreover, it revenged itself on the Christian Democrats for its elimination on the federal level by forming a coalition in Munich with the SPD; this was joined by the two other parties in the Landtag, the BHE and the FDP, so that the CSU was left alone in opposition. The strength of the Bavarian Party derived from its pivotal position in the Bavarian Landtag: it could at any moment desert the SPD and, even without support from the other parties, proceed to form a clear majority government with the CSU.[1] Both the SPD and the CSU were forced to take note of this arithmetical fact: for what was at stake was the government of the second most populous Land and the control of five seats in the Bundesrat.

Three courses lay open to the Bavarian Party after the Constitutional Court rejected its appeal against the new splinter party clause: it could seek to provoke an amendment of the electoral law; it could attempt to secure three constituency seats by arrangements with either (or in theory with both) of the major parties; and it could arrange a merger with one or more of the other minor parties of the Federal Republic. These were not alternatives, but tactically complementary courses of action. Naturally all three possibilities were explored simultaneously.

Its senior partner in the Munich Government made two moves on the Bavarian Party's behalf: a week before the Constitutional Court delivered its judgement, the SPD proposed to the Bundestag (and the Bavarian Government to the Bundesrat) a return to the rule that 5 per cent. in any one Land was sufficient qualification for entry into the Bundestag. Both initiatives were unsuccessful. At the same time the leader of the Bavarian SPD publicly appealed to the CSU to

[1] The results of the Landtag election 1954 had been as follows: CSU 83 seats, SPD 61, BP 28, BHE 19, FDP 13, making a total of 204 seats.

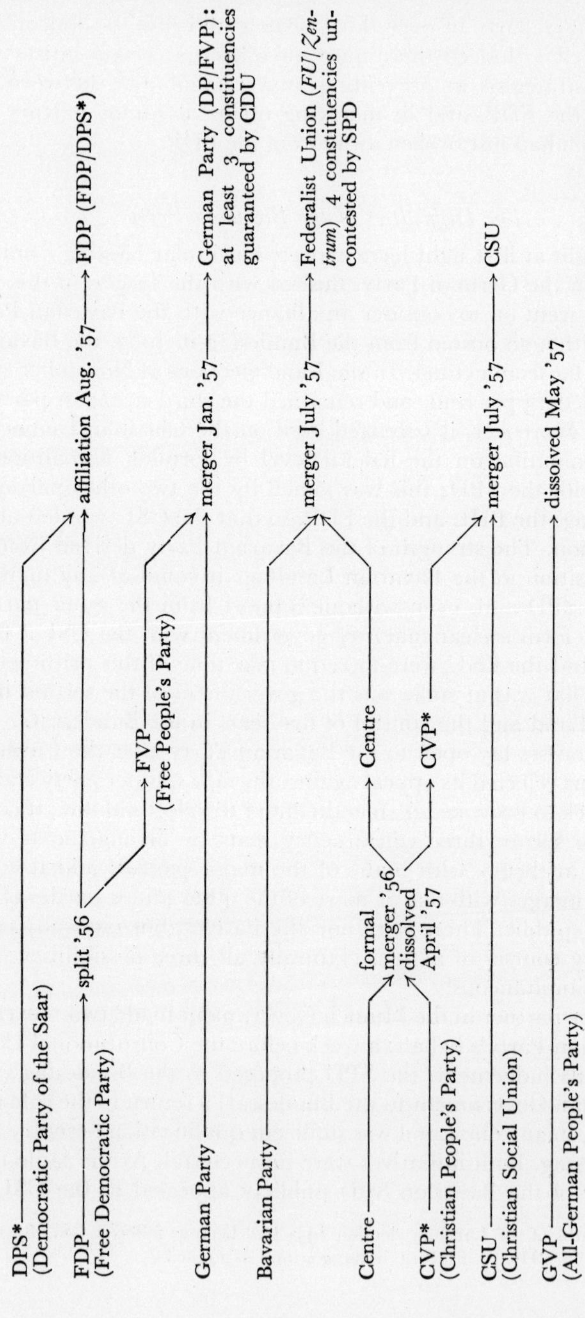

FIG. 2. Party splits and mergers, 1956–7.

help the Bavarian Party back to Bonn: if the CSU would only give the Bavarian Party two constituency seats, the SPD could contribute the third. This gesture was designed to please both the Bavarian Party and the Bavarian electorate as a whole, and also to make the CSU look ungenerous; but this piece of particularist incongruity of a socialist party pleading with one Catholic party on behalf of another was not taken more seriously than it deserved.

The CSU for its part was naturally unwilling to see a Bavarian Party group in the Bundestag elected on such a bipartisan basis: there was no guarantee that the coalition between the Bavarian Party and the SPD in Munich might not then find a counterpart in Bonn. The CSU declared that it might well supply three seats—or even make moves in the direction of revising the electoral law to read '10 per cent. in any one Land'—but the initiative must come from the Bavarian Party itself. The condition need not be an immediate restoration of CSU rule in Munich; but a promise would be required that the Bavarian Party would not support the SPD after the next Landtag election. Baumgartner, however, expressed himself forcefully in reply to this offer, declared that his party did not require the aid of those who had been its hangmen, refused to move towards the CSU, and travelled to Hanover instead to begin conversations with Heinrich Hellwege, the Minister-President of Lower Saxony and Chairman of the German Party.

Plainly there were important differences to be overcome between the Bavarian Party and the German Party, and the difficulties involved were accentuated by the still uncompleted integration of the FVP into the German Party. The Bavarian Party was hostile to Adenauer; it had in Munich gone into coalition with the SPD; it was opposed to conscription; and it was above all a federalist party that could meet with the Hanoverian element of the German Party on the common basis of loyalty to their respective homelands, but it had little in common with that centralist 'national liberalism' which Preusker regarded as the basis of the enlarged German Party.

Just at the moment, however, when it looked as if Hellwege might have problems in reconciling his new FVP allies with his prospective ones from Bavaria, Adenauer sent him an ultimatum (demanding 'full explanations by Monday') and condemned as an unfriendly act endangering the Bonn coalition any alliance with those who opposed vital items of Government policy. The CSU's interest in not losing its bait for the party that held the balance in the Bavarian Landtag may have been behind this move as much as federal considerations. Hellwege replied firmly, only to find a few days later that the Bavarian Party had for its part broken off the negotiations. The Bavarians had only then realized that in order to make the alliance effective in electoral law, they would need to call themselves 'German Party: Bavarian Land Organization'. This was more than they could expect their particularist voters to stomach. Once more the Bavarian Party declared that it would fight alone.[1]

By the end of February the Bavarian roundabout had turned full circle: the Bavarian Party was again closeted with the CSU. The plans now under discussion were more subtle than the last. None of the CSU constituency parties appeared willing to withdraw their own candidates: so in return for support for a Christian-conservative Chancellor in Bonn in 1957 and a CSU Minister-President in Munich in 1958, the CSU might either put a few politicians of the Bavarian Party among the first ten names of its own Land list (so that the Bavarian Party would at least have those few of its men in Bonn) or else it might persuade three of its own CSU members with safe constituency seats to join the Bavarian Party for the duration of the election campaign. Although these men would rejoin the CSU after the election was over, the three constituency seats thus formally won by the Bavarian Party would entitle that party to list seats corresponding to its proportion of the poll—minus, of course, the three constituency seats. It is not surprising that even the Bavarian public began to feel at this stage that its patriotic sympathy for the Bavarian Party was being strained.

The Bavarian Party itself was far from united in these parleys with its closest enemy. Some of its members could not believe that the CSU meant its offers seriously and a group round Ludwig Lallinger, the Chairman of the Munich party, may well have been prepared to sabotage the negotiations which it feared would prove a fatal embrace. In March posters appeared in the streets of Munich evoking the memory of 1866 and calling for 'Battle against the Bonn oppressors' and against 'Prussianism, Centralism and Militarism'.[2] The CSU also was not altogether of one mind. A group led by Dr. Alois Hundhammer, Chairman of the Upper Bavarian CSU, sincerely wanted an alliance with the Bavarian Party; but it was in a minority. The rest of the CSU regarded Lallinger's poster campaign as but another proof that the Bavarian Party was a tool of the Social Democrats expressly designed to split the Catholic farming

[1] It may be that the position of the two 'traitors' from the Bavarian Party who were then sitting as German Party members for Munich seats (having been nominated first by the Bavarian Party, stood on the CSU ticket, joined the Free People's Party, and then found refuge with the German Party) would have led to some embarrassment if negotiations had been taken any further.

[2] 1866 was the year in which the Prussians had defeated the Bavarians and laid the foundations for Bavaria's incorporation into the German Empire.

vote[1] and hoped this time to crush its rival for good. The CSU resumed informal negotiations until the Bavarian Party had isolated itself from the German Party beyond hope of return; then it abruptly broke them off.

It required a little time for the Bavarian Party to recover from this latest public humiliation. It had failed to obtain support either from the CSU singly or from the grotesque combination of CSU and SPD; it had attempted to amalgamate with the German Party whose return to Bonn was assured, but found this impossible; now it could only turn to other small parties whose fate was as uncertain as its own.

The Integration of the Saar and the 'Federalist Union'

At this point political developments in the Saar became relevant to the situation in Bavaria. Indeed in the early months of 1957 the press gave even more space to the internal politics of the Saar than it devoted to the difficulties of the Bavarian Party. During the years when the Saar was separate from the Federal Republic two main parties occupied most of the seats in its Landtag: the Christian People's Party (CVP) of Minister-President Johannes Hoffmann and the Social Democratic Party of the Saar (SPS). Both these parties wished to maintain the separation of the Saar from the Federal Republic and aimed at its 'Europeanization', while certain other parties, which opposed the Saar's autonomous constitution, were declared unconstitutional.

As a result of the Paris Agreement signed between Adenauer and Pierre Mendès France in October 1954 he Saar population was invited to decide whether it wished to see a European Statute applied to the Saar. In July 1955, three months before the referendum took place, the licensing of parties was discontinued. Three important parties then appeared before the public and soon combined for the conduct of the referendum campaign into a Homeland League (*Heimatbund*): the *CDU-Saar*, which defied Adenauer by opposing 'Europeanization', the *SPD-Saar*, which after the referendum quickly absorbed the SPS, and last but most outspoken among the three, Dr. Heinrich Schneider's Democratic Party of the Saar

[1] This was an old CSU theory based on the argument that Lallinger had been the private detective and bodyguard of the SPD Minister-President Wilhelm Hoegner before giving up his policeman's for a political career. A public allegation to this effect by a CSU member of the Bundestag was, however, withdrawn in settlement of a libel suit (see *Bayernruf*, 8 July 1957). Lallinger had already figured prominently in the events by which the agreement between the Bavarian Party and the CSU came to grief in 1953.

(DPS), which the FDP regarded as sufficiently close to it not to establish a branch of its own in the Saar.

When the referendum was over and only one-third of the electorate had voted for the European Statute the CVP (unlike the SPS) maintained its independent existence. It kept a hold on one-fifth of the electorate in the Landtag and the local elections, and it demanded honourable amalgamation with the *CDU-Saar* or no amalgamation at all. The *CDU-Saar* refused any merger of parties and demanded the dissolution of the CVP, promising to consider favourably the admittance of most of the CVP's members into the *CDU-Saar*. In spite of strong pressure from the bishops of Trier and Speyer, from the Chancellor and from the CDU's federal headquarters, no fusion could be agreed between the *CDU-Saar* and the CVP, and the Christian camp remained divided.[1]

More as a gesture of defiance than in any hope of thereby surmounting the splinter party clause Hoffmann thereupon concluded a formal merger of the CVP with the Centre which, as we have seen, was itself threatened with the loss of its last remaining Bundestag seat. By the autumn of 1956 Hoffmann was thus an honorary president of the Catholic party which had fought in the Federal Republic against that European Statute of which he had been the chief protagonist in the Saar; and the *CDU-Saar*, which had opposed the Statute, was a Land branch of the federal CDU whose leader had thrown his whole weight into the battle in the Statute's favour. Yet despite these reconciliations across the border, in the Saar itself the memories of the bitter referendum campaign still lingered: they even prevented the formation of a Christian coalition to take the place of the Homeland League Government which was now itself torn by personal antagonisms.

In March, when it still looked to some as if the CSU might allow the Bavarian Party three constituency seats, the emissaries of the Centre and the CVP came to Munich: they hoped to extend their own amalgamation to the Bavarian Party as well and thus to partake of the legal benefits of the three Bavarian constituencies which might be offered to the Bavarian Party by the CSU. Since the CSU's help was vital to the whole scheme it was natural that, while they were in Munich, the CVP representatives should also talk directly to the CSU. The talks between the four parties then begun were carried on for many weeks and led to a surprising interchange of partners. The Centre and the CVP, which had arrived together, left separately:

[1] It seems best to follow German usage, recognize the word 'Christian' as a purely political as well as a purely religious term, and print it without inverted commas in this context.

the Centre agreed to fuse with the Bavarian Party, while the CVP received a handsome offer from the CSU.

The Bavarian Party had by then been finally rejected by the CSU; as a last resort it found its way into the arms of the Centre, which was in the same plight. The two parties remembered the days of 1952 and 1953: in order to show the minimum number of Bundestag members required for admission to the privileges of a parliamentary party, the two completely distinct organizations in the country had then maintained a nominally single parliamentary party under the title 'Federalist Union'. This was the title they now revived jointly in order to gain entry into the third Bundestag.

Between them the two parties could not hope to obtain 5 per cent. of federal votes, having polled only half that percentage in 1953: but they hoped to be able to play the alternative card. Both were Christian parties opposed to the CDU and could be relied upon to take some votes away from it. Both were vital allies of the SPD in Land coalitions: the one in Bavaria, the other in North Rhine–Westphalia. It was thus in the interests of the SPD for Land as much as for federal reasons to help these two parties. To give each of them three seats would have been almost unthinkable, but to oblige both of them for the price of one seemed a business proposition. On 15 May the Federalist Union constituted a joint executive in Frankfurt; two days later Ollenhauer publicly confirmed that he had asked the two SPD Land parties concerned to allow the FU to win three constituency seats.

Baumgartner's ambitions now ran to the formation of a new federal party of federalists, a party of the centre that would last beyond the election campaign, reinforce federalist policies, and oppose not only nationalization but also the storage of atomic weapons on German soil and the misuse of religion for political purposes. He announced that he had found two further partners, the Schleswig-Holstein and the German-Hanoverian Land Parties; but the mass support to be expected from these quarters may be gauged from the fact that the Schleswig-Holstein Land Party at any rate did not put up a single candidate when the time came.[1]

[1] The German-Hanoverian Land Party was a small offshoot from the German Party (which it regarded as a traitor to Guelph loyalties) and considered itself the only true heir to the party of similar name founded to protest against the Prussian annexation of Hanover in 1866. A fifth possible partner for the Federalist Union was the 'Homeland League Land Baden' which had persuaded 100,000 voters—some 15 per cent. of the Baden electorate—to sign a popular initiative asking for Baden independence from Baden-Württemberg. In the event it decided not to antagonize the CDU and to remain a pressure group rather than join the Federalist Union.

From its 'separatist' history and its formal ties with the Centre it would have been natural to expect the CVP of the Saar to join the Federalist Union as a matter of course: the object of the Munich negotiations had, after all, been to bring the Bavarian Party into the Centre–CVP combination. But in fact by early April this contingency already seemed so unlikely that the Centre dissolved its amalgamation with the CVP on the grounds of misconduct: the CVP had unilaterally entered into negotiations with a third party.

Another much-publicized Saar intrigue here intervened in federal politics. In January the Homeland League coalition broke up in Saarbrücken. Adenauer and the bishops of Trier and Speyer renewed their strong pressure to bring the two Christian parties CDU and CVP together to form a Christian Government in the Saar and to agree on joint Christian candidates for the Bundestag election. In a Government crisis that lasted ten weeks it almost looked as if they would succeed: but the two Christian parties together only had a majority of one in the Landtag, and two CDU members—one of them the outgoing Minister-President—were unable to forget or forgive the CVP's separatist past. These two Landtag members wrecked the hopes of any early Christian reconciliation in the Saar.

But in spite of its rejection by the Christian Democrats of the Saar the Christian People's Party was in the end to escape the splinter party clause. The federal CDU could not recognize two opposing parties as its own branches in the same Land; but there was still its Bavarian partner with its own name and organization which was distinct from the CDU in electoral law. The Bavarian Christian Social Union offered the CVP an amalgamation and the CVP gladly accepted the proposal in spite of renewed advances from the Federalist Union. The CSU could provide a certain re-entry into the Bundestag, while the highly uncertain chance of such re-entry by the grace of the SPD's aid to the Federalist Union would have barred the way to eventual Christian unity in the Saar. The CSU for its part had the satisfaction of knowing that votes which would otherwise have been wasted or have helped the Federalist Union would yield two or three seats for the Government; nor was it unimportant to the CSU leaders that these seats would reinforce the CSU's own parliamentary strength as distinct from that of the CDU, and thus perhaps help them when it came to the distribution of cabinet posts. (The CDU was in fact a little apprehensive lest this emergency solution should encourage Munich empire-building and the cleavage between the two Christian parties in the Saar be consolidated by the CSU in order to give it even greater bargaining power in Bonn.) The CVP changed its name to 'CSU: Saar Land Organization' and its leaders could look forward to sitting in Bonn on the same benches with those CDU politicians who in Saarbrücken were keeping them in opposition.

It was not until August that the remaining Saar party scuttled for safety. Reiterating the slogan 'DPS stays DPS', Schneider's party became an 'autonomous' Land organization of the FDP with its own programme. Any link with employer liberalism was bound to reduce the electoral chances of the DPS in a working-class area like the Saar with its Catholic majority of three-quarters. But only that way could the DPS hope for two seats. Ironically enough, in the end it gained nothing from the deal: by a narrow margin Schneider's constituency seat remained the only DPS seat in the third Bundestag, and to win it Schneider had scarcely needed to join the Free Democratic Party.

Other Negotiations

Two further sets of negotiations deserve special mention: those between the Social Democrats and the All-German People's Party and those between the BHE and various other parties.

Based on Christian convictions, the All-German People's Party had been founded in 1952 in protest against German rearmament. Its founders were Dr. Gustav Heinemann, then President of the Synod of the Evangelical Church, who had been Adenauer's first Minister of the Interior but resigned in 1950 over the issue of rearmament, and Helene Wessel, a Catholic who had previously been a prominent figure in the Centre Party. The GVP had met with little popular support, the judgement of the Constitutional Court confirming the legality of the new splinter party clause sealed its fate, and the dispute over atomic weapons provided a bridge for its members to the SPD: here was an urgent issue on which, despite other differences of opinion, the members of the GVP could identify themselves with the Social Democrats.

The SPD appreciated the importance of this development: Heinemann and Helene Wessel were promised safe list seats and two other GVP men were promised candidatures, one of them in a constituency in Baden-Württemberg where the GVP had polled 16 per cent. of the vote at the last Landtag election. An agreement was reached and in May the GVP went into dissolution, recommending its members to join the SPD.

The number of voters involved was small: in 1953 the GVP had polled only just over 1 per cent. of the electorate. But what mattered was the quality of its leadership. Helene Wessel claimed that events in Hungary and Poland now made it possible for believing Catholics to vote for the SPD, and Heinemann declared that he brought with him 'at least three leading Protestant Church dignitaries, fifteen professors of theology and hundreds of pastors'. Though there were murmurs from the rank and file on the strange qualifications of these new comrades, the SPD leaders saw in their incorporation the first signs of a new era in which at last a bridge would be built between Social Democracy and that church-going middle class without which the SPD could not hope to obtain a majority in a West German Bundestag.

The efforts of the BHE either to be assured of three constituency seats or else to supplement its votes in the hope of ensuring a 5 per cent. poll were less successful. The BHE declared that it would not bind itself unilaterally to either of the big parties: since both major parties could hardly combine to give it three constituency seats, the BHE proposed an alliance of all three minor parties in the Bundestag. When this suggestion was scorned by the Free Democrats, the BHE could only approach other small parties.

One fanciful plan that apparently received some consideration was that the German Party should make over three constituency seats to the BHE and be compensated for them by the Christian Democrats. The Free Democrats, wishing to be the only third party in the third Bundestag, were determined to frustrate any such manœuvre. They alleged that the BHE had already sold itself to the CDU for £120,000 and three constituencies: in the resulting storm (including a court action) it became impossible for any such arrangement to be carried out. In fact it seems doubtful if the Free Democrats' move was really necessary: quite apart from the political absurdity of the device it was arithmetically clear that there were no three seats which the BHE even with the help of the German Party could have carried against the CDU.

The possibility of an alternative solution—the amalgamation of the BHE for electoral purposes with some other small party—was apparently discussed with the German Reich Party in an unofficial fashion, but these talks came to nothing. If it had merged with what was regarded as a neo-Nazi party, the BHE would have lost political respectability—and thereby probably also its control of several Land ministries, particularly those for refugee questions. Though the two parties between them did poll more than 5 per cent. of votes standing separately, it is also far from certain that they could have done so had they gone into the election together. As it was no further alliances were concluded.

The Balance Sheet

The preceding story has remained complicated even when stripped of its more arabesque ramifications; it may thus be worth drawing up a balance sheet of net changes in party alignments as compared with the 1953 election.

1. The Free Democrats, who allied with the CDU in various constituencies at the 1953 election and remained in the Government until 1956, then split. In 1957 they went into the election alone, and were indeed the only party to fight every constituency seat.

2. The dissidents from the Free Democrats, after founding a short-lived splinter party of their own, merged with the German Party.

3. As a result of this merger the German Party hoped to invade Länder to the south of its traditional domains and thus to extend its influence in federal politics. Owing to its arrangements with the CDU the party could face the splinter party clause with equanimity.

4. The BHE, being offered no acceptable aid from either of the big parties, hoped to come to an arrangement with the smaller ones: when these attempts failed it went into the election alone.

5. The Centre Party, which was returned in 1953 only as a result of the CDU's help, in 1956 formally amalgamated with the Christian People's Party of the Saar. In 1957 it dissolved this alliance to become one of the two mainstays of the Federalist Union.

6. The Bavarian Party negotiated with the CSU, the SPD, the German Party, and the Christian People's Party of the Saar. When all these negotiations proved inconclusive it became the senior partner of the Federalist Union, and the Social Democrats refrained in four constituencies from putting up candidates against it.

7. The Christian People's Party of the Saar attempted vainly to secure amalgamation with the Christian Democrats of the Saar and thus with the CDU as a whole; when this attempt failed it joined with the Bavarian CSU to become a second CSU Land organization.

8. The All-German People's Party went into dissolution and recommended its members to join the SPD.

9. The Democratic Party of the Saar became an 'autonomous Land organization' of the FDP.

10. All the other small parties went into the election alone.

The Government thus gained on two sides as a result of these negotiations: its Bavarian partner salvaged the CVP vote in its favour, and its ally the German Party swallowed up the FVP splinter group. The parties of the Opposition, too, secured certain gains: the Free Democrats, though they had lost the FVP group, acquired a strong branch in the Saar; and the Social Democrats swallowed up the All-German People's Party and hoped by their support for the Federalist Union to help anti-Adenauer forces—or at least to neutralize a number of votes that might otherwise have gone to the Government parties.

But the gains obtained by both Government and Opposition were only relative: and perhaps the real loser was the respect in which politicians as a group were held by the public. The tortuous course of negotiations between almost each and all did not go unobserved by the electorate, and though its impact may have been small it cannot have been favourable. Any splinter party clause no doubt provokes some device to circumvent it; but it was unfortunate (and not undeliberate) that its terms in the 1956 law, though harsher than those of 1953, were still framed in such a way as to invite inter-party arrangements. A straight percentage clause without any constituency alternative would have avoided some at least of the parties' well-publicized intrigues and reduced the prima facie inequity of the electoral law; but then, of course, it would also have eliminated the German Party from federal politics.

IV

THE SELECTION OF CANDIDATES

A DEMOCRATIC election is not merely a battle between parties for seats; it is usually also a struggle of diverse organized interests for representation, and must be a contest between individuals for membership of the legislature. Given the traditions and the political and electoral system of Western Germany, the elections to the Bundestag had very little of the character of a series of gallant personal duels with which the trappings of British elections obscure the general similarity of national swings. For the bulk of those who hoped to enter the third Bundestag the decisive contest in which their personal and political futures were decided was the selection process, and not the election itself. Much the same is true in Britain, but the character of the electoral system allowed this fact to emerge more clearly in Germany, and thus rather more public attention was focused on the selection process in Germany than in Britain.

The Position of the Bundestag Member

Th selection of candiates is a two-sided process: parties choose between contenders for nomination or try to persuade others to stand; but no less important are the questions faced by the individuals who must decide whether or not to enter the arena. Naturally those who did so were actuated largely by a sense of political responsibility and a certain liking for political life; but it is worth examining also those attendant advantages and disadvantages which together with his political functions make up the position of a member of the Bundestag in Western Germany.

It would probably be wrong to regard any legislative assembly as composed mainly of ambitious men on the bottom rung of the national ladder to executive power. Certainly this would be misleading in the case of the Bundestag: a very large number of its members consider themselves much more at the top of a local greasy pole. In the Federal Republic no less than in Britain the member is a representative of his locality and of his professional group. He is approached by local mayors and councils and by interest and professional groups to support their demands by intervening with the various ministries and in the legislature. He often remains a member of the local council and is elected or remains on the executive bodies of the various voluntary associations with which he is associated, and he is used for representational as well as for negotiating purposes. In entering the Bundestag he may in fact have come close to the summit of his particular political and often also social ambitions.

Nor is it in many cases easy to see where further political ambitions could lead. As against the eighty members of the House of Commons who are at any time associated with the executive in Her Majesty's Government, there is no analogous pyramid of paid or unpaid Government office for members of the Bundestag. Only some twenty ministers hold federal office at a time—and they need not necessarily be members of the Bundestag. Whatever the position in constitutional law, there is a much sharper psychological separation of powers in the Federal Republic than in Britain. The realizable ambitions of the bulk of members whose enthusiasm is for the work of the Bundestag thus tend to lie in the field of committee chairmanships and similar posts of legislative influence rather than in the assumption of executive responsibility.

But the slight hopes of office do not greatly affect the material position and prospects of a member. With tax-free emoluments which on average easily exceed £2,000 per annum, free postal facilities from their offices in the Bundeshaus, free transport on federal vehicles, a mileage allowance calculated for a heavy car and a special allowance for a chauffeur, members of the second Bundestag were hardly forced to earn a supplementary income and worked in reasonable conditions of efficiency.

Such an income was of course scant compensation for a professional man who wanted to return to his old career in due course and could hardly afford four years away from it. But even then—except perhaps for the smaller independent entrepreneur—there were other attendant advantages. Large firms tended to make it worth while for their senior officers to enter the Bundestag if they could. Officials of trade and professional associations could often carry out their work better on the floor of the House and in committee than in the lobbies, and found election a considerable help even in their old careers: many soon entered the supervisory boards of various firms as a result of election to the Bundestag. While some lawyers were perhaps forced to neglect their practice, others found far more briefs coming their way as a result of their Bundestag membership. Indeed there was one large category of Bundestag members who in material terms had nothing to lose and a great deal to gain from election: civil servants retained 50 to 70 per cent. of their ordinary salary on top of their full Bundestag pay while they were given leave of absence to take their seats; and university professors drew both salaries in full.

These convenient provisions for civil servants—somewhat surprising perhaps to those more used to British customs in this respect—represent the obverse of the psychological separation of powers at the top: the Bundestag was in fact regarded rather as one form of public service among others. Just as there had been ministers who were not members of the Bundestag, so high-ranking civil servants had taken leave of absence from their posts to enter the legislature. Conversely, in the absence of a House of Lords for distinguished or superfluous parliamentarians, the civil service has often been used to provide for such cases. A number of members found the Bundestag a good spring-board for an embassy or a consulate-general, private lawyers have passed through the Bundestag into Government service, and in 1957 a former BHE member who had come over to the CDU accepted a rank scarcely corresponding to that of Third Secretary in the Foreign Office. There was thus some coming and going between the Government benches of the Bundestag and the executive branch of government even apart from the fair number of Bundestag members of all parties who resigned to take over Land ministries. And SPD members if they resigned were often provided with salaried posts as mayors or as labour directors in firms subject to the law of co-determination.

Corresponding to this realization that Bundestag membership was on the whole an advantage, competition for seats became fierce in 1957. In 1949 many had watched the new political system arise with some reserve and had preferred to wait and see; in 1953 the unexpected CDU victory brought into the Bundestag a number of candidates who had not even themselves hoped to be elected, and who had been put up by the party without much reflection in what appeared to be hopeless candidatures. The election of 1957 was marked by more pitched battles in selection conferences than either earlier election. This series of contests over a fair proportion of the 2,073 list and 1,700 constituency candidatures defies any systematic analysis, nor would any such analysis be particularly meaningful. All that is attempted, therefore, is a sketch of the patterns that seem to have emerged in these battles in the two or three chief party organizations involved, and the main considerations and influences that appear to have swayed the day where candidates had a reasonable hope of success.

List and Constituency Members

A great many candidates—1,059 of the total of 2,714 men and women nominated—stood both in a constituency and on a list as well, though they were not allowed to stand for more than one constituency or on more than one Land list. Members usually preferred to be elected in a constituency. Some constituency members had a habit of emphasizing the importance of their point of view by quoting the percentage of the electorate which had cast its constituency vote for them personally. Members who were elected on Land lists without ever standing in a constituency at all sometimes felt that they were suspected of having had their seats bought for them by organized interests: 'With all my industrial connexions', one member was heard to say, 'I simply must have a constituency seat.' But by and large there was little difference in the Bundestag between the two types of members, and many probably were not sure which of their colleagues held constituency seats, and which did not.

Where local work was concerned the difference between constituency and list members was also less than might be thought. Questions about the local Bundestag representation often elicited the name of a list member either alone or in conjunction with that of the constituency member. Frequently a local dignitary was elected on a Land list and naturally kept his interest (usually also his office or post) in the locality. The defeated local candidate, if elected on the Land list, might nevertheless feel a special responsibility for the constituency even if, in the event, he was not readopted as prospective candidate there at the end of the legislative term. And sometimes where neither a local official nor a defeated candidate entered the Bundestag and looked after the constituency for whichever of the two biggest parties had failed to win the seat, that party might assign the constituency to some other list member (even from a different Land) who was expected to act as a 'step-member'—perhaps even for several constituencies simultaneously.

When a constituency member died or resigned, his Bundestag seat went automatically to the next man on the party list submitted at the last election in the Land in which his constituency lay. (After the first legislative period there were no by-elections in the Federal Republic.) Often this new list member would take over the local work of the constituency member whom he replaced, though this was not an invariable practice, particularly if the new member came from a different region of the Land concerned.

Naturally the nursing of a constituency by any list member could not go too far for fear of causing offence to the local party, which was often ready to suspect that a prospective constituency candidate might by this means be foisted upon them by party headquarters. It would be too much to say that either of the big parties had instituted a full-scale system of 'step-members'; the arrangements were too informal and incomplete to be dignified by that title; but they often seemed to work extremely well. In one case in which the CDU took special pride the Catholic 'step-member' was even elected to an overwhelmingly Protestant seat in 1957. Constituency coverage was easiest for the CDU: it had won 172 of the 242 constituency seats in 1953 and had initially 243 members of the Bundestag. The problem was much more difficult for the SPD, which had only 45 constituency members at the outset and only 151 members in all. The smaller parties were of course unable to attempt anything like such comprehensive coverage of constituencies by 'step-members' and in any case were much less interested in nursing constituencies than in securing list votes.

The nature of the work for the constituency was much the same as in Britain. Members were expected to be seen and heard frequently in the constituency. They were expected to take a lively interest in its local problems. All received a flood of mail on pension, tax, employment, conscription, housing, war damage restitution, and various other personal problems, which they answered usually in consultation with the experts on the appropriate subject within their own parliamentary party. Many had regular consulting hours in their constituency, although in some cases these consulting hours were abandoned for lack of clientele, while in at least one case a 'step-member' had to abandon them when fifty or sixty people took to appearing each time to take advantage of his professional services gratis. In rural areas the nursing might take the form of a card-playing tour of public houses till the early hours of the morning: one member with heavy responsibilities in Bonn claimed to have talked to and drunk with one in five of his male constituents in Schleswig-Holstein during the legislative period. Members often maintained an office in the constituency out of their expense allowance or contributed to the maintenance of the party office there, and in at least one case failure to do so helped seal the fate of a CSU member in spite of his diligent attendance at saints'-day festivals up and down his constituency.[1]

[1] For the attempts by one sitting member to retain his safe seat cf. *Der Spiegel*, 3 July 1957, which quotes him in the authentic Bavarian dialect uttering the plea of many a professional politician at about this time: 'Ja, um Gotteswuiln, was soll i blos machn, wenn i nimmer in den Bundestag eini kimm: i hob doch koan Beruf.' ('What on earth shall I do if I'm not re-elected: I never learnt a trade'.)

Selection of Constituency Members

The fate of this sitting member who was refused renomination was by no means exceptional. Indeed the selection procedure in this German election stood in striking contrast to British practice in that a large number of sitting members were deprived of their seats by their party selection committees.

This process can be seen most vividly in the case of constituency members. As Table III shows, nearly a quarter of constituency members were not renominated in their constituencies,[1] and it would seem that about half of these would have liked renomination. This overall ratio of over 10 per cent. of constituency members deprived of their seats against their will not by the electorate but by the party selection committees hides a certain difference between parties. The selection committees of the CDU appeared in many cases to be eager to eliminate those whom they thought unfit or who had made personal enemies. The SPD, on the other hand, when in doubt tended to give the benefit of it to the sitting member. A man was not lightly deprived of his livelihood by his comrades in the party—the more so since his alternative employment opportunities (usually with a trade union or the party organization itself) were likely to be less attractive than those of a CDU lawyer, manager, or entrepreneur who might well earn as much outside the Bundestag as within it. Only 1 of the 44 SPD constituency members was involuntarily replaced, while of the 161 CDU members some 20 to 24 were not renominated in their constituencies although they would have liked to carry on.

The reasons for which these members were not renominated were various and are sometimes not easy to analyse, being of a personal and even a momentary kind. One sitting member appears to have lost a probable renomination by his speech at the selection conference itself. Another had become involved in criminal proceedings and obviously could not hope to stand again. Several were regarded as too old for the job—a formula which was applied to members in some cases twenty years younger than the party's chairman and Chancellor, but which served its purpose in one case in spite of the expressed wish of the Chancellor himself. The remainder were refused renomination by their constituency selection committees for lack

[1] In fact in 1957 only one-third of the constituencies elected the same member for the third time. I am indebted to my research assistant, Dr. Reinhard Lamer, of Nuffield College and of the Berlin College of Politics, for the calculations on which this chapter is based; in the interests of strict comparability they exclude where appropriate the Saar and Berlin members.

TABLE III

The Fate of Constituency Members of the Second Bundestag

	CDU	*SPD*	*FDP*	*DP* *or.*[1]	*DP* *recr.*[1]	*Z*[2]	*Total*
1. Elected in 1953	172	45	14	10	..	1	242
2. Died or retired before nomination day 1957	9	1	3	1	..	..	14
3. Changed party	−2	..	−6	..	+8	..	±8
4. Sat on nomination day (1−2+3)	161	44	5	9	+8	1	228
5. Renominated for same constituency	123	37	5	5	+4	..	174
6. Not renominated for the same constituency (7+8+9)	38	7	..	4	+4	1	54
of which							
7. Renominated for a different constituency	*2*	..	..	..	*3*	..	*5*
8. Renominated on list	*5*	*1*	..	..	..	..	*6*
9. Not renominated at all	*31*	*6*	..	*4*	*+1*	*1*	*43*
10. Total (5+6)	161	44	5	9	+8	1	228
11. Re-elected in the same constituency	120	29	..	2	+1	..	152
12. Re-elected in a different constituency	2	..	..	..	..	..	2
13. Re-elected on list	5	7	4	2	+2	..	20
14. Not re-elected	34	8	1	5	+5	1	54
15. Total (11 to 14)	161	44	5	9	+8	1	228

[1] *or.*, original member; *recr.*, member recruited from a different party during the second legislative period.

[2] Centre Party.

of gifts or application either in the constituency or else in Bonn—usually for an inadequate performance in both. Some of these were CDU candidates who had been put up light-heartedly in 1953 when the party's overwhelming victory had not been anticipated, and who had themselves been surprised by their election. There were one or two cases where a man had sacrificed mending his fences in favour of his duties as a legislator. But there seem to have been no cases in which political heresy rather than inactivity was the complaint. Indeed one CDU member who had refused to vote for conscription was nevertheless renominated and re-elected.

The process of eliminating sitting members was by no means painless. In Bavaria several appeals were made against the legality of the procedure followed at the selection conferences concerned, usually on the grounds of someone voting who had no right to do so, in one case because the selection conference had met in such haste that not even the sitting member knew of the meeting until after his rival had been adopted.

Nor were the 123 constituency parties which readopted the sitting CDU member always unanimous. In possibly half of them the re-adoption did not go uncontested. In one city represented by two Catholic workers of the CDU, the CDU Land party threatened to withhold endorsement from one of these members in order to force the local party to adopt a Protestant employer whom they regarded as a better man. With the local selection committee evenly divided in successive ballots, the sitting member was finally readopted as a result of drawing lots.

Both CDU and SPD Land and federal parties in fact exercised rather an ineffectual influence on the selection of constituency candidates. In several cases where the local member was not re-adopted the Land party would have been very glad to see him back in Bonn; and conversely in several instances the Land party attempted to impose a new member on a constituency or simply to eliminate the sitting man, but were beaten—in at least one case the veto of the Land CDU being overridden by a second confirmatory vote in the constituency party.

The importance of local factors in the selection of constituency candidates is borne out by the fact that nearly four-fifths of those elected in 1957 claimed residence within the constituency (or in the same city) on their ballot paper: in nearly all cases this was a bona fide address which they had occupied well before their nomination. Those that were not able to claim a local address were almost invariably cabinet ministers or senior party officials whose parliamentary work forced them to live in the Bonn area; even some of these had lived in their constituencies until the establishment of the Federal Republic and can thus hardly be regarded as carpet-baggers (or what the French call *parachutistes*). Even if one includes list members, less than 20 per cent. of Bundestag members were born in any other Land of the Federal Republic than that which they represented (though another 20 per cent. were born outside the Federal Republic altogether).[1] The large number of members who could point to elective or other positions in local government in their constituency constitute another trace of the reconstruction of German democracy 'from the bottom upwards'.

In the case of CDU candidates, one further factor was considered of great importance. By a decision of the federal executive, a CDU candidature presupposed not so much Christian faith as membership of one of the Christian churches.[2] Moreover in the selection of a constituency candidate, the denomination was one of the vital subjects borne in mind. With very few exceptions—and these exceptions tended to be held up for admiration by party officials and speakers throughout the campaign—constituency candidates belonged to the denomination of the majority of the electorate, with a slight bias in favour of Catholics throughout, particularly where the Protestant majority was small.[3] The explanation of this bias is no doubt simple: where Protestants were only in a slight majority in the electorate as a whole, they were bound to be in a minority among that section of the electorate which voted CDU. Indeed it may be that the principal beneficiaries of the general parity system (in the civil service as much as in the CDU) were not the Catholics so much as the church-going Protestants, who, it was sometimes

[1] 'Die Abgeordneten des 3. Deutschen Bundestages nach Geschlecht, Alter, Herkunft und Beruf', *Wirtschaft und Statistik,* Oct. 1957, p. 538.

[2] A potential candidate for Buxtehude who had resigned formal church-membership as a result of a dispute with the local minister was disqualified from nomination by the federal headquarters of the party on these grounds.

[3] This tendency had been noticeable in earlier elections, and was very strong in 1957, as the following figures of CDU constituency members show:

Percentage of Catholics in population	*Members first elected in 1957*		*Members first elected before 1957*		*Total in the third Bundestag*		
	Prot.	*Cath.*	*Prot.*	*Cath.*	*Prot.*	*Cath.*	*Total*
0–40% .	29	6	31	7	60	13	73
40–60% .	..	10	8	13	8	23	31
60–100% .	3*	26	2	59	5	85	90
Total .	32	42	41	79	73	121	194

* Two of the three Protestants first elected for predominantly Catholic constituencies in 1957 were put up as the only Protestants in teams of candidates standing in Cologne and Munich: their inclusion in the team made its denominational proportions as close as was arithmetically possible to the denominational ratios obtaining in these cities themselves.

complained, were given an influence out of proportion to their numbers.[1]

It is natural that a discussion of constituency candidates revolves mainly around those of the CDU and SPD since they were in the vast majority of constituencies the only serious contenders. Even the constituency candidatures of the FDP and the German Party were for the most part nominal only, and so *a fortiori* were those of the smaller parties. Yet the serious candidates were in a minority: of the 1,700 candidates nominated in constituencies, a large proportion probably had no wish whatever to enter the Bundestag. They merely lent a locally respected or even unknown name to a forlorn cause, and their campaigning was often confined to a bow when introduced to the audience at the one or two meetings with a visiting speaker which their party may have held.

Selection Conferences and Party Lists

In 1957 it was beginning to be accepted as a general principle in both big parties, but particularly in the SPD, that on the whole the constituency candidates should be given the more hopeful places on the Land lists. The burden of the constituency campaign should bring its own reward if not in terms of the constituency seat, then at least in the form of a sporting chance of return on the list. A party which won 50 per cent. of all votes could in theory reward all constituency candidates in this way; but, particularly in the case of a party with no hopes of getting half the total seats, it was argued that with nearly 247 constituency candidates in the field, as few of the safe places as possible should go to men who did not pull their weight on the constituency side. For both parties it also seemed a point of honour to present to parts of the electorate individually those men whom the electorate as a whole would send to Bonn as a bloc. Perhaps the attempt to provide a full coverage of the country by 'step-members' was also made easier if the candidate had faced the problems of the constituency and if the electorate had at least seen the 'step-member's' name on the ballot paper at the time of the election.

The principle was by no means universally applied; indeed in a

[1] The historical character of the parity principle (which was not invented by the CDU) is illustrated by Goethe's:

> In einer Stadt, wo Parität
> Noch in der alten Ordnung steht,
> Da, wo sich nämlich Katholiken
> Und Protestanten ineinander schicken. . . .

few cases changes were made which ran counter to it. Dr. Arndt relinquished Hersfeld to head the Bavarian list: he had found conscientious attention to the problems of a fairly distant constituency incompatible with his heavy duties as the SPD's legal and constitutional spokesman, and the Bavarian SPD was glad to have a prominent man at the top of its list. But such cases were the exception in the SPD: of its 123 list members of the third Bundestag, only 18 had not also stood as constituency candidates. Given the shortage of prominent candidates in the two smaller parties all but one of the members elected on their lists had also stood in a constituency, the exception being Reinhold Maier himself. The CDU, too, saw that all but some 25 of its 241 constituency candidates were elected to Bonn.

It might be thought that this half-declared principle would impose a limitation on Land parties and give greater power to the local party: but in fact there were few cases in which non-adoption in a constituency was made to stand in the way of someone whom the Land party really wanted in the Bundestag. It merely proved easier to jettison from the list members who had not been adopted or re-adopted by a constituency party. Sometimes it was the member who hoped to retain his seat without fighting a constituency: thus one North Rhine–Westphalian CDU member who had declared in his constituency that he wished to make room for a younger man had only himself to blame if his request for a safe list seat was thereafter treated in fairly cavalier fashion. In the same Land an SPD list member who had found little time to help nurse the constituencies lying in his party region and who did not wish to nurse a constituency for the future also found himself without a reasonable place on the list and lost his seat.

The method of selection to the list differed between parties and from one Land party to another. The simplest method perhaps was that adopted among others by the Hamburg SPD. After the Land Executive had drawn up its own suggested list, some 300 elected delegates to the Land selection conference met for the secret ballot. The delegates presented counter-proposals and each place on the list was voted on in turn, a man defeated for one position being eligible to stand for the next position on the list. The nominees of the Land Executive were defeated in several cases.[1]

In a unitary Land party of this kind the parliamentary delegation

[1] A similar method was adopted in the case of the Berlin SPD, where list nomination—being subject only to the approval of the Berlin Parliament—in effect implied election. It was there stipulated that each candidate must obtain an absolute majority of delegates' votes; this was possible in the event only after months of adjournment.

could thus be planned both centrally and democratically. But such simple cases were the exception rather than the rule where the bigger Länder—and thus most Bundestag members—were concerned. It might further be suggested by this first example that in the case of list as against constituency candidatures local and social origins were replaced by political orientation and efficiency as the chief criteria of selection; but this also was true only to a limited extent.

Certainly the FDP in North Rhine–Westphalia deliberately put forward mainly such candidates as would observe party discipline and, in particular, would be ready to coalesce with the SPD. But even among the Free Democrats, where the selection of parliamentary personnel might have implied vital policy decisions, the selection was often determined largely by non-political factors. The top five candidates on the Baden-Württemberg list were a typical model of compromise between the four FDP organizations in the Land: the leading candidate was Reinhold Maier as Federal Chairman of the party, the second was a representative of North Württemberg, the third of South Württemberg, the fourth of South Baden, and the fifth of North Baden.

Geographical Quotas

Such a system of geographical quotas was applied by each of the three bigger parties, and by most of the smaller ones as well. (In the case of the BHE the original residence beyond the Oder–Neisse line also counted for these purposes.) The Land organizations of the CDU and FDP did not cut across Land boundaries, but in several cases for historical or 'ethnic' reasons one Land contained more than one CDU or FDP Land organization, and even where there was no such organizational split great care had to be taken in the more differentiated Länder to give fair representation to all parts of the Land. In the case of the SPD only three of the twenty party regions coincided with the Länder, and several party regions straddled Land boundaries. Partly for this reason and partly because of the jealous participation of a much bigger membership in the selection process, the geographical decentralization of decisions was taken to an extreme in the allegedly so centralized SPD.

It is worth exploring one example of this kind in some detail to illustrate once more the importance of local considerations in German political life. Ever since 1949 the four party regions of the SPD which cover the Land of North Rhine–Westphalia have in principle divided the places on the list into blocs of ten: the first ten places are allocated on 'supra-regional considerations'; all successive blocs of ten places are divided so that the first three go to the largest region, Western Westphalia, the next three go to the Lower Rhine, the seventh and eighth to Eastern Westphalia, and the last two to the Middle Rhine. This pattern, set in the 11th to 20th places, was repeated in the 21st to 30th, 31st to 40th and the subsequent places right down the list. Nothing came of the proposal to shunt the position of the regional places within these blocs of ten seats: indeed as the regional membership figures were roughly 85,000, 39,000, 23,000, and 15,000, the smaller regions do not appear to have been unfairly treated in comparison with Western Westphalia.

The regional quota allocation did not, however, stop there. It was carried on into the lists prepared by each region for the allocation of the places assigned to it on the Land list. This further regional subdivision may be illustrated by the case of the Middle Rhine region, which could nominate to the 19th and 20th, 29th and 30th, and 39th and 40th places, all regarded as hopeful, and to the 49th and 50th, which were regarded as marginal places. The 59th and corresponding subsequent places were available only for decorative and representational purposes.[1]

The party region of Middle Rhine itself covers two administrative counties (*Regierungsbezirke*): Aachen with four constituencies and Cologne with nine constituencies. Down the middle of the latter county there runs an important psychological barrier: the Rhine. The right bank, even within the city of Cologne, is the 'mangy side' —outstripped in commercial, industrial, social, and cultural importance by the left bank with its cathedral (in the old days Protestants had to be back on the right bank before the curfew), its business centre, its main railway station, and the rest. The difference in general economic and cultural development is just as great for the other areas of the county. With county Cologne thus divided psychologically into two, the two counties in effect formed three party subregions, and each of these was allocated certain positions on the Middle Rhine list. The third seat on the regional list (i.e. the 29th on the North Rhine–Westphalian list) was the preserve of county Aachen: not only was the nomination thus delegated from the Land party to the party region, but from the region to the four local constituency parties of one particular area.

[1] That hopeless positions on a Land list were not only used as a form of public recognition for services rendered in the past is indicated by the fact that one SPD Land list (containing ten times as many candidates as were elected) included a number of public employees, whose paid candidates' leave during the election allowed them to act as full-time party workers for that period.

On this third level there ensued further considerations of an organizational kind: Aachen-Stadt would have liked to renominate its constituency candidate; Aachen-Land objected that Aachen-Stadt had put forward this candidate in 1953 and secured his election for four years. Moreover he was now ill; it should therefore be the turn of one of the other three, and Aachen-Land for its part, claiming more votes, more members, and a better organization than Aachen-Stadt, proposed to nominate Severin Fritz Pütz, the chairman of the works council of a big mine in this mining area. With the support of the other two constituency parties, Düren and Jülich, which naturally also favoured the principle of rotation, the nominee of Aachen-Land was confirmed by the parties of county Aachen, reconfirmed by the party region, and adopted by the Land party. As a result of slight subsequent rearrangements Pütz finally appeared (and was elected) as the 28th candidate on the Land list.

This system did in theory lend itself to cheating between party regions. Any member elected in a constituency dropped out of the list in the allocation of seats. An unscrupulous party region could thus keep its candidates in safe and promising constituency seats off the party list or place them far down it, and thereby gain a disproportionate share of Bundestag members compared with the other party regions in the same Land. But since the interests of the best candidates themselves were not served by the risk involved in only having a constituency nomination, and since at least in the SPD party loyalties were more compelling than regional ones, there was little deliberately organized sharp practice of this kind. It only appears to have been used by the party region of Braunschweig, whose calculation misfired: among the constituency candidates not reinsured on the list Pastor Fritz Wenzel,[1] the leader of the conscientious objectors and a member of the federal SPD Executive, failed to return to Bonn; and there being no by-elections, the disappearance of a man not nominated on a Land list was final for the whole legislative term.

Other Quotas on the Land Lists

The system of geographical quotas was, however, only one of the criteria according to which each Land list was balanced. Every party felt the need to put forward women among the top five candidates (whose names were printed on the ballot paper). In only one case, that of the Bremen BHE, did a woman head a list, and in no case

[1] Protestant pastors were given leave of absence from their pastoral functions while occupying a Bundestag seat.

was there more than one woman among the top five candidates; but only 2 out of the 11 CDU/CSU lists and only 3 out of the 10 SPD lists were headed by five men.[1]

Most parties regarded it as essential to include refugees somewhere well up on the list: in the BHE, of course, they formed the overwhelming majority, but even in the CDU there was at least one refugee among the first fifteen candidates in each Land—three in Schleswig-Holstein and two each in two other Länder with a large percentage of refugees.

Thirdly it was in theory regarded as desirable to put forward at least one younger man, but in practice neither the CDU and Bavarian CSU nor the SPD placed a single candidate who was under 35 among the top 100 candidates on their twenty lists.[2]

When the obvious demands of women and of refugees had been met, there were further problems of balance to be reconciled with the geographical demands of the regional organizations. For the CDU in particular the problem became one of immense complexity as Catholics and Protestants, workers and employers, the professional classes, farmers and traders all demanded consideration in a multi-dimensional balancing act in which sex and geographical differentiation and the claims of the *Junge Union* and the *Exil-CDU* had to be taken into account as well. (The *Junge Union* was the youth organization of the CDU, the *Exil-CDU* the organization of those who had left the CDU of the Eastern Zone after it came under Communist influence.) One problem was solved in Hesse by simply alternating Catholics and Protestants right down the list; but in the same Land there was an open conflict between the *Junge Union* and the CDU itself when the *Junge Union* felt neglected in the nomination process. In North Rhine–Westphalia it was not until 20 July that the Land list was finally drawn up by fitting together the lists of the Rhineland and Westphalian parties on alternate positions of the Land list, certain places such as that of Adenauer himself being declared 'neutral' between the two. The lateness of the meeting was determined not merely by the difficulties experienced in the earlier stages, but also by the desire to avoid

[1] The fact that women had better chances of election on lists than in constituencies is borne out by the fact that, of the 43 women elected in 1957, 34 were elected on lists. Two of the women thus elected had been refused readoption by the constituencies for which they had sat in the second Bundestag. For a discussion of the candidatures of women in previous Bundestag elections see Gabriele Bremme, *Die politische Rolle der Frau in Deutschland*, Vandenhoek & Ruprecht, Göttingen, 1956, esp. pp. 136–46.

[2] Only the Saar CSU (CVP) nominated a man of 34 in the fifth place—a hopeless candidature.

recriminations and to foil any attempts to secure a revision of the list before nominations closed.[1]

The Representation of Organized Interests

Interest groups outside the parties themselves also sought to take a hand in the selection process. Thus the Chief Association of German Retail Traders sent a letter to its Land member organizations asking for money to help place one particular candidate high up on the Lower Saxon list: 'This as usual presupposes the supply of election finance. . . . Mr. Meyer-Ronnenberg informs us that it will be necessary to secure additional money so as to place him in a correspondingly promising position.'[2] The letter was no doubt clumsily worded and Meyer-Ronnenberg was in the event not placed on the Land list at all; but in a letter to the SPD Executive the Association of German Retail Traders very fairly put its view of the matter:

> You know as well as we do that it is part of the customs of parliamentary politics in Bonn that group interests are looked after by members of the Bundestag. . . . We do not consider this political style, which really is not confined to any particular parties, as a notably happy one, but we did not invent it and if a trade as large and important as that of retailing was represented in the old Bundestag with only three members, then you too will understand our wish that at least these three should be returned to the new Bundestag. The accusations of the SPD do not affect the Association, but only . . . a general system that has become a habit among all parties.[3]

Where the SPD was concerned, this habit was not anything like as extensive as in the case of the British Labour Party, where trade unions virtually purchase a substantial proportion of seats for their own members. The official party neutrality of the German Trade

[1] As it happened it was the party headquarters which nearly saw one of their favourite candidates come to grief as a result: they had committed the mistake of not leaving at least one 'soft spot' high up on the list in case the selection conference insisted on someone whom the executive had not considered. In spite (or more probably because) of headquarters support, Dr. Rainer Barzel was dropped to make room for just such a candidate, and the party therefore felt forced to veto some constituency candidate somewhere to secure a place for Barzel. To do so they circumvented rule No. 4 for the selection of candidates in Westphalia: 'Only Westphalians with their permanent residence in Westphalia can stand for the Bundestag in Westphalia.'

[2] See *Der Spiegel*, 17 July 1957, and the correspondence on the subject in the same news magazine of 24 July 1957, where Meyer-Ronnenberg, after pointing out that list places could not be bought, said that he knew of no candidate who was not busy with similar collections of money at that time. £4,000 is quoted in another letter as a CDU demand in return for each promising list place for a representative of the artisans' organizations.

[3] *Bonner Nachrichten*, 18 July 1957.

Union Federation prevented any direct flow of funds from the trade unions to the SPD, and trade unionists were to be found among the candidates of the CDU as well—as also to a lesser extent among those of most other parties. The German Trade Union Federation does not, however, appear to have taken any major initiative in the matter, since both the CDU and the SPD were eager to have trade unionists among their candidates and in their parliamentary parties. At least one prominent trade unionist, on the contrary, was asked by the trade unions to refuse readoption in order to devote more time to his increased trade union duties.

The non-socialist parties were equally anxious to include representatives of various business and middle-class organizations on their lists. In one or two cases the business associations which financed the non-socialist campaigns could secure the nomination of their candidates on CDU lists in spite of some resistance on the part of the party. (In 1953 one case had arisen where a business association, unable to obtain a suitable place for one of its members near the head of the CDU list, switched him to the FDP where he secured the top list seat.) More usually, however, there seems to have been a natural congruence of views between the party and the interest group when once an enterprising member of such a group had put the case for his nomination to both sides. The voluntary associations were glad to see some of their most prominent spokesmen in the Bundestag, while the parties were anxious to make special appeals to specific groups in the population through letters, meetings, and trade journals addressed to the interests in question. Such appeals were not confined to election times: indeed the great value to the parties of Bundestag members who were prominent members of voluntary associations consisted in the channel they provided for continuous contact through these organizations with wide sections of the population. The very greatest stress is laid in Western Germany on such public relations work on behalf of parties in what was referred to as 'the pre-political field' (*vorpolitischer Raum*).

Once elected, the representatives of interest groups as a rule developed an overriding loyalty to the party and its spirit and felt too sensitive to attacks of partisanship to be very vociferous on the floor of the House when issues affecting their interests were at stake. But this did not prevent them from working hard in the committees, and from thereby scoring solid successes on behalf of their groups. It was not too difficult for them to do so, since those who congregated in the Committee on Food, Agriculture, and Forests tended naturally to be those with interests in agriculture, and those who manned the Committee on Administration tended to be civil servants on leave. In connexion with these two examples it is worth noting that the Presidents of the Bavarian, Rhenish, and Hesse Farmers' Unions were all elected for the first time in 1957 while the Presidents of the Schleswig-Holstein and Württemberg–Hohenzollern Farmers' Unions were re-elected in 1957 on CDU (or CSU) lists,[1] and that the President and the Vice-President of the Civil Servants' Union were both re-elected, one on an FDP and the other on a CDU ticket. Including the Berlin members, who had no vote in the Bundestag but did take an active share in committee work, the Bundestag in fact contained some 61 farmers, 52 lawyers and accountants, and not only 52 higher civil servants but also 34 school and university teachers most of whom enjoyed civil service status. It goes without saying that industrial managers of all parties (including those belonging to the SPD) and trade unionists (including those who were members of the CDU) formed similar almost inter-party groups based on shared expert knowledge and on a natural alliance of interest, and that other smaller groups tended to form in the same way.

Planning the Parliamentary Party

Most of the legislative work was in fact done in Bundestag committees specialized according to subjects. As a result each party had its experts in various fields whom it sent to the committees in question and on whose advice it relied in debates and divisions.[2] It was thus regarded as of some importance that the party experts should be returned to the third Bundestag. Previous examples have shown that the picture of a few bosses in Bonn deciding on party lists is unrealistic for the Federal Republic, whatever may have been the case in the Weimar system: yet since the party headquarters could approach upwards of a dozen Land organizations (let alone the constituencies themselves), they were usually able to secure the return of the men they wanted. One party organization could almost always be found to agree in the end, however many others had previously refused to help. Thus the SPD was able to find seats for Heinemann and Helene Wessel who had no previous backing within the party, for a scientist with a special concern for the bio-

[1] Two other Land Presidents of the Farmers' Union had been CDU members of the second Bundestag and a third a Land minister, while a fourth stood on the German Party ticket in 1957.

[2] During the intricate debates on the pension reform shortly before the election, a vote was repeated by the Speaker after it was discovered that the whole of one party had mistaken a signal from its expert: he had only scratched his head, not asked them to cast their votes in favour.

logical consequences of nuclear tests, for a retiring Ambassador to India whom Ollenhauer had recruited while on his Asian tour, and the SPD's agricultural spokesman, who had been deprived of all his Lower Saxon party offices for not paying the Land levy on his Bundestag salary, was taken onto the North Rhine–Westphalian list. The CDU was able to nominate a well-known physicist as a counter-weight to the scientist on the SPD benches and a man like Franz Etzel, the Vice-President of the European Coal and Steel Community, whom Adenauer wished to see in his third Cabinet.

The federal leadership of both big parties was thus able to secure the return of a limited number of candidates of its own choice without having powers of direction and usually without exercising any undue pressure.[1] On the other hand the federal headquarters had no veto and was unable to prevent the election or re-election of anyone whom a regional or constituency party was determined to see elected. Decentralized decisions by large numbers on a local and Land level were thus reconciled with the satisfaction of the more important personnel requirements of the federal party. This happy asymmetry had been one of the most important advantages preserved by the retention of Land lists even when the third electoral law put the proportional system on a federal basis.

The Turnover of Membership

In the case of the constituency members, we have already seen that of the 54 not returned, 47 had not been renominated in their constituencies, some 25 or 30 of them being forced to retire against their will. In the case of list members the decision taken by the party was not a clear renomination or absence of renomination: if a man was renominated he could be given the same, a higher, or a lower place on the party list, or he might alternatively find himself nominated only in a constituency. Moreover, whatever his nominal place on the party list, his effective chance of being elected varied not merely with the result of the party vote, but also with the number of men with higher list places than himself who would secure election

[1] Where a party headquarters attempted to exercise such pressure, a violent reaction sometimes resulted: in the SPD, for example, Dr. Gerhard Kreyssig, an economic expert of the party, lost heavily in the South Bavarian regional pre-selection conference against a new candidate, Hermann Haage, but a letter from his kinsman Ollenhauer was sufficient to restore him to his original place on the provisional Land list. In the storm that followed, Haage was in the final list restored to his place; but a third candidate whom the SPD headquarters was sorry to lose was demoted on the list in order to ensure Kreyssig's return.

independently of the list.[1] The disappearance of the CSU member Edmund Leukert, for example, resulted (at first sight paradoxically) from the completeness of the CSU's victory in Bavaria. Leukert had been elected in 1953 though he had occupied only the twentieth place on the list. In 1957 he moved up to the sixteenth place, but when the CSU swept every constituency in the Land and only six seats remained to be allocated to its Land list, only the thirteenth candidate on the Land list secured election. Leukert could, however, hope that the disappearance of three Bavarian CSU members from the Bundestag would provide a seat for him later on in the legislative term.

Table IV sets out how 100 out of 259 list members of the second Bundestag failed to secure election to the third. Since the BHE with 19 list members failed to surmount the splinter party clause the analysis is best confined to the 81 list members of the four surviving parties.

The 40 list members who were renominated must have wished to return to Bonn; they thus lost their seats against their will. Nine of them were put up in the same or on a better list place, so that their parties cannot have been too unhappy at the thought of their doing so; the 31 who were put up again but on a lower list place, in a different Land, or in a different constituency and there failed re-election presumably found that their parties gave higher priority to other candidates than themselves.

Of the 41 list members who were not renominated at all a few themselves wished to withdraw from parliamentary life. Hermann Runge of the SPD, although only 55, found that his health had been too severely undermined by ten years' forced labour in National Socialist prisons for him to continue to serve the party in the Bundestag. Dr. Hans Wellhausen, who had transferred from the FDP to the CSU, was publicly offered the fourth place on the Bavarian list but then refused it in protest against the Government's fiscal policy and the hegemony of vested interests in the Bundestag; he preferred to return to his work in industry. We may reckon that about half the others were refused renomination by their parties; 5 FDP list members, 6 of the SPD, and no doubt 10 or more of the CDU list members fell into this category. They included most of

[1] In 1953 the same candidate could stand on every Land list of his party as well as in one constituency; if he was elected in a constituency, all his party colleagues below him on every Land list to all intents and purposes moved up one place in their chances of election on the list. Quite apart from the constituency prospects of a candidate's colleagues higher up on the list than himself, the change in the law on this point alone often made the same numerical position on the list in 1957 as in 1953 represent in effect a smaller chance of election.

those who had changed their party during the legislative period.[1] Few of the other list members not renominated were prominent men.

The election result enlarged the parliamentary representation of the CDU, of the SPD, and of the FDP at the expense of the smaller

TABLE IV

The Fate of List Members of the Second Bundestag

	CDU			*FDP*		*DP*		*Sub-total*	*Other*	
	or.	*recr.*	*SPD*	*or.*	*recr.*	*or.*	*recr.*	*(net)*	*(net)*	*Total*
1. Elected 6 Sept. 1953	72	..	106	34	..	5	..	217	28*	245
2. Moved up subsequently	9	..	1	3	..	1	..	14	..	14
3. Changed party	−2	+10†	..	−10	+1‡	..	+10§	+21 −12	+2‖ −11	±23
4. Sat on nomination day	79	+10	107	27	+1	6	+10	240	19	259
5. Re-elected on list	36	+2	80	13	..	3	..	134	..	134
6. Re-elected in a constituency	14	+1	8	..	..	1	+1	25	..	25
7. Not re-elected	29	+7	19	14	+1	2	+9	81	19	100
of which										
8. Put up only in a constituency or on a different Land list	3	+1	1	1	..	2	+1	9	2	11
9. Same Land list, lower position	8	+2	5	4	..	..	+3	22	5	27
10. Same Land list, same or higher position	4	..	1	1	..	..	+3	9	11	20
11. Not put up again at all	14	+4	12	8	+1	..	2	41	1	42
12. Total	79	+10	107	27	+1	6	+10	240	19	259

or., original member; *recr.*, recruited during the second legislative period from another party.
* 27 BHE, 1 Centre Party.
† 8 from the BHE, 1 from the FDP, 1 from the Centre.
‡ 1 from the BHE.
§ 8 from the FDP, 1 from the CDU, 1 from the BHE.
‖ 1 from the CDU, 1 from the FDP, both to the BHE.

parties. It would thus in theory have been possible for each of these parties to re-elect every one of its sitting members. The constituency members who lost their constituencies could have been re-elected on the Land list, the list members could have been selected for good constituencies and there was a margin for error left over, for the

[1] In fact of all the 31 members (including those sitting for constituencies) who had changed parties, only 6 were returned in 1957, 4 of the 6 being ministers who had originally belonged to the BHE and the FDP and who had stayed in the Cabinet when their parties went into opposition.

CDU membership rose by 15, the SPD membership by 16, and the FDP membership by 7 members (excluding those from the Saar) and neither CDU nor SPD lost a single seat in any Land. Nevertheless, as section C of Table V shows, half the Free Democrats, over a quarter of the Christian Democrats, but less than a fifth of the Social Democrats who had been members of the second Bundestag were not returned.

TABLE V

The Turnover in Bundestag Membership
(excluding Saar and Berlin members)

		CDU/CSU	SPD	FDP	DP	Others	Total
A. Constituency members							
sitting August 1957	(1)	161	44	5	17	1*	228
of whom: not sitting Oct. 1957	(2)	34	8	1	10	1*	54
(2) as a percentage of (1)	*(3)*	*21%*	*18%*	*20%*	*58%*	*100%*	*29%*
B. List members							
sitting August 1957	(4)	89	107	28	16	19†	259
of whom: not sitting Oct. 1957	(5)	36	19	15	11	19†	100
(5) as a percentage of (4)	*(6)*	*42%*	*18%*	*54%*	*69%*	*100%*	*38%*
C. All members							
sitting August 1957	(7)	250	151	33	33	20	487
of whom: not sitting Oct. 1957	(8)	70	27	16	21	20	154
(8) as a percentage of (7)	*(9)*	*28%*	*18%*	*48%*	*62%*	*100%*	*32%*
D. All members							
sitting Oct. 1957	(10)	265	165	40	17	..	489
of whom: not sitting Aug. 1957	(11)	85	43	23	5	..	156
(11) as a percentage of (10)	*(12)*	*32%*	*26%*	*58%*	*29%*	..	*32%*
E. Total seats gained by each party	(13)	15	16	7	−16	−20	2

* Centre Party. † BHE.

In a few cases both the party and the member himself had hoped for his re-election, but a miscalculation of the vote deprived him of his seat. Thus Dr. Joachim Schöne of the SPD fell between the two stools of constituency and list election: he had been generally expected to carry the constituency of Peine-Gifhorn (which includes Wofsburg with its Volkswagen works) and had not been reinsured on the list. Such accidents, however, were few.

We may thus conclude that of the 154 members of the second Bundestag who did not become members of the third, about a quarter (chiefly BHE and German Party members) were deprived of their seats by the election result. A smaller number genuinely wished to retire, but the remainder, representing more than half those retiring and a sixth of the second Bundestag, were deprived of their seats against their wishes not by the electorate but by their own party selection committees and selection conferences. In a few cases good men were dropped in favour of candidates with less promising qualifications: on the whole, however, the process appears to have resulted in a very healthy improvement in the calibre of Bundestag personnel which countries that give greater security to their sitting members might envy.

The undoubted rise in the average standard of Bundestag members seems in fact to have taken place more through the elimination of old members who fell below the average than through the recruitment of many outstanding new men. The first election was held under circumstances that did not favour a careful selection of candidates, and the small parties since eliminated from Bonn contributed their share of adventurers to the House. Before the second Bundestag election the parties were able to sift their members to some extent in the light of experience, but they were not yet sufficiently familiar with the working of the electoral law to be very precise in their calculations and the CDU in particular was hampered in its purge of members by the unexpectedly favourable election result. Although one member was deprived of his seat for absconding to Eastern Germany, the number of scandals of one kind or another that occurred in the second Bundestag was considerably smaller than that which had marked the first. This fact, together with the legislation achieved over the years, helped to provide a further justification of the steady rise of the Bundestag in popular esteem.[1] At the time of its election there was no reason to believe that on average the personnel of the third Bundestag would not prove the most competent yet. But it may still be asked whether the method of selection really encouraged the recruitment—difficult in any case—of the best potential legislators or of those with the greatest breadth of view and independence of spirit.

[1] See Erich Peter Neumann and Elisabeth Noelle, *Antworten*, Demoskopie, Allensbach, 1955, p. 75.

V

CAMPAIGN PRELUDES AND POLICY ISSUES

The Date of the Election

AT the beginning of 1957 Bonn was already seriously affected by election fever. The press reported the bulk of foreign and domestic news with constant reference to its bearing on the electoral battle. The Bundestag decided to withhold the usual permission for its proceedings to be photographed, broadcast, and televised. Its members were already busy in the constituencies and in the Länder preparing the way for their readoption. The quantity of legislation still left over for disposal combined with the temptation for members of all parties to frame vote-catching amendments in committee and on the floor of the House seemed to be resulting in a deterioration in the quality of the Bundestag's work. Speeches were made with a more direct appeal to the electorate than usual, the style of controversy took a turn for the worse, and it was generally said that the election—in these senses at any rate—had begun nearly a year before the end of the legislative period.

By February the rise in tension led to the widely canvassed suggestion that, now the election was on, polling day should be brought forward as far as possible in order to save the parties money and work and also spare the voter impatience with the excesses and boredom with the duration of party political controversy. This plan, however, had to reckon with the terms of the Basic Law and with such constitutional practice as the Federal Republic had already evolved.

The Federal President can dissolve the Bundestag only if there is no majority to be found in it either to support a vote of confidence in the existing Chancellor or to elect a new one.[1] He has never been called upon to use that power, and since the prerequisite conditions did not obtain in 1957, a dissolution was out of the question.

When there is no dissolution the Bundestag is subject to automatic renewal. Article 39 of the Basic Law lays down that: 'The Bundestag is elected for a four-year term. Its legislative term ends four years after its first meeting or with its dissolution. The new election takes place in the last three months of the legislative term. . . .'

[1] Articles 63 and 68 of the Basic Law.

Since the second Bundestag held its first meeting on 6 October 1953 and since the electoral law also stipulates that polling shall be on a Sunday or a public holiday the only possible dates—short of the declaration of a special holiday—were the thirteen Sundays between 7 July and 29 September inclusive.

The same paragraph of the electoral law determined that it is the Federal President who fixes the date of poll; though in fact the British model was so universally kept in mind that even the Opposition did not question the right assumed by the Government of advising the President in a sense favourable to its own electoral chances.

The only precedent had been for an election at the very end of the term of office of the previous Bundestag, and the provision of the Basic Law that the new Bundestag could not meet until the term of office of the old had expired also suggested a late polling day: there was nothing to be said for a three-month period in which either no Bundestag met at all or else one whose successor had already been elected.

In spite of these considerations, in March important members of the CDU parliamentary party came out in favour of a July election. Public opinion polls had been turning in the CDU's favour again since Christmas and there was no knowing how far the cost of living might rise by the autumn.[1] The old Bundestag could be recalled if necessary during the election or even after polling day to ratify the Rome treaties establishing the common market of the European Economic Community and 'Euratom', but would adjourn for other purposes in May. The remaining legislation could wait, and if the debates were to consist of little more than electioneering speeches these could just as well be delivered on the hustings.

This suggestion was welcomed in many quarters as sensible and realistic, though the tart comment was also heard that instead of adjourning the Bundestag in deference to the election campaign, the parties might have postponed their campaigns in deference to the work of the Bundestag.

For their own reasons the FDP, BHE, and the German Party all hoped that the election would take place in September; only the SPD, which might perhaps have thought that it would have less to lose from a summer holiday election than the others, maintained a discreet silence in public.[2]

[1] A CSU deputy added in a Bundestag speech that the election could not be held on or after 22 Sept. in any case owing to the October beer festival in Munich: with 200,000 people on the beer ground at any one time, the election would not be taken seriously.

[2] The CDU managers afterwards claimed that the discussion of this issue had given them useful clues on the state of campaign preparations among their rivals.

The dispute in fact became one internal to the CDU, with the campaign managers maintaining that they knew better than the parliamentary party. They had geared their campaign plans to a September election for two reasons. July was already a holiday month for many town-dwellers and a month of heavy work for the farmers: and a low poll was a handicap for the CDU. The relatively indifferent do not vote against the *status quo*. Moreover the public opinion pollsters had for years been asking the question 'How do you feel?' and they had always received the happiest replies around August or September. Good weather not only helped the turnout, but seemed also to be counted in the Government's favour.

Given this difference of view in the party, Adenauer reserved the final decision to himself. He came down in favour of the managers against the parliamentary party. The hope of seeing the Rome treaties ratified without a new Bundestag already standing by in the wings may have weighed with him in addition to the organizers' calculations. On 20 March the Cabinet thus decided to advise the President to fix the date of poll for 15 September, after the holidays but before the weather was expected to break.[1]

Pension Reform and Price Stabilization

The first major measure passed by the Bundestag in 1957, the reform of the pension laws, was to have an important bearing on the election. The Bundestag had spent three months completely recasting the Bill introduced by the Government; it completed its final draft on 10 January and the measure passed its second reading on the 18th and its third reading on the 21st of the same month.

This measure marked a revolution in social policy: it introduced the principle that the level of pensions should rise with the level of the national income. This so-called 'productivity pension' was to be fixed for each new pensioner with reference to the level of earnings of those still employed at the time the pension was first granted; and thereafter each pension was to partake in the annual general adaptation of all pensions to the financial position of the insurance fund and to the productivity of the economy and the income per head of the gainfully employed. The system was thus designed not merely to give a fair security of real income against inflation, but in addition to allow the pensioners to share in the rise of the real social product.

[1] Given the competition from mass entertainment, motoring, and sport, it was regarded as impossible to organize any effective popular movement of opposition in Germany between elections except in the atmosphere created by bad weather—rain being regarded as particularly favourable to opposition against any kind of nuclear experiments or atomic rearmament.

From the point of view of the election campaign, however, its importance lay not merely in this new principle, but also in the substantial immediate increase in benefits which the new formula brought to 7 million pensioners whose benefits were raised on average by about 60 per cent. This increase in pensions, moreover, was back-dated to 1 January, so that when the recalculations were completed in late spring considerable lump sums were paid out to the bulk of 7 million voters.[1]

There can be no doubt that this pension reform, for all the objections which the Social Democrats had to it in matters of detail, took much of the wind out of the sails of their propaganda on social policy. While the Social Democrats voted with the Christian Democrats in favour of the reform, the DP and FVP, though represented in the Cabinet, allowed their members a free vote. The only party to issue a whip against it were the Free Democrats. They found fault with it on many details—they had, for example, demanded that pensions be sent by post and that all pensioners should benefit immediately without exception—but their main arguments against it were that it compelled a wider range of people to join the system, that it merged the insurance of white-collar workers with the national system, that it imposed unduly high contributions on employers and employed, and that it represented a major danger to the stability of the currency.

It was argued by many observers that the pension reform was not an unmixed electoral benefit to the CDU: that the pensioners were politically less mobile than either the employed or the employers, and the compulsory contributions of both of these latter rose from 1 March by 1 per cent. of basic earnings. An even greater disadvantage to the CDU was seen in the sudden injection of extra purchasing power into the market for consumer goods during the second quarter of 1957.[2] In the early months of the year the saying was current that if Adenauer stumbled, it would be over prices; and the upward pressure on prices at the turn of the year looked dangerous to the CDU and promising to the SPD even without the back-payment of higher pensions.

If prices never became as much of a burning issue in the election as the SPD hoped, this was due to a remarkable achievement on the

[1] A pensioner whose benefits had been raised by the average proportion of 60 per cent. would thus on 1 Apr. receive 340 per cent., or on 1 May 400 per cent., of his former monthly pension.

[2] It was estimated at the time that in the first year of operation payments under the new formula would amount to £1,100 million instead of the £630 million which would have been paid under the old system.

part of the Ministry of Economic Affairs and of Erhard himself. The consumer price index based on 1953, which had risen from 104 to 106 during 1956, stayed at that figure until July, and then remained at 107 until after the election.[1]

The methods by which prices were thus held almost stable in spite of all pressures were essentially threefold: first, by a selective increase of the imported goods available to the public; second, by persuading the sellers that it was in their long-term interests to defer price increases until after the election. Both these methods were reinforced by a third—an astute psychological campaign in which Erhard combined his usual genial optimism with the threat to act 'by brutal force'.

Where imports were concerned, the Government made available cheap Danish butter and tinned meat to coincide with the back-payment of pensions; it was thought that these were two commodities on which pensioners would wish to spend heavily after their years of penury. To establish a control on the retail margins on imported goods the 'everyman import' programme was launched on 1 May whereby any citizen could import by post up to £8 worth of foreign industrial commodities, coffee, or tobacco without an import licence. Moreover a 25–33 per cent. reduction in a wide range of customs duties was made in the summer. These three measures appear, however, to have had mainly psychological rather than quantitative effects before the election.

Simultaneously Erhard embarked on a series of conferences with certain traders' associations and also with certain producers. He was unable in the Cabinet to stop Fritz Schäffer, the Minister of Finance, from having the general fares on federal buses raised by a quarter; but in his dealings with the commercial and industrial associations he was much more successful. In late March and early April first the 36,000 retailers of one association began a publicity campaign to show how many of their goods were cheaper or no more expensive than in 1955; then fifty manufacturers of branded goods published an advertisement in which they promised not to raise prices before the end of the year (a few of them appear to have raised their prices shortly before the advertisement appeared); then the leading chain stores undertook to support Erhard's crusade for lower prices by every means. The shoe industry, the building materials industry, the wall-paper manufacturers, and further manufacturers of branded goods also issued declarations joining the campaign.

For those who read their newspapers it was clear that at least one very important basic price, that of coal, would be held down not

[1] O.E.E.C., op. cit., p. 131.

even until the end of the year, but only until just after the election, and that the Government itself was considering a sizeable increase in the price of rail transport. It was realized fairly generally that the fears of the business community that the CDU might be defeated were an important factor in the success of the campaign against rising prices. Nevertheless, whatever the motive, the public was grateful for this 'closed season'.

Erhard's psychological calculation had been daring. He had, for example, objected strenuously when the price of bread rolls was slightly increased at the beginning of the year and he gave this price rise all the publicity he could. His own volubility on the subject may have made the public more conscious of the pressure on prices and raised the 'subjective price index' at the time—but the election was then sufficiently far away for it not to matter. On the contrary: if anyone was to talk about prices, it was better that Erhard rather than Ollenhauer should do so. And when all the uproar over prices had subsided and the ordinary consumer felt no price increases that seemed to justify the clamour, the CDU could more than ever claim to be the party that would hold the cost of living down.

Trips and Scandals

While Erhard was thus warding off a dangerous issue on the home front, the final round of the party leaders' trips abroad had begun. In February Ollenhauer flew to the United States, where he was briefly received by President Eisenhower. This trip, like his journey to Asia at the end of 1956, had a threefold purpose. It was designed, in the first place, to secure publicity inside Germany for the man whom the SPD hoped to present as Adenauer's successor in the autumn; it was thus to form something of a pendant to Adenauer's trip to America just before his electoral triumph in 1953. It was meant, in addition, to give Ollenhauer an opportunity of meeting the men with whom he might later have to take up official relations, acquaint himself with their views on the world situation, adapt his own position in the light of their attitudes, and then speak with greater authority on foreign affairs after his return. Thirdly, these trips were meant to allow Ollenhauer to state abroad the SPD's views on the future of German foreign policy—views to which the Asian peoples had been indifferent and which the West was viewing with deep suspicion;[1] any response that he might obtain favourable

[1] Compare, for example, an article published in the *New York Herald Tribune* on 15 Jan. 1957 by the Rt. Hon. Anthony Nutting, who until two months before had been British Minister of State for Foreign Affairs: 'How long will Russia have to wait to achieve her principal aim in Europe—the destruction of NATO? Not more

to his ideas would only go to strengthen his case before the German electorate in September.

Such trips abroad were regarded as an essential part of the electoral ritual in 1957. They emphasized not only the 'primacy of foreign policy' in the eyes of the leaders of both big parties, but also the extent to which opinions on them expressed in other countries—particularly in the United States—were still regarded as relevant to their electoral chances at home.

Adenauer spent the end of March and the beginning of April in Teheran; the newsreels and the illustrated weekly papers exploited to the full this meeting between the old German statesman and the young and beautiful Queen of Persia set against a back-cloth of Oriental splendour.[1] At the end of May Adenauer flew to the United States, and returned with an assurance from President Eisenhower: the United States did not intend to take any measures of disarmament that might prejudice German reunification, and would consult the Federal Government on all questions affecting Germany that might be discussed during the disarmament conference. In the middle of June Adenauer paid his last visit to a foreign country before the election, being received in state in Vienna. The Bonn meetings of NATO and Mr. Macmillan's visit to Bonn in May were no doubt somewhat similar in their effect to Adenauer's journeys abroad—both emphasizing before the German public his international connexions and prestige.

While both party leaders were thus anxious to suggest that they had the approval of the West, the opponents of the SPD were determined to associate that party in the public's view with special links to the Communist East. February and March in fact saw what proved to be two false starts to the election campaign.

than 12 months, I would say, if we go on as we are. Germany holds the key. What Germany does will decide the future of NATO, and this is election year in Germany. At present the chances of that great European, Dr. Adenauer, being returned look slim indeed. His Socialist opponent, Herr Erich Ollenhauer, seems an odds-on bet for Chancellor. . . . His election could mean the replacement of a statesman of proven loyalty to the Western alliance by a politician who is all things to all men and will bend whichever way the wind blows. Ollenhauer and his friends are already hungrily gulping down the neutralist bait. . . . NATO is in trouble enough with the Anglo-American split. If, on top of this, Germany should go neutral, NATO would founder. France and the rest would follow with all speed; the North African bases would fold up; and Communism would be threatening the Atlantic and Mediterranean seaboards of Europe. This is no mere nightmare. This is stark reality.'

[1] 'And Ollenhauer has himself photographed with Mrs. Golda Meir' (the Israeli Foreign Secretary), a rising SPD politician was heard to remark in despair at this juncture.

In February the CDU instantaneously blazoned a report published in the Stockholm *Dagens Nyheter* that Herbert Wehner, an influential member of the SPD Executive and chairman of the Bundestag Committee for All-German Affairs, had been imprisoned in Sweden during the war as a Soviet spy. Wehner had been a high official of the German Communist Party and had gone to Sweden from Russia to maintain contact with the underground movement in Germany. *Dagens Nyheter* hastened to publish a *démenti* of its report, the origin of which was not clear.

In the CDU's propaganda Wehner's name was constantly coupled with that of Dr. Viktor Agartz, the former head of the Institute of Economic Research of the Trade Union Federation. He was arrested in March on the charge of having over a considerable period of time received large sums of money from the Communist-dominated Free Trade Union Congress of the German Democratic Republic. (Agartz was later released and acquitted after the election, though not for lack of evidence of his receiving the money, but for lack of proof of treasonable intent.) Throughout the campaign the names of Agartz and Wehner (and in Adenauer's speeches teasing references to Wehner's 'international experience') occurred with a frequency that showed that a point had been made and that it was being driven home.

The Issue of Atomic Weapons

If in March and early April it thus seemed as if the campaign might become particularly bitter and personal just because there were no real issues to divide the parties from each other, the election entered upon a totally new phase on 12 April—the day on which eighteen leading professors of nuclear physics (including Max Born, Otto Hahn, and Werner Heisenberg, all Nobel prize-winners) launched an appeal from Göttingen to the public at large:

> The plans for equipping the federal forces with atomic weapons are causing the undersigned atomic scientists grave concern. . . . Every single tactical atom bomb or shell has an effect which resembles that of the first atom bomb which destroyed Hiroshima. . . . We know of no technical possibility of protecting large populations securely from this danger. . . .

After acknowledging that they were scientists and not politicians, the professors went on to state that their research nevertheless imposed certain responsibilities on them and that they could not be silent where some political problems were concerned:

> We do not feel competent to make concrete proposals for the policies of the great powers. But we believe that a small country like the Federal Republic

will best protect itself and do most to advance world peace by expressly and voluntarily renouncing the possession of atomic weapons of any kind. At least none of the undersigned would be prepared to take any part in the production, testing or use of atomic weapons.

The scientists' appeal had been provoked by the Chancellor's declaration that tactical atomic weapons were only a development of artillery. The Government's position was even more difficult in that Franz-Josef Strauss, the Minister of Defence, had declared earlier in the same week:

It is not as if we were trying to obtain equipment with tactical atomic weapons specially for the Bundeswehr, as is so often alleged. . . . Our point is that we demand equality of rights with the other European NATO forces.[1]

The size of the banner headlines reporting the scientists' appeal reflected the fact that in the eyes of the German public the title of a professor ranks well above that of a minister, and that the Göttingen appeal seemed to be a clearly non-party stand on a subject which the bulk of the press had hitherto tended to treat as one of the preserves in which the Government's policy was immune from open attack.

That the Chancellor also regarded this subject as one for the Government rather than for the public was apparent from his testy reply. The scientists should have come and talked to him as the man responsible for political matters; he would have told them of American experiments on the protection of armed forces and civilian populations from the effects of atomic weapons. To make policy recommendations one had to know these things which the scientists, since they had not come to him, did not know.

Very soon, however, it was realized that this ill-tempered response had been unwise. The public was genuinely alarmed, the SPD was taking the issue up on a big scale, and the political commentators felt that here might be an argument of capital importance which could turn the tables in the election campaign. The Chancellor accordingly invited a number of the professors concerned to a discussion of the whole matter. The communiqué issued after this meeting on 17 April, in which Generals Heusinger and Speidel also took part, made it clear that, in view of its treaty obligations, the Federal Republic could not produce atomic weapons of its own and that therefore the Government would have no call to ask the professors concerned to help in their production. But no mention was made of any unilateral renunciation of atomic weapons by the Federal Republic. It seems that Strauss explained that the federal forces

[1] On the Hesse radio, reprinted in Keesing, *Archiv der Gegenwart*, 9 Apr. 1957, p. 6379.

would not be effectively equipped with such weapons until 1959 in any case, but that if no general atomic disarmament had been reached by then, a renunciation by the federal forces of such arms would disrupt the whole working of NATO.

Albert Schweitzer's appeal against further nuclear tests, published all over the world on 23 April, appeared to give an added moral sanction to the Göttingen appeal, but on 27 April a threatening note from Moscow[1] cut across the domestic debate and gave it more than a party political note.

Four weeks of public discussion during which atomic questions were the overriding issue reached their climax in a dignified debate in the Bundestag on 10 May. Already earlier in April the SPD had tabled a motion which asked the Bundestag to appeal to the great powers to discontinue test explosions pending an agreement on their control, limitation, and eventual prohibition. The SPD also demanded that the Government should not equip the federal forces with nuclear weapons, should refuse or withdraw permission for nuclear weapons to be stationed by other powers on German soil, and should state the measures which it would take to protect the civilian population.

The most prominent parts in the debate were taken by Adenauer and Ollenhauer themselves, by the SPD's spokesman on defence Fritz Erler, by Strauss, and by Dr. Eugen Gerstenmaier, who abandoned his Speaker's chair for the occasion. The Bundestag rejected the motions of the Social and Free Democrats, and the CDU/CSU and DP/FVP majority in the Bundestag adopted a resolution which called upon the great powers to stop test explosions for a limited period, expressed the hope that the success of the London negotiations on disarmament would modify the problem of equipping German forces with nuclear weapons—a problem which, it stated, had not yet arisen—and declared: 'The German people expects from its allies protection and the prevention of Soviet attack. The German Bundestag therefore sees no cause to demand any restrictions on the equipment of the troops installed by its allies for the defence of the Federal Republic.'

The Social and Free Democrats naturally did not let the matter rest there, but carried it over into their election programmes. The SPD demanded both the unilateral renunciation of atomic weapons by the Federal Republic and the withdrawal of atomic weapons from its soil. The Free Democrats, while they joined the SPD in the first of these demands, were less radical where atomic weapons in the hands of foreign troops were concerned. They demanded: 'Suitable

[1] See below, Chapter XII, p. 251.

international measures of control which will prevent the stationing or storage of atomic weapons in Germany on either side of the iron curtain'—a symmetrical arrangement that might be far harder to obtain. In the Free Democrats' Berlin programme of January, the issue of atomic weapons had not even been mentioned; if 'Protect us from atomic danger' had by June become the second item in their shorter 'Programme of Action', that was the direct result of the scientists' and of Albert Schweitzer's appeals.[1]

The Seventh Party Congress of the CDU

Two days after the Bundestag debate on atomic weapons the seventh party congress of the CDU opened in Hamburg under Adenauer's chairmanship. From the point of view of campaign style the congress was notable not only for the usual corporate acts of worship which preceded it, but also for a brilliant three-hour lecture delivered to the congress itself by a Protestant theologian, Professor Helmut Thielicke, who was not a member of the CDU and was given a completely free hand. Under the title of *Conscience and Responsibility in the Atomic Age*, he hailed the Göttingen appeal as 'a moral event'—'less an argument than a confession, not a statement of science but the appeal of conscience' designed to evoke 'the ethos of the first step' in a situation in which 'the concept of a just war becomes absurd'. He went on to lecture the congress:

> It is a very serious symptom of the sickness of our time and a sign of our idolising the autarky of politics (*politischen Eigengesetzlichkeit*) if many circles, also among politicians, are no longer able even to listen to or understand an appeal of conscience as such, but either interpret it politically or use it for political purposes. If the news-sheet of one party in effect writes that the eighteen atomic scientists must be the 'stooges' (*Funktionäre*) of a very questionable controlling political agency, and if another party merely hastens to make them into the dynamo of its own campaign, changing the gold of a question of conscience and human destiny into the small coin of party politics, then I can only say that this is sad indeed, and does not serve to establish the inner integrity of such politicians.[2]

Thielicke's lecture created a deep impression and Adenauer himself rose immediately afterwards to make an improvised contribu-

[1] In early 1958 the SPD, basing itself on the Chancellor's pronouncements, claimed that the equipment of the Bundeswehr had not been an issue in the election and should be decided by referendum (an institution not known to the Basic Law for such purposes), while the CDU held that in view of the voters' rejection of the SPD programme on the matter its election mandate included the right to proceed.

[2] Helmut Thielicke, *Gewissen und Verantwortung im Atomzeitalter*, text multigraphed as a press release by the CDU in Hamburg, 13 May 1957. The quotations are taken from pp. 34–38.

tion to the debate. Assuring Professor Thielicke that his lecture had been a check on his own examination of his conscience, he drew a distinction between those who could afford to entertain theoretical considerations, and those who were forced to act. If the Federal Republic had renounced atomic weapons for the future, this would have upset the balance of war potential and reduced or destroyed the prospects of success of the London disarmament conference.

Where the CDU's orientation in domestic policy was concerned, the Hamburg congress marked the emphatic confirmation of the defeat or evaporation of the CDU's 'left' wing. Gerstenmaier, in a paper on social legislation, declared that in many fields the extreme limit had been reached which divided the socially responsible state from the welfare state, the spineless kindness-state, and the charity-state of a super-socialist type. Kaiser, the trade unionist Minister for All-German Affairs who had described himself in earlier days as a 'Socialist out of Christian conviction', was ill and could not attend. His close associate Karl Arnold, the former North Rhine–Westphalian Minister-President who had been regarded as the other trade union champion of ideas closer to the SPD than the FDP, read a paper on *Property for Each* in which he refused to envisage socialization as a means of stabilizing society. Asked at a press conference whether this paper represented a departure from the programme which the CDU had adopted at the Ahlen congress in 1947 (where it had demanded the socialization of the coal, steel, and chemical industries), the CDU's campaign manager Dr. Franz Meyers replied in terms which were to be quoted against the CDU throughout the campaign: the Ahlen programme had to be seen in its historical perspective—it had in fact even then been designed to prevent socialization.

In the place of socialization, Erhard had another plan which was indeed the very opposite: the transfer to private ownership of federally controlled enterprises by the issue of 'people's shares' (*Volksaktien*)—a plan to be applied first to the most attractive of the federally controlled assets, the Volkswagen works. The social market economy was now to enter on its second phase, when capital formation in the hands of enterprises had gone ahead far enough to allow the reform of social legislation and the formation of small capital in the hands of private individuals who were not entrepreneurs. Western Germany was in effect to become an increasingly bourgeois society. 'It is of symbolic and programmatic significance', Erhard told the congress, 'that our party thus shows its determination to transfer the ownership of the works that produces the "People's Car" into the widest circles of the people by means of the "people's share".'

The People's Share and the Volkswagen Works

This new plank which the Hamburg Congress added to the CDU platform was not to be an easy one to handle. As introduced into the Bundestag by the parliamentary party (not the Government), the Bill was designed to serve almost every known good cause in German politics.[1] One-quarter of the shares, issued at a nominal value of 50 DM (about £4) each, were to be sold at a 20 per cent. discount to individuals with incomes of less than £750 or at a 10 per cent. discount to those whose annual income was less than £1,200, provided they undertook to hold them for at least three years. There were to be safeguards against control by large shareholders (such as competing car manufacturers), and no one was to own more than £1,000 out of the £40 million of nominal capital. Within three years the federal authorities were to reduce their voting strength in the general meeting of shareholders to one in fifty thousand votes. The capital proceeds of the sale were to be held in a special account to be used for the modernization of the East German economy after reunification. Until reunification, they were to be used to help adapt the industries of the Saar to conditions on the German market, to improve water supplies and water control, and to help the middle classes. The yield from the capital was to go to finance research projects and scientific education.

In spite of these manifold virtues the Bill met with sharp opposition. The SPD argued that it was odd that this measure should only have been introduced in the last month or so of the effective legislative period. It was wrong to transfer to private ownership precisely those publicly controlled enterprises which made a profit, and thus leave the rest, which could not find buyers, as burdens on the taxpayer. Moreover, the SPD argued, the withdrawal of the State from its control over the Volkswagen works would involve a not unimportant abdication of public influence over industrial activity as a whole and over prices in the automobile market in particular.

The Volkswagen workers came out on a token strike against the Bill which, they feared, threatened the generous premiums and amenities to which the ownerless works had devoted a share of its profits, and trade union spokesmen called the scheme an election bait to distract attention from demands for co-ownership.

But the opposition did not come only from the SPD and the labour side. Schäffer, as Federal Minister of Finance, disliked the prospect of losing control over an asset whose value was rising fast;

[1] For its text see Document 3534 of the second Bundestag, which debated it on 31 May 1957.

the CDU Minister of Finance of Lower Saxony protested against the disposal by the Federation of what his Land regarded as at least partially its own property; the Volkswagen savers (who had paid the National Socialist Labour Front Reichsmark deposits on cars that were never delivered) feared that their claims might be more difficult to enforce against a privately owned works; stock exchange opinion was sceptical of the net yield on a 50 DM people's share after the various administrative charges had been met, and the legal difficulties of turning an enterprise of which the ownership was not clear into a limited company and putting its shares up for sale were formidable in themselves.

The most enterprising retort to the CDU's initiative came from the Free Democrats, who felt that they had been outbid in this case and were determined to 'test the sincerity' of the CDU by three demands: firstly, that the large federal holdings in banks and heavy industry be liquidated also, secondly, that the CDU should publicly and explicitly disavow the Ahlen programme, and, thirdly, that they should help the FDP to amend the Basic Law. Article 15 of the Basic Law states that: 'Land, natural resources and means of production may, for the purpose of socialisation, be transferred to public ownership or other forms of public control....' The FDP amendment was simply to delete the words 'means of production'. The tactics of the FDP were clever: if the amendment were passed, the voters could not fear any socialization from a coalition between Free and Social Democrats; if the CDU did not allow it to pass, then the Free Democrats could argue that private enterprise was obviously not safe in CDU hands, and the collectivist 'tacit coalition' of Catholics and Socialists could be painted in even darker hues than before. The CDU parliamentary party did not see that time could be found for this amendment any more than for the Volkswagen Bill. Like every other proposal, the Bill and the proposal to amend the Basic Law lapsed when the second Bundestag, which all but finished work in June, rose for the last time after a brief session on 29 August.

The Inaugural Rallies

The month of June saw the official opening of the campaigns of the three big parties at 'election congresses' called for the purpose. The FDP proclaimed its electoral *Programme of Action* in Hamburg on 5 and 6 June, the SPD launched its manifesto *Security for All* in Dortmund on the 16th, and the CDU formally opened its campaign at the federal congress of the CDU's youth organization, the *Junge Union*, held in Dortmund on the 30th. These congresses were designed as show-piece demonstrations of unity rather than as opportunities for internal debate; they were in fact recognized by all parties as a highly effective method of gaining publicity for their programmes and their leaders in the press, on the radio, and on television.

The Free Democrats, believing that the electorate made up its mind very early on, and anxious to secure as much publicity as possible before party congresses became boring to the public, were the first to open their campaign in this way. At their Hamburg congress Maier appeared for the first time for years without attacking Adenauer personally; he felt that it was now for the younger men to make sorties in both directions, and for him to act as a central pivot—so that in due course the party could be swung into a coalition with either the SPD or the CDU. This did not prevent more of the offensive being directed against the CDU than against the SPD: but it was made explicitly clear that the front line drawn in the election campaign might be very different from the front line after the formation of a coalition.

The demonstration of unity given at this congress was indeed remarkable for the FDP. The internal dissensions had been overcome: Dehler had been replaced, the old liberal element around Maier had been at least temporarily reconciled with the Düsseldorf 'Young Turks', the loose federation of Land parties had been tied in together under the latter's control, and the series of carefully edited little congress speeches from a row of geographically and professionally representative delegates was certainly indicative of the party's new managerial technique.[1]

'We are no longer the association of bourgeois voters we were in 1953', boasted Wolfgang Döring, the campaign manager. 'On the 15th of September we shall break the absolute majority of this Christian-Democratic state party together with its satellites, and we shall be strong enough to see that it is not replaced by a monopoly rule of socialist officials.' Deploring the attempts to make the election into a conflict of ideologies—pamphlets denouncing Liberals and Socialists as unchristian represented 'criminal methods'—Döring proclaimed the independence of the FDP from the political help of the pulpit, of the trade unions, of the federations of industry, and of the assistance of foreign statesmen, and announced the brief version of the party's seven-planked election platform:

1. At last make Germany free
2. Preserve us from atomic danger

[1] 'They left my speech just as I wrote it' one of the Free Democratic delegates announced happily in the corridors.

3. Assure a free society
4. Save the deutschmark, preserve purchasing power
5. Create a healthy peasantry
6. Prevent the omnipotence of the State
7. Never again a single-party government.

Ten days later the SPD formally inaugurated its campaign which had been gradually more and more noticeable over the weeks beforehand. Some 20,000 people came to hear Ollenhauer proclaim the party's election programme at Dortmund. This programme was very far from the original conceptions of the founders of the party, and included, for example, such demands as 'Security for Free Enterprise.[1] In some ways it was even to the 'right' of the CDU's Ahlen programme of 1947: while keeping fairly near each other in their economic conceptions, CDU and SPD had in fact both retreated from their more 'left-wing' views of the early post-war years.

In his speech proclaiming the programme, Ollenhauer set out the SPD's modest objective in the election. If the CDU again secured an absolute majority, Western Germany would become the most conservative country in Europe: therefore a Bundestag with different majority relationships must be elected. Ollenhauer never suggested that the SPD might obtain a majority of seats, but only demanded that the electorate should give the SPD 'sufficient weight'. The party plainly saw its only hope of coming to power in a coalition with the Free Democrats: and Ollenhauer's speech contained a passage openly addressed to them: 'If the FDP wants to remain true to its name, its traditions and its objective, it must know that after Dr. Adenauer's Bamberg speech it no longer has any choice.'

The CDU was the last to make its official bow to the electorate,

[1] The ten points of the Dortmund programme ran as follows:

1. Peace through disarmament and reduction in tension—an end to conscription and competitive rearmament!
2. Re-unification in peace and security—an end to inactivity!
3. Atomic energy only for the good of mankind—an end to the policy of atom bombs!
4. Stable currency and stable prices—an end to inflationary price pushing!
5. Property and prosperity for everyone—an end to the discrimination in favour of the big fortunes!
6. Security for free enterprise—an end to the abuse of power by the cartels!
7. Old age without want—an end to the confusion in social policy!
8. Security for the family—an end above all to the housing shortage!
9. Equal educational and professional chances for all—an end to the shortage of schools and colleges!
10. Protection for democracy and intellectual freedom—an end to the monopoly power of the CDU–CSU.

but its Hamburg congress six weeks earlier had already proclaimed the party programme. Moreover Adenauer himself had been fighting the election vigorously since 2 June, when he had spoken before the clergy assembled at the foot of Bamberg cathedral for a 'Civic Demonstration of the Catholic Men of Germany' and had declared that the election would decide whether Germany would remain Christian or turn Communist. Yet the spectacular congress of 30 June marked the beginning of a new emphasis not merely on the personality of the Chancellor himself but on his team of collaborators as well. On the stage of the same Dortmund hall where the SPD had held its congress a fortnight earlier, a parade of the CDU's political personalities was organized: the Minister of Posts and Telecommunications, Ernst Lemmer, called out one prominent name after another, gave a short biography, and introduced two dozen CDU personalities for the *Junge Union* to applaud. Adenauer himself spoke for over an hour in the sweltering heat and struck a note of pride and confidence that heartened the whole CDU organization.

The Issue of Reunification

It was significant that Adenauer devoted the most interesting parts of his speech to foreign affairs, re-emphasizing above all his stand that German reunification must be made part of any overall disarmament agreement. Throughout the campaign he upheld the official Western view that reunification must flow from free elections and that a reunited Germany, within whatever boundaries, must be free to join NATO if it so wished. In the meantime Western Germany must help strengthen the military, economic, and political bonds that would unite the West as a whole, and the countries of Western Europe in particular.

In contrast to Adenauer's clear-cut foreign policy demonstrated in practice over the past eight years, the attitude of the Social and the Free Democrats appeared rather more nebulous to many of the voters. For this uncertainty the parties concerned were to be blamed as much as the voters, although admittedly their case was not easy to expound with precision—being at least in part based on untested hypotheses.

The SPD election manifesto *Security for All* did not go into any great detail but merely summarized the so-called 'Ollenhauer Plan'.[1]

[1] This was the nearest the SPD ever came to stating its foreign policy conception comprehensively. It was published by *Die Welt* on 23 May.

The SPD's argument rested on the premise that the NATO powers would never be willing to accept reunification if it involved any substantial risk of a reunited Germany joining the Warsaw pact, and that the U.S.S.R. would not allow free elections if they involved the possibility of a reunited Germany forming a part of NATO. It was therefore essential to exclude both these possibilities from the start. This was to be done by international agreement on the military status of a reunited Germany—an agreement to be concluded before the first free elections ever took place, and to be binding on the reunited Germany from the very beginning of its existence.

But the SPD did not ask for a neutralization of Germany between two hostile systems of alliances. As the Dortmund manifesto explained:

> The treaties which bind parts of Germany to mutually hostile military blocks are to be replaced through negotiation by a treaty forming a pan-European security system through an alliance of every state with every other. The re-united Germany must take part in this alliance with equal rights and duties in order effectively to secure its freedom.

Members of the pact would agree to settle their disputes with each other peacefully according to certain rules, the armaments of all members would be limited and controlled, and there would be nothing in the pact that might allow of any kind of national veto. The U.S.A., the U.S.S.R., and also the United Nations would be asked to give guarantees of security to this European non-aggression pact.

For the period that might elapse between reunification and the withdrawal of foreign troops from German territory the SPD envisaged a transitional system under which the four powers that had occupied Germany at the end of the war would exchange certain guarantees with the government of a reunited Germany.

The SPD did not want bilateral negotiations behind the backs of other partners. It had always opposed any negotiations with the Government of the Democratic Republic. All it asked was that the Germans should be kept informed of the state of the negotiations between the big powers and should be consulted on them.

These negotiations should also aim at free and universal secret elections to be held under international control in Western Germany, in Middle Germany (the Democratic Republic), and in Berlin. The National Assembly thus elected would establish a constitution, form a government and wield legislative powers, define the federal or Reich powers, and secure fundamental rights and freedoms in the whole electoral area. The new central German Government would then undertake the negotiation of a peace treaty, and settle the rights of foreign troops on German soil.[1]

The ideas of the Free Democrats on foreign and military policy differed in many respects from those of the SPD: the Free Democrats voted against the Common Market Treaty, while the SPD voted with the CDU for it; the FDP voted with the CDU for conscription, while the SPD voted against it. There were sharp differences in tone and the FDP also tended to insist on German claims to territories beyond the Oder–Neisse line. But in the methods they envisaged for German reunification, the Free Democrats and the SPD were remarkedly close to each other.

In their Berlin programme the Free Democrats had declared that 'the peaceful re-unification with Middle Germany and the East German territories into a German Reich with a free constitution is our foremost aim. All domestic and foreign efforts of policy must principally serve the attainment of this objective.' This last point of the Berlin programme of January became the first point of the Hamburg programme of June: 'At last create German unity—first Germany, then Europe.' Under this heading the FDP demanded: 'negotiations with the four powers on the military position of a reunited Germany recognising the legitimate desires of our neighbours for security. A militarily diluted zone must remove the danger of conflicts on German soil. . . .' and the party insisted on 'the recognition of the right to one's homeland and the refusal of a policy of abandoning territories to which Germany has a legal claim.'

At the Hamburg congress the Schleswig-Holstein Minister of Justice, Dr. Bernhard Leverenz, delivered the keynote speech on reunification which was reprinted as an FDP pamphlet.[2] He suggested that in view of events in Hungary and Poland, Russia might now be very willing to see the Warsaw pact modified if only she received sufficient guarantees of security. He declared that without such guarantees Germany would never be reunited, and that 'anyone who still demands free German elections at the beginning, and complete freedom of decision for the all-German government to be formed at the end, is a Utopian who should keep his fingers out of politics.'

But Leverenz was careful also to strike a note of thoughtful warn-

[1] See also Ollenhauer's speech in the Bundestag on 31 Jan., where he supported his argument with the view that the events of Nov. 1956—the Hungarian rising and the Franco-British Suez expedition with their sequels—had demonstrated the flaws in both the NATO and the Warsaw pacts. For a survey of proposals on German reunification see Heinrich von Siegler, *The Reunification and Security of Germany*, Siegler, Bonn, 1957.

[2] Bernhard Leverenz, *Wiedervereinigung — unser oberstes Ziel*, FDP, Bonn, 1957.

ing. Reunification, he pointed out, would be a very different thing from the annexation of the Democratic Republic by the Federal Republic, nor would there be a single dramatic day on which it would be achieved:

> Reunification will be a long process of development, which will involve the German people east and west of the zonal border in both give and take. I am thinking . . . of the spiritual experience of the value of personal and political liberty, which our brothers and sisters in the East will be able to give to us who have become dulled and often politically and intellectually lazy in the material well-being of the West; I am thinking, where economics are concerned, of the 26 billion Marks of reparations which they have advanced to the Soviet Union on behalf of the whole German people, and which we, even at a sacrifice, must restore. Let us always remember this [he concluded] lest one day the unification of the German people be wrecked by the reunification of Germany.

Thus by the end of June the parties had taken up their political positions. They hardly modified them thereafter. There seemed to be a brief respite in July while the politicians gathered strength for the final battle. Thereafter it was the deployment of propaganda techniques by the campaign managers, rather than any new ideas from the statesmen, that held the centre of the stage.

VI

ADENAUER AND HIS TEAM

THE most thorough, purposeful, and adventurous in their campaign preparations were the managers of the CDU. It was their campaign that set the pace for the rest. In a sense of course their task was easy. Adenauer had taken over the Government when Germany's position was still far from happy, and since then it had vastly improved in every way. At home Western Germany had made a spectacular economic recovery; abroad she had been transformed from a defeated enemy too wicked for personal fraternization into the trusted outpost of the Western alliance. The record of these years was phenomenal; but no pains or money were spared to put it over to the public in a number of powerful parallel campaigns.

Campaign Preparations

The preparations for the battle had begun two or three years before: in a sense indeed immediately after the 1953 victory, for the analysis of that result and the post-mortem on that campaign served as the basis on which the 1957 campaign was planned. Half a dozen statisticians with an electronic computor were put to work for a year and a half. They analysed election results since 1871 by administrative counties (*Regierungsbezirke*) to determine the historical origins of the CDU vote and dissect it into the components derived from the Centre Party, the *Deutsch-Nationale Volkspartei*, the National Liberals, the *Christliche Volksdienst*, the *Bayrische Volkspartei*, and other earlier parties. All the towns and villages were examined in detail for past Bundestag, Landtag, or local election results since 1945 and were classified according to the percentage swing in votes which they had shown from one election to another. Recent results were compared with the population structure: if the religious, occupational, income, and other sociological data pointed to a higher CDU result than was actually obtained the party made inquiries into why the CDU vote lay below the norm and attempted corrective action in the local organization. Some of this work may have been unnecessary and had only insignificant influence on the campaign: but the distribution of prominent speakers was decided in the light of this analysis, and all speakers were issued with the relevant data for their campaign trips.

In the year preceding the election campaign the former Minister of the Interior in North Rhine-Westphalia, Dr. Franz Meyers, overhauled the party machine and tuned it to an admirable pitch of efficiency. The standard of the CDU's organization appeared high almost wherever one went; the Land officials, often graduates, were usually keen, enthusiastic, and also helpful to inquirers within the limits set by official party secrecy. For the first time every constituency party had its full-time agent usually equipped with a party car. A special effort was made in 1956 to extend the membership of the party from its level of about 230,000—though owing to the reluctance of large sections of the German population to join any party the campaign seems to have yielded very small results. The diminishing monopoly of the SPD in factory organization was also attacked (though without particular success) by the establishment of Christian-Social works cells.

The central headquarters encountered some difficulties in its intervention in the Land organizations. The CDU had originally been a collection of Land parties and had indeed won its first federal election before it even existed as a federal organization. (The federal party was founded and the federal headquarters set up only in 1950.) It was no wonder if the Land chieftains and their salaried officials did not always welcome federal intrusion in their own domains which they had built up themselves before a federal headquarters had ever been thought of at all.

But in other ways the character of the CDU above all at the constituency level was a distinct help to the organization of a tightly planned federal campaign. In many areas the party was no more than an association of local personalities known to each other socially and professionally in any case, who wished to keep local decisions within their own circle and could unite on this issue whatever their disagreements might be on others. But their influence was felt much more in the selection of candidates than in the planning of the campaign, which they had not the means to carry through themselves. CDU officials often pointed to the great advantage of a party having no members, but coming to life only at election times with all the centralized manœuvrability of an advertising firm which exists only for one purpose—the conduct of publicity campaigns. This view may contain a certain exaggeration: but at any rate the financial resources of the centre and the professional character of its party personnel—much of it on short-term contracts—allowed the new management in Bonn very largely to impose its wishes throughout the Federal Republic. Only Bavaria was a notable exception: but then the CSU, as a separate sister party, was not subject to Bonn, and its campaign was all the more conspicuous in its differentiation from the federal one as a result of the much greater central harmonization of the other Land campaigns.

Meyers was the official campaign manager of the CDU, and worked in close collaboration with Dr. Bruno Heck (known in the office as '*Der Boss*'), the Secretary-General of the Party, who bore the prime responsibility for the campaign. (Both Meyers and Heck entered the Bundestag as constituency members after the election.) They retained the services of a number of public relations experts with commercial experience, and the main propaganda contracts were placed right outside the CDU itself, with *Die Werbe* of Essen and *Dr. Hegemann* of Düsseldorf. While in the SPD's headquarters the executive and policy staff was picking its way through bales of posters and stacks of pamphlets, the CDU's much smaller headquarters was untrammelled by the technical and material problems farmed out to professionals and could concentrate on the strategy and tactics of its campaign.

In this planning the CDU laid special emphasis on a careful appreciation of the state of public opinion. For a number of years two institutes of public opinion had been supplying the Chancellor with situation reports in this field: *Allensbach* for and at the expense of the Government, *Emnid* for the CDU. Of course, neither of these public opinion institutes were run by a party any more than *Divo*, the institute which did much work for the SPD. The Allensbach Institute insisted that it first offered its services to the SPD, but found no interest for its work. But Dr. Otto Lenz, the Chancellor's first Permanent Under-Secretary of State, saw its value. Thereafter the director of the Allensbach Institute, Dr. Elisabeth Noelle-Neumann, was exploring public opinion not only for manufacturers of detergents and garden gnomes but also for the Government and its agencies, while her husband, Dr. Erich Peter Neumann, acted as public relations adviser in Bonn. *Emnid* was in fact working simultaneously for the SPD and for the CDU, putting certain questions on behalf of one and certain questions on behalf of the other party.

The statistical data, the reorganization of the party machine, the availability of public relations experts, the delegation of technical responsibilities and even the situation reports of the institutes of public opinion could not, however, be more than the elements out of which a campaign could be built. They could serve to guide the deployment of tactical resources and point to strategic alternatives: but they could not replace or themselves supply a central creative conception. For over a year before the election the Chancellor's 'kitchen cabinet', the so-called 'Wednesday Circle', met to discuss the planning of the campaign and to pool the ideas and experience of the parliamentary party, of the CDU headquarters, and of Adenauer himself—not the least seasoned and open-minded campaigner among them.

By the autumn of 1956 the strategy of the campaign had been exactly and carefully defined. The campaign managers acted on the tenet that successful propaganda must be essentially simple. If its strategic core was misplaced, all the tactical manœuvres round it could not make up for the initial inaccuracy of aim. Starting from a certain intuitive insight into the half-subconscious aspirations of the post-war West German voter, the main lines of the CDU's appeal were worked out and planned to be essentially all of one piece. It was brilliantly carried through.

The old Centre Party of the Second Empire and the Weimar Republic was remembered as primarily a Catholic party, which had united all classes in the defence of Catholic institutions. It was the natural but still revolutionary achievement of the founders of the CDU that, basing themselves on the Centre, a denominational party which had spanned social and economic differences in the interests of Catholicism, they succeeded in bridging that very denominational conflict which had been the *raison d'être* of the older party without losing the social universality of the Centre's appeal. In 1945 the CDU set out to integrate into a single all-embracing popular party both Protestant employers and Protestant workers, Catholic employers and Catholic workers, the pensioners, civil servants, and professional classes whose interests in a modern economy so often conflict with those common to employers and workers alike—and in addition the farmers whose interests very often are all their own. Moreover, while its leaders expressed their approval of the abortive revolt of 20 July 1944 (in which several of them had been involved) the party on the whole let bygones be bygones and was prepared to see men who had been closely associated with the National Socialist régime occupy highly influential posts. Cutting across so many divisions the CDU had thus broken out of that 'tower of isolation' of which the Centre Party had complained in the past, while the SPD was even more closely besieged within its own sociological domain. Gradually the CDU came to conquer most of the neutral territory between the two, making its great break-through into the Protestant areas in 1953.

Given this universal character of the party, its appeal to the electorate could and indeed had to be an equally universal one. We shall see that the Social Democrats, basing their strength on certain limited sociological and economic groups, came to lay special emphasis in their campaign on the extension of numerous distinct appeals to a large number of very different segments of the population. The CDU, for all its consideration of specific groups, essentially went out to present a single case for the acceptance of the electorate as a whole.

Where campaign issues were concerned the CDU hardly found itself attacked on the economic side; in social legislation the pension reform was a first-class (if last-minute) alibi for earlier delays; and in foreign affairs the CDU was able to counter-attack against the apparent vacillation of the SPD and to claim that only loyalty to the great allies of the West could obtain results. Thus from the very beginning the campaign was aggressive and threw the Opposition into the postures of defence. In terms of rational debate the CDU's objective in fact consisted in one thing only. It sought to inject into every single home in the country the question: shall Adenauer and his team carry on—or shall we take the risk of SPD officialdom held up on the crutches of the FDP? Compared with its stress on this single alternative before the voter all other argument was played down.

Yet the CDU was not primarily out to conduct any rational debate with any opponent. Elections, it believed, were not won that way. Only the Chancellor himself was champing to attack or rather to ridicule the SPD. Strict instructions were sent to all speakers to neglect the existence of any party other than the SPD altogether. And for the rest the campaign was to be fought on the commercial motto: 'Persil talks of Persil only.' Other parties should be left to secure their own publicity by themselves. It was enough for the CDU to delineate itself in the eyes of the electorate and to colour its image with the emotional overtones pre-selected for the purpose. Indeed in the very variations on its themes of 'Adenauer and his team' and 'Our programme consists in our achievements' the CDU pulled the stops of so many popular feelings that it composed a veritable symphony of public relations of a highly effective kind.

Most obvious of the CDU's campaign devices was its emphasis on men, not on issues—or rather, perhaps, on men as representatives and personifications of policies and achievements. In the autumn of 1956 only 34 per cent. of the population had wanted Adenauer as Chancellor for a further four years. But this had been the momentary nadir of a reputation that recovered quickly after the Hungarian rising and soared high as the summer advanced. In the words of the CDU's Secretary-General Dr. Heck, their research showed that over half the population 'revered Adenauer like a monarch', demanded his statesmanship and authority at the head of the State, almost asked for the occasional paternal rebuke, and felt secure under his clear unwavering direction of affairs.

Adenauer's person was still the greatest single asset that the party could command. Always excepting Erhard's own campaign, the CDU had in 1953 placed almost sole reliance on Adenauer as the national leader. But he was now eighty-one years old and himself wanted to be presented not as an elder statesman with a successor, but as the active leader of a strong team of men. And by 1957 a whole phalanx of names had become sufficiently known in the country to provide, singly or by the sheer weight of their numbers, an almost equally important element in the CDU's campaign.

Less obvious at first sight, but consciously and carefully planned, was the association of Adenauer—whose personality easily lent itself for the purpose—and also of the whole CDU in the mind of the voter not only with the material successes of the Federal Republic, but with the Federal Republic itself. The subtle pre-emption by the CDU of the symbols of the new State had begun early. The CDU had produced a design of a black German eagle on a gold cross in a red field for the crest of the Federal Republic. Heuss had ridiculed 'the arty-crafty efforts of the CDU' but before the 1953 campaign the party adopted the device as its own symbol instead. Together with the flag of the Republic this crest in black, red, and gold was to be found as a back-cloth at most of the party's major demonstrations. CDU meetings ended with the anthem of the Republic: *Unity, Justice and Freedom* sung in a great swell of emotion with a new-found but sober national pride. A CDU campaign film ended with the anthem while the screen was filled with the CDU's party coat of arms. In 1953 one of the most effective trump cards of the CDU had been simply a newsreel of Adenauer laying a wreath at the Arlington cemetery and a United States military band playing the German national anthem. In 1957, too, Adenauer was still represented, in the words of a CDU official, as 'the German eagle to the outside world. What party can claim *Unity, Justice and Freedom* for itself in the way we can? Wherever the national colours are honoured it redounds to our credit. Whenever a German team wins an international match, they are scoring goals for the CDU.'

The CDU was consciously building on satisfaction. Its slogan 'What we have we know' was of course largely a materialist one. But it was not clothed in materialist terms. The commentators who saw in the election result merely a decision for more and bigger cars, refrigerators and radiograms were missing an important ingredient as well as the essential packaging of the CDU campaign. The CDU appealed perhaps less overtly to financial self-interest than the SPD and never operated with fear—whether of inflation, atomic extinction, or anything else; at most it warned against uncertain experiments by an untried and unknown set of party apparatchicks. Where the SPD tended to react out of opposition, the CDU made an essentially positive appeal to what it took to be an industrious, forward-looking people proud of its recent efforts and achievements, and calculated the date of poll so as to have even the weather foster the mood of optimism and self-confidence on which it was building its campaign.[1]

The voter, in Heck's words, had 'his big and his little side'. A blatant appeal to self-interest would have left the CDU on or below the level of the SPD campaign. The SPD's attempts to sell politics with sex-appeal were in the CDU's view an attempt to call upon lower sides of human nature than those usually involved in political argument: while the CDU's campaign was designed to appear to rise to the noblest. The object of the CDU was to call upon the voter not as he actually was, but as he saw himself in his own idealization. Direct self-interest could not win against the flattery of an appeal clothed in terms of the voter's sense of honour, of national pride, and of responsibility for the whole in the hour of corporate rededication to the task in hand. The CDU was the great party of the whole German people. It was no wonder if with such a strategic conception of its campaign superimposed on its record of economic prosperity, the CDU carried its swift, confident, and masterful wooing of the electorate to a triumphant conclusion.

Parallel Campaigns[2]

The CDU started its operations late in comparison with the other parties: but its own effort was only one part of the total campaign for Adenauer and his team. It was perhaps due in large part to Dr. Otto Lenz that the CDU had for six or seven years been only one of many agencies (even if the most important one) that sought to influence public opinion to accept and support the new democratic State and the policies of the Government. Lenz as the Chan-

[1] In addition to its party cartoonists, the CDU had a party poet under contract who supplied the party's 'non-party' press services with lyrical verse designed to stimulate a happy political mood.

[2] In order to avoid the pejorative overtones of the word *Tarnorganisationen* (camouflage organizations) used by the opposition parties, a wider generic term is here used to include the activities of such bodies. For a similar term see Robert Musil's novel *Der Mann ohne Eigenschaften*, Rowohlt, Hamburg, 1930.

cellor's chief civil servant set up a whole network of State-supported organizations whose public relations work ran parallel with that of the Government, could command a wider audience, and could also be more continuous and more pervasive than purely party propaganda.

Some of the Government's public relations organizations like the 'Federal Headquarters for Internal Service' worked on a broadly non-partisan basis under councils that included members of the chief Opposition parties. Others, while able to claim a non-partisan status in the sense of not explicitly supporting one Government party against another, existed mainly to widen support for the Government's policies and therefore inevitably to rebut the arguments of the Opposition. The problem of how far a party government can use public information services to clarify its own position before the electorate is always a delicate one. Where one party or group of parties has largely built up the federal structure from scratch and the Opposition is radically opposed to such fundamental aspects of Government policy as its line in foreign affairs and military matters it is understandable that the opposition should regard almost any dynamic public relations work in favour of the Government as directed against itself. The protests of the Opposition against the use of public funds for Government propaganda in fact played a considerable role in the election.

The Government of the Federal Republic no less than that of most countries used its press and information services to justify its policy at home as well as abroad. The various ministries had their press and information departments which supplied briefs to journalists, invited them on trips, and addressed the public direct. In the early summer of 1957 the Minister of Agriculture, Heinrich Lübke, issued a letter to housewives justifying his policy and invited hundreds of them to coffee parties. Adenauer wrote a letter to all pensioners when the pension reform was passed and the booklet explaining its provisions bore his photograph as a frontispiece.

Besides carrying out such official activities the various ministries also operated through organizations or under labels which obscured the governmental origin of the public relations campaigns in question or made grants to bodies whose public relations work was parallel with their own. Early in the year a campaign took place throughout the Federal Republic to popularize German membership of NATO. Projector vans toured the villages and showed films on NATO, a large poster pictured a German soldier with the slogan: 'His comrades—our allies', a 'Working Party for European Policy' issued a poster showing the blood-stained flag of Hungary and a

Soviet tank with the motto: 'Hungary calls—defend Freedom' and a 'Working Party for Reunification' (thought to be closely connected with the Ministry of All-German Affairs) put up a double-size poster with a portrait of Adenauer and the legend: 'Adenauer guarantees a stable policy and the reunification of Germany' throughout the Federal Republic in the ten days immediately before the CDU's own posters appeared.

In addition to such activities on the part of the various ministries the Chancellor's Office had the services of the large Federal Press and Information Office with a staff of over 500 people which combined the duties of official newspaper archive, radio monitoring service, reception office for foreign journalists, and official purveyor of news. This Federal Press Office sponsored pamphlets such as an illustrated 80-page booklet *Promises Kept*, opening and closing with reports of Dr. Adenauer's declarations; dated 1957, it was to be found in large quantities in CDU committee rooms during the campaign. The Press Office also subsidized publications that might not otherwise have been produced or continued in existence: they tended to be pro-Government in their orientation. During the campaign the Press Office inspired and members of its personnel directed a new illustrated paper *Bleib im Bild* ('In the Picture') as a channel for camouflaged Government propaganda.[1] The permanent head of the Press Office, Felix von Eckhart, not only accompanied the Chancellor on his various trips abroad (one of the CDU films showed him riding a camel at the Persian court) but was also with him on his election train. The Chancellor's secret fund and in particular the funds of the Press Office were also used to subsidize non-governmental organizations whose propaganda work complemented that of the Press Office itself.

It was in this realm of what the CDU's opponents tended to term 'camouflage organizations' that Dr. Otto Lenz appears to have made his decisive contribution. It would be tedious to enumerate the various *Arbeitsgemeinschaften* and *Arbeitskreise* (Working Groups) in whose foundation or development Lenz had a share. One of the best known was the 'Working Group of Democratic Circles' (*Arbeitsgemeinschaft demokratischer Kreise*) usually known as the ADK, which described itself as a public relations organ for the Govern-

[1] It was reported that £100,000 of Government money was put at the disposal of this publication, and certainly only a court ruling prevented the plan of securing quick distribution by giving the first two issues away free of charge as a present to the newspaper trade. The paper itself contained fairly dull propaganda sweetened with large photographs of girls in the scantiest of bathing costumes competing over the greatest resemblance to the young French film star Brigitte Bardot—a feature explained by the paper's disapproval of such contests.

ment, and as the first German organization working in the political field on the basis of United States experience in human and public relations. Its initial task consisted in winning the loyalty of former soldiers and 'above all those groups which still have a "wait and see" attitude to political developments'.[1] As this function appeared to become unnecessary a new one arose: that of 'rousing the readiness for defence and removing opposition against the defence effort of the Federal Republic'.

The ADK tended to concentrate its emphasis on the foreign and military policy of the Government parties. Indeed in pronouncements before soldiers the energetic head of the ADK, Hans Edgar Jahn, tended to sound notes far more aggressive towards the East than those which the CDU would have cared to strike, and both his declarations and the ADK's subsidies to a somewhat right-wing publication led to parliamentary inquiries. The ADK maintained a dozen branch offices, at least one in each Land, sent speakers to talk to schools, to soldiers' classes on civics, to veterans' and refugees' organizations and to clubs of all kinds, organized meetings, film-shows and houseparties at which free discussion was encouraged, distributed publicity material for the Government, made its own film *The Great Error*, and published various series of pamphlets as well as the rather dry *Politische Informationen* in two editions of over 100,000 copies. Its work was continuous, so that most of it fell into the periods between election campaigns, but it sent a special exhibition train to tour the Federal Republic during the election.

The ADK appears to have been financed out of the Chancellor's secret fund for which he was accountable only to the President of the Federal Fiscal Court and out of the information budget of the Ministry of Defence. In reply to the Opposition's charges that it used public money for party purposes the ADK was able to point to the activities of the so-called *Büro Royce* in Hesse, which had used the funds of a Land governed by the SPD for its indirect SPD propaganda.[2] The ADK's reticence over the size as well as the origin of its funds makes it difficult to assess its importance: while the Opposition went out of its way to stress the role of the ADK and give it a sinister flavour, the CDU regarded it as largely obsolete and rather ineffective. Indeed in view of the target it provided for outcries from the Opposition the ADK may really have been as much

[1] A mine of information on the various bodies which form in a sense a German pendant to the unhappy 're-education programme' of the victorious allies may be found in a book on 'The Practice of Nursing Political Opinion in Germany' written by the head of the ADK: Hans Edgar Jahn, *Lebendige Demokratie: Die Praxis der politischen Meinungspflege in Deutschland*, Ammelburg, Frankfurt, 1956.

[2] '*In eigener Sache*', *Politische Informationen*, Edition B, 10 May 1957.

of a liability as an asset to the Government's campaign during the election itself.

In addition to such officially sponsored institutions private bodies of various kinds took a hand in the electioneering. An *ad hoc* 'Association for the Increase of the Electoral Turnout', financed it would seem by business firms in Hesse, attempted to place a full-page advertisement in most daily papers on the eve of poll: it showed Ollenhauer and Maier dragging the Trojan horse of Communism into the country. According to the Social Democrats there were in fact dozens of such organizations—some of them hardly more than the name of a bank account and one of a string of brass plates in front of the same office, some of them defunct, having served their turn, some latent, and some active, some privately financed, some supported by the Government, and some perhaps supported from both types of sources—which all provided alternative channels for public relations work in favour of the Government's policies and thus indirectly in favour of the CDU.

The most expensive of the private parallel campaigns was that issued in the name of Erhard and his 'social market economy'. Developed out of the similar campaign of 1952–3, it never really stopped. Its chief method between the two elections was a series of large advertisements in the daily and illustrated papers containing statements by Erhard, replies by Erhard to attacks on his policy, quotations from Erhard, and reprints of a radio address by Erhard. Comic strips in the weekly and illustrated press and specially worded appeals in the radio magazines and women's periodicals further emphasized the merits of 'Erhard's Social Market Economy'.

The Erhard campaign rose to a crescendo in the last three weeks before the poll with the issue of two posters (see Plate III*c*) and of a 16-page illustrated paper *Wir Alle* (*All of Us*) sent by post to 12 million households. It was not sent to all of them so as to give the paper some scarcity value, to make its receipt seem flattering and to arouse curiosity in those who did not receive it. Whether the postal services in fact ensured the close neighbourhood scatter on which the effectiveness of this technique depended is another matter, but the competition set in the magazine brought in a large number of replies, the list of winners being published in a CDU periodical after the election.

Since the Government denied that any of its own funds were involved, this whole campaign must have represented an effort in Erhard's favour on the part of industrial and in particular commercial circles. The CDU at times appeared embarrassed by the special emphasis placed by the Erhard campaign on the importance of the entrepreneur and by the special publicity it gave to one of the ministers personally outside the party framework. One may guess that it did not make Erhard any the more popular among his colleagues. Yet on the whole the CDU valued this parallel campaign in spite of occasional tactical disagreements with its organizers, and some may even have regarded its independent popularization of a second figure in the party as a reinsurance policy against the possibility that one day a new Chancellor might have to be found shortly before an election who would need to bring with him a certain measure of spontaneous personal support in the country.

It might be asked why material was issued under such a wide variety of different trade marks and why the CDU did not attempt to concentrate these efforts but diffused responsibility among so many parallel organizations. The answer given was that decentralization made for experiment, variety, and originality of approach; that it allowed different men to be placed in very different and flexible relationships with each other (in particular that it allowed the speedy advance of young and new men to large responsibilities without offending senior party officials); and that each of these organizations had a slightly different field of action. There were, however, a number of other extremely important considerations. It would in fact have been quite impossible from the very nature of the organizations involved to place them within an overt or indeed within any direct chain of command.

If the ADK, for example, had been subordinated to the CDU, it could neither have had access to the audiences which it was able to reach as a non-party organization, nor could it have been supported out of public funds. The same two considerations applied to many other such parallel organizations. Parties still tended to be looked upon with some reserve in Germany: appeals made by non-party bodies were heeded more readily both by the electorate and by their potential financiers. The problems of the trade mark and the supply of funds were fundamental and closely related. Over and above the fiscal reasons for this phenomenon (which will become apparent in another chapter), some firms and other bodies which were quite happy to give funds to a 'Working Group for the Increase of the Electoral Turnout' might have felt differently if asked to contribute to the coffers of a specific party; and others who were already contributing to party finance might give an additional sum to a non-party organization. On the other hand the commercial firms who made their contributions to the Erhard campaign preferred a label more specific than that of a party: they were in fact primarily reinforcing the position of the Minister of Economics and of his policies and only indirectly that of the whole CDU with its wider range of economic and social trends.[1]

The question of the subordination to the party of all the bodies that were working along parallel lines was thus partly unreal. Certainly the disagreements on tactics and the occasional conflicts of interest in the tapping of sources of finance confirm the CDU's contention that, formally speaking, the Opposition misrepresented the nature of these bodies in so far as it painted them as nothing more than the extended arm and the hidden hand of the Government and the CDU.

The Posters of the CDU

When the CDU opened its own streamlined campaign in earnest five weeks before the poll, it could thus build on years of public relations work by a wide variety of bodies, and concentrate on canalizing the carefully fostered general trends of opinion into the twin determination to vote, and to vote for Adenauer and his team. The CDU was able to watch the working of the other campaigns while it was perfecting the plans for its own and deciding what media to use and how to translate its own clear and simple central idea rigorously into these media.

Most obvious to the casual observer—and most voters must have come into that category—was the CDU's poster campaign. It was an epitome of the whole, brilliant in conception, executed professionally, centralized, expensive, and complete. The basic poster campaign was handled federally by advertising firms and placed on the usual commercial sites. Neither the Land nor the constituency parties had to trouble themselves with the basic bill-posting; they simply supplemented the posters that appeared automatically in their area. The CDU's agents secured space for two or more posters on every site in the Federal Republic, and the Adenauer portrait was up for five weeks; for the last ten days the CDU also succeeded in booking the bulk of the 7,000 large special sites in the Federal Republic, and another perhaps 1,000 large bill-boards were erected at its orders specially for the campaign. In addition to this commercial bill-posting further large posters and smaller sizes were supplied free of charge to the Land parties. At least 10 million posters (and perhaps millions more) were distributed—and there would

[1] It is, however, worth noting in this connexion that the 'Social Committees' associated with the CDU, which form at the same time its left wing and its prolongation into the field of the trade unions and industrial plants, are also financed by business circles which lay great stress on the strategic need for such a workers' wing of the CDU.

Keine Experimente!
Konrad Adenauer
CDU

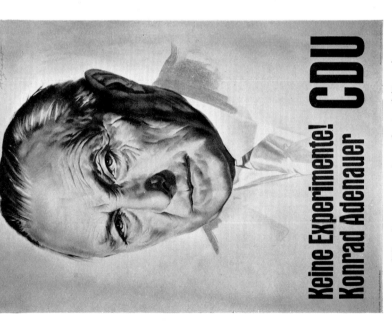

a. 'The ele:torate wants a ruler type' (*p*. 113)

b. 'HE comes': a stop of the campaign train (*p*. 120)

c. The morning after: 'Father of the entire German people'

DR. ADENAUER'S CAMPAIGN

a. Adenauer and his team: (*top row*) Adenauer, Erhard, Arnold, Schröder, von Brentano, Lübke, Strauss; (*bottom row*) Storch, Gerstenmaier, Schäffer, Lemmer (*p.* 114)

b. Two happy gardeners: Erhard and Schäffer (*p.* 118)

c. The 'Third Force' as seen by the German Party (*p.* 175)

THE GOVERNMENT PARTIES

a

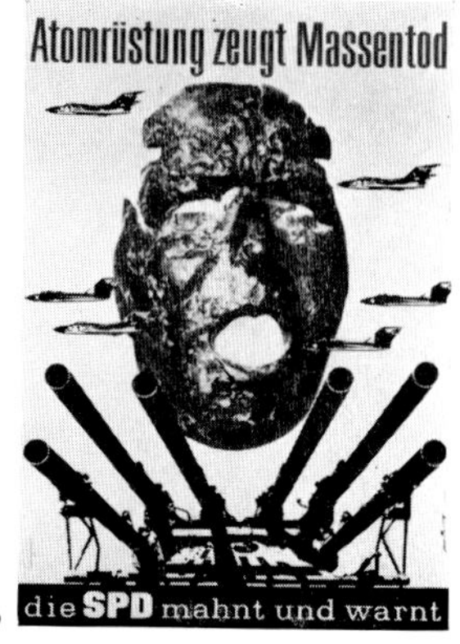

b

c

d

e

f

CAMPAIGN POSTERS

(see p. xv)

a. You can trust Mr. Ollenhauer (*p.* 135)

b. 'Don't let yourself be dazzled' (*p.* 346)

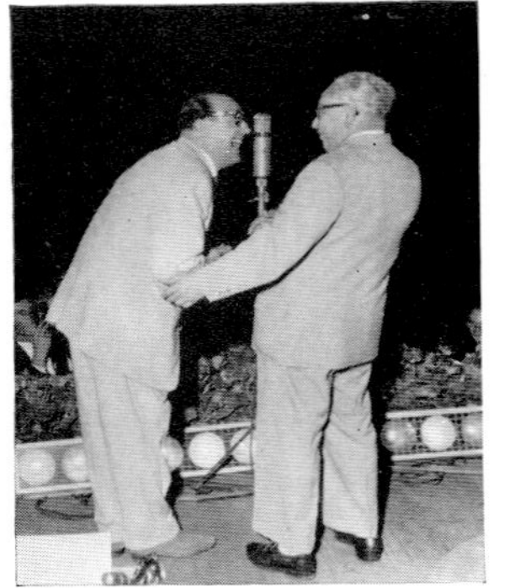
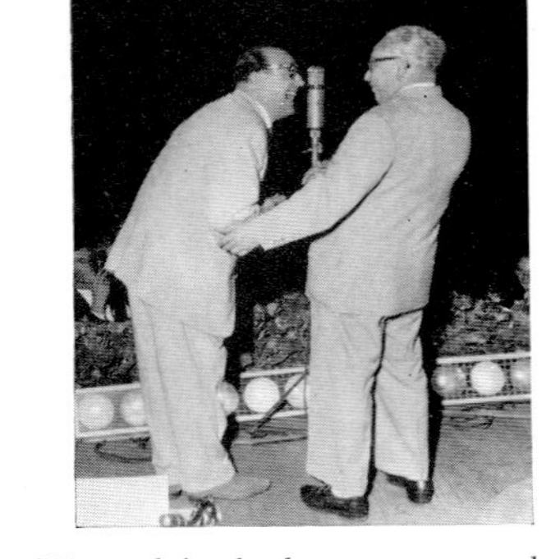

c. 'To explain the latest party resolution in the light of a music-hall turn': Ollenhauer and compère (*p.* 147)

d. 'These two understand each other': Döring and friend (*p.* 164)

e. 'We vote SPD' (*p.* 139)

f. 'It all depends on *him*!' (*p.* 162)

THE OPPOSITION

have been even more intensive coverage had not the Land parties complained that even with the help of their thousands of volunteer workers they were unable to handle further supplies. That so much could be fly-posted without a serious reaction on the part of the electorate against the campaign was perhaps made possible only by the excellence of the posters and by deliberately holding fire until forty days before the poll.

The Land parties were in fact becoming quite impatient at the absence of election material when from 7 August—after the public had grown tired of the SPD's uninteresting poster texts that had hung for several weeks without a change—they saw the whole Federal Republic blossom overnight with the white Adenauer placard (see Plate I*a*). It read 'No experiments—Konrad Adenauer', but the text was not what mattered. Their studies in America had convinced the CDU managers that the time for photographs of politicians was over: an Austrian artist, Professor Aigner, was called in to rejuvenate and dramatize the impressive face of the Chancellor, which had been immobilized on one side by an accident and plastic surgery between the wars. Freely adapting a photograph, Professor Aigner depicted him in deep earnestness, sun-bronzed, fair-haired, and with penetrating bright blue eyes that appeared to follow the voter. 'The electorate', as Heck explained, 'wants a ruler type', and excitement ran high in the whole CDU organization when the 'Big Brother' poster was released.

It was followed after a respectful interval by a whole series of half-size portraits of other CDU leaders to illustrate both the central motif of 'Men round Adenauer' and at the same time to personify the various slogans of the campaign. Thus the Minister of Finance was presented as 'Guardian of the currency' and the Minister of Defence with the SPD slogan 'Security for all'. A dozen such portrait posters were made available federally and they provided a keyboard on which various compositions of themes and of emphasis could be elaborated in accordance with the regional, social, and religious complexion of the area in which the placards were being used. In a good many constituencies candidates made use of a service provided by the Bonn headquarters to have themselves portrayed on the same antiseptic white ground as another 'man round Adenauer', and the poor job the other artists often made of their drawings only served to show up the excellence of Professor Aigner's workmanship.

These assorted posters of bronzed faces and the blue letters 'CDU' on gleaming white were posted on rows of trees, along fences, on building sites, and on hoardings until the whole Federal Republic seemed 'the bride of the CDU'. No one could help contrasting this wealth of personalities with the single and inconspicuous portrait of Ollenhauer, half the size of the standard Adenauer poster, if indeed they had noticed the Ollenhauer portrait at all. Wherever the surface area made it possible these personality posters were put up in a chequer-board effect achieved by alternating them with plain dark-blue text posters of which the best simply repeated in white 'No experiments' and in yellow 'CDU' (see Plate II*a*). This white-and-blue chequer-board pattern developed in fact a *gestalt* of its own over and above the two series of posters of which it was composed; it came to give a visual impression of the unity in diversity and ordered individualism which the party regarded as its strength.

For use by itself there was an impressive poster of burning Budapest against a night sky: 'Think of Hungary: Be prepared', and also on a curiously static map of divided Germany the text: 'The whole is what's at stake.'[1] The CDU's poster slogans thus strongly emphasized foreign affairs. There was no need to highlight the economic prosperity of Western Germany on special posters. In any case, Erhard's own private campaign and his and Schäffer's CDU portraits together with the omnibus motto 'No experiments' reinforced that argument sufficiently.

The poster strategy was so clear that four federal placards were obviously superfluous or incongruous in the series. One of them—a laughing boy—was a hardy annual left over from previous campaigns but ordered again and again by the constituencies. Others originated in the party Executive, to which the campaign headquarters had to bow for diplomatic reasons; the posters concerned were, it seems, printed in decently limited editions. The Chancellor also submitted ideas for two further posters, but the CDU headquarters was able to dissuade him from insisting on their display.

In addition to these federal posters the Bavarian CSU, always jealous of its independence, insisted on putting out its own posters: but they lacked focus both in colour and in motif. Other Land parties also occasionally printed their own designs adapted to the local milieu: the federal headquarters requested that all such posters should be unaggressive, and perhaps the most appealing of them, originating in Hamburg, showed a blond seaman at the steering-wheel with the caption 'Hold your course'.

Impressive as the series proved to be, it was not all that the CDU could do. At the beginning of the year it had experimented with even more striking montage designs of drawings and close-up photos enormously enlarged. The depth psychologists were satisfied with

[1] This text was deliberately kept ambiguous between the messages 'Reunification is at stake' and 'What is at stake is a matter of life and death'.

their work, but the advertising experts feared that the shock impact of such methods might evoke mixed reactions from the public.

It is difficult to believe that the great qualitative and quantitative superiority of the CDU in the battle of the posters remained without effect on the electorate. Whatever might be said about the other non-socialist parties, the CDU most emphatically could not be overlooked by any but electors who never ventured out of doors, and the posters were a very accurate reflection of all that the CDU wanted to say and to seem. In this case, at any rate, a traditional method regarded by some other parties at the outset as no more than a formality was used by the CDU with such vigour that the others had cause to regret that they had nothing comparable with which to neutralize its effect.

Letters, Advertisements, and Campaign Films

The CDU also used other, less traditional media with equally good results. In its campaign the personal letter and the newspaper advertisement went far to oust the impersonal unsigned and unaddressed pamphlet for general (and thus usually wasteful) distribution, while the open-air film show from a projector-van tended to supplement or give a new form to the smaller village meeting.

The personal letters of various kinds were sent through the post, which had a special service distributing letters to categories of addresses such as 'all households' or 'all radio listeners'. Pride of place must go to the two-page letter written by the Chancellor to 'My dear countrymen':

> It is a long and stony path that we have travelled together. In 1949 we were still an impoverished people without rights. . . . Today . . . we are no longer alone: the powers of the free world are our friends; they guarantee our security. They have adopted as the aim of their policy our demand for the reunification of our torn country which we cannot achieve on our own. . . .

After three paragraphs on the economic recovery of Western (as contrasted with Eastern) Germany, he returned to the consequences of his foreign policy:

> Of course we must make sacrifices for our freedom and for the security of our incipient wealth. . . . A people that is not prepared to defend its freedom surrenders itself. . . . We must stay watchful. . . . Thus it seems to me to be a counsel of prudence not to try any experiments now.

It was altogether a moderate document, which made the slogans and posters seem extracts, sub-headings, and echoes of the reasoned case the Chancellor put to each voter individually in his home.

The federal letter from the Chancellor was supplemented by others: an appeal from the Chancellor to all refugees, and letters from CDU Ministers-President, ministers, and party chairmen to their own Land or to groups within it (such as Kai-Uwe von Hassel's to the Schleswig-Holstein farmers, beginning: 'You are still in the midst of the harvest. Labourers are few and on top of that the weather is giving you and all of us cause for concern. . . .'). Election addresses were produced with greater or less lavishness; as a rule they contained half a dozen pictures of the candidate, one of them showing the candidate with Adenauer—sometimes in a ridiculously subservient attitude. An illustrated paper, *This is the place at stake*, distributed to all households showed Adenauer's chair in the Chancellory and dwelt on his responsibilities and his duties: 'Would you like to sit in that chair?' With a little caricature of Ollenhauer on almost every page—as a man for whom the chair was far too big, as a bawling baby, as an animal, as a pear—it led up to the insidious drawing of Ollenhauer negotiating with Bulganin and Khrushchev: 'Can you feel happy at this thought?' This federal illustrated paper was itself supplemented by election newspapers published on a Land, constituency, or even works basis, usually in several editions, distributed by post or as a supplement delivered with the local newspaper.

At least as important were the advertisements (often covering a full page) placed in almost all the daily and illustrated papers of the Federal Republic except those papers openly associated with the Opposition and those weekly tabloids for which the Erhard campaign had developed a special comic-strip technique which the CDU did not think consonant with its own dignity. Several dozen texts of advertisements were prepared at the party's headquarters, and individual candidates sometimes issued their own texts as well.

Long preparations went into the design, wording, and testing of the CDU's various series of advertisements. Indeed, the CDU believed that once its advertising campaign had begun, the SPD would not have the time, even if it had the money, to issue any effective reply. Advertisements were carefully adapted to the type of paper that was to carry them. The series entitled 'All of us are better off' appeared in women's magazines in such variations as 'Your lipstick confirms it' and 'Your wardrobe confirms it', and the refugee press carried an advertisement entitled 'A new life—a new home'.[1] While advertisements placed in the illustrated press carefully eschewed controversy and sought only to state the CDU's own case,

[1] The impact of this publicity may be gauged from the fact that one lipstick firm cashed in on the political slogan commercially to emphasize the superiority of its own product.

advertisements in daily papers were not afraid of ridiculing the Opposition under such titles as 'Once upon a time there was a Social Democrat...', 'What is a chameleon?', and 'Rose-pink soap bubbles'.

The coverage of the CDU's party advertisements in the fortnight before polling day was roughly equivalent to two full pages in every daily in the Federal Republic in addition to the space taken by the Erhard and similar campaigns. Though they were expensive, the CDU regarded these advertisements as highly efficient: they were bound to reach the whole electorate without involving the cost or work of distribution and the wastage characteristic of leaflets. Asked about relative efficiencies and the rationalization of propaganda techniques through polling research, officials of the CDU explained that, whatever the calculations might show, they would take no risks and not dispense with any available method of propaganda.

They therefore printed millions of leaflets and pamphlets—a dozen types on the federal and a large variety of others on the Land and local level. One federal series was enlivened with various caricatures of Ollenhauer and four lines of verse. A declaration by the Protestant Working Group of the CDU was given distribution in Protestant areas, while 16 pages of 'Words from the Pope' were distributed in the Catholic areas. Scores of similar publications, far too numerous to mention and impossible to collect systematically, were distributed at CDU meetings and film shows, in factories, through other organizations, and by post; many of them bore no party label at all, but were often produced by Government offices or parallel organizations.[1]

Like the SPD, the CDU used the cabaret to put over its point—but it had little confidence that the voter would accept such a frivolous approach to the serious business of voting. Much more interesting and important in the CDU campaign was the film-van equipped to show colour films in the open soon after sunset. The large-scale pioneer in this field had been the firm *Mobilwerbung*, founded just before the 1953 election, in which it played an active part and claimed a million viewers. It would seem that Dr. Otto Lenz had at one time planned *Mobilwerbung* and ADK as a single entity, but then a much better idea was adopted: that of establishing an independent business firm which could take commercial advertising between elections to help amortize its equipment. By 1957 the firm

[1] Extrapolation of the figures provided for one Land would suggest that 12 million pamphlets and 40 million leaflets were distributed through the party organization alone, apart from illustrated papers and brochures and—if this Land was typical—1 million balloons and 1½ million pennants as well.

was financially self-supporting although a large part of its revenues all the year round came from Government-financed public relations work. Just before the election it carried out an extensive campaign with fifty vans in favour of NATO, and some of the same films were employed in the CDU programmes that carried on where the Government campaign left off.

At the time of the election *Mobilwerbung* had some 70 or 80 vans on the road—15 of them working for the German Party, 15 for the FDP, and all but 2 or 3 of the rest working for the CDU.[1] In addition to these forty-odd *Mobilwerbung* vans the CDU had perhaps another 200 mobile film projectors of one kind or another, roughly one for each constituency. Their task was to go into the small villages not ordinarily reached by the candidates but which contained a third of the electorate, where the opportunity of a free film show might attract up to half the local population. The quality of the speakers that went with the trucks was uneven: when deployed in conjunction with a good speaker, perhaps from the *Junge Union*, or with the candidate himself, spotlighted from the projector, the use of these vans could be very effective.

The CDU had some thirty films to show in addition to the dozen of the NATO series. One of the best was *Adenauer and his Team*—an improvised newsreel of the parade of personalities at the Dortmund Party congress. Three cartoon strips illustrated the other main motifs of the campaign: *The Economic Wonder Tree* watered by Erhard, its fruits garnered by Schäffer, was drawn with gentle and not unkind humour (see Plate II*b*); *Herr Schmitz* showed the well-nourished cigar-smoking citizen of 1957 thinking back to the lean and hungry years of smoking weeds; a third—far too abstract to be effective—showed the invasion of the switchboard of politics by socialist busybodies and the short-circuit as they pulled at the NATO lever. (The election credits did not reach the CDU office before 1 April, and this inconvenience made itself felt in the hurry in which these cartoon films had to be produced.) Other documentaries showed the *Red Danger* in Eastern Europe and—in obvious exploitation of the German cult of the Queen of Persia—Adenauer's *Visit to the Peacock Throne*. 4,000 copies of such films were distributed and were seen by several million people.

The same film vans and hundreds of loudspeaker cars also used a half-hour tape-recording which combined a light touch with a

[1] The FDP claimed that only its threat to attack the whole system produced a share of vans (to which it felt entitled since it also took its part in the founding of the firm when it was still in the Government), but this story was denied vehemently from the other side.

hard-hitting attack on the SPD: introduced by South German and circus-type marching music—anything too definitely northern might have antagonized the South—it contrasted quotations from one SPD speech with quotations from another and commented in acid verses set to catch-tunes which the children could afterwards be heard singing in the streets.[1] It was curious that some prominent members of the CDU had qualms about the fairness of using this highly effective weapon of ridicule; it was much less surprising that the cars which played the tape to audiences waiting for Ollenhauer should on occasion have suffered damage from SPD supporters.

The Chancellor's Campaign

With Adenauer's portrait on the posters, his signature on the letters, his name on all the pamphlets and election addresses, and the concentration of so much of the whole campaign on his personal drawing power, his personal appearance before the widest possible audience was naturally required. The CDU was fortunate that a man of eighty-one took such delight in the battle. At the very outset he had told a sceptical 'Wednesday Circle' that he believed in meetings, and quoted the advice of an American whose opinion he had playfully demanded: 'Shake still more hands.' Many in the party, who had initially feared that meetings, attended mainly by adherents, only wasted strength better spent on preaching to the unconverted, were not fully convinced until August of how much could still be achieved by this antediluvian method in spreading a feeling of confidence among supporters and thus radiating influence among the electorate as a whole. All over the country candidates stepped up their speaking programme, many of them making over a hundred speeches, and Adenauer himself made more than twenty set speeches and dozens of smaller ones in the last four weeks of the campaign.

Before the election the saying was current that whereas in 1953 Adenauer had won the campaign for the CDU, in 1957 the CDU would have to win it for Adenauer. No prophecy could have been farther from the mark. Of course there were certain restrictions. In the interests of his lungs and throat as much as to avoid undignified interruptions, Adenauer was not to make set speeches in the open air; the police carefully protected him from draughts on his way to and from the stage, and the party always booked another major speaker for all meetings the Chancellor was to address.

[1] e.g. 'Heute so und morgen so, Einmal contra einmal pro,
So was nennt man auf die Dauer: Sicherheit mit Ollenhauer!'

Very soon, however, such precautions turned out to be unnecessary. The Chancellor insisted on making short addresses on railway platforms and outside meeting-halls (see Plate I*b*). So far from reserving his strength for his full-dress public appearances in the overflowing meeting-halls in the late afternoons and evenings, the Chancellor would spend the earlier part of the day admiring cathedrals and local museums, inspecting newspaper offices and factories, and driving through as many main streets as possible where placards saying 'HE comes', martial music, and loudspeaker announcements had assembled and 'warmed up' an audience for the triumphal procession of the black Mercedes. His speeches—in spite, it seems, of doctors' orders—soon lengthened to an hour and a half or more, so that his star colleagues felt a little sorry for themselves at the scant time left for their own speeches, and he would then return to his train, sometimes sit up after midnight with correspondents, and only rise amid a wilting staff 'to put Herr von Eckhart to bed'.[1]

It is not surprising that under these circumstances his speeches were not always very distinguished. In this very static campaign he was in any case able to repeat from a sheaf of papers and from memory much the same speech he had made the night before. It was a simple basic speech, repeating and embroidering what he had said in his letter to the voters and padded with an elaborate humorous passage confessing ignorance as to what the SPD really wanted. The journalists who accompanied the train tended to write very poor reviews of these speeches. They complained that they were jumbled and topsy-turvy, slipped from one subject to another and back again, lacked logical construction and dispensed with any processes of argumentation, often did not contain a single printable sentence, and constantly mis-stated accessory facts.[2] The corre-

[1] No account of the CDU campaign would be complete without mention of the host of anecdotes (probably true every one of them) put into circulation on the Chancellor's morale and views of his own health. Two of them related how on his eightieth birthday he had replied to the photographer who had hoped to take his picture on the ninetieth: 'That is quite possible, young man. You look healthy enough to me'; and how he had countered a similar wish with a quotation from Pope Leo XIII replying on his ninetieth birthday to a wish for his centenary: 'Why, gentlemen, do you estimate God's mercy no higher than that?' An explanation of this vigour was offered in other stories circulated, illogically perhaps, by Adenauer's opponents: thus the Free Democrats' party newspaper, in its cartoon 'Occident Express', suggested that the doctor on board the train was dosing him with the living tissues of freshly slaughtered animals (*Frischzellen*). (*Das Freie Wort*, 30 Aug. 1957).

[2] *Der Spiegel* (which does not come into the neutral category) recorded all these speeches and presented an analysis of them in its last pre-election number, quoting in detail the following example of Adenauer's self-contradictory confusion of facts.

spondent of *The Times*, who felt that the tour had 'all the characteristics of an inspection by a colonial Governor in a restive province', came much nearer the heart of the matter in acknowledging that 'Dr. Adenauer has a simplicity that calls for forgiveness'.[1]

His audiences were with him throughout. He had only to appear, be presented with a bunch of his favourite roses by the ubiquitous little girls in their Sunday best, and utter some commonplaces on the beautiful weather, the seriousness of the situation, the lovely countryside, the advantages of hiking, the merits of old-fashioned education, or to proclaim to women audiences his and his party's determination to lighten housework, and he could be sure of an ovation. The common touch he displayed on such occasions was, so the CDU insisted, a genuine expression of his personality. Yet when his audience seemed to demand it, he would rise to a high-level presentation of his case that flattered the political intelligence of the ordinary voter and absorbed even those whose knowledge and interest in politics were less cursory.

The Chancellor's adaptation to his audience and his feeling for their reactions were in fact the most impressive aspect of these speeches and one which detailed analyses trying to prove his mental decay only served to substantiate. Yet he was not playing for frantic applause and he certainly did not always receive it. Admission to his meetings was by ticket only and elaborate precautions ruled out the possibility of blocks of opponents disturbing the speech; single interrupters were in any case soon dealt with by strong contingents of stewards. But although the meetings were thus packed largely by supporters, in Hamburg, for example, a crowd of 15,000 people never gave him more than forty seconds' applause even on entering the hall, and he delivered himself of a dissertation on foreign affairs uninterrupted by any response for long stretches at a time. There was in fact nothing of a *Führer* cult, and the success which Adenauer had

An American girl employed by the FDP had written an 'Open letter to Mr. Dulles' which Reinhold Maier mentioned in a speech. This letter appeared in the following versions in the Chancellor's speeches: in Bochum on 15 Aug. Maier had written a letter to a well-known American lady. In Mannheim on the 23rd Maier 'wrote a nice letter to his aunt in America and published it here before the aunt ever got it. I don't know if it was his aunt, it might have been his cousin.' On the 24th in Pforzheim, more coyly, Maier had written 'to a lady he knew—but I'm afraid he didn't mention her address'. And on the 25th in Stuttgart Maier had, it seems, dutifully addressed the letter he never wrote to the aunt that never existed 'for publication over there'. *Der Spiegel* took all this in dead seriousness and quoted a neurological work on *Mental Senescence* to explain 'a slowing down of psychic processes, reduction in mnemonic faculties, and the necessity to fall back increasingly on the automatisms of the psycho-practical apparatus'.

[1] *The Times*, 26 and 29 Aug.

with the general public, while apparently even greater than in 1953, remained within the limits of sober moderation.[1]

In addition to Adenauer's own natural rapport with an audience, the tone of his speeches was also a matter of high campaign strategy. On the evidence of the public opinion polls the CDU headquarters decided that there was a time-lag of some two or three months before a public event made any impression on the general body of voters, while the more intelligent and discriminating public reacted much faster. In order to throw the SPD on to the defensive, the CDU planned to begin with hard blows that would impress the ordinary voter with whom little beyond the initial aggressiveness would register before the date of the poll. The nearer election day approached, the more conciliatory were Adenauer's speeches to become, and hence the more attractive to the more sophisticated section of the population, which would still react to these approaches by polling day. The CDU campaign was thus opened by Adenauer's Bamberg statement that the election would decide whether Germany was to remain Christian or turn Communist, and by his Nuremberg speech of 7 July that an SPD victory involved the ruin of Germany.[2]

Just as this rhythm of a violent start and a gentler ending was designed to exploit a division of the market according to speeds of reaction, so it attempted to exploit the regional differentiation of the German public: Adenauer's baroque early speeches were made in Bamberg and Nuremberg, where they fitted into the cultural landscape, and his sober lectures on foreign affairs were delivered in the cooler, more restrained Hanse cities of the North. (The design did not, however, work out consistently, since Adenauer also had to show himself early in some places in the North, and late in some in the South and since he himself was too spontaneous a speaker always to keep to such plans.)

[1] It may have been a little different with the local dignitaries of the CDU, who tended to welcome him on station platforms in their morning coats with 'the most unlikely looks of faithful adoration from their sparkling eyes and bows . . . that had not been so deep since their dancing lessons' (*Neue Zürcher Zeitung*, 18 Aug. 1957). They asked for his signature in their party membership books, the future Minister for Public Enterprises called out 'God save Konrad Adenauer', and in Essen he was welcomed to a meeting of the *Junge Union* as 'father of the entire German people' (*Der Spiegel*, 11 Sept. 1957).

[2] 'We are resolutely determined that the SPD shall never come to power. Why are we so resolutely determined? Believe me, it is not out of party hatred. That is not the reason; but we are thus resolutely determined to the depths of our beings because we believe that a victory of the Social Democratic Party involves the ruin [*Untergang*] of Germany.' The word *Untergang* means literally the sinking of a ship below the surface.

The Government Team

Adenauer was the star attraction of the CDU campaign. But the team that had become familiar from the poster series also took a highly active and very successful part in the election. Erhard and Strauss, von Hassel and Lemmer all addressed something like forty mass rallies in the last twenty-five days of the campaign, Strauss even speaking in Kiel one night and in Garmisch the next. Some dozen speakers toured the country according to a plan worked out in the party headquarters and even through this plan of mass rallies the CDU insisted on expressing its character as a party that integrated all sections of the population. The CDU was proud of the fact that Dr. Franz-Joseph Würmeling, the Minister for Family Affairs whose reputation as a clerical bigot was said to make him an object of curiosity in the Protestant North, was on occasions sent to speak there to show what a reasonable and charming person the 'blackest' of CDU ministers really was. Conversely, von Hassel, the Protestant Minister-President of Schleswig-Holstein, went several times to speak in the Catholic Rhineland. Indeed for the big star speakers there seemed to be no geographical barriers, Gerstenmaier's Swabian and Strauss's Bavarian accents proving no handicap any more than Adenauer's celebrated soft *g*'s of Cologne.

The performance of individual members of the team varied greatly. Gerstenmaier, though well on the 'right' of the CDU in social policy, consistently minimized the differences between the CDU and the SPD in foreign affairs, implicitly criticized the misrepresentation of the SPD's foreign policy which underlay much of the less sophisticated CDU propaganda, and did what he could to restrain tempers on both sides and secure a fair and objective campaign. Dr. von Brentano on the whole did not succeed in creating such a favourable impression: 'out of respect for the refugees' he had refused entry visas to a Moscow football team and some canoeists from Hungary; when the German Sports Federation took up the matter in a blaze of publicity, von Brentano was summoned to the Chancellor's campaign train and told to reverse his decision. It was also von Brentano who (according to SPD sources) echoed an earlier British election cry when he declared: 'If you vote SPD you can go to the savings banks at 7 a.m. on the Monday after the election and take out your savings deposits.'

Strauss, the handsome, broad-shouldered, and ambitious 42-year-old Minister of Defence in some ways had the hardest time during the campaign. His was obviously the most difficult and vulnerable of the portfolios in the Cabinet. His tough and ebullient personality was perhaps essential for some aspects of the job, but it also made him all the more a target for attack. Even some of the less sensitive voters resented his presentation of a signed portrait of himself to the 100,000th recruit, his appearances under military or police escort, and his cavalier treatment of the atomic scientists' concern for the future. He was, moreover, dogged by hard luck. On the eve of his wedding fifteen recruits were drowned in the Iller during an exercise. A few days later another recruit was killed in an explosion. His honeymoon in Italy was used by the East German *Berliner Zeitung* as a convenient peg on which to hang lurid 'revelations' of his recent private life, a Berlin paper close to the CDU recapitulated these stories,[1] and one of his most prominent opponents in the CSU attempted to force him to confirm or deny their truth.[2]

It was above all at Strauss's meetings that Young Socialists and Communists set out to create all the disturbance they could. In the packed *Hofbräuhaus* of his native Munich he was sent a parcel which, opened gingerly by the police, was found to contain an indiarubber 'for eradicating Russia from the map of Europe' in case of Communist attack—an allusion to one of his earlier pronouncements. After two hours of jeering and counter-cheers and chorus performances by serried ranks of opposition, the meeting was closed in a hurry: several interrupters had been dragged screaming from the hall by the stewards, half a dozen more had been arrested by contingents of police hidden away in side rooms before the beginning of the meeting, and for another two hours an angry crowd argued in the street in spite of police requests to 'keep to the pavement'.

The Junge Union

Strauss, von Hassel, and some of the other younger men in the CDU (including a dozen members of the third Bundestag) had risen in the party originally as a result of their leadership of the various organs of the *Junge Union*, the CDU's youth organization. The *Junge Union* had some 60,000 members (usually under thirty-five—in some Land organizations under forty), who took a very active part

[1] See *Der Kurier*, 12 June 1957.

[2] Dr. Alois Hundhammer, formerly Bavarian Minister of Culture, a bearded Knight of the Holy Sepulchre known and feared as the staunchest champion of morality, clericalism, and corporal punishment, appeared to be unique among Bavarian politicians in that Munich Radio declared: 'You could send him round the world with a bag of gold and a virgin, and he would return with both intact.' But the encounter between Strauss and this 'bronze monument of the counter-Reformation' (*Der Spiegel*, 10 July 1957) turned into the worst defeat of Hundhammer's political career: the CSU decided that Communist libels deserved no reply.

in the internal politics of the CDU as well as in the campaign. In 1956 the *Junge Union* had spoken out more clearly on the subject of its elders than most party organizations would dare to do in any country. They had declaimed against an 'evaporation of the party's stock of ideas' and a 'lack of resistance to National Socialists, militarists and opportunists', had called their party an 'agency for the brokerage of seats', and attacked Strauss's predecessor at the Ministry of Defence with an unequivocal 'Blank must go'.

Thereafter Adenauer intensified his courtship of the *Junge Union* and throughout the campaign he insisted on the importance of these younger elements in the party. The Land organizations of the *Junge Union* demanded their share of candidates in hopeful places, and when the party selection conference in Hesse did not respond to their requests engaged in a protracted dispute. During the election itself the *Junge Union* took its full share of responsibility. It worked with the Catholic youth and young mens' organizations and with the Y.M.C.A., recruited non-members for poster squads, issued a works newspaper, organized a procession of floats, ran election quiz programmes, provided stewards for election rallies, and held meetings of its own at which young people of other countries put the case for Adenauer to German audiences. The *Junge Union* also helped the whispering campaigns (*Mund-propaganda*), though it felt that insufficient use was made of this method of electioneering. Its 'Operation Parasol' put a car on the road loaded with pamphlets from the Federal Press Office, the ADK, and the *Büro Bonner Berichte* of the Ministry for All-German Affairs, which drove from town to town with a large parasol under which these publications were distributed to the population.

The Free Democrats and the Social Democrats accused the *Junge Union* of engaging in an 'SS terror' at its meetings and in the streets, but such accusations were largely the product of the time of strain at which they were made. Between the *Junge Union* and the other political youth groups there often existed a friendly rivalry and good personal relations. (After the election a meeting was held between all the Bundestag members of party youth groups in an attempt to form a united front on certain issues against their elders.) Of all the youth organizations the *Junge Union* was undoubtedly the most interesting and probably also the most active during the campaign. It is not unlikely that through the invigorating experience of electioneering it reinforced a certain political interest among a far wider circle than that of its own members and that it won for the CDU a further group of dynamic young men who will be coming to the fore in German politics in the years to come.

VII

SECURITY WITH OLLENHAUER

AT the turn of the year it might have seemed that the Social Democrats were in a very good initial position from which to open their election campaign. They had made spectacular gains in the local elections of the autumn of 1956, early in 1957 they had a slight lead in the public opinion polls over the CDU, the morale of their organization was better than it had been for years, the Free Democrats looked as if they would be only too happy to enter into a coalition with them on the federal as well as the Land level, prices were just beginning to rise, and Ollenhauer was received all over the world as a potential Chancellor of the Federal Republic.

Yet, whatever these signs may have suggested, the SPD also began the campaign weighed down by a number of severe disadvantages. However well the party might appear to do in a 'cold' campaign, these encumbrances were bound to be revealed the moment that the election was under way. And within a few months the party suffered what, compared with its earlier hopes, proved the bitterest of its post-war defeats.

The Social Democrats and their Public Image

It is worth stressing that this reverse was due not so much to specific mistakes committed by the party during the campaign as to the basic handicaps under which it was labouring. Few parties have had the benefit of so much gratuitous and often patronizing advice from outsiders and foreign observers as the SPD. It is certainly not intended to add to it here. In fact it is doubtful whether any such advice could be helpful or even relevant; for the very elements of its character and inner structure that prevented the party from attracting any sizeable new share of the German electorate also lay at the root of the unshaken loyalty of so many of its most stalwart supporters. The changes that would have been necessary to allow the SPD to fight an election campaign on an equal footing with its main rival were so radical that many of its most devoted members must have felt that the party would thereby be denying its very self.

The first of these handicaps was the SPD's name. It is the only historical party that has maintained itself in the Federal Republic and it is rightly proud of its unbroken tradition. Lassalle's flag covered Schumacher's coffin; the Weimar symbol of the three arrows still appeared in the parade of ancient flags at party congresses; and the leading ranks of the party cadre contained many of the survivors of 1933 who were liberated from concentration camps or returned from their exile in London and elsewhere after the war.[1] But this identification with past actions had its debit side. While the CDU and the FDP, the German Party, and of course the BHE could all start political life almost from scratch, the Social Democrats were regarded by large sections of the electorate as the old 'reds' or *Sozis* who failed to work their own post-Versailles system and then capitulated to Hitler without a shot being fired.

In view of the party's own insistence on its traditions the less well-informed public was hardly to be blamed if it regarded the SPD as being still largely an ideological party that derived its inspiration from Marx and hankered after the nationalization of all the means of production, distribution, and exchange. Ollenhauer with Marx, with pictures of Marx, and with busts of Marx was a favourite theme for the cartoonists. In 1953 one of the main CDU posters simply declared: 'All the ways of Marxism lead to Moscow', and no further explanation was required. As one German author put it: 'The shadow of Karl Marx obscures the SPD's uncompromising battle against Communism even today. . . . Will the SPD have the courage for the decisive leap over its own shadow?'[2]

The ideological taint with which the SPD appeared to so many voters to be marked had two specific aspects that were of particular significance: indeed the public had more solid grounds than historical tradition for ascribing to the SPD an economic policy of planning and controls, and a profoundly anti-clerical attitude.

In the immediate post-war years even the CDU was advocating the public control of basic industries, post-war misery seemed to be turning large sections of the middle class into a new proletariat, and Schumacher hoped to be able to make the SPD into a popular party of much wider appeal than ever before and to lead it to power

[1] Some 57 of the 169 SPD members of the third Bundestag had been in concentration camps, forced labour camps, the punitive military unit 999, prison, or emigration after 1933. Without in any sense making a competition of it one should perhaps also record that the same was true of 10 of the 270 Bundestag members of the CDU. In addition some 25 members of each of these parties mentioned dismissal or other persecution under the National Socialist régime in their Bundestag biographies, on which these figures are based. (For comparable figures for the Free Democrats see footnote 2 on p. 165.)

[2] A. N. Uhlig, *Hat die SPD noch eine Chance?*, Isar, Munich, 1956, p. 10.

without sacrificing anything from a full-blooded socialist programme. But economic developments after the currency reform seemed to vindicate a free-market economy, while controls were associated in the public mind with the occupation forces as well as with post-war distress; the majority of the German population did not want a return to more State control of economic life. The new prosperity under Erhard's system thus eroded the whole foundation of Schumacher's political strategy.

Schumacher, however, had two more strings to his bow. One of them was his emphasis on the rights of the German nation, which we have already discussed; the other was his suspicion of the role of the Catholic Church in political life. The partition of Germany had shifted the denominational balance of West German society sharply in favour of Roman Catholics. By phrases such as that describing the Vatican as the fifth occupying power of Germany Schumacher did not, however, recruit support for the SPD. Instead of attracting Protestants, he alienated those 'social' Catholics like Arnold who came to form the left wing of the CDU. By the time Schumacher died it was clearer than ever that neither a socialist economic policy nor the expression of anti-clerical sentiments could enlarge the SPD's support in the country.

Yet whatever the declarations of some of the more 'modernist' party leaders, the spirit of the SPD was very far removed from the Nonconformist and Christian Socialist strain of the British Labour Party. The bulk of the party membership was more than indifferent to the Churches: it felt provoked by them, and many of the older members had formally resigned their church membership at a time when the Churches—the Protestant even more than the Catholic—appeared part and parcel of the political establishment of the Second Reich and their national religion a social sedative. Membership of the SPD had been not simply a functional association for the advancement of precise and limited ends, but the corporate expression of a philosophy of life. It was as such that it could claim the devoted sacrifice of leisure and income on which its organization rested at all levels and a devotion extinguished neither by Bismarck's anti-socialist legislation (under which 15,000 SPD members were imprisoned) nor by the National Socialist terror with its uncounted torture and murders.

The SPD had begun life as a philosophical and social as much as a political community. The local party had been a working-men's club, meeting for political argument and self-education in the back rooms of public-houses all over the industrial areas, and in some of these areas it is said that even today the question at a worker's death-bed is whether his nest-egg should go to the bank account 'Erich Ollenhauer, Bonn' or to the local party organization. The appellation 'Comrade' (*Genosse*) may be used with a slight curl of the lip among some of the younger elements in the party, but the second person singular (*du*) remains obligatory throughout the organization from the youngest unskilled labourer to the most eminent intellectual. Perhaps the image of a nineteenth-century back-street conspiracy of undernourished cloth-capped proletarians has vanished; but there are still traces of it to be found lurking at the back of many judgements of the party among the electorate at large—and certainly this is the spirit which still inspires some of the resolutions sent up by the local parties to the biennial party congress, the spirit which many of the rank-and-file members themselves are sorry to see disappear and without which neither the nature of the party nor the style of its election campaign can be understood.

It had been the genius of August Bebel to create the party as an organization that could survive the severe tests to which it was subjected and re-emerge steeled each time after two periods of brutal suppression. The tight organization into regions and sub-regions, into constituency parties and over 7,500 local parties—the regions and sub-regions with their underpaid professional secretariats, the local parties with their honorary officers and collectors of membership dues—was essential for the maintenance of the SPD as a financially independent party based on a fully participant mass membership. But this same party structure also made it easy for the party's opponents to represent it as a rigid machine of cliquish party hacks. No CDU speech in the election was complete without a reference to the *Funktionäre*, the anonymous 'apparatchiks' who were running the SPD and itching to take over the country.[1] The SPD was painted as an untried and untrustworthy team of pen-pushers with a dubious revolutionary past. The Wehner and Agartz affairs only took up and inflated those popular preconceptions about the party with which the Social Democrats had to struggle from the start and throughout the campaign.

Although in domestic affairs the SPD in many ways stood well to the 'right' of the British Labour Party, the public image of the SPD in the minds of the West German voters was distinctly to the 'left' of that which the British public has of the Labour Party. Those critics who asked the SPD to become a Labour Party and thereby meant that it should move to the 'right' largely missed the point. It was already well to the 'right' of most of its voters. What was

[1] In some of Adenauer's speeches the term 'Social Democrats' never occurred: the word *Funktionäre* regularly took its place.

needed was not a shift of policy so much as an intensive effort of long-term public relations. But such an effort was beyond the limited powers of the SPD.

This image of a class-bound ideologically determined party was one of the main reasons why the SPD has never since 1920 been able to poll the votes of more than one-third of the German electorate. While prominent survivors of the old Centre Party founded a new party in 1945 precisely to escape from a similar limitation due above all to their identification with Catholicism, the SPD in its insistence on its traditional values voluntarily returned to its old coop.

The most remarkable feature of the public opinion polls taken during the year before the election was their confirmation of the theory that German voters float within but not between two camps: the socialist camp of just over a third of the electorate, and the remaining two-thirds.[1] In the spring of 1957, for example, the public opinion polls attributed less than one-third of popular support to the SPD and less than a third to the CDU, while about another third of respondents were undecided or gave no answer.[2] But, as is now abundantly clear, many of these were not undecided whether to vote for the SPD or not: they tended to be indifferent to politics generally or else undecided between the various parties within the 'bourgeois' bloc; the great bulk of them, if they cast a vote, eventually cast it for the CDU. A voter in the left camp knows where he stands, tends to declare it, and has no problem of choice between varying shades of opinion represented by different parties between which he might not choose until the campaign was well under way. Whereas the elasticity of support for the CDU and other parties in competition within the 'bourgeois' bloc was high, the SPD, though it had at least as many unwavering adherents, did not succeed in scaling the traditional palisade that separated it from wider sections of the electorate.

The Planning and the Spirit of the Campaign

Such were the fundamental handicaps with which the SPD entered on the election. Its leaders were largely aware of them and set out to overcome them by a conscientious planning of their campaign. The man in charge of the whole operation was Fritz Heine, an unassuming, scholarly, but powerful party official—one of the seven members of the Federal Executive who also held a full-time appointment in the party machine; he was an old hand at the game and proud of having managed SPD campaigns ever since 1928.

[1] Cf. Hirsch-Weber and Schütz, op. cit., pp. 163–82.

[2] See Fig. 3, p. 276.

His preparations for the battle began early. They were split into twenty-six separate tasks entrusted to different working parties, commercial firms, or individuals, who planned the tactical deployment of resources. *Divo* of Frankfurt, who had earlier been working for the United States information services, and also *Emnid*, who were simultaneously working for the CDU, provided the empirical basis (or the justification) for the strategic planning of the campaign.

The invariable courtesy shown to observers in the SPD headquarters was not merely a sign that this party had little to hide, but was also indicative of the temper of the whole organization and its activities. This was not a campaign run by business tycoons but one conducted by intellectuals and routine party officials.[1] There was something academic about the whole operation; even if the SPD did not presuppose the rationality of the voter, it displayed a belief in the extent of his reasonableness not shared by the other big parties, and it felt outraged by the campaigns of the others.

The Social Democrats in fact undertook a special responsibility for the style of German political life and the maintenance of standards in democratic controversy. Throughout the campaign they registered and exhibited with almost masochistic enthusiasm each foul committed by the other side. After Adenauer's Nuremberg speech the SPD heads of Land governments boycotted the habitual Bundesrat dinner with the Chancellor in order to mark their disapproval of his tone. In several scores of libel actions the courts were called in to deal with political trespasses: yet the legal process, if it had any real effect, was likely only to enhance the publicity given to the original attack. During the 1957 election the party published two documentary accounts of libels used in the CDU's 1953 campaign and gave them wide circulation in the hope of thereby discrediting from the start any new Schroth–Scharley affair.[2] Indeed the SPD's concern for the veracity of their opponents descended to the minutiae: when it was found that one of the photo features published in the Erhard campaign's magazine *All of Us* had used faked names and family relationships to illustrate middle-class prosperity, the SPD Federal Executive issued a special pamphlet denouncing this

[1] The fact that these officials depended on the party organization rather than on the outcome of the election for their livelihood and advancement was occasionally reflected by an almost greater concern with apparent efficiency than with real effectiveness in gathering votes.

[2] In 1953 Adenauer had stated shortly before polling day that two SPD officials, Heinrich Schroth and Hugo Scharley, had received large sums of money from the East German Communist Party—an allegation withdrawn 'with regret' after the election.

mendacity. The air of injured innocence may have been justified: but even so it was a doubtful electoral asset.

There was of course also a certain calculation behind the almost gentlemanly opening of the SPD's campaign. When the Federal Executive met to consider its election strategy in January, Heine presented it with three alternative courses of action: a sharp, aggressive campaign, such as he himself would have liked to fight, but which the Executive did not wish to see and which the sociologists and institutes of public opinion advising the party feared would home as a boomerang; an objective, positive campaign rather as it came to be fought from the federal headquarters at the outset; and a quiet campaign minimizing differences with the CDU, claiming that violent controversy was against the national interest, almost admitting that there would need to be a national coalition after the election, and speculating on a low turnout at the polls. The Federal Executive opted for the second of these alternatives; and certainly the rank-and-file membership wanted to see a fighting campaign.

As time went on the sober tone of the opening phases became sharper, and on the Land and local level the SPD became no less aggressive, sometimes indeed more so, than the CDU. The Hesse party in particular printed more virulent posters, the rank and file demanded retaliation for Adenauer's Bamberg and Nuremberg speeches, and the Chancellor's own surprisingly vigorous role forced the SPD into the one line of counter-attack which it had hoped to avoid: a personal onslaught on the Chancellor himself.

Such a line of approach might have been feasible if it had been undertaken with subtlety, recognizing Adenauer's achievements in the past but painting him as now unsuited to a changed situation. But an all-out frontal attack on the most impregnable point in the CDU's armour—the venerated Chancellor himself—was foredoomed; moreover it only invited a personal comparison between the two party leaders which the CDU was able to exploit in its turn. Compared with the effortless, even slightly cynical superiority of the Chancellor, Ollenhauer's well-meaning honesty lacked dramatic appeal. Constantly repeated in verbal propaganda but occasionally printed with unflattering 'candid camera' shots of the SPD leader the CDU used the slogan: 'If you vote SPD you vote for Ollenhauer'.[1] In fact for the last four weeks before polling day the SPD

[1] Fifteen different types of CDU advertisements directly contrasted the two personalities. The CDU also apologized vehemently in public for a remark made by one of its members, it seems in private, that Ollenhauer was a Jew and should be debarred from the Chancellorship if only on racial grounds. (A similar rumour had been heard in the 1953 campaign, when Ollenhauer was also said to have dropped bombs on German towns in British uniform.)

increasingly found itself engaged in an encounter forced upon it by its members and its opponents and not in the campaign which it had originally chosen to fight.

The plans of the Executive were really designed above all to do one thing: to make the party respectable. The campaign was to be aimed at gaining the confidence of the electorate by dispelling the fear that the SPD would nationalize and control large parts of the economy, by presenting its programme as an unrevolutionary set of adaptations to the latest developments in domestic and foreign affairs, by calming apprehensions about the party's anti-clericalism and by painting it as an experienced yet almost average association of good citizens.

By 1957 the party had called in question the very assumption that socialism could be made attractive to the German electorate. The party programme never mentioned socialism; on the contrary: 'We Social Democrats demand a free economic development, free competition and private property conscious of its responsibilities to the common good . . . our free society must be protected against economic controls.'[1] Proclaiming this programme at the Dortmund Congress, Ollenhauer explained: 'Price stops and general state controls over prices are not measures of social democratic economic policy. . . . We Social Democrats want no economic experiments.' The SPD's economic expert Heinrich Deist declared that 'nationalization of the British type' was 'such a primitive and antiquated method of public guidance of the economy' that the SPD could not even consider it, and Carlo Schmid in his election speeches openly referred to the demand for socialization as one of the 'teething troubles' (*Kinderkrankheiten*) of the party's history.

The public, however, could not quite believe that the leopard had changed his spots. Its incredulity was encouraged by the publication in April of a pamphlet by Willi Eichler, who was generally referred to by the CDU as the SPD's 'chief ideologist'—rather as if this were a salaried post. The pamphlet stated bluntly that socialization remained the objective of SPD policy. The impression of ineptitude, if not of self-contradiction, was not mitigated by hurried explanations from the party headquarters that the pamphlet was merely the reprint of an historical study contributed to a foreign newspaper eight months before. The CDU at any rate continued to operate with quotations from this essay and thus reinforced its contention that the Social Democrats themselves did not know what they wanted.

Since the SPD could not win an election fought on ideological

[1] *Sicherheit für Alle*, SPD, Bonn, 1957, p. 8.

issues, it was obliged to play down not only the economic implications, but also the philosophical basis of the Marxist element in its beliefs. It stressed the fact that many practising Christians were among its leading members. Heinemann wrote an election pamphlet explaining why he had joined the SPD, the party published a periodical called *Political Responsibility* addressed particularly to Protestant voters, and attempted in some cases to make itself a spokesman for Protestant concerns as against the alleged predominance of Catholic influence exercised through the CDU.

But the SPD also tried to appeal to Catholic voters. A Catholic communicant wrote an election brochure under the title *Christian and Socialist*. Another pamphlet for Catholic voters quoted the encyclicals *Rerum novarum* and *Quadragesimo anno* to justify the SPD's social and economic policies and emphasized the Pope's warning on the use of atomic energy for other than peaceful purposes. In fact no SPD election speech was complete without a reference to both Heinemann and Helene Wessel.

But to stress that there were some Catholics within the SPD's own ranks and that the party shared some of the Pope's views on vital issues was not enough to neutralize the political influence of official Catholicism. Here the SPD had to be anti-clerical in the strict sense of the term without seeming to be anti-religious or anti-ecclesiastical. This was plainly a difficult task. To attack the ideological basis of much of the CDU's appeal too directly would have laid the SPD open to the charge of conducting ideological warfare itself. That way lay certain defeat. 'No ideological or denominational issues are at stake' was therefore the third sentence in the Dortmund programme. But it was not always appreciated by the speakers of the SPD that attacks on Catholic institutions and even on individual members of them were, in the minds of many voters, tantamount to an attack on religion itself.

Yet, rightly or wrongly, whether voluntarily and according to plan, under pressure from the membership, or in the irritation of the battle, the SPD launched an attack on the 'theocratic pretensions' of the Catholic clergy and of the CDU. The party was careful to stress that it gave to God what was God's (and perhaps a little more). It recalled that Fritz Steinhoff, the SPD Minister-President of North Rhine–Westphalia after the 'Düsseldorf revolt', had signed a treaty with the Vatican in 1956 to set up a new diocese in the Ruhr and had thus fulfilled a long-standing Catholic demand at some expense to the tax-payer. It stressed the fact that the Steinhoff Government had done nothing to curtail the position of the Church and of the denominational schools in North Rhine–Westphalia. But at the same time the SPD insisted that no party could claim a monopoly of Christianity, and that in a democracy no clerical directions on voting ought to be given or obeyed. Its election pamphlet *Can any party hire Christianity?* concluded with an alleged quotation from Pius XII:

> The place of the good Christian man or woman has been taken by what I would call the denominational party member. Christianity, perhaps also the bourgeoisie, but in particular Catholic and Protestant blocs appear as party cadres. Perhaps they believe that one day God will come with the atom bomb in his hand to smooth the path for this pseudo-Christian social world with its democratic affectations in order that they can go on transacting their profitable business deals.[1]

Since the overriding aim of the SPD was to win the confidence of the electorate, it was not enough for the party to attempt to clear itself of its ideological taint; it had also to present itself as a trustworthy and thoroughly unrevolutionary body of men. The personality of Ollenhauer himself was in this respect a great asset: unemotional, undogmatic, almost too unpretentious, none could see him leading a revolution or deliberately thrusting the nation into dangerous feats of bravado. An honest, straightforward, but uninspiring speaker who spoke forty-five times in the last twenty-six days, his one act of showmanship during the whole campaign was to charter a yellow American twin-engined aircraft for use on his election tour. The party in fact set out to build an image of Ollenhauer as the kindly pipe-smoking husband of Martha Ollenhauer rather as the British Labour Party had run its 1955 campaign with the slogan 'You can trust Mr. Attlee'. 'Confidence in the SPD' was one of the poster legends: it was also the title of a pamphlet with a little girl on the cover, her arms trustingly around Ollenhauer's neck (see Plate IV*a*).

Unfortunately for its campaign, the SPD's attempt to put its other leaders into the limelight did not succeed. Ollenhauer was popularly regarded as one of the machine politicians, the *Funktionäre* of Adenauer's speeches, and his deputy Wilhelm Mellies even more so. The SPD could have accentuated the role of other men who had come to it only after the war or who were under no suspicion of having a machine mentality. Professor Carlo Schmid, as an international figure who in Mannheim polled 6,000 more votes than his party; Fritz Erler, as the party's expert on defence who enjoyed

[1] It was not entirely the SPD's fault if one of the Pope's doctors, who had allowed this quotation to be printed on his authority in a German illustrated paper, later denied its authenticity.

respect even in the ranks of the CDU; Waldemar von Knoeringen, the popular and successful party leader in Bavaria—these and others could all have been given greater publicity and it might not have been as unwise as many no doubt feared to have given the former Communist Herbert Wehner the public stature which his standing in the party warranted. The party headquarters did in fact make some attempt to publicize Schmid, Erler, and Wehner—the three men who after the election became vice-chairmen of the parliamentary party. But here again the SPD's decentralization was a handicap: the party regions had requisitioned the services of at least the first two speakers before the headquarters could arrange for a nation-wide programme like that which they organized for Ollenhauer and for Mellies, the two leaders who toured the whole Federal Republic during the campaign.

It was in particular a great pity that none of the men who wielded power as the heads of Land governments—Hinrich Kopf, the highly popular Minister-President of Lower Saxony from 1946 until 1955, Dr. Georg August Zinn, the Minister-President of Hesse since 1951, Wilhelm Hoegner, the Minister-President of Bavaria, and Fritz Steinhoff, the Minister-President of North Rhine–Westphalia, were ever popularly regarded as belonging to the inner circle of the party. These men, although they had proved themselves in governing four of the five largest Länder of the Republic, were not fully harnessed to the federal campaign; and Max Brauer, who had governed Hamburg from 1946 to 1953 and Wilhelm Kaisen, who had headed the Bremen Government without interruption since 1946, both had excellent reputations but remained popularly associated with Land politics only. They could perhaps have spoken with the self-confidence and the authority that comes from responsibilities borne, decisions made, and concrete successes achieved. Yet since they were never presented to the public as a clearly defined shadow cabinet, the bid for power in the Federal Republic as a whole was bound to sound a little unconvincing.

Specific Appeals

Such were the main attempts to overcome the handicaps with which the SPD was faced before the election. Over and above these general efforts to dispel distrust, the SPD hoped to escape from the electoral limitations of a sectional party by appealing quite specifically to further sections of the electorate.

The SPD could not afford an expensive blanket coverage of the whole population; the comparative paucity of funds therefore made a concentration on marginal voters essential. Casting about for further classes of voters to woo, the SPD based its calculation on the 6,000 interviews carried out for it by *Divo*.[1] The SPD's analysis of these interviews divided the electorate of 35 million into eight categories: 5 million non-voters, 9 million firm SPD supporters, 3¼ million 'soft' SPD voters, 3 million voters quite undecided, nearly 2 million voters who might be weaned away from the small parties (these latter two categories constituted the 'target group'), 1 million firm supporters of small parties, 3¼ million 'soft' CDU voters, and 8½ million firm supporters of the CDU. Either this analysis ignored the 'bourgeois' bias of those who refused to give a definite answer, or else the SPD must have lost all its 'soft' voters during the election and gained none elsewhere.

The analysis was then concentrated on the 'target group' of 5 million people; it was hoped to combine economy and effectiveness by concentrating the propaganda effort (both in content and in distribution) mainly on these marginal voters. 'Our electoral strategy', the analysis continued, 'must be based on an exact knowledge of the social and ideological structure of this group.'

These marginal voters were sociologically very similar to the voters of parties other than the SPD, although there was among them a large number of refugees, and their tenuous personal relationship to the Churches was much more like that of SPD voters, as was their domicile (in the medium and large towns) and—in so far as they already had slight sympathy for the SPD—their propensity to discuss politics with working colleagues rather than in the home. Being on the whole not very interested in politics, they could hardly be reached by the conventional methods of electioneering: only 30 per cent. of them had ever been to a political meeting, and it was not to be supposed that they read newspapers with more attention than the rest of the population.

From this analysis a number of conclusions were drawn on both the content and the form which the SPD's propaganda should take. It is true that much of the strategy and the tactics of the campaign had been laid down before the *Divo* interviews had been carried out and interpreted. Nevertheless the results of the poll may have provided confirmation or correctives to the activities already planned on more 'intuitive' evidence. Thus the report on the working-class

[1] For the SPD's interpretation of the *Divo* findings, cf. in particular three roneo reports: *Parteien und Wähler im Spiegel der Meinungsforschung*, *Fragen und Antworten — Ergebnisse einer Meinungsbefragung*, and *Die Arbeiterschaft vor der Bundestagswahl*, all prepared between March and July 1957. One of them declared flatly: 'An overwhelming victory of one of the two big parties is almost unthinkable.'

element in the 'target group' concluded: 'The task of our campaign must be to overcome this apathy by persuading the employed workers . . . to carry the political discussion into their family circle.' This recommendation can only have strengthened those in the party's headquarters who laid heavy emphasis on the 'oral propaganda' which the party's 54,000 volunteer helpers had been requested to spread in their immediate surroundings at work, in public transport, during recreational activities, and in the home. They were supplied with letters, documentation, and 'talking points' throughout the campaign from March onwards.

The dominant impression left by the analysis of the marginal voters as they emerged from the *Divo* interviews was the heterogeneity of the target group. This picture was thought to confirm the party's view that a decentralized, varied, and flexible campaign was needed and that a large number of separate, very carefully aimed appeals should be made to different, even quite small groups of people. Coffee parties for university professors to meet Ollenhauer and special meetings for professional groups like civil servants, letters to doctors and master-artisans, advertisements aimed at the employees of foreign armed forces, letters to sports fans and leaflets for football lovers, one brochure on farmers' pensions, another on farmers' contributions to the scheme for childrens' allowances, pamphlets for wine-growers and for single, divorced, and widowed women—such was the outcome of this approach.

The central conception of the SPD campaign thus stood in sharp contrast to that of the CDU. While the CDU was carrying through a strategic offensive and found itself on the defensive only in a few tactical engagements (such as that for certain farmers' votes), the Social Democrats were strategically on the defensive and were able to undertake sorties only on a few restricted sectors of the front. And while the CDU appealed from different sides and under a wide variety of labels to the whole single mass of the electorate, the Social Democrats issued their appeals under their own name to a large variety of differentiated groups, opposing, one might almost be tempted to say, the multifarious origins and the single objective of 'centripetal' Government propaganda with their own diversified 'centrifugal' campaign.

The Poster Programme

Broadly speaking, the campaign media used by the Social Democrats were of necessity the same as those of the CDU; but there were interesting differences in the emphasis which each party laid on one or other means of carrying its appeals to the public—differences closely related to the character and resources of each party and to its own central conception of its campaign. The SPD regarded the poster as a defensive rather than an offensive weapon: it was expected by its supporters to be well represented visually, and the party leadership, as we have seen, was prepared to adapt its campaign a good deal in order to sustain the morale and ensure the co-operation of its supporters. While the CDU believed more in advertisement than in brochures and regarded the cabaret as a luxury of limited value but films as essential, the SPD published a variety of earnest booklets of documentation, was prodigal with its leaflets, and spent a surprising amount of time and manpower on music-hall shows. The poster, the newspaper advertisement, and the public film performance with their relatively undifferentiated coverage (and greater cost) could be contrasted with the cheaper brochure and the music-hall cabaret with their less universal but perhaps more specific appeals. Such differences of emphasis should not be overstated: but the extent to which they did exist is borne out by a more detailed examination of the use made by the SPD of these various techniques.

The SPD's poster campaign was based on two series: one of black text posters in yellow script and one of photographs on a light-blue ground. Both series might have been issued by the Labour Party. The black text posters were graphically good and most were brief: 'German unity—so SPD', 'No conscription—so SPD', 'Down with Prices', 'More homes instead of barracks', 'Security for all—SPD', 'Confidence in the SPD', 'This time—SPD'. Perhaps an extract from the propaganda catalogue conveys the best impression of the blue series: 'No. 9) Young couple, No. 10) Middling couple, No. 11) Older couple'. These 'milieu' posters, it was explained, were designed to appeal to the subconscious and lead through identification with the group representatives portrayed to identification with the resolve expressed by the text: 'We vote SPD'. Four worthy but singularly unattractive women (see Plate IV*e*), a grandfather and child, a family and a little girl illustrated further slogans such as 'Old Age without Worry' and 'Security for the Family'.

In the same blue series posters of Ollenhauer with Eisenhower and Ollenhauer with Nehru demonstrated that the SPD leader had been travelling too. While the one symbolized the SPD's attachment to the West, the other suggested a more neutral orientation; yet the inferiority implied in Eisenhower's patronizing smile and the insecurity that seemed attached to the third force concept in world politics made both posters less effective than the SPD had hoped.

The Ollenhauer portrait itself, on a dark ground, bore a close resemblance in style and technique to the Adenauer portrait of four years before, though it was reproduced from an oil-painting. None of the many photographers who attempted the task proved able to achieve a portrait sufficiently inspiring for the purpose.

Conspicuous by its absence was any sort of poster series that could balance the CDU's personality chess-board. In the last ten days or so of the campaign a few colour photographs of Carlo Schmid, Erler, and Mellies became noticeable, but even Ollenhauer tended to be rarely seen. The absence of anything like a shadow cabinet proved a deficiency nowhere more than in the SPD's visual propaganda, which thus failed to portray the party in personal terms.

In fact even here the party's appeal remained in part a negative one. The most graphic of the posters was one showing the mushroom of a nuclear test and the slogan 'Stop that'. Whether, as some public relations experts believed, this associated the SPD in the public mind with the explosion is difficult to say. By the same theory perhaps the pleasing design of German cathedrals and the message 'Don't drag religion into the election campaign' may have had the success it deserved, though printed late and only thinly distributed.

This poster programme of the federal headquarters seemed too tame for the fighting spirit of several of the party regions, which proceeded to print other designs that were not always happier. One originating in Hanover (where cartoon posters were used by most of the parties) showed a tank firing atomic missiles; it had the face of Adenauer. Another displayed the head of a corpse disfigured by radiation: 'Atomic armament begets mass death' (see Plate III*b*). The message was no more violent than that of the federal poster which declared, 'Whoever votes for the CDU risks high prices and inflation, final division, atom bombs and atomic death'; but the picture proved too much for many members, who refused to use it.[1] Overloaded with text, unfair, but at least generally noticed was a placard saying, 'In Nuremberg, Hitler declared. . . . In Nuremberg, Adenauer declared . . .: In twelve years Hitler ruined Germany: don't give Adenauer twelve years!'

Nor was co-ordination between the various party organs always as good as it might have been. A blue Hesse poster showing a mark piece with a section sliced off and declaring 'The mark is only worth 82 pfennigs now—stop depreciation' was posted cheek by jowl with the federal SPD's strangely gratuitous blue poster showing a newly

[1] In Hamburg, so one was told, stocks of this poster were held in reserve and its issue threatened if the CDU should become too unfair in its local campaign. One SPD advertisement also declared: 'The atom-bomb Chancellor must go.'

minted piece and the slogan 'The mark must retain its stability.' Yet where decentralization and local initiative were most urgently needed—in the Saar—the standard federal posters demanded reunification (which the Saar had just achieved), abolition of conscription (which had not yet been introduced), and lower prices (which, since the Saar was still in the franc area, were the concern of Paris rather than of Bonn). Be it said to their credit that the Young Socialists, always anxious to lighten the earnestness of their seniors, produced one witty drawing on a car sticker aping the road-safety campaign: 'Listen to your wife—vote SPD'.

Most of these posters were equipped with the standard SPD sign: this suggests strength and reliability through the massive, almost squat shape of the three-dimensional letters; solidarity through their cohesion; and dynamism through their ascent from the level of the S via that of the P to the D.

In its solidity, its lack of genius, its multiplicity without a central theme from which all else could flow—even in the occasional loss of its sense of proportion—the poster display was just as illuminating of the whole SPD campaign as the CDU's posters of the campaign of the Government. Where the wealthier Government parties could obtain unquestioned obedience by paying professionals, the SPD offered its party regions 2½ million posters free and hoped that most of them would be displayed. There was undoubtedly a fair wastage. The other 2 million posters were sold just below cost price to the party regions in accordance with their orders; but there were thirty models—perhaps far too large a range in any case—and the federal headquarters could not lay down which of them should be ordered. The Social Democratic Executive was in fact reduced to employing the price mechanism to reinforce its propaganda recommendations: it subsidized the posters it regarded as most effective out of slightly higher rates charged for the posters it did not value so highly.

The independence of regional and local party organizations also made it impossible to implement any central plan for the staggering of posters: the campaign as a result began rather too early and showed no discernible rhythm. It did, however, often have the great virtue of implying a personal commitment: in the few cases where election posters were to be seen in the windows of private homes or on poster sites in private gardens they were usually posters of the SPD, and sandwich boards and 'walking columns' proved a cheap and effective means of publicity. In one constituency the sitting member himself planned to picket the railway station in a sandwich board to encourage his team. More use could have been made of this method—though many party workers remain shy of publicly proclaiming their party allegiance (and *a fortiori* of making a public spectacle of themselves) and plainly there were certain considerations of dignity involved which would have put an upper limit to its effectiveness. (It is worth noting that the CDU, which had ordered thousands of campaign buttons in the American style with a portrait of Adenauer and the motto 'I vote CDU', completely failed to persuade its adherents to wear them.)

Other Propaganda Methods

Like Adenauer, Ollenhauer sent one letter to every pensioner and another to every household. To the pensioners he recalled the SPD's constant pressure on the Government in favour of higher benefits, listed six sources of dissatisfaction with the 1957 pension reform, and concluded:

> The CDU majority must be broken in this election, so that a new battle of the pensions can be fought in the next Bundestag with greater hope of success. . . . Put your trust in the Social Democrats.

His general letter was much briefer than Adenauer's. Dated 31 August and beginning 'Dear Voter', he stated quite bluntly:

> If someone votes for the CDU, he will have to put up with prices rising further, Germany remaining divided, and our living under the atom bomb and perhaps dying by it.
>
> My political friends and I have worked out a government programme. We shall strengthen the currency and assure stable prices. We shall safeguard a free economic development and small and medium properties in town and country and protect them by public control of the mammoth enterprises.
>
> A government led by the SPD will advocate a disarmament treaty, abolish conscription and help to see that atomic energy is used only for peaceful purposes. In close co-operation with our Western allies we shall propose a security system for the whole of Europe to make possible reunification and give us more security than we have today.

After a reference to six Länder whose governments had been led by the SPD, Ollenhauer concluded his letter by writing:

> The only issue on the 15th of September is whether we refuse the CDU's claim to monopoly power because it would mean the end of democracy in the Federal Republic.

Like the CDU, the SPD put out an illustrated newspaper: *Illus* A, B, and C were printed in 3½ million copies between them and *Illus* D in nearly 6 million copies. This last, an 8-page number, was laid out according to an obvious scheme. It contained three pages of pictures of middle-class people who all declared that they would vote SPD, and one page showing SPD leaders with bishops of both Churches. Another inside page contrasted Adenauer's Nuremberg declaration with a map showing countries with strong socialist parties as bulwarks of freedom; the sixth was filled with caricatures. The front page sported the face of a laughing girl, the back the portraits of two dozen SPD politicians.

The party's list of election propaganda bears eloquent testimony to the differentiation in both the style and the destination of the appeals with which the SPD hoped to attract specific sections of the electorate. The publicity material varied from a serious historical study of the SPD's attitude to conscription since the nineteenth century to 100,000 red cardboard gliders marked 'For our children—SPD'; from documentation on the Churches' role in the election to a book of cartoons of Ollenhauer (many of them highly unflattering); from accounts of the CDU's party finance to a rubber ball marked 'Security for all'. The black-and-yellow poster series was reproduced in the form of millions of small stickers used particularly to seal letters—a publicity technique over which the party clashed with the Federal Ministry of Posts and Telecommunications—and a gay leaflet announced a prize for the most accurate prediction of the SPD poll: a free trip to Naples, Athens, or Marrakesh. In all, the Bonn headquarters dispatched 9 million illustrated papers, 17 million election newspapers, and 15 million pamphlets with perhaps another 20 million leaflets and similar material, and local organizations must have added further dozens of millions of copies of their own productions as well.

Of the greatest interest among such local publications were of course the constituency candidates' election addresses. They tended to be standardized throughout a party region in format, style, and partly even in text, with wide differences between regions. Only occasionally would an enterprising candidate strike a more individual note. The election address of one candidate showed his little daughter on the phone: 'My daddy? But he's in Bonn . . .' and that of a professor of economics pictured him engaged in his hobby of cutting semi-precious stones. Dr. Schöne's election address in Peine-Gifhorn put the emphasis on his services to the locality and the areas abutting the zonal border, not only in the Bundestag but also in the Common Assembly of the European Coal and Steel Community; he never mentioned his party in the text, relegated the party initials to the back page, and also used a personal poster that was devoid of any party symbol.

In his case there was an overt attempt at presenting the constituency member as a personal representative of the locality irrespective of party; but imitations of the 'camouflage' propaganda of the Christian Democrats and the Communists were also tried. A news and features service was supplied to local newspapers by a 'camouflage' party agency and 'non-party' lectures were organized; several party organizations distributed highly unflattering photographs of Adenauer and Strauss without indication of origin and the simple legend 'Him?' Such attempts, however, did not go very far. The *Hints for Women* (home-made face packs of yeast and cucumber rinds, 'and the best beauty treatment: to think more of others than of oneself') only had a non-partisan cover page, the rest being straight propaganda signed by the SPD Executive.

Just as the CDU issued its workers with a lavishly produced *SPD Mirror* containing quotations from the speeches of SPD leaders, so the SPD helped its workers and speakers by a table setting out the voting record of every member of the Bundestag in every division up to the last weeks of the legislative period, and by a voluminous handbook confronting *CDU Words—and Deeds*. The SPD's large reliance on voluntary helpers is borne out, too, by the brochures on poster display, on the conduct of a local campaign, and even on how to reproduce the party monogram, and by the specimen speeches, specimen letters, and other aids to local parties.

But in spite of all the concessions it may have made to the rank-and-file members, the SPD Executive was in several respects disappointed by their response. If the campaign managers of the CDU had gone to the United States for inspiration, so those of the SPD had hoped to import one distinct Anglicism into their campaign. Canvassing to locate supporters and knocking them up to ensure that they turned out to the polls may have been more difficult in Germany than in Britain if it was true that voters were more reluctant to declare their intentions to party workers; it may also have been less useful than in Britain, given the very high turnout in the second and third Bundestag elections. But the SPD leadership had asked local parties to organize a canvass, and had supplied detailed instructions and specimen canvass returns for their use. They met with blank non-co-operation. The bulk of the local parties realized that they could not complete the task and did not see the advantage of a partial canvass; they did not like the assignment, and they feared that to engage in it might rouse memories of the National Socialist system of political 'block wardens' and thus do the party more harm than good. Perhaps hardly a fifth of the local parties even began the task.

There were also other difficulties on the local level. While the

CDU had the financial resources and contact with a reservoir of suitable personnel which could take up temporary posts with the party organization, the conservatism and reserve of local Social Democratic organizations in the face of outsiders ruled out the employment of temporary election agents in most local branches. The elected local officers of the party could often not take much holiday, and in some cases, so the party complained, were also unsuited to organizational jobs of any complexity. A few party officials were imported from Berlin, but for the rest the ordinary staff of the party (which consisted of some 300 administrative officers, and perhaps as many other employees again), coped with that side of the election with little but part-time volunteer help. It must always be remembered in this context that a party which is largely controlled by its members, one-tenth of whom are active in local or Land government, will not always regard the Bundestag elections as the ones that matter most. In many instances the party felt it could detect a certain withholding of local resources for other occasions when the people who held the local party purse-strings would be candidates themselves.

But there was one task at any rate about which the membership was enthusiastic: the showing of films. Whereas the CDU largely employed professional personnel for this purpose, the SPD could rely on its members to go round themselves with the party cartoon and documentary films and save it such expenditure. On average the organization appears to have had the use of at least one projector per constituency, in many cases of several. But there were only ten film vans capable of playing to outdoor audiences, which were used particularly in the 'black' Catholic areas such as the diocese of Münster. The SPD claimed that voters in these areas would be frightened of attending indoor meetings which might brand them far more clearly in the eyes of the clergy and of their neighbours than loitering in a car park watching a film: in fact there may also have been other reasons why outdoor audiences there tended to be four or five times the size of audiences at comparable indoor showings.

The SPD had rather fewer films to show than the CDU. *Handshake with America* was an imitation of the 1953 film on Adenauer's transatlantic trip. *In times like these* presented an unvarnished view of drab life in 1957, worries over prices and pensions, a research worker and his wife unable to afford a baby, letters from the Eastern Zone, and the tragedy of cousins enlisted in opposing armed forces—all blended with a television cabaret and interviews with SPD politicians. The film opened and closed with a campaign chorus to security. *Atoms this way and that* and *Don't forget* brought the number of documentaries up to four. Five further films showed Schmid, Erler, and Deist speaking on various subjects, and twenty-five of the party candidates had their own personal films for use in their constituency. Five cartoon films and two films of puppets completed the range of federal films, though the Saar party region also produced a tense cloak-and-dagger account of its underground work during the Hoffmann régime.

In addition to these sixteen general and twenty-five candidates' films (with over a thousand copies in all), the SPD made extensive use of what it termed the poor party's cinema—a series of slides for projection together with a script or a tape-recording which the slides were designed to illustrate. Nine such series were at the disposal of party organizations, and they appear to have been impressive when properly used.

Nothing gave the SPD more work and trouble, Fritz Heine declared during the election, than its cabaret programme. The SPD had for some time put a special emphasis on this method of propaganda in the belief that the cabaret, as an essentially destructive weapon, was ideal for an Opposition party.

Post-war Germany had seen a fair revival of the professional political cabaret. The best-known groups, such as the 'Porcupines' and the 'Islanders' of Berlin, appeared on radio as well as playing nightly to packed 'live' audiences in their tiny cellars or improvised theatres. Their script-writers were intellectuals and they found a ready-made target in those who were doing well under the *status quo*, in rearmament and in all things American, in big business, and in inadequate provision for education and for the pensioners. Their ridicule was no less venomous when the Berliner's jealousy of the upstart 'federal village' played into their sketches in which Frau Pappritz as governess to diplomatic society was made the indispensable symbol of the *nouveau riche* pretentiousness of the post-war Republic.[1] The cabarets were thus natural allies of the Opposition,

[1] Frau Erika Pappritz, Deputy Chief of Protocol in the German Foreign Office, had become a national figure early in 1957 by appearing as joint author of a book on etiquette which included such dicta as: 'A lady who smokes in the street is either an American or no lady', 'Long underwear remains unmanly and unbeautiful, even if seen by hardly anyone', 'The famous chain should be pulled during and not after use...', and: 'We should bath every day.... "Do you know that exciting feeling of just having washed?"' Questions were asked on the matter in the Bundestag, no cabaret was complete without a ballad, a lampoon, and a host of references to this senior civil servant and her book attracted sufficient international attention for the German Foreign Minister at a press conference in Australia to allow correspondents a glimpse of his own long underwear.

and as such all the more effective for being formally uncommitted to any party line.

It may be asked whether sending such professional cabaret groups on tours of the Federal Republic under the auspices of the SPD and paying some of their star members to join special SPD cabaret groups was really in tune with the quasi-constitutional position as touchline critics occupied by the professional cabaret on the Continent. Their overt employment by the SPD may even have represented the destruction of a capital asset from the SPD's own point of view. But then it was not for the voter to grumble at such politically sponsored (even if slanted) entertainment; and the observers of the election, too, had reason to be grateful for some little light relief.

The SPD's main federal cabaret was entitled *Next One, Please.* Preparations were made over nine months and 300 candidates and others had been carefully worked into its programme, usually in witty interviews with a compère (see Plate IV*c*). *Next One, Please* was seen in sixty-four performances by some 100,000 people. It was not on the whole a very highbrow entertainment: one of its main attractions was the most popular of German child stars, a winsome 14-year-old singer in spectacles, and much of its matter was non-political. In and around Munich, on the other hand, 'The Timefuses' presented a first-rate programme. Two men and two girls had the stage to themselves for over two hours, the local candidate introducing himself in the interval; with one or two lapses into the tear-gland sentimentality that seems inevitable at a certain point in every German cabaret its wit and speed were up to the most exacting taste.

Apart from these and similar professional cabarets, the SPD had for some time been running another hundred amateur groups 'multiplying like rabbits', and published a two-monthly magazine devoted entirely to helping the 2,500 amateur cabarettists whose work reached a crescendo during the election campaign. This beautifully produced *Treasure Trove* contained songs, sketches, and essays on the theory of humour and on the tactics of its political use together with careful instructions on all kinds of detail of organization, staging, and acting.[1] The eighth congress of SPD cabaret groups

[1] See, for example, *Die Fundgrube*, no. 20, of May–June 1957, which contains an article entitled 'Every joke has two sides' on the danger of popularizing an opponent while making fun of him, and an essay on cabaret shows for women which specified: 'Children always get across', but 'we have discovered that the simple mixture "children's ballet plus Erich Ollenhauer" remains unsatisfactory'; the two elements must be fused and it was the task of the compère 'to explain the latest party resolutions in the light of a music-hall turn'. As the editor insists: 'When the laughter has died down the question looms up: "Has this laughter been of political use?"'

took place just before, the ninth just after the election. The party estimated that another 200,000 people were reached by these amateur groups, which were willing to go almost anywhere to carry their political message and help with an evening's entertainment in women's clubs, at trade union rallies, and at works festivities.

Other entertainment programmes were provided in various places, usually by the Young Socialists; in Bremen they engaged the local beauty queen and Max Schmeling the heavy-weight boxer; in Saarbrücken they booked the radio band for three evening dances in the largest hall of the Land and organized a display of model aeroplanes. A large proportion of the attenders at such functions must have been below voting age, but they were regarded as an investment for the future. It seemed important to convince the voters of 1961 that *Sozis* could still be quite civilized people, and some felt that this was just the sort of long-term public relations work which, while financing itself, could do more to help the party out of its social and ideological isolation than any quantity of laboured documentary brochures.

The SPD was given a certain amount of more or less independent support from a number of intellectuals. Some 300 writers, actors, and artists of the 'Franconian Circle' published an appeal six days before the election which went rather further than the SPD—it demanded readiness to negotiate with the Government of the German Democratic Republic—but which was obviously designed to aid the party:

> For the sake of the good of the people it is no longer military armaments, but culture and science that must have priority. This involves a higher evaluation of intellectual achievement, worthier conditions for students and the complete abolition of privileges in education. Schools are more important than barracks. . . .

A commercial address firm also sent 'predominantly to members of the so-called educated classes'[1] 50,000 copies of a pamphlet consisting essentially of a reprint of one chapter from a well-known journalist's full-length jeremiad published in July.[2] It was the chapter which attempted to analyse Adenauer's personality:

> Adenauer, educated by a father who was the living example of absolute authority before his son's eyes, . . . can see in the apparatus of parliamentary democracy always only the infra-structure for his personal power, [and] has never in his life of eighty years, fifty of which have been spent in public affairs, uttered a single constructive political thought.

[1] Erich Kuby, *Verehrter Mitbürger*, München, Amalienstrasse 15, Anfang September 1957.

[2] Erich Kuby, *Das ist des Deutschen Vaterland, 70 Millionen in zwei Wartesälen*, Scherz & Goverts, Stuttgart, 1957.

Complaining that 'the daily chop lay like a thick plank in front of the brains of most Germans', Kuby concluded:

> I opt for the 'ruin of Germany' because I regard a third Adenauer government not as the ruin of Germany—no—but as the condition for the final triumph of nationalist and militarist tendencies in our midst.

The Party, its Members, and the Electorate

Throughout the campaign the SPD lamented its lack of funds. But it may well be asked whether even with as much money as the CDU the SPD would really have conducted a much more effective campaign, and polled a decisive number of extra votes.

There are several things that should be remembered. The SPD could not by its very nature have run the type of campaign which the Christian Democrats were able to launch. Its large and active membership, its internal structure, its attitude to the voter and its concern for democratic processes would have hamstrung any such exercise, and the public as well as the party itself would have regarded anything too slickly American in style as out of keeping with its character. A party that is concerned with establishing its respectability must err on the side of stodginess rather than of high-pressure salesmanship. In seeking to give the party a character of straightforward conventionality the campaign left it devoid of all glamour.

Perhaps it is in the nature of socialist parties, particularly in prosperous economies, that they find it difficult to make a romantic appeal. The SPD's opponents might have been tempted to see its humdrum harping on social self-interest as a reflection of a vestigial materialist view of man. Certainly the statistical barrier with which the SPD was faced was largely the reflection of a psychological one. It was not only the image of the SPD in the mind of the electorate—to which the party was so sensitive—that was faulty, but also the image of the voter as seen by the party that was distorted by naturalistic theories derived from the past. While the CDU believed that the voter demanded emotional satisfaction no less than material well-being, the SPD for its part searched the electorate for potential Socialists pre-conditioned by their class situation whom it then set out to convince by its reasoning. The party's occasional non-rational appeals by the provision of music-hall shows could not fill this emotional void. Here quantitative public opinion polls were a misleading guide which only obscured the half-conscious aspirations and less self-regarding impulses of the citizen of the sober post-war Republic.

Yet perhaps it was neither lack of funds nor campaigning style that lost the SPD the election. Given the initial situation there was perhaps no possible SPD campaign that could have resulted in a majority even for the SPD and the FDP combined. There are times when the advertising expert's best advice is not to change the publicity but to change the product. The SPD went a long way in adapting itself to feelings in the country. It could hardly have gone much further without ceasing to be a party whose leadership reflected the views of its members. Most of the money and the physical effort came from the members, and they could not be disregarded: nor would the leadership have thought it right to abandon old views too fast for the rank and file.

While the CDU and FDP could afford to neglect their membership and concentrate on the electorate, the SPD was serving two masters, and was proud of it. The SPD might just possibly have won the 1957 election if very different decisions had been taken four years, six years, or a decade earlier: but given the position a year before the poll, the SPD could not then have cynically abandoned its attitude both to the electorate and to its members.

A few days before polling day a small scene took place which was not part of the election campaign and was yet profoundly significant of the temper of the party. Passing near Munich at the height of the battle Ollenhauer interrupted his election tour to lay a wreath on the memorial to the victims of the Dachau concentration camp. The members to whom the SPD felt responsible were not only those of the present, but also those of the past. Its leaders remembered many who did not survive the Hitler régime; the portrait of Schumacher, crippled by Nazi tortures, hung on the walls of most SPD offices; and even the present members of the SPD have been marked far more than those of the other parties by their experience of the rulers of the Third Reich. No one seems to have suggested that Ollenhauer's gesture ought to hurt his electoral chances: but a good many newspapers went out of their way to speculate whether it would. In spite of its cabarets the SPD's campaign was far from brash. If it had been, then something perhaps still of value would have been lost from German political life.

VIII

THE MUSKETEERS OF A THIRD FORCE

The Free Democrats and their Leaders

THE history of German liberalism—and not of German liberalism alone—is strewn with internal divisions. Political liberalism could reconcile the demand for civic freedom and responsible government with championship of the national idea against petty principalities up to the creation of the Second Empire; thereafter the emphasis on German unity and strength began to clash with democratic and internationalist principles. Economic liberalism could reconcile the advocacy of *laisser-faire* policies with the advancement of the middle classes until the emergence of large combines, trade unions, and tariff protection. Both in the political and in the economic sphere there was thus a range of attitudes which claimed to represent the essential liberal tradition, and different economic could be combined with different political views. Given the liberal pride in individualism it was no wonder that it was never possible either in the Second Empire or in the Weimar Republic to constitute a united liberal front.

Both the main liberal parties of the Weimar Republic were reduced to the size of splinter groups well before Hitler's take-over of power, and after the war many of their adherents joined the CDU, though a few, like Professor Alfred Weber, entered the SPD. Both the national and the liberal trends, however, were also represented in the Free Democratic Party which at least in Württemberg-Baden was founded before the CDU. In addition the FDP increasingly drew on other elements which had stood further to the right in the Weimar constellation or had not been politically active before 1933 at all: some of its leaders also consciously regarded the party as a bridge by which former adherents of National Socialism could cross over to the new democracy. Although twelve years had passed since the foundation of the FDP the party had not become an integrated unit. Even the split of 1956 cut across ideological lines. Several members of the dissenting group represented the more democratic liberal tradition; and if the representatives of big business and the more nationally minded wing of the party were in a majority in the splinter group, the FDP also continued to have a strong 'right' wing of a slightly different kind.

The relative importance of different trends within the FDP varied from Land to Land, largely for historical and sociological reasons. In the Hanseatic cities of the North the FDP often represented the old patrician families and the Protestant middle class of shippers and traders with their international outlook. In the bucolic communities of Lower Saxony, where neo-Nazi elements had scored substantial successes in the early years of the Federal Republic, the FDP was largely influenced by right-wing elements, who in turn regarded their party associates in the traditionally democratic area of Baden-Württemberg as 'stone-age Liberals'. In Bavaria the party saw its role at least on the Land level as largely anti-clerical, in Hesse as largely anti-socialist. In the Rhineland-Palatinate, perhaps largely for opportunist reasons, the FDP tended to be on good terms with the CDU, while in North Rhine–Westphalia, though much of the money came from small and medium enterprises, the parliamentary party had put the SPD in power. In its planning of the campaign the FDP was thus forced to take into consideration not so much the views of its membership, which was small, but the divergence of outlook between its various Land committees and Land parliamentary parties.

It was no easy matter to lead a party so heterogeneous in its political origins and orientation, and when Reinhold Maier replaced Dehler in January 1957, he was the fourth leader of the party in eight years. For six years he had headed a coalition which included both CDU and SPD in the original Land Württemberg-Baden and had then presided over the first cabinet of the new Land Baden-Württemberg, in which the CDU was not represented. Maier was a canny tactician. He seemed staid and elderly, and even when the Chancellor rejected his proposal of a month's election truce until 10 August he was determined to fight the election like a country gentleman, refusing to give up periods of rest in his chalet at Arosa. But when in the fray he laid about him with vigour, twice toured the country by what the FDP emphasized (in contrast to Adenauer's train and Ollenhauer's plane) to be 'means of transport available to every private citizen', and spoke in his heavy Swabian accent in small but usually packed halls in the larger cities.

Maier concentrated particularly on the party's domestic proposals: the sale of nationally owned enterprises into private hands, a more effective control over cartels, more disinflation, less Government spending, tax reform, and certain changes in agricultural policy. This might seem at first sight a jejune programme; but a party which wished to restrict the functions of the State could hardly be expected to put forward a very elaborate Government programme. Having once made clear its fundamental *laisser-faire* conception, it could concentrate on denouncing the activities of the Government.

This Reinhold Maier proceeded to do. 'We need much less state than we think' was one of the most eagerly applauded sentences in his standard speech, echoed in the poster: 'Less laws, less civil service, less taxes—FDP'. Maier ridiculed the constant demand for more State policing: 'The law on the equalisation of war damage is longer than the whole of the Bible. Our milk is kept healthy, pure and good by two hundred and twenty legal regulations. The tax laws constitute a secret science.' Parallel to the conversion of the whole Federal Republic into 'one grandiose comprehensive workhouse' the psychological needs of the inmates were met as well:

> Cast all your cares on your Kaiser or your King, your Bismarck, your Hindenburg, your Adenauer! They will see that everything is all right. . . . 'With us you are as safe as in Abraham's bosom'. And, lo and behold, as the young chicks gather under the feathers of the mother hen, thus the voters seek refuge under the wide-open tailcoat skirts of security.[1]

Maier provided a respected figure-head for the party and did much to retain its traditional electorate. Many, however, regarded him as a stalking-horse for the little junta which had engineered the 'Düsseldorf revolt' and which, by skilfully exploiting the financial difficulties of other Land associations and the wealth of the North Rhine–Westphalian organization, had taken over and consolidated the seats of federal power in the party. These 'angry young men' of the war generation had initially planned to keep in the background, but as the campaign went on they more and more openly set the tone. They provided the thirty-seven-year-old campaign manager, Wolfgang Döring, whose personal and political style bore the imprint not only of his professional tank officer's career in the *Afrika Korps* but also of his admiration for the American way of life.[2] He and his friends matched Maier's traditional South-West German liberalism with the brisk radical tone of the North Rhine–Westphalian party at home and with demands for a more flexible reunification

[1] Quotations taken from the multigraphed standard speech distributed to journalists at Maier's meetings, pp. 4, 11, and 24, and *Das Freie Wort*, 23 Aug.

[2] Döring's contact with Americans began while attempting to escape from captivity; in his election address he printed three pictures of himself in America alongside four taken during his war service, and at one point in the campaign flew in an American jet fighter and used photographs of the event in his campaign. (Adenauer thereafter joked about American transport for FDP electioneers.) The dominant adjectives in the self-characterization by the 'Young Turks' in their election addresses and party newspapers were: youthful, sporty, adventurous, brash, outspoken, adaptable, astute.

policy abroad; and it was they who administered the efficient new party headquarters set up at their insistence in Bonn.

Campaign Strategy

This party leadership prided itself on its realism. It was plain that the party could not hope for a parliamentary majority, and the Free Democrats determined not to fight as if they could imagine such a contingency. They set themselves other, more restricted objectives, but such as would still promise them a key position in German politics: they would attempt to hold the balance in the third Bundestag between the CDU and the SPD, and if they could threaten at any moment to put the other party into power, they could extort from any coalition partner the satisfaction of their own policy and personnel demands.

Whether the Free Democrats could occupy such a strategic position did not, of course, depend on the success of their own campaign alone. They could hope to exercise a decisive influence only if neither big party (taken together with any satellites) obtained an absolute majority of seats and neither big party (taken together with any satellites) fell short of an absolute majority by more seats than the Free Democrats commanded themselves. These arithmetical conditions implied in practice that the Free Democrats must be the only independent third party in the Bundestag.

While such a balance in the Bundestag would be largely the net result of the voters' reactions to the two big parties whom the FDP liked to call 'the unscrupulous and the uninspired', there were certain conclusions the Free Democrats could draw as to the tactical objectives they must set themselves in their own campaign. Firstly, they must attempt to reduce the votes cast for the party that happened to be in the ascendant; secondly, they must attempt to eliminate other smaller parties from the parliamentary scene; thirdly, like any other party, they must strive to strengthen their own representation in Bonn.

This political strategy of holding the balance resulted in campaign declarations which to many electors seemed very curious indeed. Whenever the Free Democrats were asked which of the two big parties they would put in power, which relegate to the role of Opposition, they had only one answer to give: 'We cannot or will not tell you until the day after the election.'

Their evasion of what to most voters seemed the one vital issue made the Free Democrats appear to many to be fighting a disingenuous campaign. A vote for them seemed a blank cheque which they could pass on either to the CDU or to the SPD as they wished. But the Free Democrats really felt they had no alternative. Only thus could they keep the free hand they would require after the election; the patchwork quilt of Land organizations with different political ideas might have been strained all too visibly at the seams had they given any straight answer to this fateful question; and the electorate might have decided that if a vote for the FDP was in effect a vote for one or other major party, they might as well vote for that major party itself.

The Free Democrats felt that in 1953 this had been their greatest handicap: as junior partners in the Government they could neither effectively attack the Government's failures nor fully reap the rewards of its success. They felt they lacked a distinctive image of their own, and the desire to construct an independent character for themselves before the 1957 election had become so much of a complex that it was no doubt largely responsible for their withdrawal first from the Düsseldorf and then from the Bonn coalition. Liberated at last from the electoral and propagandistic limitations of sharing in what cabinet responsibility had yet evolved in the Federal Republic, they were now determined to keep their free hand.

Only once did their determination not to answer the coalition question waver. In July 1957 Dr. Erich Mende, one of the party's vice-chairmen, grew tired of being reproached with ambivalence and demanded that his colleagues take up a more explicit stand. According to the opinion polls, a coalition with the SPD would prove arithmetically impossible, while to leave this theoretical possibility open would only cost the party some of its anti-socialist votes. In the ensuing discussions within the Executive Döring proposed a third solution: the demand for a National Government as a means of simultaneously shaming the CDU and reconciling all elements within the FDP. But this last alternative would have meant a radical reversal of the party's proclaimed doctrines on the role of an opposition within a democracy, and both Döring's and Mende's suggestions were rejected. The Free Democrats could hardly maintain their violent offensive against the CDU while declaring that they would enter a coalition with it straight after polling day.

The Concept of a Third Force

To bolster their position of independence between the two biggest parties and explain their refusal to answer the coalition question in advance the Free Democrats elaborated a theory of government which identified a two-party system with single-party rule: for a single party whip then controlled an absolute majority in the legislature. The feeling that at least in Germany single-party government was incompatible with democratic processes and that party bargaining must take place within each cabinet as well as within each legislature had been implicit in much anti-CDU propaganda; but it was left to the Free Democrats to draw the logical conclusion and indeed to elevate their tactical demand for an alternative system to the rank of a constitutional doctrine.

A two-party system, they argued, might work in the Anglo-Saxon States, which looked back on a long democratic and freedom-loving tradition, and which had no ideological parties. But it would not work on the Continent. Either it would result in the permanent rule of one party, and 'given the willingness of our people to accept authority, there is the constant danger that the rule of one party may become the rule of one man';[1] or it would result in sudden changes of course affecting the entire ideological basis not only of the State but of the whole of society; or else—as in Austria—it would result in permanent 'national governments' that left no room for healthy opposition at all.

The two-party system, therefore, was to be condemned. But a multi-party system would engender weakness and confusion. Only a third force could provide a way out of this dilemma.

This necessary third force was to be more than merely a third party. The German Party could not be a third force, for it was dependent on the CDU for its survival in the Bundestag. The BHE could not be a third force either, for as a pressure group turned party it represented no independent set of political and ideological principles of its own. Only the Free Democrats could constitute the third force. They represented the concept of liberty against single-party rule or permanent all-party coalitions; they represented the concept of the nation against socialism and denominationalism: 'With the FDP as a third force between CDU and SPD, the Germany party system finds those bearings which are indicated for it by history. The socialist, the liberal and the conservative-clerical elements form the foundation of the three-party system in Germany.'[2]

Implicit in much of this constitutional doctrine there was, of course, the claim that the FDP should be the final arbiter of policy or should

[1] Karl-Hermann Flach, *Dritte Kraft, der Kampf gegen den Machtmisbrauch in der Demokratie*, FDP, Bonn, 1957. The quotations are taken from pp. 5, 7, 9, 15–17, and 20.

[2] The matter was put most succinctly in the party advertisement 'Zwei Stimmen für die dritte Kraft—gegen Rom und Planwirtschaft' ('A third force vote is two in one—'gainst Rome and 'gainst an economic plan').

at any rate (failing the dreaded 'black–red' coalition between clericals and socialists) share permanently in office: 'Neither of the big mass parties will be able to rule without being forced to tone down its extreme demands in a coalition with its liberal partner.' And if this would seem to give an influence to the Free Democrats quite out of proportion to their electoral strength, lack of support was made almost a political virtue: 'For once, even in politics, not quantity but quality will have the decisive voice. The disproportionately stronger position of the third force would merely redress the unequal balance between mind and mass.'

The Attack on the CDU

In accordance with their doctrine of a third force, the Free Democrats had announced that they would enter no federal coalition in which their partner was not dependent on them for his majority; they had thus in effect cut themselves off in advance from the line of retreat envisaged in Mende's proposal. Moreover a slightly less pessimistic reading of the same public opinion poll figures cited by Mende in fact suggested the opposite conclusion and reinforced the need to attack the Government parties. Only the highest SPD and the lowest CDU poll still conceivable would allow the FDP to hold the balance of power in Bonn, and anything that would lower the CDU's poll even without increasing that of the FDP itself would be to the Free Democrats' advantage. Attacks on the SPD as distinct from socialism in the abstract were practically confined to the local level (except perhaps in Hesse, where the FDP had long been in opposition to a government under SPD leadership). The main offensive was directed against the Chancellor and his party.

Apart from calculations of coalition arithmetic there was a second reason for this line of action. It is a generally accepted principle of electioneering in multi-party systems that it often pays a party to attack its closest competitors with the fiercest determination. The Free Democrats recognized that they could not win votes away from the SPD: Socialism might be the enemy, but the CDU was the rival for votes. Only within the anti-socialist camp could the FDP hope to make converts.

The CDU was thus accused of being too much of a socialist party: in the early post-war years some of its leaders had demanded 'Socialism out of a sense of Christian responsibility' and von Brentano had pledged the CDU in Hesse to a socialist economic system. The Free Democrats liked to claim that Erhard was really their man and that only their influence had prevented him from reimposing controls at the outbreak of the Korean war. Even in 1957 the CDU had not secured the passage of the Free Democrats' amendment to the Basic Law directed against possible future socialization. Obviously, so the FDP argued, private enterprise was still not safe in CDU hands. One pamphlet by Dr. Max Becker, the leader of the parliamentary FDP, went so far as to argue: 'Only recently the chairman of the SPD, Ollenhauer, has been asking for nationalisation again. That was an offer to the CDU.' And whether socialist or not, the Christian Democrats were painted as a corporative party of 'Catholic welfare romantics, left wingers from the trade unions . . . state capitalists and friends of cartels from the right'. Both the CDU and the SPD were leading Germany towards 'the total welfare state'.

At the same time as they were accusing the CDU of being too socialist the Free Democrats also accused it of too clerical an outlook. They gave great publicity to articles published in the periodical *Neues Abendland* (New Occident) in an issue to which Adenauer had contributed a foreword and which had been sent free of charge to addresses supplied by the Federal Press Office. Calling for 'an occidental view of history', these articles appeared to the Free Democrats to drop the mask from the Government's long-term objectives and to embody all they most hated in the CDU: a clericalism of the counter-reformation that accused Protestants of wanting German reunification mainly for the sake of regaining 'the heartlands of the Reformation' and a two-thirds majority over Catholics, a Carolingian disregard for the 'colonial territories' beyond the Oder–Neisse line, a hankering after a Roman Catholic 'Little Europe', and an anti-democratic authoritarianism that despised the Basic Law as being 'founded on the quicksands of Jacobin democracy'.[1]

For most of August quotations from these articles alleged to foreshadow 'clerical–fascist dictatorship' were one of the Free Democrats' main weapons against the CDU, and they printed half a million

[1] The Free Democrats also quoted other passages like: 'Adenauer's occidental policy lacks the foundation of a historical explanation in popular consciousness. . . . How can his voters understand why the Chancellor is leading them into a completely different direction where they see nothing but fog and the uncanny mystery which frightens any man without a grasp of history?' and 'For the sake of four years of secure rule it is worth fighting without regard for men or material. And then—four years of secure rule give many opportunities for an active and determined party leadership that does not suffer from scruples to create the conditions for the next election victory' (Dr. Otto Roegele, 'Autumn of Illusions', and Eugen Falkner, 'Germany History and Politics', in *Neues Abendland, Jahrbuch für Politik und Geschichte*, vol. xii, no. 2, pp. 99–118 and 157–66).

copies of a leaflet on the subject under the title *Who is preparing the ruin of Germany?* They demanded an explanation from the Chancellor:

> This is a central question of German politics. For years the Free Democrats in the Bonn coalition had the uncanny feeling that the Chancellor and the caucus of his party were pursuing very different aims from those laid down in the Government programme. Now we have it demonstrated in black and white.

On the evening of 31 August, the party's teleprinter in its nightly situation report from Bonn flashed instructions that for the last fortnight of the campaign all propaganda should be concentrated on this danger of single-party rule. Döring argued that another Bundestag majority for the old Government parties would mean 'the end of the second attempt to construct a democratic state in Germany' and that Adenauer represented 'the greatest danger to German democracy since Adolf Hitler', and Maier himself warned the electorate that the CDU was 'preparing to take over total power in the State'.

The Birth of an 'Opposition'

Under these circumstances it was not surprising if the Free and Social Democrats, whatever their ideological differences, began to feel partners in a tacit alliance. Both were violently opposed to the Chancellor and the CDU, and both believed that the future of German democracy no less than the interests of their own parties demanded a change of government. Successful coalitions on the Land level might be misleading, for where educational and personnel rather than broad economic policies were at stake, it was easier for 'left' and 'right' to meet behind the back of the 'centre'. Yet on the federal level also, developments within the SPD had reduced concrete differences between the two parties in matters of nationalization and controls, and there were two larger questions on which they were moving along parallel lines. Both demanded a more flexible and enterprising policy towards reunification, and both feared the equipment of the federal forces with atomic weapons as an obstacle to German unity.

The Free and Social Democrats in fact found themselves in a curious relationship of mutual aid. While the Social Democrats were hoping that the FDP would wean as many anti-socialist voters as possible away from the CDU, the Free Democrats hoped that the SPD campaign would prevent people from voting for the CDU who, hesitating to vote for the SPD, would then turn to the Free Democrats as being neither 'red' nor 'black'. The Free Democrats were thus disappointed that the Social Democrats did not fight a more vigorous campaign and almost felt it necessary to do so for them; by the end they were working in very close contact with the SPD and on the eve of the poll one of the campaign organizers of the FDP, still weary from the night of the 'Trojan horse', was heard to say: 'Last night it was we who took over the leadership of the opposition.'[1]

The Fight against Small Rivals

The Free Democrats were all the prouder of such activity in that it was their aim not merely to hold or increase their vote and to hold the balance in the third Bundestag, but also to be the only third party there, and to monopolize the position of third force for which they had argued so vehemently on constitutional grounds. The Free Democrats refused any kind of arrangement with the BHE, and involved themselves in a libel action to sabotage any arrangement that the BHE might attempt to make with any other party.

Particular bitterness characterized the Free Democrats' relations with the German Party. They saw in it a rival for the votes of those who stood to the 'right' of the CDU. They saw in it a travesty of a third party, which survived only by subservience to the Chancellor. Worst of all, they now saw within it their own former colleagues Blücher and Preusker, whom they accused of selling their liberal inheritance for cabinet seats, and the other 'traitors' of the abortive Free People's Party. The Free Democrats might not be able to prevent their return to the Bundestag: but they could do everything possible to reduce the votes of the German Party to a minimum and thus, they hoped, to induce the CDU in the long run to dispense

[1] It will be remembered that an 'Association for the Increase of the Electoral Turnout' attempted to place a full-page advertisement in all German newspapers of the Saturday before the election showing Ollenhauer and Maier dragging the Trojan horse of Communism into the Federal Republic. The SPD and FDP had wind of this plan, and throughout the Friday co-ordinated their activities, Heine providing some of the tactical experience on the timing of telegrams and legal *démarches*, the FDP headquarters working through much of the night to press home an application for an injunction based on criminal libel after one based on civil libel had failed. In Frankfurt the Chief Public Prosecutor issued an interim injunction, the police entered the newspaper offices of the *Frankfurter Neue Presse*, lorries distributing the paper were seized by the police at the city boundaries and the offending page was torn out of every copy and littered over the country-side. The injunction was lifted next morning, and the advertisement, together with an account of the actions of the Hesse police (which is controlled by an SPD Government), was sold as a special edition.

with its existence on the federal level. In some parts of the country, in North Hesse and in Lower Saxony in particular, it almost looked as if there were two separate election contests being fought simultaneously: one between the CDU and the SPD, and another between the Free Democrats and the German Party.

Sometimes this private war was conducted with a certain elegance; when the German Party organized a 'homeland rally' in Hesse which had previously taken place under Free Democratic auspices, the FDP hired an aeroplane to shower 100,000 good-humoured leaflets on the crowd. But, as the campaign went on, the light touch was supplemented with heavier artillery. In a pamphlet issued in Hesse but distributed beyond it, Becker uttered direct personal warnings: 'If the libels of the bankrupt Free People's Party do not cease forthwith, we shall publish the real reasons why one or other of them left the FDP, or why he was forced to leave it.'

The federal headquarters put out two posters directed specifically against the German Party. One of them, 'Treason over the German Saar', listed the names of individual leaders of the German Party who had voted in favour of the Europeanization of the Saar. The FDP knew that posters of this kind would probably lead to court action, but welcomed the free extra publicity which such proceedings could provide. Indeed a week after the release of the 'Treason' poster the German Party obtained a court order forbidding it to be displayed.[1] Then a cartoon poster 'Don't be taken in', showing Hellwege as a babe in Adenauer's arms waving the Guelph flag, was stuck over it. The latter poster had already been used with particular zest in Lower Saxony and elsewhere in the North; it was not supplied to the southern Länder, where Hellwege and the Guelph flag were practically unknown.

Campaign Techniques

The rest of the FDP's poster campaign was fairly simple. Their private sources of information told the campaign managers that all the other parties would eschew the colour red. For this reason and because they thought it a provoking colour they decided to use red for their main poster: the black rising eagle of the FDP (affectionately known in the organization as the 'bankruptcy vulture') on a red ground, often with the slogan 'It all depends on *them*'. The headquarters had attempted to secure a federal compromise for a

[1] The German Party, for its part, was ordered in another court case to withdraw its poster equating the formula of the Düsseldorf coalition with the East German Socialist Unity Party: 'SPD+FDP = SED'.

unitary colour scheme that would satisfy both the national and the liberal elements in the party: both white and yellow (or gold) should figure on all their announcement posters using black and red.[1] Four colours would, however, have complicated this emblem excessively; the eagle was therefore issued in two versions, one in the republican, the other in the imperial colours.

As the campaign progressed and Maier became better known in the country, a second federal poster appeared: but while Adenauer had been rejuvenated in a drawing and Ollenhauer dramatized in an oil-painting, Maier appeared on the posters in a colour photograph on which not even the warts on his neck had been retouched (see Plate IV*f*). It was typical of the 'Young Turks' that months before the campaign they had taken care to secure the advertising sites opposite the Chancellery in Bonn; throughout the later stages of the campaign Adenauer when entering or leaving his office was faced by a whole row of these canny faces with the slogan 'It all depends on *him*'.[2]

In the last fortnight before polling day the FDP put out a final series of posters nicknamed, for their three-quarter-length view of various men and women, the 'fifty-shilling tailor' series. A young woman, a worker, a mother and child, a prospering entrepreneur, and a well-to-do artisan stood out against the yellow background (regarded as impudent) and pointed to the black eagle on a red ground. They were saying: 'We're lucky that we've got them' or 'It all depends on *them*' and the combination of the young woman's photograph with the word *Glück* ('luck', or 'happiness') was expected to be particularly effective. The federal headquarters issued 1½ million posters in all, and the lower party organs about another million.

The posters issued by Land and local associations varied in quality. One showing a gold triangle between red and black and asking for a vote for 'the golden mean' had a certain inherent plausibility; but the Hamburg poster of a sharp yellow wedge cleaving a red-and-black block, though pictorially striking, presupposed the fear of a coalition between Socialists and clericals of

[1] It will be remembered that the 'struggle of the flags' in the Weimar Republic had contrasted the republican black, red, and gold of 1848 with the imperial black, white, and red under which the first world war was fought (and which were taken up again by the Third Reich).

[2] Döring in particular was out to annoy the CDU leaders personally, calling Adenauer for example 'a remarkable mixture of *Sportspalast* demagogue and sybil of ruin, of Rhineland carnivalist and professional funny man (*Büttenredner*)'; von Brentano returned the compliment by his declaration: 'That fellow learnt from Goebbels. People like him should keep their dirty fingers out of politics.'

which very few voters could at that moment have seen any signs. The Bremen FDP depicted the party eagle against the background of the Brandenburg Gate to illustrate the slogan: 'With us for a united Germany', and their design—basically similar to the eagle and Brandenburg Gate of the BHE—was ordered by other Land associations as well.

The FDP made its own film entitled (in the words of a soldiers' drinking song) *Thus do we live*. The party leadership was very reluctant to show it to journalists: when this became unavoidable, Döring explained that the film was designed to be shown exclusively in the smaller villages where only a bare minimum of political knowledge could be presupposed. It was produced in Land editions, substantially the same text being spoken by the respective Land chairmen, although having been shot near Munich it was based on the Bavarian milieu and opened with a view through the bottom of a beer mug. (South German habits of living tended to be viewed with more indulgence in the North than North German characteristics in the South.)

The film ranged in black-and-white pictures and equally black-and-white arguments over the FDP's case. It attacked Adenauer almost to the exclusion of the Social Democrats. Adenauer was blamed for spending £20 million on building a temporary capital. When he was shown signing treaties, the 100-mark notes which he was signing away rained from the ceiling in a thick storm in front of him. To symbolize the extravagance of the régime and to raise a cheap and not entirely innocent laugh Adenauer was shown at a reception, drinking champagne with the wife of a coloured diplomat who was amply proportioned by European standards; pictures of life in refugee camps were flashed in by way of contrast. Where reunification was concerned 'The aged Chancellor, he takes his time . . .'. Forty-nine copies of this film were made, and shown in conjunction with trailers of horse-racing or of postage-stamps to attract audiences to the fifteen *Mobilwerbung* vans used for outdoor performances.

The FDP issued a dozen small leaflets appealing to women; they contained only ten or fifteen words of text and were sold to shopkeepers and employers for inclusion in parcels, paper bags, and wage packets. On the whole, however, the FDP worked less with leaflets than the other parties; leaflets might have been regarded as too cheap to be worth reading by those to whom the party was making its main appeal. It put much more emphasis on brochures. The most popular in its appeal was called *Why you can't manage on your money* and distributed in 3½ million copies. It complained of taxation and inflation, illustrated Government extravagance by 'candid camera' shots of Frau Pappritz and of luxurious banquets and buildings, warned against atomic dangers, and demanded reunification. A similar pamphlet, with a smiling child amid flowers on its cover, was designed to court the women's vote.

But such pamphlets with the large editions and relatively small demands on the reader, though reminiscent of the film, were only one aspect of the Free Democrats' campaign. The brochures of the party's main series, distributed in editions of 10,000 to 20,000 copies, seriously discussed problems such as reunification, pension reform, and agricultural policy. Though the text was illustrated with cartoons, it presupposed some political or technical knowledge, and was designed to appeal particularly to the views and interests of the middle classes. 'Without us', as Maier declared, 'the middle strata would be politically defenceless.'

This distinctively middle-class appeal of the FDP's written propaganda was sometimes not completely devoid of a snobbish tint. A letter from Dr. Haas, the Bavarian chairman, sent to all telephone subscribers (a useful working delimitation of potential FDP voters), began: 'Dear Ladies and Gentlemen, So much of your time, I am sure, must be taken up by your professional and social engagements . . .'. Reinhold Maier sent a personal letter addressed 'Dear Professor' to all members of university staffs and enclosed a copy of the *FDP Principles for the Advancement of Science and Research* printed on embossed vellum-type paper with rough edges. Organizers were also instructed that 'it is just as wrong to announce a meeting on economic problems for entrepreneurs in an ordinary restaurant as it is to put a workers' meeting into a luxury hotel', though to obviate comment from the general public 'if at all possible, ostentatious columns of cars outside meeting places should be avoided'.[1]

It was perhaps a class difference, too, that while the SPD propagandists felt that children's ballets and children's photographs would appeal to their type of electorate, the Free Democrats squarely put their trust in dogs (see Plate IV*d*). Of the eight election addresses supplied as a sample by the party, seven featured the candidate's own or a borrowed dog—the dog appearing, sometimes by itself, in up to four photographs in the same election address. (The eighth of these election addresses was that of a farmer and showed cows and a calf; but the other seven also included a horse, a cat, ducks, and chickens.) Solid prosperity was further stressed by photographs of the candidate's own factory, of holidays abroad, of expensive

[1] FDP, *Wahlkampf und Werbung, Leitfaden für Wahlkampfleiter, Propagandisten und Redner der Partei*, FDP, Bonn, July 1957, pp. 31, 34.

hobbies, of recently furnished interiors, and of antiques and old books.

Parallel Activities

This championship of the middle class enabled the FDP to enlist the help of one small but not entirely insignificant body which generally fostered the candidature of non-party candidates at local elections, the Federal Association of Independent Electors. It issued proclamations in most Länder asking its members to vote for the FDP, and this appeal appears to have been heeded in certain country areas and small towns. The Taxpayers' Federation also organized meetings in a number of constituencies to which it invited all the local candidates. It goes without saying that, in the summing-up presented by the Taxpayers' Federation itself, the FDP with its demand for 'less taxes' tended to emerge as the favourite party.

But the most widespread as well as the most interesting parallel campaign for the FDP came from a slightly different quarter. The FDP was itself making a discreet but unmistakable appeal to former National Socialists. Publicly this effort went little further than demands that all should be equal before the law (regardless of past party allegiance). Privately, but with the full knowledge of members of the party Executive, a selective campaign was run from the Cologne office of an organization founded a few months earlier under the title *Aktion Die Ehemaligen* ('The "Ex–s"'). 25,000 copies of a 31-page *Confidential Communication to all 'Ex–s'* were distributed by post in the Federal Republic: 'There are so many "Ex–s", those of the Kaiser's Empire, those of the Weimar Republic, and those of the Third Reich.' Former members of the National Socialist Party were warned against voting for the German Reich Party or other splinter groups: 'To cast a vote for them would be like a platonic declaration, suitable for teenagers but not for us: we have burnt our fingers once before and have left our romantic period behind us.' The FDP was to be their party on the fourfold grounds that it stood for equality before the law, for a national social order (*Volksordnung*), for German reunification, and for ideological freedom.[1] Four letters in a similar vein were sent *To Our Political Friends* in Lower Saxony by a Braunschweig group led by Karl Glorius, an FDP candidate determined to draw votes away particularly from the DRP.[2]

[1] The *Aktion Die Ehemaligen* explained (in a letter to the author) that its support for the FDP in this election did not imply its commitment to that party on future occasions.

[2] The Bundestag biographies of 1957 reflected this appeal. Four or five Free Democratic members explicitly mentioned their membership, date of entry, rank or function in the National Socialist Party or organs such as the Hitler Youth, and the

The Role of the Opinion Polls in the FDP Campaign

One further aspect of the Free Democrats' campaign is worth special notice. The argument which 'The Ex–s' used against the splinter groups of the extreme right, that a vote for them was a vote wasted, was one that the FDP had itself to face. While the two biggest parties found that it was mainly the morale of their workers that was affected by election forecasts, the FDP had to fear the desertion of its voters: for some of the opinion polls published had attributed only 4 or 5 per cent. of support to the party. During the war of nerves to which the party was exposed in the whole year preceding the election 'favourable predictions', as one of its organizers emphasized, 'were absolutely essential for us'. Determined to leave nothing to chance or to its opponents, the party set out to investigate public opinion for itself, and engaged a small and only recently founded institute of market and advertising research called *Intermarket* to supply them with soundings of public opinion.

Though four-fifths of *Intermarket*'s revenue was derived from commercial contracts, the link between this institute and the party was close. At least one Bundestag member on the FDP Executive—himself a business consultant—sat on the board of *Intermarket*, and its head office in Düsseldorf was, according to the FDP, housed in premises that belonged to the North Rhine–Westphalian branch of the party. Indeed it would seem that just as *Mobilwerbung* had been founded to help the Government but also engaged in large-scale commercial publicity to reduce overhead costs, so *Intermarket* was founded not least with the FDP's own requirements in mind.

Intermarket prepared a series of confidential *Political Analyses* for the party's federal executive, each ending with recommendations to the party's campaign management.[1] The popularity of the party's

length of their internment after the war. *Per contra* what in Dehler's biography of 1949 had figured prominently as 'from 1933 until 1942 membership of a group of opposition to Hitler, which later had contact with Dr. Goerdeler [who was executed after 20 July 1944], arrested in 1938 and sent to a forced labour camp in 1944' appeared in the 1957 biography as a plain 'legal practice in Bamberg'.

[1] 'The election demands arguments of foreign and of social policy and the creation of a distinct party image (*Profil*) which would silence the question about the potential coalition partner' ('The Return of the Pendulum', *Politische Analysen*, viii, Feb. 1957, p. 15). 'The CDU could still be isolated. This would require careful public relations work on a broad front. The lever would have to be inserted at the desire for security . . . but at the same time the desire for security requires a careful guarding against any arguments that could even remotely be termed pro-Eastern. In view of hard personal experiences the fear of the East weighs more heavily than that of an atomic conflict' ('Problems of Atomic Armament', *Politische Analysen*, x, Apr. 1957, p. 12). 'Adenauer's authority appears unbroken, regardless

leaders was investigated from time to time—and it would seem that before Maier's election, Mende, as a forty-year-old holder of the Knight's Cross of the Iron Cross, might have been the most popular leader in the country at large. *Intermarket* also tested the slogan 'It all depends on *them*' just as a powerful cigarette firm with friendly links to the party invented and tested the slogan 'We're lucky that we've got them'.

Thus the role of *Intermarket* was broadly analogous to that of the other institutions working for other parties on motivational and propaganda research. But its further utility to the Free Democrats lay in the possibility it gave them to counteract the fears of a wasted vote. *Intermarket* did not publish any series comparable to those of the other institutes, but contracted to hand over its results to the FDP for publication as the party saw fit. There was thus no obligation on the party to publish discouraging results, but it could publish all the encouraging ones.

Broadly speaking the *Intermarket* results agreed with those of *Allensbach* until June. But in April *Allensbach* as well as *Intermarket* were attributing twice as much support to the FDP as *Emnid*; and from the end of May the *Emnid* figures showed a steady rise by one point in each poll to finish a full point above the actual election result.

The most serious divergences appeared in the crucial months of July and August when *Allensbach* and *Emnid* seemed to unite against *Intermarket*. The Free Democrats' party newspaper itself highlighted the contrast in its front-page article entitled 'Public Opinion Polls—Guided Missiles in the Election Campaign':

> It is important to know who is the customer for such an opinion poll. Radically different results can be obtained through the formulation of the question, the factors of uncertainty taken into account, and so forth. Thus *Emnid*, working for the customer we have already mentioned, gave the FDP 4 per cent of votes, while *Allensbach* at any rate reached a figure of 6 per cent . . . *Intermarket* calculated 10·8 per cent for the same month, while a few weeks ago, admittedly with a smaller sample, it even reached 13 per cent.[1]

The Free Democrats hinted freely at 'doctoring' of polling results by other institutions, and suggested that the curious rise in the

of what he may say. . . . As against this it is difficult still to find any convincing arguments. The interventions of the Church into daily politics are as little to the voter's liking as conditional aid given to political parties by interest groups. Here would be a foothold, since the campaign management no longer has any impact or scope outside the purely economic field of prices, finance and taxation' ('Six weeks before the Poll', *Politische Analysen*, xiii, July 1957, pp. 9–10).

[1] *Das Freie Wort*, 2 Aug. 1957.

Emnid figures before polling day represented an attempt by that body to save its own reputation. The other parties, to give credence to similar suspicions about the *Intermarket* figures, pointed to the various types of sponsorship effect that could result from the close connexion between *Intermarket* and the Free Democratic leadership. The newspapers indulged in witticisms and there was further protest against the misuse of an instrument of social study to help form rather than gauge public opinion.[1] In fact, however, the solution of the problem was simple. Though *Intermarket* did not see fit to comment on such statements at the time,[2] its calculations never gave the FDP more than the already comparatively high figure of 9·7 per cent. with a sample of 500, and 9·0 per cent. with the normal sample of 2,000 interviews. The higher figures originated in the Free Democratic headquarters.

Conclusion

Karl Arnold, when he fell from power in North Rhine–Westphalia, called the Düsseldorf group 'amoral technicians of power'.[3] Certainly the managers of the FDP displayed some tactical resource, if not perhaps much finesse. They planned their campaign like a military operation, they supported it with parallel appeals, constitutional doctrines, and their own statistics, they attracted attention by calculated violence of language and libel suits, and they translated their central conception even into colour schemes and paper quality. Their campaign almost looked like a smaller, cruder, and fiercer version of that of the CDU. Yet Arnold's characterization of them was not perhaps the whole truth; there was a certain moral element in their indignation; and if they were technicians of power, their techniques brought them no success.

Every other party that entered the third Bundestag had increased both its absolute number of votes and its share in the total; only the Free Democrats lost 400,000 votes compared with the 1953 election and suffered a drop by one-fifth in their share of the poll. Perhaps the split in the party can account for most of the absolute loss in votes, though the German Party gained only a fraction of that total.

[1] The cult of the public opinion poll had come under heavy fire in public discussions earlier in the year; see, for example, Wilhelm Hennis, *Meinungsbefragung und Representative Demokratie*, Mohr, Tübingen, 1957.

[2] 'We had no influence on the form in which our customer made further use of the results of our research, any more than we have any influence on how a cigarette firm uses the results provided by us for its commercial purposes thereafter' (letter from *Intermarket* to the author).

[3] The phrase appears to have been coined first by a CDU Bundestag member.

But to argue that the magnetism of the two big parties was solely responsible for the rest is only to say that the FDP—unlike the German Party and even the DRP—was unable to hold its voters. Nor can financial considerations be held responsible; as one of the federal organizers declared: 'We certainly did not fail for lack of funds.' The prime causes must be sought with the party itself.

There can indeed be little doubt—and *Intermarket*'s reports confirm this—that the electorate was not convinced of the basic view which the FDP held of its own role in German political life. For the ordinary voter the party was too difficult to 'place'.[1] Its evasion of the coalition question alienated those who feared the SPD as much as those who thought the Government's foreign policy in need of a change. Its adroit manœuvres did nothing to inspire confidence; and to many the party appeared too clever by half.[2]

Yet this much at least must be said in their favour. The Free Democrats fought a colourful and adaptable campaign which, for all its sorties in various directions, was unified in their own eyes by the central concept of an anti-authoritarian and anti-collectivist third force. They brought some movement into the static West German political scene in the year before the election, and without them the Social Democrats could not even have hoped for the chance of taking over the Government in 1957; their sniping was responsible for many of the small surprises that saved the campaign from being too much of an inevitable crushing of one giant by another; and more than any of their constructive ideas on reunification or on economic policy it was their spirited assault on what they felt was resurgent authoritarianism in Western Germany that did most to make the country, in the summer of 1957, seem a lively democracy with imaginative and vigorous groups in healthy opposition to the established preponderance of the Government party.

[1] The FDP found itself, for example, fighting one rumour that it was a party of Jews simultaneously with another that it was one of Hitler youths.

[2] It was no accident that nine months later the FDP suffered the most crippling defeat of its existence in the Land elections in North Rhine–Westphalia, where the electorate decisively reversed the 'Düsseldorf revolt' and reinstalled the CDU with an absolute majority.

IX

THE EFFORTS OF THE MINOR PARTIES

THE Christian, Social, and Free Democrats were by far the most important parties contesting the election, but they held no monopoly of public attention at this time. It is true that the vote for all other parties combined diminished from 28 per cent. in 1949 to 16 per cent. in 1953 and 10 per cent. in 1957. But they were still very much alive. Two of them had been represented in the second Bundestag and in the second federal cabinet, and while the Refugees' Party polled considerably more votes than the German Party, the German Party secured re-election to the third Bundestag and two cabinet seats. These two parties thus fall into an intermediate category between the large and the really small parties; and the first part of this chapter is devoted to them.

The second part of the chapter seeks to sketch the electioneering of two Saar parties which, though amalgamated with larger parties in law, in fact fought quite distinct campaigns of their own. Both these parties had held seats in the Bundestag at the end of the second legislative period and both were to be represented in the third Bundestag as well.

Yet in addition seven other parties were able to fulfil the conditions of the electoral law for the nomination both of Land lists and of at least a number of constituency candidates. A description of these groups should not suggest that any one of them has as spectacular a future before it as had the National Socialists in 1928, when they failed to poll even 3 per cent. of votes. But they are interesting phenomena in themselves. They illustrate the historical and the regional factors at work in the eighth year of the Federal Republic, and by their very lack of inhibitions some of them reveal fears, misconceptions, and prejudices held in greater or less degree by wider sections of the population than their own voters, which the 'responsible' politicians of the larger parties would never voice as freely. No earlier study of West German elections has devoted any great space to these small parties, and it may be that not many future ones will be able to do so. The last part of the chapter therefore includes at least a brief passage on each.

A

The German Party

Through the Düsseldorf revolt of 1956 and the withdrawal of the Free Democrats from the Government coalition, the Bonn Government had lost its liberal and predominantly non-Catholic ally against the SPD. Perhaps the business community felt this shock as severely as did the CDU: for it had always regarded the Free Democrats as the guardians of its own special interests. The FDP had simultaneously mopped up votes to the right of the CDU and channelled them towards the Government, and it had represented business interests with the leverage that comes from party independence—thus providing a counterweight to any left-wing trends in the CDU. Given the reputation of the BHE as buccaneers exploiting every situation to gain office for themselves and social payments for refugees, only two other parties were available in the Bundestag to play this role: the dissidents from the Free Democrats who had remained loyal to the Bonn coalition and constituted themselves into the Free People's Party, and the German Party. The amalgamation of these two groups at the beginning of 1957 created a new unit that seemed capable of assuming the mantle of the 'traitorous' Free Democrats. Even when the business community resumed its substantial payments to the FDP, the German Party—being obviously the more reliable of the two—was still supplied with ample resources. Thus one of the most interesting experiments of the campaign began.

This experiment was really of a dual nature. On the one hand a party which had a membership basis only in Lower Saxony and Bremen was to be extended to the rest of the country by the use of financial resources and advertising techniques; on the other hand the Hanoverian farmers' party, which had largely retained its Guelph sentiments, was to be transformed even more than it had already been into a modern streamlined party of middle-class conservatism which was also quite ready in some Länder to absorb elements farther to the right. The two aims were intended to interact; the new outlook and techniques were to bring in the new votes, and the new votes were to consolidate the position of the modernists who would revolutionize the party for good. The financial support which was in the obvious interest of the industrial and commercial sponsors and of the Free People's Party also appealed to the German Party itself, which had long been attempting to extend its basis among the electorate to the rest of the country and had already moved very far towards the change in political concepts involved.

In terms of slogans and programme the new DP/FVP was naturally forced to take responsibility for the actions of the last eight years of government and was for the most part proud to do so. It was the only party other than the CDU whose members had supported the Adenauer Governments throughout the existence of the Federal Republic, and particularly in foreign policy the German Party endorsed the CDU's programme whole-heartedly.

The leaders of the CDU had in fact expected the German Party to confine its attempts at differentiating itself from them to matters of sentiment. They might appeal to loyalty to the Lower Saxon soil and declare that 'wealth is no substitute for consciousness of statehood'; they might perhaps make a special bid for former National Socialists and other die-hard elements who would be favourably impressed by Seebohm's declaration that they 'bowed to every German symbol... under which German men had sacrificed their lives';[1] and they might exploit the series of bank robberies that occasionally thrust even the election off the front pages by advocating the reintroduction of the death penalty which had been ruled out by the Basic Law.

To its pained surprise, the CDU was to discover that the German Party took a far more independent line than that. The German Party felt forced to differentiate itself very sharply from the CDU in order to persuade the electors to vote for a junior Government party without Adenauer when they could vote for Adenauer's party itself. It therefore set out on a vigorous if limited attack against its senior partner, and advanced against it along three different lines: it presented distinctive demands in fiscal and social policy; in some Länder at any rate it claimed to represent a more uncompromising stand against the SPD; and above all it appealed to the farmers by repudiating the Government's agricultural policy altogether.

Much play was made with the German Party's middle-class appeal which closely paralleled the Free Democrats' demands: lower taxes and a simplification of the tax laws, fiscal encouragement for the formation of private capital, and detailed proposals of various kinds of immediate interest to shopkeepers and intellectuals.

Secondly, the German Party cast on the CDU the same suspicion with which the CDU was campaigning against the Free Democrats: that of being prepared to enter a coalition with the SPD. Such an argument would have been flimsy on the federal level; but it could be illustrated with local examples in Baden-Württemberg and in Bremen, where such coalitions were in office, and even in Hesse, where the CDU had been in coalition with the SPD until 1951 and was now visibly tiring of the Opposition benches.

[1] H. C. Seebohm, *Drei Vorträge*, p. 16, quoted in Lange *et al.*, *Parteien in der Bundesrepublik*, p. 410.

The agricultural campaign was, however, the most lively of the attacks on the CDU. Until a year before the election there was little sign of it; indeed the Permanent Under-Secretary of the Ministry of Agriculture and Food was a prominent member of the German Party. Then suddenly the German Party developed its own agricultural policy; the leaders of the Farmers' Unions in several Länder proffered a big agricultural vote to whoever attacked Heinrich Lübke, the Minister of Agriculture and Food, and one of the best-known of them joined the German Party and stood for it in the election. The German Party's attacks on Lübke were undoubtedly enjoyed: 'Farmers', declared a letter sent by some of Lübke's and Schäffer's cabinet colleagues to every farmer in the Federal Republic:

> If you vote CDU/CSU, you support Schäffer, who declared that in the North farmers come to the fields on a high horse and [*sic*] in a flashy car to make sure that others are working on their behalf. Farmers! Such a policy cannot save your fortunes. Never again Lübke, an end to his CDU agricultural policy.[1]

But the German Party's alternative suggestions (where they rose above direct subsidies on diesel fuel and fertilizers) were, so the party itself afterwards felt, psychologically inept. A 'price to cover costs' was a double-edged sword, and inefficient farmers in particular appeared much more eager for subsidies of all kinds, low interest rates and direct investment aid, than for mere price supports. Moreover the German Party's support for the Common Market also cast some suspicion on the compatibility of its foreign policy with a restriction of food imports, another of the farmers' demands.

The local basis and campaigning style of the German Party in its strongholds will be described more fully elsewhere.[2] The campaign around the Lüneburg Heath was not, however, typical of the centralized, schematized, and professional operation launched in the rest of the country from the new headquarters in Bonn. These two campaigns were superimposed on each other in North Hesse, Lower Saxony, and Schleswig-Holstein: elsewhere only the national operation made any impact at all.

Of these national initiatives by far the most striking was the poster campaign. It was managed by Günther Mundt, a high-pressure advertising expert who set out by the use of modern publicity techniques not so much to spread ideas as to imprint the label of the firm on the consciousness of the electorate.

[1] The Free Democrats for their part, pointing to the fact that the German Party was after all in the Government, issued posters with the slogan 'A vote for the DP is a vote for Lübke'.

[2] See Local Study A, pp. 317–29 below.

Only three posters (and a fourth as a framework for announcements) were federally printed. Each used a deep blue already familiar from the Senoussi cigarette advertisement to spread a feeling of well-being and thus (it was claimed) arouse sympathy for whatever was printed on this satisfying ground. Each printed the letters DP in bright impudent yellow and in vaguely gothic script, the D slanting to the left, the P to the right; indeed the letters DP were the only party initials (other than the well-known SPD sign) to develop a distinctive *gestalt* of their own. The first of the series (see Plate III*d*) used three dice to attract attention (a margarine firm had lately had some success with this motif); the second, designed as a *détente*, showed a family beaming with health and bore the greeting 'Happy holidays!', while the third, striking a warning note, showed an inverted red triangle and the word 'STOP'. Each poster had a few further words to justify the use of the dice, the family group, and the traffic sign and to link it with politics, the last, for example, reading 'STOP: Not black, not red, not chequered; vote DP'.

These three federal posters were released one at a time, the first for ten days, the second and third each for a fortnight, and were put up almost entirely by advertising firms. Even the fly-posting was done by a curious firm of motor-cyclists who papered over the country-side (and other people's posters) in areas where there was no party member for miles around. (They had included the fines for doing so in their original estimate to the party.) Had there been a vigorous campaign of explanation and political argument to fill the symbol with content this poster campaign could have been valuable. But coming almost completely by itself in many parts of the country, familiarity with the symbol alone did not yield political returns.

In the Länder where the German Party had a good organization the federal posters were supplemented with local efforts. The North Rhine–Westphalian DP issued a surrealist version of the party initials, which, while decorative when put up in long series, failed to signify anything in the more conservative and particularly in the country areas. In Hesse the parties showed two red nightmare hands clamping down on a farm and on a busy town: 'Prevent this', and, much pleasanter to look at, a series of peasant costumes: 'For a healthy farming community.' (Great care had to be exercised in the precise local distribution of these posters, as traditional costume varies from area to area and a tactless slip would have been only too easy.)

The Lower Saxons fought the most unorthodox of the German Party's poster campaigns. It was here and in Hesse that the main tussle with the FDP was taking place, and the personal enmity of old colleagues in the coalition and the rivalry for third place in the

Bundestag produced a rash of cartoons from all parties. In Hanover the German Party showed Hellwege as the steady second man on Adenauer's tandem (a doubtful position, one would have thought, in which to capture new votes) and in contrast old Reinhold Maier as a skittish and disreputable woman on a swing teasing both 'Konrad' and 'Erich' (see Plate II*c*). A poster bearing the portrait of Hellwege roundly declared 'Lower Saxony votes for the party of its Minister-President'. The Lower Saxon party thus had one poster which the federal party felt that it sadly lacked—the face of a leader to balance those of the other parties. But Hellwege's reputation was too local for the poster to be useful outside Lower Saxony, and Preusker, who would have been the natural choice for the purpose, had apparently refused to have his portrait placarded. Other posters simply pointed to the different list numbers the party bore in each Land, and the acme of unreasoning suggestion was reached with the lapidary slogan: 'German Party—Your Party.'

The poster campaign was amplified by many Land and four federal advertisements: in varying combinations an intellectual, a farmer, a housewife, a shopkeeper, or a refugee said 'If you ask me . . .'. More personal in their appeal were five letters sent through a commercial address firm—three to some ½ million farmers, one to over a million middle-class, and another to 150,000 professional people. Four and a half million brochures (including one of cartoons) and further pamphlets and brochures issued on the Land level completed the range of printed election material.

The German Party had no proper film of its own, though it used sixteen *Mobilwerbung* trucks showing much the same films as the CDU but also one concentrating on the work of the German Party's ministers in the Government. It ran no cabarets, but—originating as a 'homeland' party and still appealing most directly to the farmers—it carried through a number of farmers' days in which costume groups, peasant orchestras, folk dances, and fireworks fostered local 'homeland' feelings and framed a few political speeches that advertised the party and its basic sentiments. The party claimed an attendance of 20,000 people for one such rally.

The federal headquarters of the party paid around £150,000 for its campaign, the money being supplied predominantly by the central Civic Association in Cologne.[1] At least as much again was spent by the Land and local parties on their campaigning and supplied by the Land political funds. As a result the money was unevenly distributed: while some campaign managers below the federal level were openly amazed at the money they had available and expressed some doubts

[1] See Chapter X, pp. 212–15.

as to their capacity to spend it, others were obviously short of the resources they would have needed to give a local basis to the national campaign. After spending about £350,000 in all, the party received only a bare million votes—one vote for every seven or eight shillings that it had spent. What disappointed the German Party most, however, was the poor response of the farming community whose grumbles the party had made into its own distinctive platform. In fact the German Party's experience was only analogous to that of the others: the sectional appeal was none too effective in the 1957 election.

The GB/BHE

In comparison with the advertising activities of the German Party the GB/BHE (which was to secure rather more votes than the German Party) fought a quiet campaign. So at least it looked from the outside; the party leadership itself, being small, was straining hard. The campaign was managed by Frank Seiboth, one of the party's parliamentarians, who was at the same time among the most active speakers in the campaign and absent from the headquarters for long periods at a time. But then it was a straightforward campaign which, once the initial preparations were over, practically ran itself.

Some of the officials of the party were quite glad that it did not put on a tremendous display of posters and other publicity methods. Many of their members were among the poorest in the electorate, and would not have appreciated a campaign in the American style financed, as they might have thought, out of their own small contributions. They preferred to do the work themselves, occasionally getting some pay for it from the party; since a great many of them were pensioners, they had the time to help and appreciated the odd 5-mark piece for doing so. Only on the eve of the poll as a last gesture of bravado a solitary plane circled over the Cologne area trailing the appeal 'Vote BHE'.

The BHE claimed by far the highest ratio of members to voters of any party in the Federal Republic: and of 170,000 members, 130,000 it claimed actually paid up sums varying from 10*d.* a month upwards according to income. The party's candidates—themselves often pensioners and far from smartly dressed—were usually unable to contribute to campaign expenses, so that in addition to perhaps an average of £30 of subscriptions retained at the local level, grants of around £25 were made from the Land parties and the federal headquarters for constituency use.[1] The accent of the whole campaign was on canvassing: no other party laid such emphasis on the personal touch of one individual talking to another: and in consequence it was a campaign that was easy to run in the countryside and above all in the areas where housing programmes for refugees had been carried out—but difficult or impossible to organize in towns where refugees were dispersed and more easily absorbed into the general economic and social milieu of Western Germany.

There in fact lay the great problem before the BHE. Its voters had been above all the unintegrated refugees from beyond the Oder–Neisse line. Already in 1953 there had been a significant difference between the country and the city. Only a bare quarter of refugees voted for the party in the big towns, while over a third of them voted for it in the smaller towns and the villages.[2] And since 1953 the movement of refugees from the Schleswig-Holstein, Lower Saxon, and Bavarian country districts to the cities of North Rhine–Westphalia and Hesse (and to the smaller industrial towns of Baden-Württemberg) had proceeded further. A refugee moved was usually soon a refugee integrated, and this in turn tended to mean a vote lost to the BHE. The very success of the party's social concern was sealing its fate. Moreover the older refugees—the hardest cases that could not be absorbed in Western Germany—were dying out, and the younger ones perhaps tended to feel no analogous ties to their parents' homes beyond the Oder–Neisse line.[3] Two demographic factors were thus simultaneously threatening the existence of the BHE.

Of course the party had from the beginning attempted to appeal to a somewhat wider section of the population. Its very name—'Block of the Homeless and those Deprived of their Rights'—was designed to appeal also to those who had suffered from bombing and denazification. But they, too, were now feeling less of a grievance, and in any case other parties appealed to them with greater *élan*. As in earlier elections, the BHE made an effort to address itself to the

[1] In some cases these aggregate grants appear to have reached £60–£80. The Land organizations, afraid of a curtailment of their federal subsidies, did not always declare the funds they had received themselves, so that there were some disparities in the money available.

[2] See Fig. 6, p. 296.

[3] In its sample surveys (described in Chapter XIV, pp. 285–96) the Federal Statistical Office found that in 1953 16 per cent. of all valid votes, and 15 per cent. of BHE votes, were cast by those under 30: in 1957 17 per cent. of all valid votes, but only 12 per cent. of BHE votes, were cast by that youngest age-group—which by then contained the generation which had been between the ages of 9 and 18 at the time of the expulsions of 1945.

refugees from the Democratic Republic, but with no success: such refugees tended to vote for the SPD on the grounds of their working-class status or for Adenauer as the arch-enemy of the East German régime. The party in fact realized even before polling day that its attempt to gain new votes by sectional appeals was a failure.

For these reasons—and because of its sensitivity to the charge of being nothing but an interest group—the BHE particularly re-emphasized two aspects of its general policy which it hoped would make it more of a party and less of a pressure group and give it a chance of gaining votes in the electorate at large. The first point was its concern for the socially weak in general, not only the refugees but also all pensioners, the aged, and the invalids. It attempted in fact to be a non-socialist but 'social' party and stressed its demand for the creation of 'small positions of economic independence' such as small farms and workshops not only as a means of absorbing further (particularly agricultural) refugees but also as a shield against the spread of Communism in the West.

But far more important than such domestic proposals was the distinctive position of the BHE in foreign policy. It demanded 'an active policy of reunification and the sharpest fight against the politicians of surrender . . . who give away for nothing what does not belong to them—other peoples' homes'. Negotiations were to begin only on the basis of 'the legally incontestable possessions of the German Reich in 1945—including the Memel and Sudeten lands' as well as Danzig. Its election programme was headed unequivocally 'From the Saar unto the Memel'. No concessions or surrenders were to be made in advance. The emotional feeling for the old homeland from which they had been driven only twelve years before was of course very strong among the older refugees, and indignation at speculative remarks on the Oder–Neisse line by von Brentano and Carlo Schmid boiled over at one meeting after another: theirs was seen not only as a national but also as a very personal betrayal.[1]

Accordingly the BHE campaign began with six mass rallies on the twelfth anniversary of the Potsdam Conference. As the party's official newspaper declared in a curious foreshortening of history: 'From that 2nd of August 1945 dates a world full of fear and

[1] As a Bavarian election pamphlet put it: 'The hunters of souls are at large again in the land, bought and besotten fools. Millions of Deutschmarks are ear-marked from Pankow to Bonn to gut your inmost selves and to befog your reason. They accost you in daily and illustrated papers with their glistening hypocrisy and out of the radio sets their satiated fatty voices boom: *You are to abandon yourselves, are to deny your destiny and turn traitors to your homes!*'

anxiety.'[1] After such early national demonstrations, the campaign was transferred to small meetings on the local level, where the newspapers gave it scant attention. This lack of press publicity was an undoubted disadvantage to the BHE in its campaign, and it was really only broken when the FDP's accusations of political prostitution were discussed in court. The BHE, so the Free Democrats alleged, had been bought for £120,000 as a coalition partner for the CDU. The FDP eventually withdrew its statement that conditions had been attached to this money. The money in fact came from the big political funds—half of it from the Civic Association in Cologne, the rest from the Land political funds.[2] One high official of these organizations, confirming that no explicit pledges had been exacted, expressed the hope that the BHE would nevertheless realize what honourable dealing would demand after the election.

Throughout its printed propaganda and at its meetings the BHE was anxious to clear itself of the charge of nationalism: opposition to a 'national sell-out' was a very different matter. Who would uphold Germany's rightful claims in the Bundestag, BHE speakers asked, if their party were no longer represented?[3] Adenauer with his Carolingian aspirations had by his own confession always regarded Berlin as a heathen city in colonial territory. On the other hand refugees from the Eastern lands were particularly well qualified to understand the Slav mentality, and to make their knowledge available in the interests of future peace. (More study of East European problems was one of the suggestions often put forward by the BHE.) The party also made foreign policy demands of a more concrete and immediate kind: there were to be no relations with Poland; and before Gomulka's Government received aid from Germany, Poland's victims should have relief. Nearly a million of them had died already before receiving any compensation worthy of the name from the two successive governments led by the CDU. In fact since the voices of the thirty or so refugees in the CDU parliamentary party had not been heeded, a vote cast for a refugee in one of the big parties was only a vote wasted. As there were 9 million refugees from territories under foreign administration in the Federal Republic, the BHE must be able to overcome the 5 per cent. clause.

[1] When Sir Winston Churchill had been presented with the Charlemagne Prize at Aachen in 1956, a rally of protest was held there against the 'frontier of shame' and the man accused of surrendering European territory to Communism.

[2] See Chapter X, pp. 207–18.

[3] A BHE advertisement asked the electorate also to remember and to vote for the cities of Middle and Eastern Germany:

> Denkt auch an Eger, Breslau, Königsberg und Stettin.
> Wählt auch für Dresden, Leipzig und Berlin!

The national headquarters prepared four posters to be released one at a time in four phases. The first showed a honeycomb design with the legend: 'Social, national—BHE'; the second, which was said to have greatly appealed to women, showed a little girl eating a slice of bread with the inane slogan: 'Lower prices give joy'; and the third bore four hands clasped athlete-fashion on a black, red, and yellow ground. The last carried the same slogan as the one of the CDU's: 'The whole is what's at stake'—but the dynamism of the drawing differentiated it sharply from the CDU's analogous but curiously static poster on which two parts of Germany had simply been contrasted in blue and red. Here two strong hands were fitting together three parts of Germany, firmly marked as belonging together, the Oder–Neisse territories included, with just a finger conveniently hiding the Polish Corridor (see Plate III*e*). The CDU's poster, moreover, had been ambiguous when it came to the Eastern territories: for the CDU, the BHE remarked, it was only three-quarters that was at stake. Nothing could have been a more effective expression of the BHE's position than this well-drawn poster on reunification—and nothing more tragic for its supporters than its political unreality.

For the rest, the BHE put out half a million copies of an illustrated paper contrasting the ostentatious luxury of the cities with the misery of the 400,000 people still in camps, and the politicians of surrender with the men who had fought for better pensions: the party also put out four or five numbers of an election newspaper with an edition of 400,000 each, a series of pamphlets, and postcards of 'the homeland never to be forgotten'. It received much help from at least one of the two big refugees' organizations and they and their personnel were a considerable asset to it. In 16,000 mostly very small meetings it claims to have addressed about 900,000 people. It received 1·4 million votes—250,000 less than in 1953 but less than 100,000 short of the 5 per cent. it required to re-enter the Bundestag.

Whatever its role continued to be in various Länder, the BHE could hardly hope to reappear on the federal level and was financially forced to wind up its federal headquarters in Bonn. For all the scandals at the top and its very sharp (though on the whole dignified) tone—which must be seen against the background of personal suffering and the forlorn hope of return to homes beyond the Oder–Neisse line—there must yet belong to the BHE the credit of having organized sections of the population that were ready for a swing to real radicalism, of having helped to make them feel that there was a place for them in West German politics, and of having led them to participate in the processes of the new democracy.

B

The political integration of the Saar into the Federal Republic and the consequent application of the 1956 electoral law had forced two small but locally powerful parties to conclude formal amalgamations with larger parties in the Federal Republic. In fact, however, both these parties fought independent campaigns and concentrated almost exclusively on issues peculiar to the Saar. While the Saar CDU and the Saar SPD scarcely troubled to adapt their propaganda to the specific problems posed by the continued economic association with France, both the Democratic Party of the Saar and the Christian People's Party largely retained their old character and techniques even under the new labels FDP/DPS and CSU. They therefore require a brief special mention of their own.

The Democratic Party of the Saar

In his dynamic referendum campaign Schneider had united middle-class and workers' votes on the basis of nationalism—a well-tried recipe; that he was now forced by the electoral law to ally with a liberal party of employers made him highly vulnerable to attack in a country of workers who were predominantly Catholic. Both the Social Democrats and the Christian People's Party exploited one or other horn of this dilemma (or both simultaneously) to the full. What might elsewhere have served as a recommendation was used in the Saar as a warning: 'Behind the mask of the DPS there lurks the *liberal* FDP.' How much this argument hurt the DPS may be read off not merely from the constantly repeated slogan 'DPS stays DPS' but also from a special letter sent to every voter in which each Free Democratic (DPS) candidate pledged himself to the 'inviolable maintenance' of denominational schools and the principles of a truly Christian State.

As a result of its participation in the Saar Government the DPS faced a second dilemma. The party had entrenched itself in the Saar as one of violent opposition to the autonomous régime by demanding immediate return to the Homeland. Now Schneider had become Minister for Economic Affairs and had first refused to vote for political integration with Germany on the grounds that certain economic demands had not yet been met, and had then insisted on the maximum period of adaptation before complete economic return to Germany. His enemies accused Schneider of a political motive for a lengthy transitional period: after economic reunification there would be no reason for Catholic workers to continue supporting a non-Catholic non-socialist party. As late as 23 August

Schneider declared that only a charlatan could ask for immediate economic reunification. But a few days later he went sharply into reverse. Erhard had taken the opposite view in a mass-meeting in the Saar itself and the German Party was subjecting Schneider to radical competition on his other flank.[1] Under these circumstances a somersault three weeks before the poll, however awkward it might be to perform, seemed forced upon him.

The party's basic *raison d'être* of course lay in the past: in the glorious days of the referendum campaign, when Schneider's energy and showmanship had become the symbol of the second return to Germany. It was thus not by accident nor simply out of personal enmity that the DPS was driven to fighting in 1957 the battle it had already won in 1955. The formal amalgamation with the FDP was not followed up by any great comradeship in arms. With the exception of the FDP's placard 'Treason by the Saar' not a single poster, not a single pamphlet or leaflet or speaker from the FDP was used in the Saar, and Schneider himself only made one of his eighty speeches of the last four weeks in any other Land—on Assumption Day, for which the Saar parties had agreed a truce. Instead of federal problems (except that of reunification—for which Schneider appealed in Ludwigshafen curiously enough on the grounds of West German economic self-interest) the twice-weekly *Deutsche Saar* and the illustrated pamphlet sent to all households devoted page after page to the misdemeanours of the CVP before 1955 and warned the country that CVP members of the Bundestag would be 'listening-posts for France'. With such paraphernalia of obscenity as lavatory pans, cows' udders, and jack-boots in opponents' buttocks the cartoons and articles of the DPS continued its feud with the 'Hoffmann clique' and thousands upon thousands of words and a court case were

[1] The German Party had gone about its first appearance in the Land with shock tactics. They were led by Hubertus, Prince zu Löwenstein-Wertheim-Freudenberg (an FDP member of the Bundestag only a few weeks earlier until he was disappointed in his hopes of renomination), who had been arrested in St. Wendel in 1951 for waving the black, red, and gold flag in the autonomous State of the Saar. The prince took up residence in St. Wendel before nomination day and the *de facto* devaluation of the franc provided him with his cry: 'Immediate economic reintegration—honest money for honest work.' Bareheaded he marched down the main street of Saarbrücken bearing banners with this bold device, and bought time on the commercial television service (run in the Saar by a French company) to be interviewed on the football ground at half-time in the big match on the Sunday before the poll. The DPS was seriously worried (various acts of rowdyism including the slashing of German Party car tyres were attributed to the DPS) and not without reason: for the German Party's intervention and its poll of 4,000 votes undoubtedly cost Schneider's party the expected second seat which only another 300 votes more would have ensured.

devoted to determining whether the CVP's top candidate, Dr. Mathias Goergen, was entitled to the professorial title he claimed in his election literature (the court decided that he was not). In the claustrophobic atmosphere of a small political unit which had seen such a complete political revolution only two years before, the personal tone of the campaign was perhaps understandable; at any rate the other parties began to reply in kind, the SPD depicting Schneider as a maggot worming his zigzag way and the CVP in its turn publishing details of Schneider's political pluralism and the resulting personal income.

The Christian People's Party

The CVP's problem was in fact not much easier. Just as the DPS had to teach its voters to mark their cross in the box marked 'FDP/DPS', so the CVP was faced with the even more difficult task of identifying itself with the new and non-composite title of 'CSU'. Like the DPS the CVP existed only because of the survival of old hostilities and loyalties: it could differentiate itself from the Chancellor's party only by accusing the CDU of unchristian behaviour in demanding that the CVP disavow its past, when in fact (as the Chancellor had certified in a letter which they quoted with pathetic frequency) they had been just as good Germans as the CDU itself. As the only way to keep a grip on its voters who were attracted by the federal CDU the CVP, too, intended to fight its Bundestag election predominantly on Saar issues.

Its hopes of doing so were, however, disappointed. The Adenauer campaign and a triumphal visit by Erhard made the election a federal one, and the CVP in the end found itself vying with the CDU in the use of Adenauer magic. In violation of the agreement made between Munich and Bonn the CVP obtained 500 Adenauer posters from the Bavarian CSU; it launched them ten days before the poll with the overprint: 'Saarlanders vote List 3.' Placards with the same Adenauer portrait thus appeared side by side wooing the electorate for two different parties, and popular aversion to this comedy may have cost both parties some votes. The CDU countered with stickers to obliterate the words 'List 3' and 'CSU' and to demand votes for the CDU instead: on the last night before the poll, when traditionally all the remaining posters are pasted on no matter what vertical surface, a free fight between rival teams of Christian bill-stickers ensued.

For the rest, the CVP fought the campaign mainly with its own posters, which were much superior to those of the Bavarian CSU.

Indeed no poster series in the whole election shows the restful calm of the CVP's graduated blues and blacks: 'Christian homeland' (a view of country and town), a Bethlehem motif under the legend 'Mother and child' and, with the most blatant use of religious symbolism in the whole Federal Republic, a luminous cross surmounting the globe with the legend 'CVP now CSU' (see Plate III*a*).[1]

The Saar thus really saw two battles carried on simultaneously—one between the SPD and the CDU, who regarded this as a German federal election, the other between the DPS and the CVP, both determined to retain their special position by once more fighting the battles of the past. The voting figures suggest that neither gained votes by this calculated if far from collusive antagonism: but the CVP did better out of these tactics than the DPS. The CVP nearly kept its share of the total while Schneider emerged as the one clear loser of the campaign.[2] On 1 January 1957 the Saar had been allotted ten Bundestag seats: its valid votes now entitled it only to

[1] Two thousand copies of each of these posters were put up by the two advertising agencies that between them monopolize the business in the Saar; a fourth poster—a black reminder that the CVP was now the CSU—had to be printed in double that quantity as the expectation of life of posters in the last of the four ten-day periods had appreciably diminished. The poster campaign cost the CVP 2,400,000 francs in display expenses; the printing cost cannot have been excessive since the posters were produced in the Saarländische Verlagsanstalt, which also issued the party's daily newspaper, in whose offices the party had its headquarters, in which the Hoffmann family had shares and from which a part of the CVP's funds were derived. Some of the election finance, it appears, came from Munich—and for the rest the CVP maintained many of the good relations it had built up before 1955 (when it was the governing party) to some of the bigger firms such as the Boch porcelain works and to much of medium-sized industry.

[2] The following were the election results in the Saar:

Party label		*Votes Landtag election Dec. 1955*		*Votes Bundestag election 1957*		*Seats in the Bundestag*	
1955	*1957*	*'000*	*%*	*'000*	*%*	*Jan. '57**	*Oct. '57*
CDU-Saar	CDU	150	25	184	33	3	3
DPS	FDP/DPS	143	24	100	18	3	1
CVP	CSU	129	22	117	21	2	2
SPD and SPS	SPD	119	20	138	25	2	2
Others	..	50	9	12	2	..	..
Total	..	589	100	552	100	10	8
Electors	..	664	..	662	..	..	..
Turnout	..	..	90	..	89	..	..

* Attributed on the basis of strength in the Landtag elected in 1955.

eight. The two that were lost were lost (narrowly) by Schneider—a first sign perhaps of some return to normal or rather some approach to German conditions in the political life of the Saar.[1]

C

The German Reich Party (DRP)

Whereas all the parties we have so far discussed had been represented in the second Bundestag, the German Reich Party (which had won five seats in 1949) was defeated in 1953 as a result of the new splinter party clause. But since it occupied six seats in the Lower Saxon Landtag it was exempt from the provision that forced most other small parties to collect signatures before they could present candidates at the election. It was thus able to submit lists in every Land and candidates in all but twenty constituencies. This was a feat for a party which claimed no more than 7,000 members, and it is clear that party activists were generous both in their financial contributions and in the time and energy they devoted to party work.

The German Reich Party called itself nationalist and was commonly regarded as the rallying-point of neo-Nazism. One of its main protagonists had been prominent in the National Socialist farmers' organization; the former National Socialist Minister-President of Oldenburg was its candidate in the constituency of Oldenburg; and at all levels of its organization the proportion of former officials of the National Socialist Party tended to be relatively high. Nevertheless it would be wrong to regard it as no more than a club of old National Socialists and the party boasted that 38 per cent. of its members were still under the age of thirty-five.

The German Reich Party set out its basic principles as follows:

> The DRP is the community of Germans who, overcoming social, particularist and denominational divisions, demand the restoration of the German Reich in the whole Europe.[2] It defends the true value of the national character (*Volkstum*) as expressed in all epochs of German history. It subordinates special interests to the good of the people and stands for the German national community (*Volksgemeinschaft*). The DRP does not seek the restoration of obsolete forms. It takes its stand on the Basic Law and decisively rejects totalitarian tendencies. It acknowledges an honest and free democracy.

[1] For a broader account of the campaign see 'The Saar Revisited' in *Young Europe*, Dec. 1957.

[2] A phrase unintelligible even in German.

The party's election programme demanded the establishment of an independent government in the national capital Berlin, the restoration of the historic frontiers, and the withdrawal of foreign troops. It denounced the Common Market as a foreign device designed to control and exploit the strength of the German people, it rejected atomic weapons and NATO and demanded German neutrality. If it seems at first sight paradoxical that right-wing elements should demand arrangements with the Soviet Union and neutrality, it should be remembered that only reunification and independence from the great powers would, in their view, allow Germany to regain her national stature. The neutrality which the party demanded was in any case not to be unarmed: the DRP asked for a professional army under German supreme command to guarantee German independence from East and West and 'instead of constant talk of soldiers of a new type and of a break with German soldiering tradition, the DRP demands the cultivation of the traditional values of the German soldiery in the Bundeswehr'.

There followed the demand stressed at length in every meeting for equal justice for all, the release of German war criminals, the abolition of all measures of discrimination against former members of the *Waffen-SS*, and the transfer of fiscal and cultural sovereignty from the Länder to the Federation; an end to 'the uncritical and undignified adoration of even the feeblest expressions of foreign art and literature', a federal ministry of health and 'a year of domestic service for female youth'. More generally the party sought 'the restriction of legislation to questions of principle and far-reaching freedom of decision for an executive conscious of its responsibilities' and, lastly, the reintroduction of the death penalty.

While the electoral programme was thus formulated fairly cautiously, other literature was addressed with a more forthright appeal to former members of the National Socialist Party and of the *Waffen-SS*, to farmers and to the middle classes.[1] Something of the same dichotomy between the more respectable official pronouncements of the leadership and the shriller tones farther down the line could be observed at the meetings of the party. Official speakers tended to use careful, often metaphysical and always highly ethical

[1] 'Comrades!' said one pamphlet, 'since 1945 you have been persecuted, stripped of your rights, and slandered. . . . Comrades! Will you vote for your own hangmen?' A pamphlet for farmers, pointing out that only the DRP had a farmer for its party chairman, struck the same note: 'The Government has made us ridiculous in public and degraded us to the status of paupers. . . . With our ballot-papers let us see to it that this Government does not make us into serfs for another four years. "Only the stupidest of calves vote for their own butcher." '

formulations[1] and to disclaim any wish to see another Third Reich: indeed they appeared on some occasions to be embarrassed by the anti-democratic and anti-semitic utterances of their supporters in the discussion, and by the loud applause such sentiments tended to receive. Nevertheless it was the usual practice for the organizers to have a bookstall in their meeting-halls to sell the productions of certain publishing houses which specialized in war memoirs, memoirs and biographies of prominent National Socialists, and the works of foreign apologists of war-time Germany.

The DRP leaders were in fact placed in a curious double dilemma. Whatever they would have liked to say, they could not risk being outlawed as unconstitutional or compromise their eligibility for collaboration with other parties on the Land level by the expression of extremist sentiments in any very clear form; on the other hand the rehabilitation of the former members of the *Waffen-SS* was their most popular cry, and their supporters often publicly minimized the culpability of the SS for such operations as the extermination of over 5 million Jews. Similarly they felt bound at meetings to conform to the most democratic procedures by allowing a general discussion after the main speech; but they had little control over their usually middle-aged supporters and more to fear from their utterances than from the interjections of the party's opponents. Since such opponents—particularly young members of the bigger parties—were sometimes also present in force, DRP meetings often ended in uproar, and on several occasions the police had to dissolve them to prevent bloodshed.

The colours of the DRP were unequivocally black, white, and red and its emblem the eagle of the Reich, worn as a badge by its members and displayed on most of its posters: 'We call Germany' 'Politically, militarily, neither East nor West! Vote German!

[1] Thus Professor Kunstmann, who took the place of the party's official leader Adolf von Thadden when the latter was debarred by the North Rhine–Westphalian Minister of the Interior from speaking in that Land, tended to lecture on the philosophical basis of the πόλις and to demand 'a phenomenological interpretation of National Socialism', while the Lower Saxon party fought its 1956 Landtag campaign with a poster bearing *Ten Commandments of German Renewal*, including the following: 'First Commandment: Thou shalt love thy people and serve it! Thou shalt despise the repentant, for they want to make money out of Germany's misfortune. Second Commandment: Thou shalt honour the soldier from the front, and punish the traitor. . . . Fifth Commandment: German boys, be brave; German girls, be fresh and clean. Such youth will bear our future! "Samba-youths" and "pin-up girls" are the expression of western decadence! Sixth Commandment: Thy queen shall be the mother of thy children, not the beauty-queen or the sex-bomb! . . . Tenth Commandment: Respect Europe, but love the Reich!—What we need is a moral rearmament.'

DRP.' The North Rhine–Westphalian party on one of its posters showed a naval officer with the Iron Cross holding the naval flag aloft over his sinking ship: 'Yet always true to Germany' (see Plate III *f*). In Lower Saxony the party issued cartoon posters that were small and cheap and were yet bound to be noticed. These showed Adenauer as the old pied piper with most of the other anti-socialist parties dancing to his tune, and a nightmare election slot-machine: a vote for any of these parties always delivered the same old man again. These placards were also reprinted on postcards with home-made verses of the type: 'For unity the people strives with might, and on election day votes for list 8.'

The most effective of the party's posters was undoubtedly that issued one day in the last week of the campaign. It showed much the same map of Germany divided as had been used by the BHE, and bore a remark attributed to Adenauer by the American magazine *Newsweek*: 'Please do not forget that I am the only German Chancellor who prefers the unity of Europe to the unity of his own country.' It was symptomatic of the weakness of the DRP and of the determined treatment it received from the other parties that this poster did not survive the night after it was put up. The party received a bare 300,000 votes in the whole Federal Republic, only 12,000 more than in 1953.

The Federalist Union

The Federalist Union, compounded for electoral purposes out of the Bavarian Party, the old Centre Party, and the diminutive Lower Saxon group that took up the original heritage (as well as the original name) of the German-Hanoverian Land Party was ruled to constitute a new party and therefore forced to collect signatures in support of its candidates. It was able to put up lists only in three Länder: Bavaria, North Rhine–Westphalia, and Lower Saxony—while the even more insignificant Schleswig-Holstein Land Party, although a member of the collectivity, never presented even a single candidate.

The new party held a congress in Frankfurt in July, proclaimed Christianity and federalism as the basis of its policy, and announced a seven-point programme. This programme demanded the control of the central power of the Bonn bureaucracy by federalist forces true to their homeland; a struggle against the monopoly power of one party; a positive German attitude and activity in the disarmament question including the renunciation of atomic weapons, the abolition of conscription, a controlled 'diluted zone' of comparative disarmament in central Europe, and a pan-European security system.

The platform went on to advocate the free development of the Churches and the loyal fulfilment of treaties between the State and the Churches; in economic matters the party demanded a true 'social market economy' with special reference to family enterprises among farmers and artisans; it also asked for lower taxation and the increase of social security through healthy capital formation among the middle and lower income groups.

As a highest common factor in the conceptions of very disparate groups this programme was not badly written, though it is unlikely that it won over a single new voter: but it did satisfy the law on the unity of the party as an organization, and thereby helped it to retain voters who would otherwise have seen no hope at all of the component parties overcoming the splinter party clause.

The Federalist Union never became a single unit but operated on a Land basis with three different campaigns in the three Länder in which the component parties had been able to submit lists. In Bavaria the party still regarded its original programme as operative, but its image of a Bavarian federalist party of sturdily homeland-loving peasants became very much blurred in the course of the campaign. Its change of name to Federalist Union was relatively unimportant, but its alliance with the Social Democrats was difficult to explain away. The party took legal proceedings when its opponents alleged that it was committed to voting for an SPD Chancellor, and it stressed that the voters were electing not a government but a legislature. Yet the Federalist Union had made common cause with the Socialists over conscription and the issue of atomic weapons, and had put anti-militarism in the forefront of its campaign. It was no wonder that from representing a Bavarian variant of political orthodoxy which could fight for Bavarian privileges within the Christian conservative camp, the Federalist Union in Bavaria had seemed to be moving over to the Opposition. It may thereby have gained a new audience from those who still deeply felt the effects of the last war, but it lost much of the prosperous farming vote. Its Bavarian poll—nearly 1,300,000 in the 1954 Landtag election—fell to 168,000 votes.[1]

In North Rhine–Westphalia the party appeared under the label '*FU/Zentrum*', and it used the same name in Lower Saxony, where its Land list was made up for the most part of members of the Centre. Throughout the campaign the party stressed that it was bound to

[1] For a fuller account of the party's campaign in one part of Bavaria see Local Study B, pp. 330–40.

overcome the splinter party clause because of its alliance with the Bavarian Party: but 'Each party remains what it is and has been! Centre remains Centre!' The party had given no undertakings to the SPD, and it provided a Christian alternative to the CDU. It was opposed to conscription and bent upon helping the middle classes as a party of the centre not dependent on contributions from big industry. Its propaganda put reunification and peace at the head of its programme: middle-class policies took up the bulk of space. Its opposition to the centralization of power was only one part of the last point on its leaflets; on some leaflets indeed it was omitted altogether.[1] In North Rhine–Westphalia the party polled 70,000 votes—less than 3 per cent. of the total.

In Lower Saxony the appeal was broadly parallel with that in North Rhine–Westphalia, though the inclusion of four members of the German-Hanoverian Party on the second, fifth, seventh, and ninth places of the list added a certain Guelph note. Starting almost from scratch and in a Land in which the German Party had already weaned the homeland enthusiasts away from the narrower dynastic loyalties to a rather wider conception of the contribution of Lower Saxon attitudes to the Federal Republic's political life, it failed to obtain any success worth mentioning: its 14,000 voters represented less than half of 1 per cent. in the Land.

The League of Germans

If the German Reich Party represented in effect a neutralism of the nationalist right and the Federalist Union an anti-militarism of the Catholic centre, the League of Germans was the main advocate of neutralism on the extreme left. The 'League of Germans—Party for Unity, Peace, and Freedom' was founded four months before the 1953 election by the former Centre Party Chancellor of the Weimar Republic, Dr. Joseph Wirth, who had signed the Rapallo treaty. Many of its party leaders also appeared like a stage army on the governing bodies of a host of sports, cultural, and other organizations

[1] For the sharp tone of the FU Centre Party's propaganda compare its newspaper *Kurier am Sonntag* of 8 Sept. 1957: 'Almost the same election slogans! Today as then! On all the poster sites, larger than life, the portraits of the leaders! Today as then! . . . Powerful financiers in the background! Today as then! Whoever raised a warning voice became an outcast! Today as then! We warn you! Be on your guard!' But the party also commanded the mood of the fatuous doggerel, as proved by a poem on the same page beginning:

Wer die FU/Zentrum wählt
hat die Richtung nicht verfehlt
Wer FU/Zentrum unterstützt
Hat seinem Volke sehr genüzt . . .

which whether rightly or wrongly would in Britain no doubt have been labelled 'fellow-travelling'. The party defined its objective as 'the united, independent and democratic Germany of peaceful work and welfare for all, of social justice and national security, a Germany free from unilateral military ties, bound in friendship to all states that respect its independence and self-determination'.

The League of Germans attacked the CDU for its policy of rearmament. Political pacifism played a large part in its declarations: it denounced NATO; it made much play with the cost of maintaining Western troops in Germany; it used the declarations of Schweitzer and the eighteen German scientists to advocate a zone free of atomic weapons and ultimately the banning of atomic weapons altogether; it demanded good neighbourly relations and trade with East and West; and it objected to the Common Market as involving Germany in the policies of the colonial powers and thus reducing German prestige and commercial opportunities with the emerging nation-states of Asia and Africa. The reinstitution of the plebiscite was to prevent important decisions being taken against the will of the people; and the savings effected by disarmament were to be spent on social and cultural advance.

It was generally assumed that the inspiration, if not also the finance, of this party was supplemented from East German sources; but no concrete evidence was ever offered on this point during the 1957 election. The banned Communist Party certainly did not regard the League as a possible successor to itself. The party published four periodicals including the *Deutsche Volkszeitung*, a well-produced 16-page weekly newspaper which could hardly have been maintained without subsidy; it may well be that the publicity they gave to Russian and East German affairs and the type of cartoon they published also at first sight encouraged suspicions of support from Communist sources.

For the bulk of the electorate the League of Germans can have been known by little except its red oak-leaf poster which was widely displayed in the towns. Although it had submitted a list in every Land it polled less than 60,000 votes.

The 'German Middle Class'

The party which cumbrously called itself 'German Middle Class (Union of German Middle-Class Parties—UDM)' was founded in June 1957 as a combination of various small political groups which had no illusions about even their collective chances at the polls; but it was designed at least 'to stir the conscience of all those who had promised the middle class so much in previous elections without keeping their word'.[1] The decision to appear as an independent group in the election campaign was strongly opposed by the German Middle-Class Block (*Deutscher Mittelstandsblock*), the permanent pressure-group organization to which the Farmers' and Civil Servants' Unions and the four Associations of Artisans, Retail Traders, Hoteliers, and House and Property Owners belong: the Block believed that only by working through the other parties and not by competing with them (and thus perhaps antagonizing them) would the middle classes reap the maximum benefit from their political strength. The Union of German Middle-Class Parties took the opposite view. It believed that 'the complete dissipation of middle-class forces among almost all parties' was the main cause of 'directly anti-middle-class economic, fiscal and domestic policy'.

The party's programme, in forty points, was signed by a butcher, a doctor, and a retail trader: it called for the defence of the self-employed, of private property, and of private initiative. It demanded fewer taxes, fewer laws, the reinstitution of the tax on chain and department stores, and a tax on co-operatives above a certain size. Five hundred thousand copies of this programme were printed in a 4-page leaflet, together with two articles and the following appeal:

> Middle class, awake! Your hour has come! Or will you once more believe the parties that have never yet kept their word? For eight years they have betrayed you. They have put all the burdens on you. And now like whores they solicit your vote once again. Middle class, you are strong enough to take your fate into your own hands. Vote your own party into the Bundestag! You are the 'third force' if only you stand by your party.

The party was obviously very short of funds; but it succeeded in putting out a weekly newspaper with an edition of 10,000 copies called *Die freie Mitte* ('The Free Middle'). Printed by one of the party members, it contained articles attacking the 'double-faced' Middle Class Block and a woman's and a motoring page. The party also put out 50,000 copies of one poster: it showed a lifebelt marked with the party name and the appeal: 'Middle class, vote for your party!'—an appeal heeded by 37,000 voters in the three Länder in which the Union had been able to submit a list.

[1] Letter from Dr. Wilhelm Schmitz to the author. It may be noted that the Economic Party (*Wirtschaftspartei*) of the Weimar Republic led by the baker Hermann Drewitz was regarded as something of a precedent for this new party.

The South Schleswig Voters' League

If the Union of German Middle (*SSW*) Class Parties had tnin and widely dispersed class support, the South Schleswig Voters' League (*Südschleswiger Wählerverband*—SSW), which polled almost the same number of votes, was the only legally recognized party of a national minority and based its vote on the strip of country that lies south of the Danish frontier. This had been the second referendum zone in 1920 in which 52,000 inhabitants had opted for Germany, and 12,000 for Denmark. (The northern referendum zone, where 75,000 opted for Denmark and 25,000 for Germany, has formed part of Denmark ever since.) The question was kept alive to some extent in the inter-war period: on the whole, however, it was German support for the minority to the north of the frontier rather than Danish support for that to the south of it which characterized this period.

At the end of the second world war the position suddenly seemed reversed, though the Danish State acted with great prudence throughout. The fresh memories of the Hitler régime, the destruction of the German economy, the opprobrium that appeared to be attached to German nationality, and the hope too, no doubt, of escaping the flow of refugees from the East all made annexation by Denmark a seductive prospect. Although the British occupation authorities attempted to discourage the movement, the 'Danish list', which had polled some 5,000 votes in 1933, polled nearly 100,000 in the Landtag elections of 1947. The term *Speckdänen*—'Danes for the sake of the bacon'—came into use again as after the first world war. Even in 1957 the opponents as well as the supporters of the SSW pointed to the manifold and social services provided by publicly financed and private Danish organizations for the less prosperous sections of the South Schleswig community. Nearly 6,000 children attended Danish schools, poorer children were sent on holidays to Denmark, a health service was provided in Germany by the Danish Red Cross, there were sports and musical exchanges, and Danish was taught to adults in nightschools. The various organizations which provided these advantages were grouped together in the South Schleswig League (SSV) of which the SSW was in its origins the political arm.

As the immediate consequences of the war were slowly overcome, so the poll of the SSW fell to 75,000 in 1949, 45,000 in 1953, and 32,000 in 1957. Indeed, by 1957 the SSW's appeal was no longer primarily one of integration with Denmark, but had been reformulated to appear in its election programme as: '1. The full recognition of our national rights, the recognition of the right to self-determination and self-administration for South Schleswig.' But much more to the fore in party literature even than this demand were three other themes: firstly, anti-militarism and an 'uncompromising stand against conscription'; secondly, an emphasis on the economic development of this strip of frontier on the margin of the German economy; and thirdly, not so much a pro-Danish as an anti-refugee feeling.

The anti-militarism of this regional party paralleled that of the Bavarian Party and sprang no doubt from much the same source. More interesting was the economic argument: indeed while we have noted instances of what were essentially pressure groups attempting to paint themselves as political parties, the SSW was a political party trying to turn into or present itself as a pressure group. Time and time again it was argued that the SSW was 'not a party in the usual sense'[1] but represented

> the interests in the first place of the national minority of our homeland, but over and above that the total interests of our homeland in a way which no other party does or can, since their main interests are dispersed over wide areas and very little remains for the 'appendix' Schleswig.

'One independent SSW representative', it was bluntly stated, 'can obtain more for South Schleswig than one of 200 in a large party.' 'We too want our share of the economic miracle at last' was the motto. The CDU had not done enough. But a vote for the SPD was no solution either:

> No, because in that case a CDU majority in Bonn would be peeved. . . . Schleswiger, be bright: think of your homeland! Stick a pistol in the chest of Bonn! Vote SSW!

The economic demands of the SSW included compensation for the heavy transport cost to distant markets and suppliers, cheap agricultural credits, and a housing programme. The latter two demands at any rate contained a distinct note of hostility to the refugees. One 4-page pamphlet filled three of its pages with a catechism that ran:

> Why is every second farm on the new polder given to a refugee? . . .
> Why is no cheap housing being built for native inhabitants? . . .
> Why cannot a native inhabitant open any competitive business? Because he does not get the cheap credits available to a refugee. . . .

It was no doubt out of the same local patriotism that, in the most interesting of the constituency contests fought by the SSW, a photograph of the Bonn doorbell of the incumbent, the young

[1] *Forposten—Meddelelser fra Sydslesvigsk Forening*, Sept. 1957.

CDU whip Will Rasner, played some part in the campaign: 'The bell to Rasner's door is to be found 500 miles from his Flensburg constituency.' The SSW candidate there (who had been faced by a 'German bloc' in 1953) found that the BHE candidate publicly asked BHE supporters to vote not for himself but for the CDU candidate, but he claimed to quote the SPD candidate as saying, 'I myself don't have any chance of winning the constituency. . . . Of course all the workers can now give their votes to the candidate of the SSW.'

The literature of the SSW was written partly in Danish, a smaller part still in the local *Platt* dialect, but mostly in German. Its main publicity carried the picture of a girl athlete in a team, hands outstretched, with the Danish flag sown to her tunic: the main poster depicted a flight of five swans over the waves of the sea—a symbol of the appurtenance of Schleswig in the eyes of the party to the five countries of the Scandinavian North.

The German Community, the Fatherland Union, and other Splinter Groups

An even smaller group was the German Community (*Deutsche Gemeinschaft*), which claimed Stein and Fichte as its spiritual forebears and was led by 'the pioneer fighter of the German freedom movement', August Haussleiter. This (mainly South German) party had been represented in the Bavarian Landtag from 1950 until 1954, where it had sat to the left of centre between the SPD and the BHE, though some had wished to place it to the right of the CSU.

The German Community demanded an end to the 'bargain sale' of a Germany threatened by Eastern materialism from without and Western materialism from within, the restoration of a free and peaceful, social and independent German Reich, and the recognition of the enduring validity of the Weimar constitution over the whole of German territory. It demanded an end to 'the rule of the Communist and of the capitalist internationals over German soil'. One of its election posters told foreign troops bluntly: 'Go home! Germany for the Germans.' Since Germany had now in fact become colonial territory and 'the playground of foreign agents' the party demanded the closest collaboration with Afro-Asian peoples, in particular close friendship with the Arab States.

In economics the German Community called for 'an end to reparation payments to the allies and to Israel', the control of foreign trade in the interests of national policy, and special taxes on chain and department stores and mail-order houses. The party consistently prophesied economic disaster with a conviction that allowed it to print the (epistemologically curious) boast: 'We alone have correctly foretold the economic crisis that is to come!' It claimed such experts as the former President of the Reichsbank Dr. Hjalmar Schacht as its advisers in working out plans for a national economic order to oppose Communism not merely by force, but by a better system of social planning.

For the rest the German Community shared with the German Reich Party its concern for the welfare of the denazified and former members of the *Waffen-SS* and its lamentations over the decline in the morals of the rest of their countrymen. This the German Community attributed to the Morgenthau plan for the 'De-germanisation of the Germans' and to official encouragement of 'the repulsive mass orgy' of the carnival, where the centres of shamelessness were identical with the centres of piety—'and that under a Government which calls itself Christian'.[1]

The party had its national headquarters at the back of a Munich flat where the visitor was requested to 'ring three times for the German Community'. It was obviously poor, its red-and-white oak-leaf poster was seen little outside Bavaria, and though it claimed a membership of 16,000 it polled only 17,631 votes in the five Länder where it was able to submit a list.

Smallest of all the parties that presented a list of candidates was the Fatherland Union (*Vaterländische Union*) of Karl Feitenhansl, which stood only in Bavaria. Describing itself as the organized upsurge of the German people for the defence of freedom and the restoration of the unity of the Reich including all the territories of which it had been robbed, the Fatherland Union advocated a presidential form of government and a plebiscite to speed up the creation of a European Confederation of States. Among its other demands for 'a traditional German policy' were an economic system in which private profit was subordinated to the needs of the people, the recognition of the unique achievements of German soldiers in two world wars, 'draconic punishment' for any form of recruitment for the French Foreign Legion, less officialdom, less taxes, and a progressive social policy. Its poster demanded: 'Shall Germany remain the milch-cow of the world?' Its total poll, however, was only just 5,000 votes.

[1] Dr. Renate Maluche at the party's Göttingen congress—reported in *Die Deutsche Gemeinschaft — Kampfblatt der Deutschen Freiheitsbewegung*, 2nd April edition, 1957. Among other causes taken up by the party was the candidature of two of its members in protest against the odours of a fish-meal and of a varnish factory in Hamburg.

In addition to the thirteen parties admitted to the election on the Land level the 'parties' of two independent candidates who succeeded in obtaining the 200 signatures required for a constituency nomination and also a few other small groups distributed literature demanding action at the polls. Otto Strasser, one of Hitler's early rivals in the National Socialist Party, had come from Canada to form a German Social Union. His party congress was cancelled after trade union protests, he put out a pamphlet urging an invalid vote, and immediately after the election applied for a visa to return to Canada. A Free Social Union under the motto 'Count us out' quoted *Die Welt* on the electoral system: 'Throw the monster into the abyss of wolves' and concluded with the unanswered rhetorical question: 'Now do you know what to do with your ballot paper?' A 'League for German Unity', claiming that behind the CDU stood high finance, political Catholicism, and an industry estranged from Germany by foreign capital, asked that only candidates opposing atomic weapons and Bonn separatism be elected; and no doubt there were other minute political groupings which called themselves 'parties' but whose activity consisted in the main in distributing pamphlets outside the halls in which the bigger parties held their meetings.

Such groups might well have cluttered the ballot paper but for the signature requirements stipulated by the electoral law. The other minor parties were no doubt hampered by the splinter party clause, which not only kept all but the German Party out of the Bundestag, but which also reduced their poll through the fear that a vote cast for them would be a vote wasted. In both these ways the electoral law kept the number of parties that could appeal for a vote and that could enter the Bundestag within manageable proportions. The number of parties who submitted lists has remained much the same at successive federal elections, but the proportion of votes cast for any but the three large parties has sunk steadily, and the number of parties securing membership of the Bundestag has dropped from ten in 1949 to six in 1953 and four in 1957—a development that reflects not only the success of the bigger parties, but also a certain prudent scepticism on the part of the German electorate in the face of splinter groups of all kinds.

X

CAMPAIGN EXPENDITURE AND PARTY FINANCE

THE carefully calculated depth-psychology and the sheer dimensions of the CDU's campaign in 1957 represented a new phenomenon in European political style. It goes without saying that an operation of such scope and intensity could not be waged without considerable financial resources. Various SPD regions declared that they, too, had spent a multiple of the money available in 1953, and the FDP headquarters were satisfied with the material resources they were able to throw into the fray. Not unnaturally the amount of propaganda launched in the last few weeks before polling day led to a good deal of speculation both within the Federal Republic and outside it, and various wild estimates were put about as to the cost involved. The Free and Social Democrats, confused by the bewildering variety of sources from which pro-Government propaganda was converging on them, pointed to the size of the CDU's funds as proof of the sinister purchase of political influence by anonymous business capital. They pointed to the comprehensive coverage of the electorate by the CDU and the Government campaigns as proof of the monopoly rule of an undemocratic executive power. (No doubt their managers were also anxious to cite the CDU's material superiority as an alibi for their own impending defeat.)

The electoral law imposed no limitation on campaign expenditure and no obligation to declare its amount. The provision of the Basic Law which demands that parties must give an account of the origin (though not of the destination) of their funds had remained a dead letter.[1] In contrast to the SPD, the CDU published no accounts

[1] Para. 21 on the political parties states: 'They must publicly account for the sources of their funds.' Subsection 3 runs, 'Details shall be regulated by federal legislation', but though the question of a law to regulate parties had been under consideration since 1950, the difficulties inherent in the problem proved to be such that the Cabinet rejected a draft Bill proposed by the Ministry of the Interior in 1952, and an expert commission on the subject was appointed which reported very shortly before the election. (For its report see *Rechtliche Ordnung des Parteienwesens, Bericht der vom Bundesminister des Inneren eingesetzten Parteienrechtskommission*, Metzner, Frankfurt, 1957.)

whatever. Its managers were at pains to explain that any real figures would be incomprehensible to the man in the street, would invite further questions, and would thus distract attention from the main message of their campaign. The more persistent inquirer might be asked to believe that the CDU's campaign manager had less than £600,000 to spend, but when the SPD came out with a detailed estimate spread over seventeen pages to show that the pro-Government campaigns had cost £10 million the CDU issued nothing more explicit than an emphatic but unreasoned denial. Nevertheless it is possible by piecing together fragmentary evidence to discuss campaign expenditure in terms that are precise enough for the purpose of political studies.[1]

Problems of Definition

At the outset of any such inquiry it is essential to ask what precisely is its object, and what therefore are the definitions of expenditure relevant to the purpose in hand. A whole range of alternative concepts of campaign expenditure could be used; none of them will do justice to the individual situation of each party; yet a uniform standard must at least initially be used for them all.

The problem may be attacked either in monetary or else in real terms. The party treasurer will be interested in the money disbursements from his coffers, and this purely monetary concept is also of interest to the student of political affairs: cash expenditure can serve as a useful pointer to cash receipts, and hence as an aid in the investigation of the nature and relative importance of different sources of party finance. On the other hand such cash outlay may bear scant relation to the amount of goods and services which a party can in point of fact command, and the impact on the voter depends on the total of the real resources employed and the effectiveness of their use. A party with less money which can rely on its members to bill-post its placards may not be handicapped as against another with larger funds which needs professional agencies to distribute its material. The very prices charged by printing offices attached to party newspapers or by polling institutes or advertising agencies with party sympathies may reflect concealed subsidies to the party machine. An estimate of how far material superiority was an advantage in a campaign must therefore be based on the second concept.

[1] A number of Germans concerned with party finance were kindly willing to discuss the present argument after it had been written on the basis of circumstantial evidence; while suggesting modifications of detail or of phraseology, they confirmed the orders of magnitude indicated by these calculations.

Whether the calculation is to be based on financial or on 'real' transactions, two further problems arise from the period of time that is to be regarded as relevant and from the distinction between a party's general overhead costs and its specific election expenditure. If one party maintains a large permanent establishment for which an election involves small additional costs and another party with ordinarily small overheads vastly expands its machine at election time, then comparisons confined to the additional cost directly attributable to a single campaign miss the wood for the trees. An ideal comparison should be based on the cost at market prices of each party's total propaganda effort over a period which, in the German case, should cover the full round of quadrennial federal, Land, and local elections.

Even then, however, the complexities of the problem are not exhausted. Some components of each party's election campaign may be wholly or partially self-financing. The SPD charged an entrance fee for its cabarets: if the amount had been of any importance—the total yield lay under £10,000—it would have been worth while asking whether the revenue thus derived should be deducted from campaign expenditure or added to election funds. Pamphlets were sometimes bought from a party by its sympathizers or by primarily non-political bodies, and only a part (if any) of them passed on to the public; presumably here only the excess of revenue over cost to the party should be entered on the credit side of the party's accounts. Several widely distributed party publications carried advertisements just like those in the commercial magazines. In such cases only a comparison of commercial charges with the party's charges for such advertisements and perhaps even an inquiry into the motives of the advertisers would allow us to classify the transactions involved for the purposes of our purely monetary definitions.

There remains, moreover, the important problem of 'parallel campaigns'. If plain in their intention and effect these must be taken into the calculation in full; though since in some cases they benefited more than one party they are naturally to be treated with care. The public relations work of Government agencies posed further difficulties. In the final summing-up no doubt one would wish to keep such spending in a separate category, though a suitable proportion of it—and in particular all that part which reached a definite climax during or just before the election—should be related to the party and private campaign figures involved. But this problem in particular is, as we shall see, a highly theoretical one.

In a sense indeed it is a question of degree where one draws the lines of demarcation between a party campaign, a parallel campaign specifically organized to benefit one or more parties in the election, the influence (reinforced perhaps at election times) of primarily non-political organizations such as Churches and trade unions, and the general activities of these and similar bodies which did as it happened favour one line of policy or even one type of party as against another. Even a theoretical division into 'normal' public relations activity and supplementary activity in the period defined as 'the campaign' is an arbitrary line of demarcation and will tend to underestimate the importance of such activities as it is financially and otherwise possible to pursue even between elections. Ideally here, too, a calculation covering the whole period between two federal polling days would be demanded.

In short the farther one moves away from the monetary estimate of expenditure by the parties themselves, the less meaningful do any final figures become. Once one begins taking the cost of producing church newspapers into the reckoning—as the SPD tried to do—one is not far from terming the Catholic clergy 'unpaid black party secretaries'[1] and is in fact passing from the consideration of an inter-party conflict to that of the social context within which it takes place. Elections are not staged in a vacuum as debating contests in which the prize goes to the party with the most convincing arguments; they are fought in a universe of pre-existing ideological persuasions, economic interests, and social prejudices of which the party campaigns are themselves an expression. The relative force of these given factors can hardly be calculated in monetary terms, and can only be gauged by the complete description of an election, from historical considerations right through to the analysis of voting behaviour.

The present passage must therefore leave all these very general considerations aside for discussion in later chapters. Over and above a brief comparison of the scale of this West German campaign with a typical British election, the prime object of the calculation is to provide a quantitative framework for the discussion of party finance. It can thus afford to confine itself to cash transactions and to obvious subsidies in kind.

Even then all sorts of difficulties remain, and in the German case these are not only of a theoretical but also of a very practical kind. There are no detailed and comprehensive figures for the electoral period from 1953 to 1957 or even for the 1957 election alone. The parties themselves probably do not possess any such figures except on the federal level: Land organizations are either not anxious to reveal their financial state to the federal headquarters or else wish

[1] *Junge Gemeinschaft*, Feb. 1957.

to paint it in the darkest possible colours. Even the SPD—the only big party to publish its accounts—cannot provide figures in the detail and over the range of local expenditure to fit our theoretical concepts. Given in addition the secretiveness of the party organizations over what figures they do possess, one is ultimately thrown back on estimating the quantity of effort expended by each party and multiplying it by the prices ordinarily charged for such services.

The Sums Involved

The Appendix sets out a calculation of this kind for the CDU and similar estimates for the other parties.[1] If this reasoning is correct, the sum spent by the parties themselves and by obviously *ad hoc* private parallel campaigns in the last three and a half months before the poll lay in the region of £5 million; but it should be emphasized that this figure disregards any expenditure incurred by Government agencies. These £5 million were divided roughly as follows:

CDU and parallel campaigns	£3,000,000–£3,300,000
SPD	£700,000–£850,000
FDP	£600,000–£700,000
German Party	£350,000
Refugees' Party	£230,000
Other parties between them less than	£230,000

The reckoning would thus suggest that the FDP spent at least as much in the 1957 campaign as one of the major British parties; certainly its publicity efforts looked roughly analogous to a British party's campaign, the difference of course being that the FDP was able to poll only 8 per cent. and not 50 per cent. of the equally large electorate. The Social Democrats appear not to have spent very much more than the FDP; but they were able to run a substantially larger campaign thanks to their access to both permanently salaried and voluntary manpower. The CDU spent at least three times as much as the SPD and five times as much as the British Conservative Party in any post-war election. Altogether the money spent in 1957 by all West German parties together appears to have been four or five times as much as was spent in the previous British General Election by all three British parties involved.

Party Finance: the Role of the Membership

£5 million represents nearly three shillings per elector and more than £5 for every member of any party in the Federal Republic.

[1] The reader disinclined to take the figures on trust should perhaps examine the Appendix (pp. 304–14) before reading further in the main text.

In particular if the private pro-CDU campaigns cost £3 million this represents over £10 for every party member of the CDU. The question thus arises: From where did this money come? It was a question constantly asked, and answered in a fashion, by the SPD's propaganda. Perhaps the finance of the campaign did not in 1957 become an issue to quite the extent that it had in 1953, when the SPD had issued a pamphlet under the title *Businessmen's Millions Purchase Political Power*[1] and the Chancellor had counter-attacked with the charge that SPD officials like Schroth and Scharley were receiving Communist funds. Nevertheless the financing methods of the Government parties were heavily criticized by the Social Democrats; they again published a pamphlet on the subject,[2] and in July the Federal Constitutional Court was invoked against one of the chief devices by which the anti-socialist parties were financed.

The question of campaign funds is best approached through a consideration of party finance in non-election years. This already reveals a very marked contrast between two types of parties: those which could rely for the bulk of their ordinary revenue on fixed dues and levies exacted from their members as part of the duties of membership, and those which were heavily dependent on large donations of all kinds. The SPD and the BHE were parties of the first type, supported in very large measure by the regular subscriptions of their own members: the FDP and the CDU were parties of the second type, relying predominantly on other sources of finance.

With less than 250,000 members the CDU could barely raise £100,000 from membership dues and these were retained by the local organizations. Bundestag and Landtag members and other office-holders were expected to subscribe fairly heavily to party finances. £200 per annum was a little exceptional but £100 per annum was probably below the average for a Bundestag member, half that amount being demanded of a Landtag member. Altogether this source of income could hardly come to more than another £150,000. The remaining £150,000 or £180,000 needed even in a non-election year to support a running expenditure of around £350,000 or £400,000 came from donations and payments of one kind or another on a Land or a federal level.[3]

[1] *Unternehmermillionen kaufen politische Macht*, SPD, Bonn, 1953.

[2] *Die Finanzierung des Wahlkampfs 1957: Eine Untersuchung über die Abhängigkeit politischer Parteien von wirtschaftlichen Machtgruppen*, SPD, Bonn, 1957.

[3] Cf. also Arnold J. Heidenheimer, 'German Party Finance: the CDU', *American Political Science Review*, vol. li, no. 2, June 1957, pp. 369–85, which is the most detailed piece of research on the problem of CDU finance between elections published so far. The present author's estimates lie slightly below Dr. Heidenheimer's.

The Free Democrats, like the CDU, published no accounts even between elections. It may, however, be regarded as certain that membership dues never reached the federal headquarters and almost everywhere remained with the local organization that collected them. Both the Land and the federal organizations were thus supported in their entirety by donations of various kinds; but since the geographical distribution of FDP supporters who had funds to spare was extremely uneven, some Land organizations were very much better placed than others. Perhaps there was no party in whose internal politics money played such an important part as the FDP. The financial resources available to the North Rhine–Westphalian party proved a considerable asset to it, and this party organization probably subsidized not only the federal party, but one or two other individual Land party organizations as well—all with excellent effect on the acceptance by the whole party of the men and of the policies which the North Rhine–Westphalian organization had to offer.

The financial structure of the SPD was radically different. Its nearly 600,000 members contributed on an average just over £1 per annum, each member in accordance with his own estimate of his income. The membership dues rose to £50 per annum for those with incomes of over £1,500. These dues were collected monthly by the sale of membership stamps in various denominations, and in 1955–7, for example, 94 per cent. of the number of monthly stamps which the membership figures warranted were in fact sold. The denomination of the stamp was not always that appropriate to the real income of the party member concerned, and admonitions to honesty in self-assessment for subscription purposes figured regularly in party reports. Nevertheless, while the party's membership sank between January 1949 and January 1957 from 850,000 to 600,000, the total of membership dues collected rose from £560,000 in 1949 to £720,000 in 1957. The SPD thus raised from membership dues alone nearly twice as much as the whole CDU spent in a non-election year.

The distribution of the dues collected varied between party regions: perhaps the ratio of 5 per cent. to the collector as a commission, 25 per cent. to the local party, and 55 per cent. to the party regions was the most typical. The regions thus had a steady income from subscriptions of over £350,000 per annum and perhaps another £100,000 or more from office-holders—quite sufficient to finance their ordinary party activities. By a decision of the federal party 15 per cent. of all membership dues were sent to the federal headquarters, which thus had a steady income of £100,000 derived from its rank and file.

Table VI sets out the accounts of the federal party headquarters for the whole four-year cycle ending three months after the election: it shows an extreme constancy in all the non-election items on the income side (amounting to some £200,000 each year) and a similar constancy in the non-election items on the expenditure side (amounting to between £200,000 and £220,000 each year). Even the federal headquarters derived over half its ordinary revenue from dues and levies imposed on the membership. The political importance of this financial structure has already become apparent in the discussion of the SPD's election campaign.

TABLE VI

The Finance of the SPD's Federal Headquarters, 1954–7 ('000 of DM)[1]

	1954	*1955*	*1956*	*1957*
A. *INCOME*				
15 per cent. of party membership fees	1,058	1,079	1,137	1,245
Dues of Bundestag members	291	282	220	330
Contributions for public relations from associated enterprises	667	510	533	505
Restitution payments	..	240	..	..
Collections and other income	208	146	178	178
Sub-total	*2,224*	*2,257*	*2,069*	*2,258*
Election contributions	498	413	1,031	4,170
Total	2,722	2,670	3,101	6,427
B. *EXPENDITURE*				
Administrative and similar items	1,273	1,414	1,442	1,690
Public relations	792	801	813	716
Subsidies to lower organs for 'agitation'	320	247	441	131
Sub-total	*2,385*	*2,463*	*2,696*	*2,537*
Election expenditure	296	254	148	4,117
Total	2,681	2,717	2,844	6,654

[1] 11·75 DM = £1; 4·20 DM = $1.

Source: *Jahrbuch der Sozialdemokratischen Partei Deutschlands 1954/1955*, Neuer Vorwärts, Hanover and Bonn, 1956, pp. 209–10, and *Jahrbuch der Sozialdemokratischen Partei Deutschlands 1956/1957*, pp. 253–4. (In both these yearbooks the items 'Party membership fees' and 'Election contributions' are presented as a single figure: the segregation of the two has been carried through in accordance with the data presented on pp. 217–18 of the first and on pp. 260–1 of the second volume cited.) The slight apparent discrepancies in the totals are due to the rounding of the component figures.

Party Fund-Raising Activities

All parties claimed in public to be short of funds. Their claims were taken seriously enough by sections of the public for both the SPD and the CDU to be embarrassed by diminutive amounts of money sent sometimes by poor pensioners with touching letters of support for the party cause. Whatever the moral value of such small gifts, they could not be expected to have any appreciable effect on the finance of either big party. A whole gamut of other methods of party finance have therefore been evolved, which played an appreciable role in the budget of the SPD and an overwhelmingly important one in the case of the CDU, of the FDP, and of the German Party. They aimed for the most part at tapping impersonal sources of funds and augmenting the supply of contributions by allowing them to be offset against individual income and particularly against corporate taxation.

One obvious method of giving money to parties and recovering tax on the sums involved was that of advertising in newspapers and other publications linked with the party to be financed. This practice is of course current in most countries, though in the case of one CDU paper it was alleged that the bills tended, at least for a time, to be written and paid without the advertisements ever appearing.

A second device consisted in the sale by the party or by an affiliated organization of some service—usually copies of a newspaper—at a price greatly in excess of its cost to the party and of its usefulness to the customer. Payments for such services were entered in the books of the subscriber as a business or other expense to be set against taxable income, but on the publisher's side they could be treated as receipts for purposes benefiting the common weal and therefore once more claim tax exemption.

For just this purpose the SPD ran a news service supplied at differential prices, though it seems to have yielded only an insignificant addition to revenue. The CDU was naturally much more successful in this type of operation. Its best-known enterprise was a weekly 16-page roneo broadsheet, the *Wirtschaftsbild*, for which firms paid £50 per annum per copy; they tended to order it in bulk, annual payments of £5,000, £6,000, and £8,000 not being unusual. (The periodical also received donations outright, one gift of £70,000 being reported in 1954.) The *Wirtschaftsbild* was not taken seriously as a purveyor of news[1] but recognized as a primarily financial

[1] The managers of the *Wirtschaftsbild* were unwise if they gave the obviously erroneous impression that subscribers—particularly to Edition A sold at £100 per annum per copy—would be receiving very special economic benefits from their

device and discussed as such in the Bundestag early in the year of the election: the SPD tabled a formal request that the Government should not allow the publicly controlled Volkswagen Works to subsidize the chief Government party to the tune of £5,000 per annum in the guise of paying for 100 copies of the broadsheet; the Government, however, declined to take any action in the matter.[1] (SPD supporters who were shocked by the Volkswagen subscription to the *Wirtschaftsbild* should in this connexion have remembered that municipal funds were often expended in advertising the amenities of SPD-governed cities in SPD-controlled papers whose readers would hardly have taken investment decisions of equivalent benefit to the town.)

The Sponsors' Associations

But even these two methods of fund-raising played a subordinate role in the finances of the non-socialist parties represented in the second Bundestag. By far the most important source of their income were the political funds maintained by West German industrial and commercial firms. These political funds existed by 1957 in two distinct variations: the older type commonly known as Sponsors' Associations (*Förderergesellschaften*), and the later variety known as Civic Associations (*Staatsbürgerliche Vereinigungen*). Common to both

relations with the paper: 'We give information and news on the work of the Bonn ministries, the Bundestag and its committees . . . this is in many cases confidential information which must not become public too early. . . . Our staff will set to work to give subscribers valuable tips on the allocation of contracts by public authorities, such as those of the occupation forces, the Israeli Purchasing Mission in Germany, the Federal Frontier Force, etc. The *Wirtschaftsbild* with all its apparatus is at subscribers' disposal for detailed consultation on such matters.' (Quotation taken from *Der Spiegel*, 5 Sept. 1956, pp. 13–14.) On the other hand the Free Democrats, who maintained a similar information service, admitted that: 'As a result of the FDP's going into opposition it has become much more difficult this last year to obtain such information.' (*Das Jahr der Selbstbehauptung*, FDP, Bonn, 1958, p. 30.)

[1] See Documents 2799, 2833, and 2916 of the second Bundestag, and the debate on the subject during the 182nd sitting of the second Bundestag, 10 Jan. 1957, pp. 10123–8. It would be interesting but complicated to set out the curious chain of events reported concerning the *Wirtschaftsbild* between then and election day. It included among other incidents the arrest of a counter-espionage agent of the Gehlen organization who had been shadowing the wife of a former employee of the *Wirtschaftsbild* after the theft (during the carnival) of the bulk of the accounts and other records of the publication. Alleged photostats of the missing books (in particular of receipts of large payments made by firms said to be supplying the nascent armed forces) were hawked around the Opposition parties for some time before they were published by the organ of the Socialist Unity Party *Neues Deutschland* on 10 Sept. 1957 with the cloak-and-dagger story that the burglary had been carried out on CDU instructions, but that the burglars had in their own interests made photostats of the records before destroying them.

was the task of collecting money from businesses in a form that secured tax relief for the donor, and of then distributing this money to more than one party simultaneously.

Sponsors' Associations were founded under slightly varying names in all the Länder of the Federal Republic in the year preceding the 1953 election. They were designed to act as intermediaries between the parties on the one hand and individual firms on the other. They not only mobilized new and potentially more stable sources of funds through being run by businessmen and appealing to the solidarity of the business community, but they also increased the effective amount of money available by allowing the sums paid to the Sponsors' Associations to be deducted from taxable income: for the Sponsors' Associations were formally trade associations. As such they raised their income by a fixed membership levy determined usually in proportion to the payroll in the case of an industrial undertaking, and the turnover in the case of a commercial firm. These levies were varied from time to time to provide adequate funds for election years. Firms had the right to designate the party to which they wished their contributions to go, but whether the contributions thus earmarked were deducted from the general pool before its distribution to the parties (thus upsetting the party ratios) is not clear.

The distribution of money between non-socialist parties was carried out according to various criteria, often the relative strength of the parties in the Land concerned. Membership figures of one kind or another, votes polled at the last Bundestag election, votes polled at the last Landtag election, or seats in the Landtag could furnish different bases on which to calculate their relative importance. The level of funds placed at the parties' disposal could, however, also be affected by the prospects they offered of a coalition policy acceptable to the donors. Moreover, not all the anti-socialist parties were in regular receipt of such funds. The DRP only had an occasional lump sum payment to settle its debts and to secure its aid in ousting the SPD Government of Lower Saxony, and in contrast to earlier occasions the Federalist Union received nothing from the political funds for its 1957 campaign.

Before the third federal election the managers of these political funds proceeded not so much by dividing a given sum between the parties, as by negotiating with each party individually, asking each to justify its budget, and meeting only those campaign expenses which they felt were reasonable and lay within their financial power. The resources available to the funds were not entirely inelastic: they depended on the level of business prosperity, on organizational factors, and also on the climate of business opinion on the internal political situation. Thus while the CDU headquarters (as distinct from the whole party and its parallel organizations) had at the beginning of the year budgeted for an election campaign costing £800,000, the party managers were forced down to a budget of £400,000 in the discussions of the spring. After the Göttingen appeal of the atomic scientists the situation seemed to have become much more grave; the CDU felt it necessary to launch a large-scale advertising campaign and asked for further credits specifically to make such a campaign possible. The Civic Association decided to relent, passed the hat round again, and provided the extra finance which allowed the CDU headquarters in the end to spend £600,000, though it seems that the Civic Association as well as the CDU went slightly into debt for the purpose.

It was no doubt the hope of the Sponsors' Associations that with a cartel hold over such an important part of the finances of a whole range of anti-socialist parties they would be able to obtain certain minimum terms for industry. They could at least demand that their money was not wasted on anti-socialist parties fighting each other: and the Sponsors' Associations certainly had some influence on agreements between parties. For the first time also the business community could have a say on the ways in which its money was spent, though it does not seem that precise accounts were demanded.

In a sense indeed these political funds were defence leagues of business against the very political parties which they were supporting. Instead of having to open the door to three, four, or more different anti-socialist parties and to decide on whether to give to one or several of them and how much to each, business men now bought a measure of protection against such competing direct approaches. (Householders' charitable associations in many German cities unsuccessfully attempt to fulfil just this function against the private beggar and miscellaneous charities.) The parties, on the other hand, instead of being able to play off firms against each other, were to be faced by a common front of business.[1]

[1] This aspect of the Sponsors' Associations is strikingly illustrated by a CDU report on the 1954 Landtag election in North Rhine–Westphalia: 'Before the foundation of the Sponsors' Associations we in the Rhineland were always able to finance every election adequately and on time. Even in the [1953] Bundestag election the Sponsors' Associations did not disappoint us within the framework of acceptable conditions. But this time the election could not be financed in time and then only very inadequately, in spite or because of the Sponsors' Associations. If the Sponsors' Associations do not keep to agreements and deadlines, we cannot for the future feel bound by the condition that we abstain from our own collections. And in other respects also collaboration with the Sponsors' Associations this time raised really very displeasing problems.' (One may guess that these 'displeasing problems' involved, *inter alia*, the expression of preferences in the party's selection of candidates.)

The Issue of Tax-Exemption

The foundation of the Sponsors' Associations in the year preceding the 1953 election was facilitated by an opinion which the Federal Fiscal Court expressed in May 1952. In reply to questions posed to it by the Federal Ministry of Finance, the Court then declared that if a subordinate proportion of the funds of a trade or professional association were passed on to political parties or to election funds, contributions to such organizations did not for that reason cease to be exempt from taxation.[1] Subsidies to political parties were thus recognized as a legitimate business expense and the political defence of business interests as one of those functions performed for firms in common by their trade associations.

But the victory was not yet complete: only a part of the tax-free funds of such associations could be passed on to political parties. In practice it was assumed that a quarter or a third of the total remained within the limits of a subordinate proportion, and the remaining income of the Sponsors' Associations had to be employed for more general purposes. They ran information services, political and economic lectures, courses for members of works councils, and engaged directly in such public relations work in favour of free enterprise as, perhaps, the Erhard campaign. The SPD would no doubt class such activities as camouflage campaigns, but only a change in the law could make possible what from the anti-socialist parties' point of view was to be a more efficient form of organization.

Just over a year after the CDU's victory of 1953 the income-tax law was therefore amended: donations for political purposes were listed among those for charitable, scientific, and other purposes which could be deducted from taxable income.[2] Twenty-two CDU

[1] 'Gutachten des Bundesfinanzhofs ID 1/52 S', of 17 May 1952, reprinted in *Bundessteuerblatt III* of 5 Sept. 1952, pp. 228–32.

[2] For the brief debate on the subject see the Official Report of the 55th sitting of the second Bundestag, 16 Nov. 1954, pp. 2671, 2683–4, 2700, and, for the voting, pp. 2728–32. The new paragraph 10 (*b*) of the Income Tax Law of 1955 thus read as follows:

'Expenditure for the advancement of charitable, church, religious, scientific and political (*staatspolitische*) purposes and of purposes benefiting the common weal which are regarded as especially worthy of support may be deducted [from taxable income or profits] as special expenditure up to a level of 5 per cent. of total receipts or 0·2 per cent. of the sum of total turnover and of the wages and salaries paid during the calendar year. For scientific and political purposes this percentage rises from 5 per cent. by an additional 5 per cent.' (*Bundesgesetzblatt I*, 1954, p. 373.)

The following was the relevant paragraph of the Order on the implementation of this clause:

'*Paragraph 49—Advancement of political purposes*

'Sums expended for the advancement of political purposes can be deducted [from taxable income or profits] only

members of the Bundestag joined the SPD and some other members in voting against this amendment. But it was passed by 193 votes against 180, and as a result for every 55 DM (net of tax) sacrificed by a corporation to a political fund or party, the latter received 100 DM, the State losing 45 DM in revenue. Forty-five per cent. of the contributions made by corporations to those political parties which they supported were thus in effect passed on to the State; but the State, of course, bore no part of the membership dues that played a much larger role in the finances of some parties than of others.

The CDU could claim that this system had a precedent: it had been introduced by the Socialists themselves in order to strengthen democratic institutions immediately after the first world war, though it was quickly abolished again when its different effects on different parties came to be grasped. In fact neither the 1954 amendment nor the Order issued under it were accepted without question. As leader of the All-German People's Party Heinemann appealed to the Federal Constitutional Court against subsection (1) of the implementing Order. He argued that it violated the principle of equality between parties implied in Articles 3 and 21 of the Basic Law by practically confining the tax privilege to parties already represented in a legislature. In February 1957 Heinemann won this appeal. In one passage of its judgment the Federal Constitutional Court threw out a hint that it might be prepared to go even farther: 'constitutional grounds of objection might perhaps be argued against the application of the tax relief provisions of the income tax law to political parties'.[1] The Socialists were slow to take their cue, but then in June 1957 Minister-President Zinn appealed in the name of Land Hesse against the constitutionality of the tax exemption itself.

'(1) *a* If they are given to a political party on whose nomination at least one representative was elected to the Bundestag or to the representative assembly of a Land at the last election, or to a political party of the Danish minority . . .

'(2) If they are given to a legal person which according to its statute and actual conduct serves exclusively political purposes and the resources of which are used for the purpose defined in sub-section (1) . . .

'(3) If they are given to legal persons which according to their statutes and actual conduct serve exclusively general political purposes and which are designated by the Federal Government with the assent of the Bundesrat. General political purposes within the meaning of this Order are such as are directed towards the general support of the democratic form of government in the region to which the Basic Law is applicable and in West Berlin; activities which seek to further only certain specific interests of a political kind do not serve general political purposes. . . .'

[1] 1 BvG 241/56.

Zinn argued that the 1954 amendment in effect obliged the State to contribute taxpayers' money to whatever party the donor claiming tax relief happened to designate; the law thus represented an abdication on the part of the State of its right to decide itself on the distribution of public funds to political parties. The amendment violated the equality of political parties guaranteed by the Basic Law, since it disregarded the radical differences in the social structures of different parties; and Zinn complained that

> The legislator consciously and deliberately shaped the provisions on tax exemption . . . in such a way that the financial assistance of the State must flow overwhelmingly towards the present Government parties.

In addition the law violated the equality of individuals' political rights, and led to a grotesque revival of elements of a class franchise:

> The system which makes the level of the State's share depend upon the level of the [private] contribution, taken in conjunction with the progressivity of taxation, gives the rich man more State assistance in the pursuit of his political aims than the poor one.

Worst of all was the fact that the State always contributed 45 per cent. of any donations decided upon by the anonymous managers of business corporations:

> Since the amount of donations given by corporations probably vastly exceeds that given by individuals, the provision leads to the paradoxical result that legal persons, which are excluded from the most important form of political decision, the franchise, are given greater support in the pursuit of their political aims than the private citizen who has the vote.

This appeal came too late for the Constitutional Court to take any decision on it before the election.[1] But quite apart from its merits, and even if it came too late to discourage firms from political contributions by its threat of retroactive taxation, Zinn could hope that it would at least focus public attention once more on the political and fiscal problems of party finance, which were an important ingredient in the SPD's election campaign.

The Civic Association and the Land Funds

In 1957 direct donations to political parties could thus be deducted from taxable profits. Nevertheless most firms (as distinct from individuals) preferred to continue making their contribution

[1] In June 1958 the Court allowed Zinn's appeal: the amendment of 1954 discriminated between parties in favour of those 'whose program and activity appeal to moneyed circles', and discriminated between citizens 'since those with large incomes save a larger absolute and relative amount of tax as a result of their political donations' (2 BvG 1/57).

through the organized funds, which had become all the more efficient politically through the 1954 amendment. For now the existing Sponsors' Associations, which consolidated their tax privileges in accordance with paragraph 49 subsection (3) of the implementing Order, were replaced or supplemented by a new form of organization, the Civic Associations, which derived their tax immunity from subsection (2) of the same paragraph and devoted the whole of their income to party political purposes. Sponsors' Associations subsisted in a number of Länder, even in one or two cases where Civic Associations were formed alongside them: but by far the most interesting phenomenon was the emergence of a new central body, the Civic Association run from (though not formally by) the headquarters of the Federation of German Industry in Cologne.[1]

This central Civic Association represented the answer to the problem of how to finance the federal headquarters of the leading anti-socialist parties. Until 1956, while the political funds were run as Land Sponsors' Associations, it was not always easy to obtain contributions from each Land to the parties' federal headquarters. The North Rhine–Westphalian and Baden-Württemberg Sponsors' Associations were naturally prosperous and able to help finance federal party organizations, but the Sponsors of Schleswig-Holstein regarded themselves as too short of funds to be able to spare money for federal purposes, and there were difficulties in Hesse that may not have been unrelated to the existence of a strong SPD Government in that Land.

When the central Civic Association was founded the field was therefore divided. The Civic Association was to support the federal party organizations by tapping a restricted number of large insurance companies, banks, and very big industrial and commercial firms; all the rest were to be left to the Land Sponsors' and Civic Associations. In 1957 the central Civic Association not only paid money to federal parties, but in one or two instances also helped Land organizations; Schleswig-Holstein in particular was in difficulties after the metal-workers' strike at the turn of the year. Co-ordination between the central Civic Association and the Land Sponsors' and Civic Associations was close, and their officers tended

[1] It seems that this central Civic Association was the only one legally recognized as entitled to benefit from the new subsection (2) of paragraph 49 and that the receipts issued by the Land organizations were drawn up in its name. (Cf. Order of the Federal Government of 27 Feb. 1956, Document 166/56 of the Bundesrat, accepted without discussion at the 159th sitting of the Bundesrat, 18 May 1956, p. 183.) The official seat of the central Civic Association was later moved from Cologne to Koblenz.

to meet three or four times a year to discuss current problems of the kind that required settlement in the light of more general considerations than those of Land politics alone.

The Civic Association in Cologne and the political funds in the Länder were largely run by men who were simultaneously officers of the Federation of German Industry and of Land industrial and commercial associations. But these personal unions between the ordinary industrial and commercial associations and the political funds were far from complete, and a number of otherwise independent business men also took their share in the running of the political funds. There was no party uniformity among their officers: while the majority supported the CDU, there were also some who personally favoured the FDP, and the President of the Federation of German Industry was himself known to be a supporter of the German Party. These men were of course united by their opposition to socialism and the Social Democrats; nor can there be any doubt that the views of the Federation of German Industry tended to determine the conduct of the political funds.

It remains to attempt an assessment of the relative importance of this source of finance to the different non-socialist parties. The CDU's total central campaign cost it something in the region of £1,100,000–£1,250,000 and it would seem that 40 per cent. of this total came from the Civic Association in Cologne. The CDU thus financed some four-fifths of its headquarters campaign of £600,000 (as distinct from the Adenauer campaign) from this one source. The *Wirtschaftsbild* funds went to finance the Adenauer campaign rather than that of the CDU headquarters; the bulk of the remaining CDU money thus came from direct donations, as did the rest of the Adenauer campaign. Adenauer's close connexion with the heads of various banking firms allowed him to collect large funds even without using Government money. Indeed the foundation of the Cologne Civic Association may have somewhat reduced the fund-raising importance to the party of the Chancellor himself.

It is more difficult to know how much of the Land campaigns was financed by the Sponsors' and Civic Associations. In Länder like Schleswig-Holstein and the Rhineland-Palatinate the political funds were almost the sole source of campaign finance; in North Rhine–Westphalia, on the other hand, the direct contributions of individual firms played a considerable part. The Land Civic and Sponsors' Associations probably did not contribute more than another £1,000,000 between them. Altogether the political funds must thus have contributed something of the order of £1,500,000 to the CDU.

The federal headquarters of the Free Democrats received

£120,000 from the Civic Association in Cologne. Originally the Land organizations were to have received in addition an equivalent amount, but in fact they succeeded in obtaining nearer £200,000—though the secrecy maintained between different Land organizations of the party makes a more precise figure difficult to obtain. The Refugees' Party received £55,000 from the Cologne Civic Association and about another £80,000 on the Land level. If the German Party received some £300,000 in all, the three smaller parties supported by the political funds received about £800,000 from this source; the total resources of the political funds distributed in 1957 must then have lain in the region of £2,000,000–£2,500,000: just under £1,000,000 in the hands of the Civic Association in Cologne, and perhaps not quite twice as much again in the hands of the Land funds. More than half the total campaign funds of the four bigger non-socialist parties thus came to them through the Civic and Sponsors' Associations.

The Working of the System

The size of these political funds combined with the very efficient methods of persuasion of the electorate which they could buy represented a source of great actual and perhaps ever greater potential influence on Western Germany's political future. Quite apart from the legal issue of tax-exemption the Social Democrats regarded it as a caricature of equality that firms should pay money to the SPD's opponents in accordance with the number of their workers and employees (who might largely be Social Democrats) and thus redress the formal equality of the voters by an effective inequality of the means of persuasion. They regarded it as undemocratic that parties should be financially dependent for their very existence on the funds contributed by pressure groups representing anonymous business capital. As one of the SPD advertisements stated: 'Whoever is in receipt of millions from the lords of the big business concerns cannot but pursue their policies thereafter.' The reality of these dangers is crystal clear and need hardly be laboured. It is all the more interesting to ask in what terms the situation was described on the other side, in the quarters responsible for the working of the whole system of party finance.

The trade association officials and businessmen who administered the political funds did not regard the arrangement as ideal. They were acting as brokers between the business community and the parties, and there were difficulties on both sides. The business organizations did not relish appealing to their members for money by the meetings, circulars, and personal approaches which were needed; their member firms would no doubt have preferred to retain the funds involved in their businesses or pay them out to the owners. On the other hand the officials were dissatisfied that something like half of the business community was resisting their appeals and refusing to contribute at all, and they were afraid that a slackening of business prosperity would cut down rather than raise the sums available for political action.

Relations with the parties, too, were not wholly satisfactory. Since party membership dues in the leading non-socialist parties were as a rule retained at the lowest levels of party organization, Land and federal headquarters depended for their daily upkeep (and Land and federal officials for their monthly salaries) on the continuance of support for the party by the political funds. Each party headquarters had fixed overhead commitments, and the political funds felt morally obliged to continue payments though they sometimes saw no real political returns for them or even heartily disapproved of the policies pursued. Thus after the 1957 election the Refugees' Party was assured of sufficient funds for it to meet its running commitments and to wind up its federal headquarters over fifteen months.

In fact financial activity of this kind tended to develop an impetus of its own. Once one party in a coalition was supported, it was natural that its coalition partners should also ask for funds; and once these had been given, the party could exercise some pressure for a continuance of payments even after it had gone into opposition. Only a few weeks after the 'Düsseldorf revolt' the political funds were forced to resume negotiations with the Free Democrats, however disgruntled their subscribers may have been at the thought.

The leaders of the business world were in fact acutely aware of such pressures as parties could exert on their source of funds, particularly when they were managed by men not used to the nature of gentlemen's agreements. On the other hand the businessmen also felt that their financial sacrifices were ill rewarded. Bundestag members were less interested in the sources of their party's finance than in its popularity in the country; just as the political funds stood between the individual donor and the party, so the party organization shielded the individual politician against direct pressure from the sources of political finance. The business community might make prominent representatives available to the parties, but businessmen complained that, once in the Bundestag, these members often put party loyalty above the interests of their trade association, and even where they retained close links with their business associates members dared not speak too openly on their behalf in public. Few members of the Bundestag elected with the funds supplied by the employers spoke the kind of language on social and trade union matters which many employers might really have liked to hear. The political funds could on occasion give or refuse money for specific types of propaganda between elections; they were able to help a few business representatives into legislatures on the Land and federal level who might otherwise have found the going more difficult; but broadly speaking they professed to see themselves as the horse rather than the rider of the alliance.

Nevertheless the leaders of the business community did induce their colleagues to surrender substantial sums every year for their political experts to use for such purposes as they thought fit. The desire to keep out the Social Democrats was no doubt uppermost in the minds of those who signed the cheques; but the duty of the business community to patronize political no less than cultural life tended also to be quoted. On the whole readiness to contribute to the political funds decreased with the size of the firm. Indeed the deliberate nature of the decision to contribute should not be overestimated: the size of the funds available in 1957 resulted not simply from fiscal and organizational changes, but also from the fact that the main boom for German business had occurred after 1953, and in as highly organized a business community as the German the slight contribution (of, for example, 1*s.* 8*d.* per annum per employee) was made almost automatically as one of those very minor business expenses, trade association dues, and cultural, sports and religious donations on which no great decisions of principle needed to be taken at board level, particularly if the other firms were paying them too.

Over and above this trend to conformity and the feelings of joint responsibility for the cost of protecting the political and economic system as it had evolved in the post-war Federal Republic there was, however, in many cases a further motive at work—particularly where funds were not channelled through the political funds but given direct to the parties. Even the SPD obtained funds from business firms, especially where it was in control of local or Land governments—a fact which suggests that more specific favours of one kind or another were expected from the recipients and, as one can only presume by the persistence of the practice, were not always expected in vain.

It should be noted that the Sponsors' Associations, by encouraging the solidarity of the business community and by making the individual donors anonymous *vis-à-vis* the parties, attempted to represent a certain safeguard against the last of these possibilities. But they failed to 'corner' political contributions. The Erhard campaign was not financed through them but represented a private venture agreed upon between the promoters of the campaign and certain large predominantly commercial rather than industrial firms. (Commercial circles had a greater interest than industry in Erhard's programme of cartel laws and import liberalization.) The Civic Associations indeed discouraged 'parallel campaigns' of all kinds. It was their view that the parties should make their own propaganda on their own budgets and not seek to spend more money (and perhaps do so less effectively) by also running parallel campaigns on parallel budgets. The Civic Association refused to support the 'Trojan Horse' advertisement, yet this campaign also managed to collect sufficient funds for its purpose. Money was thus still flowing directly between business firms and political propagandists and by-passing the political funds.

Indeed the money flowed not only between business firms and parallel campaigns, but also between firms and the parties themselves—the more so since, under subsection (1) of paragraph 49, even straight party contributions could be deducted from taxable income. The CDU received large direct contributions for its election campaign, and the Free Democrats appear to have done particularly well out of such direct support. They ran their own fund-raising 'Association for Economic and Social Policy', which collected contributions particularly from the small and medium-sized patriarchal firms; these tended to support it even in North Rhine–Westphalia, where they are as typical of the Land as a whole as the big firms are of the Ruhr. Some of the big firms also took out a 're-insurance policy' by direct contributions paid simultaneously to the Free as well as to the Christian Democrats.

The Finance of the SPD Campaign

In addition to their share of the pro-Government funds the FDP also drew a small sum from the 'Association for Democracy and Reunification', the political fund of the Opposition. This body collected perhaps £10,000 after an outlay of nearly half that amount. The SPD took most of the profit, but also gave a token sum to one small party of the Opposition which had earlier made an unsuccessful attempt to claim money as of right from the Civic Association. The SPD received certain limited funds from its friends in business, from firms—particularly those with labour directors on the board—who found it difficult to defend too partial a policy of donations, and from those who wished to establish or maintain certain personal contacts which might prove useful one day. Breweries and department stores in particular found it difficult to resist SPD appeals for expensive advertising space: a fair proportion of their customers were, after all, SPD supporters. In Hamburg in particular the Social Democrats approached business circles with marked success. But the SPD never asked for money from the political funds associated with the Federation of German Industry. It would have been even more embarrassing to have received a small sum from them than to have had nothing, and the party could not afford to have evidence of any approach on its part published while it was simultaneously attacking the system as a whole.

It is therefore worth asking how, without the support of the political funds, the SPD was able to finance a campaign that must have cost something like £700,000–£850,000 in money terms. From the published accounts of the central party headquarters set out in Table VI it is quite clear that the party did not save money for three years in order to spend it on electioneering in the fourth, but that there were two sources of funds for propaganda purposes: 'contributions for public relations', a stable annual item of about £45,000, and 'election contributions', which expanded dramatically from £20,000 in 1955 to £360,000 in 1957.

The stable 'contributions for public relations' were almost the more revealing item. They came from the party's own business firms. It was not generally realized that the SPD had in fact very extensive interests of its own and was indirectly an entrepreneur on a large scale. By 1914 the party already owned a large number of newspapers; after 1945 when the British authorities gave licences to representatives of German parties to establish newspapers in the British zone, the SPD retained the ownership of most of these licences so that the licensee only acted as a trustee on the party's behalf. While large fortunes were accumulated by some individual licensees of other parties, in the SPD's case the party itself thus received the benefit of the growth in value of the newspapers in question. These newspaper companies and others outside what had been the British zone joined in the SPD's servicing company *Konzentration G.m.b.H.*; between them they employed 15,000 persons and accounted for some 10 per cent. of the total West German newspaper circulation. *Konzentration G.m.b.H.* had its own firm of newsprint importers and suppliers and, in addition, administered the premises owned by the party. In accordance with the party statutes these enterprises were obliged to contribute an annual sum fixed by the party Executive as 'contributions for public relations'. With an annual turnover of over £12 million it was not difficult for them to provide the party with £40,000 every year.[1]

The item 'Election contributions', on the other hand, comprised collections made specifically for the campaign, the proceeds of the sale of campaign stamps, payments made into the publicly advertised 'campaign account', and payments made on the blank 'campaign cheques' (naming the party as payee) which candidates and organizers presented to individuals and to business firms for their signature. It is not fanciful to suppose that a membership which year in year out paid £600,000 in ordinary membership dues should also have contributed an appreciable share of the not much greater total cost of the election. But certainly a substantial proportion of these funds also came in large single amounts from business firms, and legal persons of various kinds accounted for some of the medium-sized contributions.

A certain clue to the sources of the SPD's other financial backing may perhaps be found in the way in which the party financed the issue of its Yearbook of 1956/7. This carried a detachable appendix of 160 pages of advertisements, about 90 pages being bought by local governments with SPD majorities and by their municipal works, 20 pages bought by private industrial firms, 10 by trade unions, 10 by newspapers and publishing houses, and the remainder by miscellaneous advertisers such as co-operative, insurance, and funeral societies (as well as British European Airways). Contrary to the impression current in some circles, the SPD hotly denied that the co-operative societies and similar banking and insurance institutions played any appreciable role in financing its campaign.

Conclusion

It is at least as easy to condemn the system of party finance practised in Western Germany as it is to attack the systems evolved in other countries.[2] Where some parties are concerned description without comment might even seem sufficient criticism in itself. Yet the system must be seen against the background from which it grew. Given the reluctance of German electors to join a party after their experiences from 1933 until 1949 and given also the state of the law, the Civic and Sponsors' Associations were perhaps not the worst solution of the problem, though no one would claim them to be the

[1] The party also ran a workers' travel agency, but lack of adequate profits prevented this from making any appreciable contribution to party funds.

[2] For a brief note on the British practice see R. T. Mackenzie, *British Political Parties*, Heinemann, London, 1955, pp. 594–7.

best. But then the law is not so much a datum of the situation as an instrument for regulating it. Whether the law should be changed, whether parties should be made to reveal the size and sources of their funds, whether something like the British system of restricting campaign expenditure could be introduced, and whether such reforms would really result in unmixed advantage—these are a cluster of questions that exceeds the scope of the present study.

XI

THE CHURCHES, TRADE UNIONS, AND OTHER INTEREST GROUPS

PREVIOUS chapters have described the indirect intervention of the West German business community in the election campaign: trade associations, individual firms, and *ad hoc* groupings bore a very important part of the expenses incurred by the party organizations, and in addition they financed and operated parallel campaigns of their own. Their direct intervention, on the other hand, appears to have been less significant than in 1953: and indeed there was a general decline in the influence which primarily non-political organizations attempted to exert as compared with the previous Bundestag election. Both the Trade Union Federation and the Social Democrats noted the greater neutrality of the trade unions; both the Roman Catholic organizations and the CDU agreed that the Catholic Church had taken a smaller part in this campaign than in previous ones since the war. But even this reduced non-party participation in the campaign represents (except for the trade unions) a remarkable contrast to British practice, and was indeed one of the most interesting phenomena of the election.

Religious Observance

Undoubtedly the most important of these primarily non-political bodies were the Churches, whose active membership was also the largest of any such organization in Western Germany. Church-going is no sufficient index of either faith or works, but the criterion of active church membership is the most relevant to the present purpose, and it is worth noting that while in Britain perhaps less than 15 per cent. of the population will be found in church on any Sunday, the figure in Western Germany would seem to be nearly twice as large.

A sharp distinction must however be made between the denominations. In the Germany of 1937 about two-thirds of the population had been Protestant and about one-third Catholic. We have already noted that the division of Germany resulted in a sharply different ratio in the post-war Federal Republic: 51 per cent. of the population were taxpaying members of the Evangelical Churches, 45 per cent.

of the Catholic Church, and the remaining 4 per cent. belonged to other or no denominations.[1] The statistics would suggest that 50 or 60 per cent. of the nominal Catholics attended church 'regularly'—which in the case of Catholics tended to mean once a week—but even a slightly lower figure would still be worthy of note. Hardly 10 per cent. of Protestants in the towns and 20 per cent. in the villages attended church 'regularly'—at least once a month in their case. Sixty or 70 per cent. of Catholics and perhaps 20 per cent. of Protestants claimed to take Holy Communion at least once a year.[2]

The main reasons for the spectacular contrast in active religious observance were largely structural. The high proportion of Catholics in the population is what chiefly raises the national average of church-going figures so far above the British, and the virtual equality in the numbers of nominal members of both denominations may also add to the zeal displayed on both sides. As in Britain, the habit of church-going is stronger in small communities and rural areas;

[1] Church taxes were collected by the State and passed on to the authorities of the denomination of which the taxpayer declared himself a member. The Evangelical Church disliked the term 'Protestant' on the grounds that it had a positive doctrine of its own. In view of the very different meaning of the word 'Evangelical' in English, the word 'Protestant' is, however, used elsewhere in this study except where specific reference is made to the Evangelical Churches themselves. Similarly the term 'Catholic' is used for brevity's sake instead of 'Roman Catholic' without thereby implying any reflection on the Catholicism of the Church of England.

[2] Erich Reigrotzki, *Soziale Verflechtungen in der Bundesrepublik*, Mohr, Tübingen, 1956, pp. 19 and 26 ff.; Erich Peter Neumann and Elisabeth Noelle, *Antworten, Politik im Kraftfeld der öffentlichen Meinung*, Demoskopie, Allensbach, 1955, p. 89. These figures refer to the years 1952 and 1953; that they remained valid is suggested by the figures for December 1956 published in Elisabeth Noelle and Erich Peter Neumann, *Jahrbuch der öffentlichen Meinung 1957*, p. 29. These are the figures quoted in the text. The figures for Catholics shown on the basis of a church census (in *Kirchliches Handbuch: Amtliches statistisches Jahrbuch der Katholischen Kirche Deutschlands*, Bachem, Cologne, 1956, pp. 357–61) lie about 10 per cent. below those quoted by the public opinion polls, but make no adjustment for the infirm and those otherwise prevented from church-going on the particular Sundays in question, so that they tend on the whole to confirm the polling results. For the British figures compare the forthcoming study by Michael Argyle, *Religious Behaviour*, Routledge & Kegan Paul, London, 1959. Unlike the Catholic authorities, the Evangelical Church, at least at the time of writing, has published no figures of church attendance. (For the reasons why church attendance figures are not published compare the article by Oberkirchenrat Dr. Zieger, 'Statistik des Gottesdienstbesuches', in *Evangelische Welt*, 16 June 1957.) Information supplied direct by the Office of the Representative of the Evangelical Church to the Federal Government and by the Church Statistical Office suggests that not more than 8 per cent. of nominal church members can be found attending a service on any ordinary Sunday, and that the number of those who attend with some regularity at least once a month lies only in the region of 10 per cent. of adults in the large towns and 20 per cent. in the smaller villages.

since one-third of the West German population lives in communities of less than 3,000 inhabitants this introduces a further social factor making for a high percentage of religious observance.

But over and above such structural factors there is evidence that the events since 1933 allowed the Churches to grow in conscious reaction against the period of persecution, in national defeat and amid personal tragedy.[1] This same experience of Nazi domination and the disasters that followed it evoked among large sections of the Protestant Churches the conviction that to limit their activities to the care of souls might be to commit once more those sins of omission to which they had publicly confessed after the war. The Catholic Church, too, in its concern to fight Communism and to prevent another disaster, was determined to return to its long tradition of political activity and to exercise its influence again not only on purely educational and family matters but also on general social and hence economic policy and—especially after West European unity came to offer an ideal with a particular appeal to Catholics—in foreign affairs as well.

The Catholic Church

At the end of the second world war and immediately afterwards few organizations except those of Christians and of Socialists possessed the confidence of the occupying powers as they marched into Germany. Particularly in the rural areas the clergy were often consulted on the personnel to whom local civilian administration should be entrusted, and in any case there was a large reservoir of able Catholics ready to take over the tasks of local government. With the growth of the new political system 'from the bottom upwards' the Catholics who had shouldered responsibilities in the first period of post-war confusion naturally rose from this ground floor and came to take part in the wider affairs of the new Länder and finally in the establishment of the Federal Republic.

During the period of persecution under the Third Reich the links between the clergy and the politically conscious laity increased in intimacy, and in the early months of the occupation it was sometimes

[1] 'In 1935 Church attendance, Easter Communion and annual communion in Germany reached their highest level since the beginning of church statistics in 1915 . . . all three percentages fell considerably until the year 1946, but they then recovered steadily and constantly until the year 1952. . . . Considering the great pastoral burdens preceding the second world war, during that war, and after it (refugees from the East, expellees, destroyed churches, lack of priests), these figures, particularly in comparison with those of other countries, may be described as not unsatisfactory' (*Kirchliches Handbuch*, p. 357).

the clergy who became the spokesmen for the local population *vis-à-vis* the occupying powers. The support of the Church for the inter-denominational CDU as against the resurrected Centre Party was initially perhaps as much of an experiment as a very deliberate long-term decision: but at least from August 1945 it was given whole-heartedly—Cardinal Archbishop Frings of Cologne became a member of the party for several years—and the relationship then established has never broken down since.

In the CDU the Church now felt it saw the men who were active members of its own flock and who shared its concern for Christian morals and for the realization of a Christian social order; in the CDU's foreign policy it saw the strongest defence against any further territorial advance of Communist materialism; and from the CDU it could expect the most favourable treatment of its own special concerns in schools legislation and in such administrative questions as tended to arise in the relationship between Church and State on the local, Land, and federal level. The CDU recognized the enduring validity of the Concordat of 1933 concluded between the National Socialist Reich Government and the Vatican and wished to see it implemented by the Länder, whom the Basic Law had given sole responsibility in religious and schools questions.[1] The SPD and FDP had contested the validity of the Concordat and continued to oppose its implementation by the Länder. It would be difficult to assign any particular weight to each of these various considerations that linked the Church and the CDU.[2] This was not a functional alliance, but a long-standing relationship of mutual trust.

The SPD, on the other hand, was extremely suspect from the Church's point of view. It was Marxist, materialist, and godless in its origins. A spirit of hostility to the Church as such was still constantly reappearing in pronouncements made at lower levels of the party's organization, and like the Free Democrats the Social Democrats violently opposed the Church's attempts to influence political

[1] The *Reichskonkordat* laid down, *inter alia*, that denominational schools (over whose personnel and religious instruction the bishop must be consulted and had a certain veto right) must be set up where there was a reasonable demand, and that —provided a corresponding agreement was reached with the Protestant Churches— the Catholic clergy would take no part in political life. In a judgment delivered on 26 Mar. 1957 the Constitutional Court ruled that the Basic Law did not supersede the Concordat, but 'left it to the Länder to decide on their own responsibility and by their own free decision how they would shape their schools legislation in view of the fact that the Federal Republic of Germany was bound by international law to observe the *Reichskonkordat*'. For the full text of this complex decision of the Constitutional Court see its document 2 BvG 1/55.

[2] In the words of an official of the Central Committee of German Catholics: 'You might as well ask me why I married my wife.'

affairs. In a whole range of concrete issues such as the denominational character of State schools the SPD was obstructing what the Church regarded as the vital interests of its members, and like any organized group the Church felt not only a right but a duty to warn its members against parties that might violate their concerns. Both because of their foreign policy and because of their essentially secular spirit the Free Democrats seemed no less dangerous than the Social Democrats themselves.[1]

Just as the CDU tended to feel that it was part of its function to see that the demands of the Church received a fair hearing from the State, so the bulk of the clergy felt that the CDU should receive the support of their congregations. The over 11 million Catholics to be found at Mass on any Sunday all the year round included a quarter of the West German electorate.[2] However illegitimate the comparison, it might well be said that not all the German politicians put together could secure anything like as large a personal audience as the Catholic clergy could command every Sunday of the year, and the 3 to 5 million Catholics who were adherents of Catholic organizations (including youth groups) represented a membership total ten or twenty times as great as that of the CDU. The influence of the Church on the election could therefore be substantial; and its clear stand made it a major force on the side of the Government—both between elections and during the campaign.

The first episcopal pronouncement on the election came in early July. The Bishop of Münster in a widely publicized address stated that electoral rights implied electoral duties, and the exercise of these duties was 'a question of conscience and not a question of purely political judgement'.[3] In accordance with the encyclical *Quadragesimo anno* a Catholic could not be a socialist, the SPD was still of its essence a socialist party and therefore neither a Catholic worker nor any believing Catholic could reconcile it with his conscience to vote for it. Moreover 'You will already have felt that the SPD is not the

[1] Indeed after the election an influential Jesuit from the Vatican told the Social Democrats at a conference called to consider their relationship to the Church that Catholic objections to their party were based not on its socialist, but on its liberal principles: 'If the Pope concludes that every type of socialism is incompatible with the doctrine of the Church, it is in the last resort because of the conception of socialism as a laïcist secularising form of proletarian Liberalism' (Gustav Grundlach, S.J., 'Katholizismus und Sozialismus', in *Christentum und demokratischer Sozialismus*, Zink, Munich, 1958, p. 23).

[2] Compare the remark made by an Italian socialist minister after the Easter blessing of 1956: 'We may not think much of the Pope, but we certainly envy him the audiences that turn up for his meetings!'

[3] Dr. Michael Keller, Bishop of Münster, *Bischofsworte zu aktuellen Zeitfragen: Kann ein Katholik sozialistisch wählen?*, KAB, Recklinghausen, 1957.

only party to which we cannot give our approval'. It was not clear even to experts whether this statement was delivered as part of the bishop's pastoral functions or not; but whatever the position in canon law, the impression was certainly created that a vote for the SPD or FDP would be a matter for confession.

While one or two individual bishops were thus prepared to speak out very clearly this did not seem a unanimous policy when the bishops met for two days in June to consider their attitude to the political questions of the day. Indeed it is possible that the sharp reaction provoked by the Bishop of Münster's early, very definite stand made the rest of the hierarchy even more cautious in its pronouncements. At any rate the pastoral letter read in all Catholic churches on the Sunday before the election was phrased in more general terms than the pastoral letter of 1953. Dated 30 August 1957, it quoted the Pope:

> It is clear that the voice of conscience commands every upright Catholic to cast his vote for that candidate or that list which offers truly adequate guarantees for the protection of the rights of God, of the family and of society in accordance with God's law and the Christian doctrine of morals.

and exhorted the faithful:

> Do your electoral duty!
>
> Only vote for men and women whose basic Christian principles are well known and whose public activity corresponds to these principles.

This pastoral letter was commented on in many churches, in which the Sunday sermons had in any case often touched upon questions of civic duty for some weeks before.

It was usual in the villages and the small towns for the local priests to appear at CDU meetings (where they were often specially welcomed) and not to attend the meetings of other parties. Catholic politicians were invited to deliver frankly political speeches just after or even before the episcopal blessing at a pilgrimage, a Catholic congress, and at similar church functions. Such juxtapositions of religious ceremonial and political personalities were part of the traditional social pattern in many parts of Western Germany. The Opposition attacked it as 'clerical interference', but in doing so they directed their fire against old local customs rather than any deliberate new political initiatives on the part of the Church.

It was only occasionally that children were told in scripture classes to remind their parents that they must vote for Adenauer, that priests made political or personal attacks on candidates of parties other than the CDU in or out of the pulpit, and that CDU posters were displayed in church porches or CDU pamphlets found among the devotional literature sold or distributed inside or outside the churches after Mass. With some 20,000 Catholics in Holy Orders in the Federal Republic, it was only natural that some were more active in their advice to their flock than others, and both the Free and the Social Democrats saw to it that publicity was given to those cases where they felt unfair use had been made of supernatural sanctions or ecclesiastical authority to influence the voter at the polls.[1]

Such cases were, however, the exception and not the rule. Indeed it may be asked how far the correlation of active Catholicism with a vote for the CDU is really dependent on the specific public declarations of the hierarchy or even of the parish priest. The religious influence on voting behaviour is a structural datum of German politics; and given the usual exhortations to vote, the influence of the Church can hardly be adduced to explain the outcome of one particular election as against the rest. The faithful understood and mostly shared the support of the Church for Adenauer and his party regardless of particular pronouncements, and the social position of the priest as a leader of public opinion, particularly in the villages, may even have made overt public declarations in favour of one party largely unnecessary. They might raise the turnout at the polls, but they also immediately roused anti-clerical cries. Indeed one explanation offered by Catholic circles for the pronouncements made during the 1957 election was simply this: that they were expected by the faithful, and that it would have been taken as a sign of something amiss if they had not come.

Catholic Organizations

The declarations of the clergy in their role as teachers and as spiritual and moral advisers to the faithful were, however, only one of the ways in which the influence of Catholicism was felt during the

[1] Among the incidents thus publicized was the reply given to a questioner by a priest who on principle used forceful expressions as a pastoral technique: 'Come here you dirty dog (*Schweinehund*), as a priest I shall not be ashamed of seizing you by the throat.' One Bavarian Don Camillo denounced the Social Democrats from the pulpit as 'red devils', 'red bloodhounds', and 'red swine', and declared after the service that they should all be strung up. Another priest, adapting the Italian warning that 'God can see you in the ballot booth—Togliatti can't', declared that God went into the ballot booth with each voter, and one Sunday sermon was reported to have urged the faithful to vote for Christian candidates on the grounds that they —unlike non-Christian politicians—could by divine grace foresee the future. A church magazine on the Sunday before the election carried a 'Socialist creed' beginning, 'I believe in Karl Marx, the mighty creator and father of freedom and socialism; and in my party leader, his son our Lord, who has conceived the socialist spirit . . .', while another church magazine wrote: 'In the last resort it is a decision between God and Satan.'

election. The work of individual Catholics, laymen and clergy, acting on their own initiative in the political field hardly requires elaborate discussion. But a further type of activity gave rise to much misunderstanding: that of the various Catholic organizations which marshalled their members to canvass votes for a political party over and above their voting for it themselves.

An almost all-embracing range of Catholic organizations was rebuilt in Western Germany after the war and practically every activity in a Catholic's life 'from the cradle to the grave' that calls for formal group membership can be exercised within a Catholic group. There are Catholic kindergartens, Catholic schools exist almost everywhere and are fully maintained by a number of Länder, there is a Catholic parents' organization, and there are professional groupings such as Catholic young farmers' leagues, Catholic traders' associations, and a society of Catholic publicists. The reading of Catholic newspapers is strongly encouraged by the clergy, and these papers are supplied with news by the Catholic news agency KNA (*Katholische Nachrichtenagentur*). The general attempt to set up Catholic bodies rivalling the 'neutral' and 'comprehensive' organizations initiated under occupation auspices in the early days after the war was also carried over into the trade union field in the autumn of 1955 with the re-establishment of a Christian Trade Union Movement, the CGD (*Christlicher Gewerkschaftsverein Deutschlands*) as a competitor to the German Trade Union Federation.

The role of the clergy in these organizations varies roughly with the date of their formation: in the Kolping Family, as one of the earliest, a priest is head of the organization, in the League of Catholic Women—almost a suffragette offshoot of the Catholic movement—the priest is little more than a chaplain. Where the president of the organization was not a priest he was frequently a member of the Bundestag or occupied some other political position—his political work often arising out of his social concern.

Where such a close personal link existed between a Catholic organization and a CDU candidate, the Catholic organization tended naturally to give its assistance to its officer in the election. Several Catholic organizations—but with only a few hundred thousand members between them—prepared for the election contest on a federal basis and a good deal was heard of them during the election. The rest remained quiescent except on a local level, issuing perhaps an appeal to their members to vote but not arranging for them to take part in any electioneering activities as a body. Little more need be said here of such organizations; it is the few active ones that require further description. Chief among them were the Catholic Workers' Movement and the Kolping Family.

The Catholic Workers' Movement (*Katholische Arbeiterbewegung*—KAB) had one CDU member of the Bundestag for its Chairman and another for its General Secretary; it took a very direct part in the work of electioneering. Four-fifths of its 150,000 members were concentrated in the three dioceses of Münster, Paderborn, and Cologne, so that they represented an appreciable body of helpers in North Rhine–Westphalia; a fortnight before polling day 15,000 of them from the diocese of Cologne went on a pilgrimage to the shrine of Our Lady of Neviges to pray for a happy outcome of the election.

The KAB's fortnightly organ, *Ketteler Wacht*, sent free to all members, printed highly political banner headlines and front-page leading articles in almost every 1957 issue until after the election, using such titles as 'Election Strategy' and 'After the Victory'. The KAB also put out a special pamphlet for its members analysing Landtag and Bundestag election results in each constituency of the Länder in which it was strong:

> We must now investigate where the causes of the advances of the SPD and other parties lie. We must ask ourselves where we have ourselves failed and how far immoderate criticisms, slogan propaganda and misrepresentation by political opponents have led to signs of disintegration in our own ranks.[1]

Thirty members of the KAB were elected to the third Bundestag, six of them full-time officials, and the KAB felt it necessary to declare afterwards that it had not been among those groups which had demanded special recognition in the distribution of cabinet posts.[2]

The German Kolping Family, which until 1933 was called the 'League of Catholic Artisan Journeymen', might be regarded as the upper working- or lower middle-class equivalent of the KAB. The Kolping Family had over 2,500 local branches in Western Germany and around 210,000 members—nearly as many in the CDU. Since half of these members were young unmarried men, the Kolping Family was able to give the CDU very active support, or rather:

> the Kolping Family does not itself participate in the election campaign, but its members do . . . naturally our Kolping Houses will put premises at their disposal for the purpose.

[1] *Wählen heisst Wägen, Die Ergebnisse der bedeutendsten Wahlen seit 1948 in Nordrhein-Weslphalen, Hessen, Niedersachsen und Rheinland-Pfalz*, KAB, Cologne, 1957, p. 3.

[2] *Ketteler Wacht*, 15 Nov. 1957, p. 2.

Kolping sons could win floating voters by three methods: by argument, by influencing the general climate of opinion, and by pressure:

> Glowing optimism must be exuded by those who want to win over others. . . . Anyway, who can say how an election will end? There have been the wildest surprises in the past. So why give up hope? . . . Only the carcass merchant cares for dead dogs. . . . Our watchword must be: posters at every corner, leaflets in every hand and everywhere meetings and demonstrations that get talked about.

Pressure was not ordinarily a method open to Christians:

> But one means of pressure can sometimes be legitimate and lead to good results: namely fear. Fear of Communism, of political adventures and of unreliable individuals can undoubtedly keep a people out of dangerous experiments.[1]

Kolping sons formed an important contingent of the CDU's stewards in the Rhineland, the organization held meetings of its own, such as one of 10,000 people in Dortmund addressed by Arnold, and the only precise description of the British system of canvassing and knocking up supporters to be publicized as a model during the election by anyone but the SPD was that issued as a guide to the Kolping Family.

The Kolping Family (which, like many other youth organizations, received a grant from the publicity funds of the Ministry of Defence) was specially thanked by the Chancellor on the day after the election for its work. Thirty-two of its members entered the Bundestag. Since eleven of them were simultaneously members of the KAB, the combined strength in the Bundestag of these two organizations thus consisted of fifty-four members. The bulk or all of them were simultaneously members of the 'Social Committees' of the Christian Democratic Workers (CDA), to which a number of Protestant workers' representatives in the CDU parliamentary party also belonged. (These 'Social Committees' constituted the principal organized expression of what was usually referred to as the 'left wing' of the CDU.)

While the Catholic Workers' Movement and the Kolping Family were the most active throughout their organizations, other bodies did election work only on a local basis or confined themselves to appealing to their own members. The Catholic Men's Organization (*Katholisches Männerwerk*) declared that it was and remained untied

[1] Theo Rempe, 'Kolpingsfamilie und Bundestagswahl', in *Erbe und Aufgabe, Führungszeitschrift der deutschen Kolpingsfamilie*, no. 44/2 of May 1957.

to any party, but that in the decision at the polls it pledged itself to Adenauer. 'All the world over, Catholic men in particular expect us to stand by him in loyalty.'[1] The Central Committee of German Catholics, which grouped some 300 Catholic organizations, issued a guarded but unequivocal appeal: 'God will demand an account of your electoral decision also. Examine whether the parties that ask for your votes are capable of understanding and fulfilling the demands made by our conscience, ask yourselves whether for them God is the Lord also of our time.'[2]

It would be tedious to multiply the instances in which election appeals were issued by existing Catholic organizations. In addition, new organizations were set up in one or two dioceses specifically in order to influence the election. Thus in the diocese of Münster the 'Working Group of Catholic Organizations' (claiming half a million active members in the diocese) set up an organization called *Aktion '57* which was to hold meetings, distribute leaflets, and 'help create the proper confident atmosphere among the Catholic people' to return Adenauer's Government to power.

The Church press, with a weekly edition of 10 million copies, attuned itself carefully to the Government's election campaign. On 26 and 27 June the Committee of Editors of the Church Press Group held a two-day meeting in Bonn to discuss 'questions of political principle in the face of the coming Bundestag election'. They were addressed by Adenauer and by Strauss and inspected a tank and an artillery battalion of the Bundeswehr. As the Government Press and Information Office afterwards reported: 'The main theme for the month of August in the Catholic Church press is the Bundestag election of the 15th September. Detailed reports highlight the great achievements of the present Government in all domains.'[3] Pictures of Adenauer, Professor Aigner's poster drawing of him, articles by cabinet ministers, and CDU party advertisements could be found in many of the large church papers and of the smaller church magazines.

The Catholic Church press concentrated its attacks on the SPD almost exclusively on its foreign policy and on its 'godless attitude' drawn from Marx and Engels. In domestic policy very little was said except on concerns that affected the Church's position in a very

[1] *Mann in der Zeit*, Sept. 1957.

[2] When the Social Democrats interpreted this wording as 'a hand held out to the SPD' they received a sharp rebuff: 'They do not even hesitate to misuse and misinterpret for their purpose the appeal of the Central Committee of German Catholics.' (*So sind sie wirklich*, Cologne, 1957—a 32-page pamphlet issued against the SPD on behalf of an important church dignitary.)

[3] *Spiegel der katholischen Kirchenpresse*, 31 Aug., p. 5.

immediate way, in particular on the schools question.[1] *Mann in der Zeit*, a monthly newspaper with an edition of 575,000 copies published on behalf of the German bishops and sold at church doors after Sunday mass, printed moderate but distinctly personal attacks on individual SPD and FDP leaders, and a supplement issued in Greven to the official organ of the Kolping Family compared SPD leaders to Vyshinsky in their duplicity. Different organs of the Catholic press were geared to the election campaign to a different degree, but no active Catholic can have been ignorant of what was expected of him. Finally, in the light of all the evidence thus presented, Catholics were advised to ask themselves with due care: 'How will I wish to have acted in the hour of my death, face to face with God sitting in judgement?'[2]

Criticisms of Political Catholicism during the Campaign

A great many believing Catholics were profoundly disturbed by these political activities. The city priest who took great care always to have a Social Democrat on his parish council in order that 'a social democratic worker is not forced on his death-bed to send for a priest whom he regards as a party enemy'[3] was concerned with one side of the problem. Men with as acute a sensitivity to all shortcomings in post-war Germany as Walter Dirks and the small circle round the *Frankfurter Hefte* felt that not ideological roots—whatever they might be—but their fruits in policy were what mattered:

> For many Konrad Adenauer is the Christian state leader sent by God, for others he is a clever seducer who has been largely responsible for the fact that the German people has chosen a less Christian way than God offered to it in the opportunity of its defeat. . . . The rearmament policy of the Chancellor is at the heart of the electoral decision. . . . How can one really go so far as to bring pressure to bear on the conscience of those who trust Carlo Schmid and Elisabeth Lüders more in this matter than Franz-Josef Strauss?[4]

If practising Catholics close to the CDU were unhappy about the Church's intervention in the election, it goes without saying that further opposition came from other groups: from practising Catholics

[1] The *Neue Bildpost* of 1 Sept. was, however, not alone in adding at least one issue of doctrine by quoting an SPD report of 1947: 'Woman must be accepted unconditionally as the life and love companion of man . . . the invention and spread of good contraceptive devices must be furthered.'

[2] *Paulinus*, 15 Sept. 1957.

[3] W. D., 'Die Kirchen und die CDU', in *Frankfurter Hefte*, June 1957, p. 378.

[4] Ibid., pp. 380 and 381. Elisabeth Lüders was the senior FDP member of the Bundestag and (in view of the Chancellor's unwillingness to accept that honour) its *doyenne d'âge*.

in the SPD who felt that they were being thrust into a moral dilemma; from practising Protestants in the CDU who feared that their party might thereby come to be stamped as a denominational one; and from those who were neither Catholics nor CDU supporters and who felt that democracy itself might be menaced by the alliance of the Church with the governing party.

The Catholic Working Groups of the SPD's League of Christian Socialists issued a declaration that the pronouncements of the bishops could have been made only out of a false view of modern democratic socialism, and Helene Wessel claimed that the Vatican did not regard the British Labour Party as socialist in the sense condemned in the papal encyclicals.

When the Evangelical Groups (*Arbeitskreise*) of the CDU met in Kassel at the end of June, strong misgivings were expressed over the intervention of Catholic dignitaries in the political campaign. Dr. Otto Schmidt, a Bundestag candidate and a former North-Rhine Westphalian minister, freely admitted that

> the SPD has undergone a change . . . it is in our interests that Christians who are convinced by the social and economic conceptions of Social Democracy should be able, for the sake of democracy and of the future of our people, to find their home in the SPD without prejudice to their church ties.

Warning against anything that might make the CDU seem a Catholic party and tend to make the SPD a Protestant one, he stressed the need even for liberal forces within the CDU, since 'neither a state-directed Christianity nor an ecclesiastically directed State are aims worthy of a Christian democratic party today'.[1] Liberals and others in the CDU also expressed their concern that they should receive such conspicuous support from the Catholic Church, and Gerstenmaier—himself an ordained Evangelical theologian—speculated whether the word 'Christian' should not be dropped from the party label.

Members of the Evangelical Church who stood outside the CDU expressed themselves even more strongly. The *Sonntagsblatt* published by the Evangelical Bishop Hanns Lilje felt it its duty to warn against 'the hypocrites who want to cover the nakedness of their political decisions with a cloak of piety' and to remind them of the second commandment: 'Thou shalt not take the name of the Lord thy God in vain.'[2]

The most emphatic protest against what they recognized as a most powerful and regarded as an entirely illegitimate influence on

[1] Otto Schmidt, *Die geschichtlichen Kräfte des deutschen Protestantismus und unser politischer Auftrag* (multigraphed text), pp. 5, 6, and 14.

[2] *Sonntagsblatt*, 7 July.

the electorate naturally come from the other parties. Little purpose is served by printing a selection of the often quite immoderate anti-clerical reaction to the apparent identification of the Church and party, though several of them were picked out for the limelight by Catholic publications. Thus the SPD's cabaret *Next One, Please* quipped: 'The hooks of the hooked cross [swastika] have gone, but the cross remains', and the organ of the SPD's youth organization 'The Falcons' called the Pope 'a very little manikin'. In *Der Spiegel*, on the other hand, 'Jens Daniel' (believed to be the Free Democratic owner, Rudolf Augstein) turned his wrath on the party rather than on the Church:

> Very old people have told us that even in the Kaiser's day the servility towards the sovereign in Berlin did not take on as bizarre and despicable forms as the utter hypocrisy, the piety calculated according to denominational arithmetic and displayed for career purposes, that is flaunted in Bonn. . . . The economic miracle, with the help and applause of prelates and moderators, has made of [the CDU] a monster of disingenuous mentality, a bastard of so-called occidental spirit and tax reductions for export. They talk of God and mean their racket.[1]

To those not used to the ways and aware of the problems of political Catholicism, the intervention of the Church in elections may seem to be a fit subject for rather simple cut-and-dried value judgements of the kind in which *Der Spiegel* felt free to indulge. But neither the SPD's cry of a misuse of religion for political purposes nor the FDP's picture of a party misused for ecclesiastical purposes quite did justice to the complexity of the problem.

If we wish to look at their activities through the eyes of the actors themselves we must in fact discard the categories of Church and party and concentrate on the responsibilities of the individual. For the clergy there was no reason why voting should be an exception to the duty of the faithful to obedience on doctrinal and moral issues, and they felt obliged to speak very clearly:

> Given the present deadly threat to humanity by atheist Communism and practical materialism, the Church would be failing in its holy duty in a decisive hour if it were to be silent or if it were to speak only on fundamental questions and thus seem equivocal or unintelligible to many.[2]

Much the same was true of many lay members of the Church working in the various Catholic organizations and involved in the day-to-day issues in which the CDU would be the most helpful

[1] *Der Spiegel*, 12 June 1957, p. 10, in the editorial entitled '. . . Und meinen Kattun'. (Literally: 'They talk of God and mean cotton'—originally a comment on British colonialism.)

[2] *Katholisches Sonntagsblatt*, 11 Aug. 1957.

party and the one in which their own leading members had considerable influence. Many of them had come to the CDU through their Catholic activities and they regarded their combination of political office with their leadership in Catholic organizations as all of one piece and derived from the same spiritual source. It was thus easy for them to dispute the existence of any valid distinction between associations for political and associations for social purposes. It was, after all, of the very essence of Christian democracy to seek an integration of all these spheres simultaneously in terms of human relations governed by the message of the gospels applied in the context of modern society.

The Protestant Churches

The 'Evangelical Church in Germany', founded as a single organization in 1948, remained a confederation of twenty-seven Land Churches: eleven otherwise independent Churches, the ten Churches of the Lutheran Church of Germany (*Vereinigte Evangelisch-Lutherische Kirche Deutschlands*) and the six Churches of the United Church (*Evangelische Kirche der Union*).[1] Varying in size from 90,000 to nearly 5 million members and from twenty to over a thousand pastors these twenty-seven Land Churches enjoyed internal autonomy and freedom in matters affecting doctrine and liturgy. On the basis of the Augsburg compromise *cuius regio eius religio*, each of them had its own clearly defined geographical sphere of competence. But this organizational patchwork only obscured a substantial unity of outlook in which the Lutheran element seemed to be dominant. Indeed it may well be said that the Evangelical Churches of Germany have never in their history been so united as after the second world war. This essential church unity deserves to be stressed although the

[1] The formal membership of these Churches is estimated to have been roughly as follows in 1954 (in millions of members):

	Western Germany	*West Berlin*	*Democratic Republic and East Berlin*	*Total*
Ten member Churches of the Lutheran Church	10·0	. .	7·5	17·5
Six member Churches of the United Church	6·4	1·6	7·5	15·5
Eleven other Land Churches . .	8·7	. .	0·5	9·2
All twenty-seven Land Churches of the Evangelical Church in Germany .	25·1	1·6	15·5	42·2

differences between the members of the Evangelical Churches were not confined to theological doctrine, but also to be found in the conception which individual members of the component Churches had of the role which they as Christians should play in political life.

Indeed their experiences under the National Socialist régime led to a partial 'horizontal' split that cut across the theological and geographical barriers. When after 1933 the 'German Christians' took over the official church government except in Hanover and the South, a 'Confessing Church' organized its 'Brethren's Councils' (*Bruderräte*) in opposition to the official church government. Without the income derived from church taxes and without official authority these Brethren's Councils secured wide acceptance for their decisions in spiritual matters, and organized unofficial seminaries, examinations, and appointments to curacies on the voluntary contributions of its members who carried the 'red card' of the Confessing Church. Karl Barth's theology and the leadership of men like Pastor Niemöller have kept their concern with Christian action in world affairs alive even after the Confessing Church as such declared its emergency powers extinct in 1948.

But there was also a fairly wide range of attitudes on this question in the Evangelical Church. There were some who feared that too great an involvement by what they termed the 'welfare Christians' in the day-to-day satisfaction of man's desire 'not so much for a merciful God as for a merciful neighbour' might obscure the mission of the Church to be 'interested in the first place in men's salvation, and in their welfare only for that reason',[1] and who, while they might share the feeling of Christian responsibility for the future of society, are more reserved on the methods by which Christians as such should affect the world.

It would be a mistake to over-estimate this divergence of views in the Evangelical Church on the question of political action. On one subject at any rate its members were all but unanimous: that the Church should do whatever it could to bridge the gulf between Eastern and Western Germany. Although only eight of the twenty-seven Land Churches were principally situated east of the zonal border, their membership accounted for some 40 per cent. of that of the Evangelical Church in Germany. Developments in the Democratic Republic thus necessarily took up as much of the attention of that Church as those in Western Germany, the 'elections' in Eastern Germany earlier in 1957 were as important to it as the West German elections in September, and in its activities the Evangelical Church

[1] Propst Asmussen, quoted in Karl Thieme, 'Die Lage der evangelischen Landeskirchen in Deutschland', in *Kirchliches Handbuch*, p. 495.

was forced constantly to have regard to the attitudes of two German governments and not only of one. Its concern particularly with the fate of the population of the Democratic Republic and with the future of German unity made its German Evangelical Church Congresses (*Deutsche Evangelische Kirchentage*) of great significance on both sides of the zonal border. Hundreds of thousands of Evangelical Christians from the Democratic as well as from the Federal Republic united in prayer and discussion under mottoes such as 'Yet we are brethren' and it was a great disappointment to the Evangelical Church that its congress planned for 1957 in Thuringia could not be held as a result of the attitude taken up by the East German Government.[1]

As there was no unanimity of views on the extent to which Protestant churchmen should be politically active, so also there was a divergence of tendencies when they did decide to enter the political field. Many of them did so, particularly in the early years after the war, out of their concern never to repeat what they had formally confessed to have been sins of omission during Hitler's rise and at least his earlier years in power, when too many of them, they felt, had for too long remained prisoners of an uncritical interpretation of Lutheran tradition and neglected the problem of the Christian's attitude to a non-Christian State. The individual decisions taken after the war cannot be classified according to neat rules, though perhaps Lutherans often tended to take up a position on the more conservative, the few Reformed and some of the United churchmen perhaps on the less conservative side of German politics. At any rate Protestant laymen and clergy were scattered over the main parties of the Federal Republic, and leading ordained and lay members of the Evangelical Church sat on the CDU and on the SPD benches (as well as in the Speaker's chair) of the second Bundestag.

In fact there are good reasons for believing that the vocal minority of prominent Evangelical Christians which tended towards the SPD was not matched by any equally important section of ordinary church-attenders. Those who went to church were often apt to be conservative in general outlook and to vote also for a Christian party. Much of the Protestant middle class had come to the CDU as the great party of reconciliation between the two denominations after the defeat of their common oppressors. They were not perhaps

[1] Theological and political doubts have, however, on occasion been voiced within the Protestant Churches that these congresses might give religious sanction to a political aim and that they might by their implications ignore 'the possibility that a prolonged partition of Germany may be your contribution to the peace and unity of Europe' (Ecumenical Commission for European Co-operation, 1951).

always happy about their Catholic allies in the party or about every feature of the party's policy. Yet here for the first time a specifically Christian party in which Protestant Christians played an important part had pursued a fruitful policy and its efforts had been crowned with success. There can indeed be little doubt that the bulk of pastors and of Protestant no less than Catholic church-going Christians intended to vote for the CDU.[1]

It was the church leadership that was rather more divided. Bishop Dibelius of Berlin-Brandenburg was a well-known member of the CDU. Yet many intellectuals, particularly after 1945, had opted for the SPD out of a Christian Socialist ideal. Dr. Adolf Arndt and Pastor Hans Merten were to be found among SPD members of the Bundestag, while another such Bundestag member, Pastor Wenzel, had joined the SPD already in 1930. After 1950 these Christians opposed to the CDU found themselves reinforced by those who feared German rearmament and took a view of reunification policy much closer to that of the SPD than that of Adenauer. Heinemann, who had been President of the Synod of the Evangelical Church from 1948 until 1955, first while Minister of the Interior in Adenauer's Government and then for some years after he had founded the All German People's Party, was by 1953 plainly committed against the CDU, as was Pastor Niemöller, President of the Land Church of Hesse-Nassau. Given these divisions, the attitude of the church leadership to the election was rather less explicit than that of the relatively 'monolithic' Catholic Church.

The potential influence of the Evangelical leaders was in any case limited by the fact that the proportion of the nominal membership which felt any real ties to the Evangelical Church was small. It is unlikely that more than 2 million people at the outside attended even one Evangelical service in the last month before the election. And it is implied in the very spirit of Protestantism that any advice which they might have received there would have been of comparatively minor influence on their voting behaviour.

In fact no organ of the Evangelical Church government issued any statement in support of any of the parties during the election. In one or two Land Churches members were urged to vote, on occasion also to examine carefully the candidates presented to them, and even to remember the objectives of peace and of reunification. But no partisanship can be traced in any of these official declarations.

[1] In so far as the replies to questions put to 314 regular Protestant church-goers in July 1953 are any evidence, some 38 per cent. of them favoured the CDU and only 14 per cent. the SPD, while 29 per cent. gave no definite reply (Reigrotzki, op. cit., p. 133).

Such 'positive neutrality' on the part of the official church organization did not deter individual groupings within the various Land Churches from issuing declarations of their own binding no one but themselves. But their unofficial character, their restricted audience, and the contradictions between them severely limited their effectiveness.

For what little it was worth the support of several Brethren's Councils went to the Social Democrats. But these former organs of the Confessing Church were now no more than small groups of highly active Christians who had no financial or organizational backing in the parishes, and the sharp wording of some of their declarations may have stood in inverse ratio to their influence on the church-going public.[1] One such body in Württemberg declared: 'We as members of the Church are resolved to deny our votes to the CDU at the coming Bundestag election and to reject that party for as long as it is not ready to delete the word "Christian" from its party name.'[2]

Their resolution had hardly been published when another group of ministers and laymen from the same Land Church issued a counter-declaration: 'Not those who call themselves Christian, but those who deny others the right to bear the Christian name commit a slander and discredit their own ecclesiastical name.'[3]

The role played by the Evangelical Churches and their lay members in the election was thus rather different from that played by the Catholic Church. Yet their influence was not for that reason unimportant. The prominent positions some of them occupied in the CDU proved that that party was more than one of Catholic clericalism; the conspicuous presence of men like Heinemann in the SPD prevented the appearance of a country divided between Christians and socialists. Which of the parties gained more from this phenomenon it would be difficult to say; it is also comparatively irrelevant.

[1] Thus the Rhenish, Westphalian, and North-West German Ecclesiastical Brotherhood was perhaps the most explicit: 'The CDU is becoming more and more a Catholic party . . . they wish to leave open the possibility of a military use of nuclear energy. . . . For these reasons we must ask everyone seriously whether they can at the moment take the responsibility of voting for the CDU. It is misleading still to represent the SPD as an atheist party. In these fundamental questions the conduct of the SPD and also that of the FDP has been the more considered and sober. It was therefore indefensible and a poisoning of political life when the Federal Chancellor declared in Nuremberg that a victory of the SPD involved the ruin of Germany.' Similarly in the Palatinate, a 7-point declaration obviously aimed in the same direction was issued against, *inter alia*, 'the renascent spirit of nationalism, militarism and anti-semitism' and against 'clerical and denominationalist tendencies spreading ever more strongly in Church and state'. (See *Junge Kirche*, 10 Aug. 1957, pp. 485–7.)

[2] Declaration of 1 July 1957, reprinted ibid., p. 487.

[3] *Frankfurter Allgemeine Zeitung*, 12 July 1957.

More important is the fact that a large number of leading Protestants—like one or two of the leading Catholics also—even where they deepened the conflict, made it both more earnest and less partisan, and that by their very presence on both sides of the political fence they exercised a healthy influence on the country's politics as a whole.

The Trade Unions, Christian Unionism, and the Campaign

If the political importance of the Churches was greater in Germany than during a British election, the role of the trade unions was of somewhat smaller significance. Only about a third of labour was organized in Western Germany as against nearly half the workers in Britain. Of the 18 million wage and salary earners in Western Germany less than half a million belonged to the purely white-collar German Salaried Workers' Union (*Deutsche Angestelltengewerkschaft*) and the sixteen comprehensive industrial unions which are members of the German Trade Union Federation (*Deutscher Gewerkschaftsbund*—DGB) had some 6 million workers between them.[1]

In addition to this lower degree of organization the very character of German trade unionism was the main reason why the unions were less conspicuous in the German 1957 campaign than in a British election. Before the elimination of trade unions by the National Socialist régime there had been separate socialist Christian and Liberal trade union movements, and the socialist trade unions had been a considerable asset to the SPD. The common experiences after 1933 convinced trade unionists of all these persuasions—many of whom had begun to think in these terms already towards the end of the Weimar Republic—that they must unite into a single, ideologically tolerant movement that would represent the interests of the working masses as a whole both against the employers and against any future danger to democracy. The occupying forces encouraged this new unity, and in due course the employers, also, came to be not dissatisfied with having to deal with a single trade union movement and not with rivals tempted to compete for members by outbidding each other in militancy. When the sixteen component unions and their zonal groupings joined together at the establishment of the

[1] For accounts of German trade unionism written in English cf. Philip Taft, 'Germany', in Walter Galenson (ed.), *Comparative Labour Movements*, Prentice-Hall, New York, 1952, pp. 243–312; Clark Kerr, 'Collective Bargaining in Postwar Germany', in Adolf Sturmthal (ed.), *Contemporary Collective Bargaining*, Cornell (Reprint No. 10, n.d.), pp. 169–209; on their political views Otto Kirchheimer, 'West German Trade Unions: their Domestic and Foreign Policies', in Speier and Davison, *West German Leadership and Foreign Policy*, Rowe, Peterson & Co., Evanston, 1957, pp. 146–94.

Federal Republic in 1949 to found the DGB this new federation was bound over to ideological tolerance just as much as the component unions themselves.

Ever since the establishment of the DGB the large majority of its officials (and also many officials of the Salaried Workers' Union) have been card-carrying Social Democrats and in some cases SPD members of the Bundestag. Willi Richter, the President of the Trade Union Federation, was an SPD member of the Bundestag until 1957, and at one time all sixteen heads of the component unions were active Social Democrats. Given this personal union it was not unnatural that in 1953 the DGB had been tempted to intervene directly in the Bundestag election to the extent at any rate of issuing millions of copies of an illustrated paper and of launching the slogan: 'Vote for a better Bundestag.' Among the minority of DGB officials who supported the CDU there were some who regarded this slogan as a criticism of the Government and protested against any such violation of political neutrality. By 1957 the DGB was thus forced for the sake of its own internal cohesion to avoid any political stand of too partisan a kind.

Such neutrality between parties was not always easy to maintain when tensions developed between the trade unions and political bodies or governmental agencies. The SPD was frequently forced to restrain itself from invoking the loyalty of SPD trade union officials who could have helped the party in its political aims but did not wish to threaten the formal neutrality within the DGB; and this neutrality was watched over jealously by the non-socialist element in the DGB, particularly by the Christian Social Group (*Christlich-Soziale Kollegienschaft*) associated with the CDU.

By 1957, however, the DGB was no longer the only trade union movement to claim the loyalty of Christian workers. In the autumn of 1955—partly perhaps as a result of the disputes over the DGB's political activity during the 1953 election—a rival Christian Trade Union Movement of Germany (CGD) had taken up again the traditions of the Christian unionism of the Weimar Republic. The Christian Trade Union Movement was founded by two CDU members of the Bundestag, Johannes Even and Bernhard Winkelheide; both had been active in Christian unionism before 1933. Its third founder was a Protestant; but it remained a predominantly Catholic organization, and it was politically hostile to the SPD. The Catholic bishops issued a guarded statement in the CGD's favour at its foundation, and individual bishops gave it strong support thereafter. Nevertheless, a year after its foundation it still had only 11,000 members. The incorporation of the Christian unionists of the Saar in 1957 may have helped the finances of the organization (which were heavily dependent on the Brussels headquarters of the International Federation of Christian Trade Unions) but it did not save the Movement from the doldrums into which it passed almost immediately after its birth.

In the middle of May the DGB counter-attacked the Christian organization. A group of over a hundred Catholic officials of the DGB sent a letter to Cardinal Archbishop Frings as chairman of the bishops' conference and asked him whether a Catholic could be a member of a comprehensive trade union, whether he could be an official of such a union, and whether he could take part in schooling courses organized by such a union. A clearly positive answer would probably have resulted in the extinction of the CGD. Yet a clearly negative answer might have split the Catholic Workers' Movement (of whom only a slight percentage had left the DGB for the new union) and might not have been obeyed. Several well-known Jesuits were, moreover, supporting the DGB in this matter, and Johannes Even of the Christian movement complained: 'As a layman I can hardly dispute with a priest like Father Reichel.'[1] After consulting the bishops, Frings replied two months later that 'There is to be no further statement on this subject for the moment' and urged Christian trade unionists, whatever their organization, not to denigrate each other. It appears that the problem had been given some consideration in the Vatican, and that the Holy See also had no wish to see a new trade union struggle among German workers.

By the time the 1957 election arrived, therefore, Christian trade unionism was no danger to the DGB and its formal neutrality cannot be explained to any extent by fears that Catholic members would leave the DGB if it took up too partisan a position. Such impartiality as the DGB maintained was much rather the result of other factors: a desire to avoid any renewed tension within the organization such as that resulting from the activity of 1953; some scepticism as to the value to the SPD of any stand the DGB might take up; in the case of several trade unionists no doubt a feeling that the SPD was not militant enough to deserve any support which would jeopardize the little working-class unity that existed; and certainly everywhere the desire not to risk another defeat equal to that of 1953, which could not strengthen the position of the unions. Nevertheless, the DGB and its constituent unions were vitally interested in the outcome of the election, and ideological tolerance and independence of party did not result in indifference to the campaign.

[1] *Süddeutsche Zeitung*, 8 July.

On May Day the DGB issued an appeal for German reunification which seemed broadly parallel to the SPD's views on the subject. In particular it complained that the 'emergence of restorative and neo-fascist tendencies' in the Federal Republic hampered the pursuit of the paramount aim of German unity. Thereafter the DGB Federal Executive came out with only one major statement, the election appeal of August, which, after stressing the importance of the election, declared that ten demands—all of them parallel to the policy of the SPD—were to be met by the new Bundestag.

> In accordance with the decisions of the Hamburg DGB Congress we expect that all workers, white collar employees and civil servants, all pensioners, war victims and their families, will give their votes to such candidates—regardless of their party affiliation—whose support may be expected for the legitimate interests of all employees, pensioners and war victims.

At the end of August the DGB published *Information on the Price Increases to be expected after the Election in the autumn of 1957* which could not but embarrass the CDU, and sent an open letter to the Chancellor asking him to lose no time in counteracting this threatened rise in prices. Whatever their formal neutrality, it was clear from their pronouncements that the majority of DGB leaders wished to see the Social Democrats strengthened from the election.

Of the component unions, the most influential and politically active during the campaign was that of the metal-workers (*Industriegewerkschaft Metall*). It was this union which had been involved in the bitter four months' strike in Schleswig-Holstein at the turn of the year and naturally it was in Schleswig-Holstein that relations between the *IG Metall* and the CDU were at their worst. The *IG Metall* organized a meeting in Kiel at which a CDU candidate—like all other candidates—was to have ten minutes in which to answer five questions which, unlike the SPD candidate, he could not have answered with a simple 'Yes'. The CDU in its letter of reply gave six reasons why it could not accept this invitation which it termed not far removed from blackmail and hoped that co-operation would become possible again after 15 September.

The *IG Metall* also came out strongly against the CDU in Lower Saxony with an election pamphlet which declared: 'We have no reason to be satisfied with present policy', quoted allegedly unkept ministerial promises, and concluded that 'for four years profits policy has taken precedence over social policy'. It quoted the voting record of various Lower Saxon Bundestag members, and mentioned two parties with approval: 'Equal rights also for the worker—only the Bundestag members of the SPD and of the BHE wanted that.'

But relations between the parties and the unions differed from area to area and from union to union. In general the other fifteen unions of the DGB appear to have taken much less part in the election than the *IG Metall*, and it is difficult to obtain evidence of any formal election activity on their part at all. This does not necessarily imply that there was none; but it was not organized on the federal level, occurred mainly within industrial plants and largely by word of mouth, and was thus difficult for any but close local observers to trace. Moreover, since no one was anxious to antagonize the unions, no particular publicity was given by their opponents to such breaches of party neutrality as may have taken place. Only where trade union officials and members stood on the SPD ticket was direct electioneering activity obvious.

Just as the Catholic organizations gave local aid to their prominent members who were standing as CDU candidates, so the local DGB and union organizations gave mainly non-financial aid to their members who stood on an SPD ticket: personnel, premises, office equipment, and cars were placed unofficially at the disposal of such SPD candidates, and the union made the recruitment of volunteer helpers less difficult. Officially the DGB's and most of the unions' help was, however, confined to the organization of meetings at their own expense which, even if addressed by all the constituency candidates, naturally gave the most sympathetic hearing to the one who could show the greatest solidarity with the unions and their demands. The presence of CDU members at all levels of the organizations made other official activity difficult, and in at least one city the DGB Land Secretary, who had cleared his desk in preparation for electioneering work, found himself—much to his chagrin—an idle spectator during the campaign.

Industrial, Middle-Class, and other Organizations

The Federation of German Industry, to which virtually all industrial firms in the Federal Republic belong, and the Federation of German Employers' Associations (*Bundesvereinigung der Deutschen Arbeitgeberverbände*) have from the very beginning of the Federal Republic openly declared themselves in favour of the general policy of the Adenauer Government and have always helped and promoted this policy as far as possible. In 1951 the Federation of German Industry and the Employers' Associations founded an institute of research and public relations to further their work in these fields, and to 'help lay the foundations of the entrepreneurial conception of economic and social policy and to make it part of public consciousness'.

In 1953 this Institute of Industry took a very active part in the campaign of the non-socialist parties by means of its weekly *Letters to Entrepreneurs* (*Unternehmerbriefe*) and its *Staff Letters* (*Mitarbeiterbriefe*) written for managerial employees. Compared with 1953, the Institute of Industry, the Federation of Industry, and the Employers were remarkably restrained in 1957. The employers' journal, which had struck a highly polemical note in 1953, exuded calm and confidence in face of the election:

> No one will expect us to be socialists. . . . Of course we take sides in the economic and social debate of this election campaign, and we are opposed to socialism. But this precludes neither the recognition of real achievement and worthy motives on the other side nor respect for the function of an opposition in both fields. Should there be a federal government led by Social Democrats, then we should of course give to it as much political and human loyalty as to any other legitimate government; we should rejoice in its successes for our people and we should objectively criticise its measures when we considered ourselves entitled to utter such criticism.[1]

In 1953 the Institute of Industry had regularly discussed the election campaign in its *Letters to Entrepreneurs*; there was much less discussion of the 1957 campaign, but of course the Institute's political views were unchanged:

> Socialism remains opposed to the entrepreneur and to the liberal economy in which he can develop and act in the interests of all; latterly, however, it has more and more been the bourgeois, watered-down version of it which is spreading like cancer. . . . Thus our watchword should be: see to it by all permitted and available democratic means that everyone votes, that they vote intelligently, that they cast their votes to the right of socialism, and that moreover no party cheats the voter by a pact with socialism after the election. . . . During this summer, just as four years ago, the chief political concern of entrepreneurs and their associations must be the psychological preparation of the election under the motto: *Tua res agitur!*[2]

In August the Institute of Industry provided for its subscribers a letter addressed to a 'Dear voter in perplexity', issued free of charge and intended for wide distribution. The letter drew attention to the fact that the Socialist Unity Party of the Soviet Zone was advising all former members of the West German Communist Party to vote for the Social Democrats in the federal election. One therefore had to reckon with eleven extra SPD members from this source alone. The undecided elector was now faced by the following question:

> Is democratic-marxist socialism (a genuinely revolutionary paradox) to shape Europe? Whom does socialism really benefit? Please think about this

[1] *Der Arbeitgeber*, 20 July. [2] *Unternehmerbrief*, 23 May.

thoroughly. Wealth and prosperity are created by experience and skill in a free economy imbued with a climate of liberty, responsibility and personal initiative. When inexperience and lack of expertise lay claim to the power of direction, this is always at the expense of the general public. Is it still necessary to show that the welfare state means collective inefficiency and the failure of productivity? Socialisation remains the SPD's declared aim. Leading Social Democrats continue to maintain that a new ordering of productive capital is urgent and that the need for decision on a class basis has not been overtaken by developments.

But taking it all in all one may say that the industrial associations intervened only on the periphery of the election. Industry's main contribution to it was of a financial kind, and the rationalization of effort led the industrial organizations, on the whole, to leave political propaganda to those whose job it was and whom they were paying to carry through the campaign.

The German Farmers' Union (*Deutscher Bauernverband*), on the other hand—to which practically all German farmers belonged—took an active part in election preparations at Land and federal level. The Union backed the general policy of the Government, but as a strong interest group with a membership of over one million, it also hoped to obtain as much material benefit for them as possible. German agriculture has been supported by protective tariffs and large subsidies for many years, but these did not altogether satisfy the Farmers' Union, and some of its leaders hoped that the election might improve their chances of obtaining further concessions in two different ways: by altering the balance of power within the coalition that assured Adenauer's majority, and by the election of more farmers' leaders to the Bundestag. The President of the Farmers' Union of Lower Saxony was plainly in favour of the German Party, on whose list the President of the Westphalian Farmers' Union was standing in the neighbouring Land:

The Farmers' Union of Lower Saxony has always refused to lay down a party political line for its members. It has always confined itself to the representation of the professional interests of its members and knows full well that other considerations play a part in an electoral decision and that they may even be more weighty than agricultural considerations. But perhaps a leader of the occupational group, who has deliberately kept out of party politics in order to preserve his full freedom of action, may be permitted an expression of what he would like to see: a strong CDU, but not one so strong as to need no allies. I should therefore welcome a growth of the small parties, possibly in conjunction with some tidying-up by mergers. Such a constellation would seem to me to give the best chance of a successful parliamentary policy for agriculture.

In a last declaration of 14 September the Farmers' Union asked all farmers to use their vote:

Some presidents of farmers' associations are standing as candidates. Our hopes are with them. Where they stand, they should be voted for; for we need the certainty that the men who receive our votes will really put work for the agricultural community first.

In addition to such declarations from industrial and farmers' associations, the Central Associations of German Tradesmen and Artisans, the Civil Servants' Union, the Central Association of House and Property Owners, and a host of other similar associations published election appeals of one kind or another, asked their members to cast their list votes only for parties friendly to their interests, and reported on the candidatures of their officers and members.

The number of associations of the most diverse kind which felt called upon to show their allegiance to the new democracy by calling on their members to vote, or which hoped also to advise their members on how best to vote, was legion.[1] But by comparison with the previous federal election such sectional appeals seem to have been less noticeable: even the poster of the Middle-Class Block showing the letters SPD as hooks on a line out to catch a green carp-like representative of the middle classes was confined to one or two Länder. Apart from fund-raising, the most effective political work done by these associations consisted in their long-term public relations efforts, in providing a forum through which the parties could appeal at meetings to wider sections of the population, and in thus acting as a supplementary link between the State and the people in a country where the population had become shy of party membership. They certainly attempted to affect the outcome; but by 1957 the main visible initiatives came from the political parties themselves.

[1] While the majority of associations of all kinds were probably favourable to it, the CDU reported that electoral appeals directed against it were printed in a nudist magazine and in a journal for homosexuals.

XII

FOREIGN INFLUENCES AND COMMUNIST INTERVENTION

Western Influences

THE reduced interference in the campaign by primarily non-political bodies within Germany was matched, indeed exceeded, by the decline in foreign or at least in Western interventions. In 1953 the cry had gone up from the SPD that the Chancellor was receiving massive electoral aid from the Western powers. The Foreign Relations Committee of the U.S. Senate had passed a resolution which Senator Wiley hoped would be useful for Adenauer's electoral effort, Adenauer was able to read out at election meetings a letter from President Eisenhower on reunification, and John Foster Dulles declared at a press conference three days before the poll that if the Government coalition under Adenauer were not maintained, this would be disastrous for Germany and for its hopes of reunification.

In 1957 the Western powers were rather more reticent in their support for the Government during the election campaign. Ollenhauer as well as Adenauer was received in Washington. Dulles carefully avoided committing himself too obviously to the Chancellor—although when pressed hard by correspondents, he gave a reply which was quoted in the German press as meaning that Germany had to decide on 15 September whether she was grateful for American help.[1] The NATO meetings in Bonn and Mr. Macmillan's visit to the Chancellor were regarded by the Opposition as deliberate electoral support for the CDU, but certainly the visit of a Republican campaign manager to the CDU's headquarters during the closing stages of the contest was not the American intervention which the Opposition attempted to pillory.[2]

[1] The officials record of the press conference reads: 'Now, if there are those in Germany who think it is a matter to be appraised as to whether or not the policies of Germany and the United States coincide, whether American policy is helping Germany, that is a thing for the Germans to decide.'

[2] Mr. Bernard Lamb, a manager of President Eisenhower's 1956 campaign, spoke no German and arrived far too late to affect the planning of the campaign; his own urbane reply to the SPD's clamour against foreign intrusion was to express the hope that while in Bonn he could also see his 'old friend Fritz'. (He had once

The only official document of any importance issued obviously to influence the vote was the twelve-point declaration published in Berlin on 29 July and signed by von Brentano together with the British, French, and United States Ambassadors in Bonn. While emphasizing the concern of the Western powers for German reunification and promising that the Western powers would not join any disarmament agreement which would stand in the way of German reunification, the declaration insisted on free elections in all Germany and on the freedom of an all-German government to decide its own foreign policy as prerequisites of reunification. There could be no question, the British Ambassador stated, of their abandoning these two demands. The three Western powers thus once more joined the German Government in expressly rejecting the foreign policies advocated by the parties of the Opposition.

Both the SPD and the FDP were unhappy at being put in this embarrassing position: for both had declared that they would not break treaties, but only withdraw from them with the agreement of the partner States. Maier was thus missing the point, presumably deliberately, when he commented on the Berlin declaration: 'If the Berlin declaration has an aim, then that aim is not reunification, but the membership of the whole of Germany in NATO. Only for that membership is anything offered in return', and he objected that the Federal Government had 'made the holiest concern of our nation, namely reunification, the object of an unsuccessful election stunt and a propaganda demonstration'.

Even if their support of the CDU was more tactfully expressed than in 1953, the official sympathies of the Western powers were clearly on the side of the Government in so far as foreign policy was concerned. Unofficial opinion, however, whatever it may have been in the U.S.A. and in France, was less unanimous in Britain. A final 2-page CDU advertisement, aimed in particular against the Free Democrats, quoted a testimonial from 'Don Salvador de Madariaga, Oxford', Honorary President of the International Liberal Union: 'Western Germany must choose whether the only living statesman of world stature is to remain in office. . . . If Adenauer were beaten, not only Germany, not only Europe, but the whole world would be the loser.' The SPD and FDP, on the other hand, were citing the Bonn correspondents of *The Times* and *The Manchester Guardian*, who had become alarmed at the overwhelming superiority and the occasional

met Heine at a cocktail party in Washington.) Lamb's campaigning was, according to his hosts, confined to the distribution of 5-mark pieces to those who courteously answered 'yes' to his question 'You for CDU?' and to walking down the streets of Rottweil holding Heck's hand aloft and exclaiming 'I'm for my old friend Bruno!'

excesses of the CDU's style of campaign. Other British papers and similar reports from Swiss journalists were also quoted against the CDU.

It is perhaps not surprising that even in 1957 the German public was sensitive to foreign comment on its internal affairs, particularly when it came from the Western allies. To have won their support for the Federal Republic (and for himself) was after all one of the achievements with which the Chancellor was making most play in his campaign. Yet that sensitivity may have been less acute in the more self-confident Western Germany of 1957 than in earlier years.[1] The close links in foreign policy between the Government and its Western allies were undoubtedly one of the greatest sources of strength to the CDU throughout the campaign; but it is very much less certain that the explicit electoral support for Adenauer from abroad was in 1957 worth anything like the million votes which Mr. Dulles's declaration was said by one CDU politician to have swung in 1953.

The Influence of Soviet Diplomacy

Much more blatant interventions in the election campaign came from the East, and though their tone was one of abuse for the Adenauer Government it is quite possible that these interventions were for that very reason at least as great an advantage to it as the declarations of the Western powers. At the beginning of 1957 the Soviet Union launched a diplomatic offensive on Western Germany which alternated the promise of carrots of a kind with the display of a very heavy stick. Earlier in April there had been a good deal of reference in Russian pronouncements to 'the spirit of Rapallo'.[2] Then on 27 April—after the Göttingen appeal and before the Bundestag debate on atomic questions—the Soviet Foreign Minister Andrei Gromyko handed a note to the German *chargé d'affaires* in Moscow which declared: 'If the nuclear weapons were used, the whole of Western Germany would become one single cemetery . . . for the Federal Republic this is in essence a matter of life and death.' Mellies, on behalf of the Social Democrats, declared that he could not but underline every word of this Note on the atomic danger and that the Russian announcement only went to substantiate the views

[1] Cf. the remark overheard by Alfred Grosser in 1957 made by one workman to another: 'These English would like us to get rid of Adenauer, I suppose, so as to weaken *our* Mark.' Cf. Alfred Grosser, 'Le plebiscite du 15 septembre', *Revue française de science politique*, vol. vii, pp. 839–63.

[2] Cf. *Die Sowietunion heute*, published by the Soviet Embassy in Bonn, 10 and 20 Apr. 1957.

of the SPD. The Federal Government, on the other hand, denounced the Note as an attempt to intervene by threats in the internal affairs of the Federal Republic. Its reply, dated 22 May, stressed that the Federal Republic was the only State in the world to have formally renounced the production of atomic, bacteriological, and chemical weapons, and re-emphasized that it did not possess any such weapons. But:

> The Federal Government has not heard of any declaration made by the Soviet Government as to how it intends to equip its forces in the future. The Federal Government is not prepared to accede to the unilateral and completely unjustified demand by a foreign government for such a declaration on its part.

Moreover the Federal Government felt that to renounce the stationing of atomic weapons in both parts of Germany prior to a general agreement on disarmament would not be conducive to guaranteeing the security of the Federal Republic.

The whole question of the forces to be stationed in Western Germany was simultaneously being examined by the United Nations Disarmament Sub-Committee at its meetings in London through the summer. The Social Democrats felt that the continuance of these negotiations beyond polling day would prevent either their success or their failure from being claimed by Adenauer as a justification of Western policy. Adenauer for his part felt it necessary at one stage to defend himself against accusations that his insistence on coupling the problem of reunification with that of disarmament might be hampering the London talks, but argued that any unilateral renunciation of nuclear weapons would throw away a bargaining weapon in the hands of the West. For the bulk of the electorate, however, the complications of the various proposals and counter-proposals made in London by other governments appeared to be only indirectly relevant to their own electoral choice.

Rather more notice was taken of three other events that took place in the last two months before the election: Khrushchev's visit to East Berlin in early August, the intermittent negotiations between the Federal Republic and the Soviet Union that took place in Moscow, and the Russian Note on reunification delivered a week before polling day. All these, as the Opposition afterwards complained, made it easy for Adenauer to paint them as suffering from hallucinations: the Soviet Union appeared in fact to be doing its best to live up to the CDU's description of it as an implacable negotiating partner from whom no concessions were to be obtained.

On 7 August Khrushchev was given a conspicuous reception on

his arrival in East Berlin and on the 8th he made a big speech before the People's Chamber of the Democratic Republic. He declared that disarmament and reunification were completely separate questions, and that the responsibility for reunification lay with the Germans themselves.

> While all previous German states were the tools of the aggressive policies of Prussian *Junkers*, bank lords and the magnates of imperialist monopolies, the Democratic Republic is realising the principles of peace and friendship between peoples . . . . We regard its proposals as right and we support them.

Otto Grotewohl, the Minister-President of the Democratic Republic, repeated these proposals: a confederation between the two German States with a consultative All-German Council was the only path to peace and reunification; only such a confederation could implement a common policy which would allow both German States to withdraw from military alliances, to renounce atomic weapons, and to secure the withdrawal of foreign troops.

Khrushchev also concerned himself directly with electoral questions:

> What free elections can there be in the Federal Republic when the Communist party is outlawed, the progressive organisations of workers and fighters for peace are hunted and persecuted by the police, while war criminals and Hitler fascists play an increasing role in political life?

A resolution by the People's Chamber called upon the population of the Federal Republic to clear the path for peaceful and democratic reunification by their electoral decision, and Walter Ulbricht, the First Secretary of the Central Committee of the Socialist Unity Party, declared that if a new government were formed after the West German elections, the German Confederation could be launched on 1 January 1958.

After the photographs of Khrushchev's triumphal reception by the People's Chamber in East Berlin, the picture of a German diplomat, Dr. Rolf Lahr, constantly landing or taking off from Bonn or Moscow airports symbolized German–Soviet relations for the public at large during the rest of August. In his almost cordial letter to Adenauer of 5 February, Marshal Bulganin had proposed that the Soviet Union and the Federal Republic should improve their relations and conclude agreements for a substantial increase in trade, for cultural and scientific co-operation, and for consular arrangements for 'the protection of the interests of their nationals, thus facilitating the solution of questions concerning the repatriation of nationals of both countries'.

When negotiations began in Moscow on 23 July, the electorate cannot but have recalled Adenauer's own journey to Moscow two years earlier, when he had secured the release of nearly 10,000 German prisoners of war. Indeed it soon became clear that the German delegation, led by Lahr, was interested above all in securing the repatriation of German civilians said to be in Russia and regarded this as a prerequisite for any expansion in trade. Lahr was recalled a week later when the Russians declared that there were no further Germans in Russia to be repatriated; he was sent back to Moscow in August for a week, only to be recalled again when the Russians insisted that this item on the agenda had been exhausted and that trade relations between the two countries should now be discussed. Although Lahr returned to Moscow again briefly at the end of August, the impasse remained unresolved when Western Germany went to the polls. Whatever the motives on both sides the impression given to the German public by these negotiations must have been one of Russian intransigence.

That impression was deepened when, just a week before the poll, Gromyko handed the German Ambassador in Moscow a Note which re-emphasized the Russian view of reunification with a blunt appeal to the electorate:

> The Federal Republic is now faced with the choice: Either it renounces its NATO policy and its war preparations and establishes the unity of Germany gradually by peaceful means, or else it continues its present political course, pregnant with extreme danger for the population of Western Germany, and takes responsiblity for the maintenance and the accentuation of the division of Germany. There is no third alternative.

On the publication of this Note, the Social Democrats, while rejecting the idea of confederation, made a last attempt to use Russian pronouncements in their own favour: 'In the United States efforts are being made to explore new paths in German policy: yet Bonn digs itself in in the trenches of the cold war and refuses to see the signs of the times.' But the tone of the Soviet Note evoked almost universal irritation and it was certainly not calculated to suggest that new approaches to the Russians would yield any very attractive returns. As the FDP Press Service assessed the situation: 'This abrupt *Njet* could hardly help those forces in the Federal Republic which are working for the relaxation of tension in the world and understanding between the West and the Soviet Union.'[1] The Social Democrats, too, could not but note that the Soviet Union had pursued very similar tactics during the 1953 election, and was now for the second time seriously—even if indirectly—embarrassing their campaign.

[1] Quotations taken from Keesing, *Archiv der Gegenwart*, p. 6633.

Direct Communist Intervention

Such direct intervention from abroad as took place during the election came almost exclusively from the Democratic Republic. At least several million brochures and leaflets produced in the DDR were addressed to private individuals selected at random from (often obsolete) directories, to soldiers, to young voters, to people who had visited the DDR, and to similar groups, and were posted in small batches by couriers who toured the Federal Republic. A few of these couriers were intercepted and given prison sentences as 'traitors to the constitution': often whole sacks of such material were found abandoned by agents who had decided to give up their mission. Further material was stacked in inter-zonal trains or distributed to travellers leaving the DDR by car. A week before polling day some hundred and fifty different types of material had been registered by the West German security authorities, and in the last week another sixty or seventy further titles were intercepted.

The most obvious and straightforward type of propaganda consisted in coloured stickers with crude mottoes such as 'While Adenauer reigns in the land, riches and hunger go hand in hand', 'Whoever votes for Adenauer, votes also for atomic war'.[1] A weekly paper of the 'National Democratic Party of Germany' printed extracts of Khrushchev's speeches and stories of misbehaviour and violence on the part of British and American soldiers alongside obscene cartoons, and greeting-cards from the 'Peace Council of Gera' sent out for 1 September, the 'Day of Peace', said: 'May you on the 15th of September decide for a government that supports security and peace and the unity of our German country.'

But the great majority of the Communist material that was distributed in Western Germany was of three different, less ingenuous kinds: what might be called 'jack-in-the-box' material, parodies, and forgeries.

The first type of material at first sight looked like something else but when opened revealed straight Communist propaganda. There was an imitation 10-mark note close enough to the original to be

[1] Cf. for example the painful pseudo-versification, the obvious misstatement, and the misspelling of:

> Heussinger, Strauss, Speidel,
> und andere Hitler-Generale,
> das ist nicht unsere Wahl.
> Wir wollen nicht der Bundeswehr Qualen!

and, slightly less clumsy:

> Wenn die Volksmassen bei der Wahl entscheiden,
> müssen Adenauer und Speidel Schiffbruch erleiden!

picked up by a pedestrian in the street (and to be passed on as money by a few enterprising West Germans) which opened out to reveal a text saying:

> This note of course is not genuine. But have you ever thought about the fact that . . . of every 10-mark note the government takes away 2.50 DM? . . . Not a vote for the CDU/CSU, the party of tax blackmailers and re-armament hyenas. Vote SPD!—The Communist Party of Germany.

What at first sight looked like a catalogue for a well-known make of small car with the question: 'Who 's at the wheel?', opened out to argue that through the CDU, the monopolists and militarists steered Germany's course. But there was more often no such link between cover and content. Thin ivory paper imitating that on which the Federal Post Office printed its notices was used for *Instructions for the Use of Post Office Savings Bank Accounts*: the inside of this leaflet consisted of the manifesto of the 1957 KPD Congress. Under the cover of Remarque's *All Quiet on the Western Front* were to be found thirty-two pages of a Communist version of the Hungarian revolt and eight pages of photographs of subjects such as the corpses of Hungarian victims of the 'white counter-revolution'. A brochure entitled *High-yield Soft Fruit Cultivation* masked a 'Journal for the Theory and Practice of Scientific Socialism'. Further Communist material was put out inside covers depicting the American film actress Marilyn Monroe in deep décolleté in the hope presumably of thereby easing and speeding its circulation in Bundeswehr barracks.

Quite clever and even witty at times were the various parodies of Western publications put out from the DDR. *A word to all housewives of the Federal Republic* embellished with Erhard's signature and the drawing of him used by the Erhard campaign caricatured his usual declarations; a fake edition of the Bonn local paper *General-Anzeiger* (with a very creditable imitation of its typography) included some amusing mock news. A *Neue Bild-Zeitung* copied the Hamburg *Bild-Zeitung* in its layout and features, but presented straight Communist propaganda within this form. A puzzle magazine and a pamphlet advertising Coca-Cola both developed into propaganda against the CDU.

Lastly there was material which was intended to deceive as to its origins rather than merely attract attention and conceal the nature of the publication at first sight: 'A group of frontier police' was said to be responsible for a pamphlet against the CDU, ostensibly printed in Cologne, which was sent to many members of the frontier police. A 'Committee of Peace-loving Sportsmen' called on sports enthusiasts to vote SPD. A 16-page *Trade Union Information* on the

Iller tragedy was made to appear as the publication of a West German trade union. A chain-letter appeal from a spurious Protestant organization to vote only for Protestant candidates was sent to many Protestants with a request to make at least three copies and pass them on; a leaflet calling on Catholics to put a stop to the rise of Protestants in the CDU was sent as if by mistake to Protestant CDU supporters. And, as an attempt less to influence the election directly than to cause dislocation and 'show the flag', a large number of conscripts received official-looking letters exempting them from conscription regardless of any further communication which they might receive.

In addition to all this printed propaganda, the continuous campaign of private letters sent from the DDR itself reached a climax in August and September. A Leipzig newspaper reported on a conference of 700 activists of that city:

> From this party activists' conference strong impulses must now reach out to support the West German working class in its election campaign. It will be the task of the party organisation, the works trade union leaders and the National Front to see that tens of thousands of personal letters, agitation material and newspapers are sent to the workers of Western Germany. . . .

Shortly before the election, the East German authorities had forbidden students to travel to the Federal Republic, but during the election parties of students appeared at West German meetings and in West German universities.[1] Many of them spoke in the discussion at meetings—often in crude and violent, sometimes in rather skilled and subtle terms. As Ulbricht himself had declared at the KPD party congress: 'We must see to it that in the election meetings the political discussion takes a different course from that foreseen [even] by some members of the SPD Executive.'[2] It was reported that 4,000 agitators had received special briefings on their role in the West German election at an academy near Berlin, that 500 officials were employed in a special administrative department 'Electoral Agitation Western Germany', and that a number of schoolboys had been told that their entrance to the East German universities in the autumn was made dependent on their 'proving themselves' in the West German election during the summer. No figures are available of the number of East German agents at work in Western Germany

[1] It appears (on other evidence) to have been an East German student whose peroration of 'Whoever fought shoulder to shoulder with the SS, may his shoulder rot' set off a free fight in one DRP meeting near Bonn which the police had to break up after blood had begun to flow.

[2] Quoted in *Feinde der Demokratie*, a multigraphed periodical issued by the Lower Saxon DGB Executive, vol. vi, no. 10, p. 19.

during the election, but the degree of organization involved may be gauged from the fact that a tape-recording of the uproar at one of Strauss's meetings in Munich was broadcast from Berlin less than 24 hours after the meeting had occurred.

Moreover, the German service of Moscow Radio, the *Deutschlandsender* in Berlin, and 'Freedom Station 904', which the DDR had put at the disposal of the Communists of Western Germany immediately after their party was declared unconstitutional and which used American jazz tunes as its main bait for listeners, all carried constant appeals against Adenauer and for the SPD. Max Reimann, who had been the KPD leader in the first Bundestag, declared in a broadcast a week before the election: 'Not one worker, not one enemy of the Adenauer party must stay away from the polls on the 15th of September. Everyone must help to beat the Adenauer party and this time secure the victory of the SPD.'[1] Similar special appeals were made to particular groups such as to young voters and to artists, and the East German CDU and the East German Liberal-Democratic Party apostrophized West Germans to vote against CDU and FDP.

The East German authorities also offered the Social Democrats any amount of free radio time on their powerful stations beamed to the West and all the facilities of East German propaganda. The offer was made publicly—much to the embarrassment of the Social Democrats, who found the whole campaign in their favour a most unwelcome 'kiss of death'. It was the SPD's loudly proclaimed theory that the entire Communist offensive was designed to sabotage its electoral chances and ensure Adenauer's return to power. Inevitably the question occurs as to what precisely can have been the motive behind this whole expensive and self-defeating campaign. It was a question which itself became one of controversy between West German parties during the election.

The CDU maintained bluntly that the Communist rulers of the East German Republic wanted to see the SPD in power: that after all was only natural between parties which both drew their inspiration from the same source, and since the SPD's foreign policy would play straight into Eastern hands they had every incentive for making any contribution they could, regardless of expense, to further an SPD victory. Eight different types of CDU advertisement ensured that this argument should not be lost on the electorate, and one CDU poster stated: 'Moscow commands: "Get rid of Adenauer." So now, to spite them: CDU.'

The Social Democrats insisted on just the opposite view. The

[1] *Feinde der Demokratie*, vol. vi, no. 10, p. 22.

Communists could not possibly be so blind, they maintained, as not to realize that their intervention was bound to antagonize floating voters and turn them away from the SPD. If the Communists really wanted to help the SPD, they could have done so by less blatantly provocative means. They were obviously determined to sabotage the SPD, their closest and bitterest historic enemy. Their main concern was to maintain the *status quo* in which they held Middle Germany in their power. It was natural that Ulbricht should wish to see Adenauer returned to office. Both depended for their political existence on the division of Germany. Their public and real antagonism entailed, as the other side of the medal, a mutual dependence: each, if the other did not exist, would have to invent him.

Perhaps neither of these obviously partisan explanations is adequate. 'The Communists' may not have been as monolithic in their tactics as some liked to maintain. One need not go so far as to postulate three different agencies taking three different lines: disinterest in the issue of the election in Moscow, anxiousness to depose Adenauer among the outlawed KPD, and a readiness on the part of the East German rulers to give the KPD all the rope it wanted and help Adenauer all the more certainly back into power. But the result of this particular election in Western Germany was hardly the only consideration which led the Communists to intervene in the campaign.

It was of the nature of the Communist Party that it could not stand aside from such a political battle. The underground cadres of the dissolved organization could only be held together by activity, and a spectator's role while the SPD was fighting would have resulted in a further lowering of morale. In part at least the intervention was a remedial exercise for the disintegrating Communist cells in the West.

In the Democratic Republic also the rulers of the régime were forced to show passionate interest in the conflict or they would appear slack in their fight against capitalist bosses and militarists for peace, disarmament, and reunification. Short of an absurd 'tactical' reversal (which would hardly have been worth while), they could only campaign against the Chancellor, however much they simultaneously reviled the SPD. The Communists' propaganda may thus have been perfectly 'sincere'; and no doubt they entertained some hopes that in the long run their arguments might come home to the West German population. And if the more sophisticated East German leaders realized that their efforts, if they had any short-run effects, tended to help the Chancellor, then they may even have welcomed the disservice they rendered to the Social Democrats thereby.

XIII

CAMPAIGN PUBLICITY AND ELECTION NIGHT

THE preceding chapters have tended to regard the campaign from the point of view of each party headquarters in turn, and to describe the activities in which various other organizations were engaged. Finally an attempt must be made to paint a comprehensive picture fitting together the cumulative influences converging on the electorate during the last few months before polling day. It must begin with an account of the West German press and radio, through which the bulk of the general political background, of preliminary party manœuvrings, and then of the campaign declarations passed on their way to the voter.

The Press

Any study of the role of the press in the election is seriously handicapped by the fact that Western Germany lacks a national press.[1] Over a thousand daily papers were produced on a local and regional basis in 1957—but there was only one in the whole Federal Republic with an edition of more than 400,000, the *Bild-Zeitung* published by Axel Springer in Hamburg, which sold an edition of 3 million copies. This only mass-circulation tabloid carefully avoided taking any party political stand; when Adenauer visited the publishing house, the Springer newspapers printed his photograph with the caption that Ollenhauer would be visiting them too.

Three good political dailies, the *Frankfurter Allgemeine Zeitung*, the *Süddeutsche Zeitung*, and *Die Welt*—with a circulation of 170,000, 200,000, and again 200,000 respectively—came closest to what would in Britain be regarded as national daily newspapers. The leader-writers of the *Frankfurter Allgemeine* clearly sympathized with the Government while the *Süddeutsche* sympathized mainly with the Social Democrats. *Die Welt*, published as a prestige paper by the Springer organization, was in many ways the most interesting of all the dailies. On the morning of the CDU's Hamburg congress it

[1] For a more detailed account of the post-war German press written in English cf. W. Phillips Davison, 'The Mass Media in West German Political Life', in Speier and Davison, op. cit., pp. 242–81.

caused considerable though purely temporary embarrassment to the CDU: it printed a report from Washington according to which President Eisenhower had abandoned his standpoint that the reunification of Germany must be a condition of any agreement on disarmament. One of its main leader-writers, Paul Sethe, had delivered himself of a forceful attack on Adenauer's reunification policy a year before the election;[1] and under the title *Ave Caesar* he then wrote the one leading article of the campaign that was to prove of any importance.[2] Its effect, whatever its intention, was to sap Opposition prestige and once more to reassert the effortless supremacy of the Chancellor. The CDU used it on its platforms, the rest of the press reprinted it in whole or in part, editors and leaders of local opinion regarded it as a turning-point in the campaign and even in their own voting intentions, and an official of the political funds declared after the election that he would have been willing to pay £85,000 for that article signed by that author to be published when and where it was. (It goes without saying that no such offer would ever have been made or accepted.)

Certainly there were papers which pursued a straight party line, or which represented the expression of some wing within a party. There was a range of newspapers of pronounced CDU sympathies, and the SPD, through its *Konzentration G.m.b.H.*, itself controlled some

[1] Paul Sethe, *Zwischen Bonn und Moskau*, Schleffler, Frankfurt, October 1956. 3rd edn., March 1957.

[2] The article—somewhat unusual in style—appeared on 2 Aug., after some sections of the FDP (in contrast to the party's campaign manager Döring) had seemed to be wavering in their determination to assail the Chancellor:

'Only one man still stands upright in the turmoil of battle. Wolfgang Döring, bleeding from many wounds, fights on . . . his eye falls on a white flag and a feeling, half fear, half joy, courses through his veins. . . . It is not good to cling to the victorious chariot of the conqueror—but it is better, surely, than to be mangled by its wheels? . . .

'And in the meantime from the other side loud cries ring out, raised by Erich Ollenhauer: "Come unto me, all you who also know not what you want, and I will lead you, for I am flesh of your flesh. Get out of NATO; no, stay inside it for the moment! Give me the control of industry. What is that? I do not know, the experts do. Come unto me, all you who fear to have power and to exercise it. Together let us ride to defeat. . . ."

'On his Field Marshal's hill stands the old man of the Seven Mountains [Adenauer]. The lines of contempt for mankind round his mouth have deepened. Wistfully he thinks of the years when he had a worthy opponent: "If only Schumacher still lived. . . ."

'And as he stands in reverie a little troop approaches from the edge of the battlefield, at its head an upstanding man, his hob-nailed shoes covered with the dust of Arosa. . . . [From Maier's mouth Adenauer] hears what he wished to hear but cannot value: "We greet thee, O Caesar . . . Doomed tomorrow to die, we bow to thee, O Caesar. . . ."'

twenty-eight papers with a combined daily circulation of 1½ million copies. The total number of dailies sold which took up some sort of stand on controversial political issues came to around 4 million copies out of a total 17 million. But even these papers tended to express their bias in editorials and features rather than by the manipulation of news stories or space to the extent to which this practice is current in Britain.

The editors responsible for the bulk of the remaining daily circulation of 10 million copies carefully avoided taking any particular political stand. Their aim was to attract as many and repel as few customers in their area of circulation as possible. They gave a fair hearing to the bigger parties and to their local candidates. They reported local meetings briefly, and mentioned the more important campaign moves on the federal level and in their Land. They sometimes printed letters to the editor, taking good care to balance one expression of views against another. For the rest, the only political appeals which they carried were the advertisements paid for by the parties and parallel campaigns. The importance of this advertising should not be underrated. Many readers, above all in country areas, studied the advertising pages with a care which they would not have bestowed on any editorial or on anything more than the headlines of the political news. The lion's share of this advertising space was bought by the supporters of the Government.

Election news was thus handled carefully by most of the press. It was not until the very end that main headlines were devoted to the election: for the campaign was too static for such treatment. But the more significant moves in the campaign were reported in objective fashion. Most of the news came over the wires of the non-German agencies Associated Press and United Press or of the *Deutsche Presse-Agentur* (*dpa*). This agency was owned communally by the papers themselves and obliged by its statutes to preserve impartiality; and since most of the papers were too small to allow extensive coverage by individual correspondents, technical reasons also contributed to the fair and indeed monotonously standardized treatment of news. The fact that many German dailies lacked a clearly defined political standpoint only made it easier for them to report the election not perhaps very thoroughly but at least without grinding any axes of their own.

This view of the press was not one professed by the political parties. The CDU complained that it had the 'big' intellectual papers against it.[1] The SPD felt journalistically outnumbered and

[1] A member of one CDU Land Executive explained that the pro-Government campaigns were designed to cope with this problem and to curb editorial irresponsi-

lamented the fact that the run of local papers was unaware of the watch-dog function of the press in a democracy and unreceptive to the SPD's ideas. The Free Democrats protested that a conspiracy of silence was depriving them of the share of space which their spirited campaign deserved; they called a special party congress a fortnight before the poll to attract more limelight to themselves.

By and large these impressions seem to have been about equally subjective. Between elections news tended to be made by the Government, and the Government had the resources of the Press and Information Office and of the information departments of the various ministries to brief journalists and supply them with free hand-outs and pictures. The SPD, on the other hand, had not been particularly successful in its relations with the press. When the Government was faring badly in the winter, the CDU began an intensive campaign of personal approaches to journalists asking for their advice; but when the SPD was criticized, its leaders tended to withdraw into a hedgehog attitude of private resentment. The absence of any strong political controversy in the press was no doubt an asset to the Government. But the fault, if such there was, arose less out of any conscious partisanship on the part of the bulk of editors than out of their submission to the balance of impacts upon them and their over-faithful reflection rather than leadership of the mood in the country.

The weeklies were politically more articulate, but their circulation was usually well below 100,000. The *Rheinischer Merkur* was commonly regarded as Dr. Adenauer's personal mouthpiece, *Die Zeit* was managed by a CDU member of the Bundestag, the (twice-weekly) *Deutsche Zeitung und Wirtschaftszeitung* tended to express views held in industrial circles, the *Sonntagsblatt* was the organ of Bishop Lilje of the Evangelical Church, and *Welt der Arbeit*—the only one of these weeklies whose nominal circulation exceeded 100,000—was run by the DGB. None of these swayed many votes in the campaign.

A unique position was held by *Der Spiegel*, which began as a German version of *Time Magazine*. It was owned and directed by Rudolf Augstein, who was first nominated as ninth candidate on the FDP's North Rhine–Westphalian list and then withdrew his candidature. But *Der Spiegel* did not print anything designed explicitly to gain support for the Free Democrats. An organ of opposition *per se*

bility. There is little evidence that this really was the prime motive, though the CDU considered that the advertising campaigns had had an appreciable and beneficial effect of this kind. The space bought by the CDU and Erhard campaigns was valued (according to list prices) at £400,000, though quantity discounts considerably reduced the sums actually paid. (See Appendix, esp. pp. 307, 309, and 310.)

without any visible constructive policy of its own, it was the only paper that habitually sent its reporters to ferret out facts for themselves. It lived on exposure, and prided itself on not having lost a libel suit yet. The accuracy and relevance of its factual information (as distinct from its slant and the tone of its comments) once even stirred the Bundestag into setting up a special Commission of Inquiry (the *Spiegel-Ausschuss*). During the election campaign *Der Spiegel* rather lost its composure. It used every trifling incident against the Chancellor; in election week its cover showed his portrait as that of an enfeebled dotard, and it devoted eighteen pages to a textual analysis of his campaign speeches. *Der Spiegel* sold a quarter of a million copies. Nevertheless it may be doubted whether its highly entertaining if sometimes petty attacks on the Chancellor cost the CDU any votes. By focusing attention on the Chancellor as a person rather than on policy issues it may inadvertently even have contributed to his victory.

By far the most widely sold organs of the weekly press were the fifteen big illustrated magazines, which were read or looked at by more than half the population. Pictures of royalty and of film stars, war stories and memoirs, crime, medical information, and sporting events tended to be the staple diet of their readers. Most of these illustrated magazines took up no position in the campaign. The Chancellor and his ministers had naturally figured much more largely in their pages before the election than the parliamentarians of the Opposition, though the gruesomeness of atomic radiation had also provided much material for pictorial journalism. Only one of these papers, the *Neue Illustrierte*, came out with a feature in election week which was obviously designed to arouse sympathy for Ollenhauer and his party.

Radio and Television

By September 1957 the Federal Republic had issued licences for 13 million radio sets—almost one set for every two electors. The radio was thus a medium of great potential force in the campaign.

Chartered under Land laws, the eight West German radio stations were obliged to uphold democracy and freedom, to observe party neutrality in their news reporting and to put their microphones at the disposal of the main political parties at election time. The radio stations were each under the supervision of a radio council representing the parties, the religious denominations, and other groups.

News during this as during earlier elections was selected and treated on purely journalistic criteria, election reports being included where they concerned an important new argument or a new element in the situation. There were unofficial protests from time to time that the reporting gave more publicity to one or another party, but the radio councils appear to have been satisfied with the impartiality of news bulletins, and in one or two cases they congratulated the stations on their work.

Where party broadcasts were concerned the radio stations adopted much the same procedure as during previous elections. Over a period of five weeks before polling day parties were allotted time on the air to put on their own programmes. Each party was allowed the microphone usually for five minutes at a time and always during the peak listening hours between 6.0 and 8.30 p.m. according to the station. The total time allotted to each party was settled by agreement between the radio stations and the parties; in the case of the North and West German radio stations the ratios laid down were still essentially those agreed between the parties and the old North-West German Radio in 1949, which had then been based on the previous Landtag election results in the area covered by the old station. The established small parties reaped a distinct comparative advantage from this schedule.[1]

While no particular difficulties arose between the radio stations and the five parties which had been represented at the end of the second Bundestag, the smallest parties felt that their exclusion from broadcasting time altogether represented an illegal and indeed unconstitutional piece of political discrimination. Already during

[1] Thus the North and West German radio stations allocated the following number of minutes on the air to the parties:

	Joint Medium Wave Programme North and West			*Very High Frequency*	
	Party broadcasts	*Eve of poll appeal*	*Press conference*	*North*	*West*
CDU	100	4	30	30	50
SPD	90	4	30	30	40
FDP	45	4	30	15	25
BHE	35	4	30	15	15
DP	30	4	30	15	10

The schedules of other stations were established on analogous principles, with less time for the essentially northern German Party and time instead for such South German regional parties as the Bavarian Party, which received 30 minutes on the Bavarian Radio, and the Christian People's Party, which was given time on the Saar Radio.

the 1953 election the North-West German Radio had refused to allow time to the Communist Party, although it was then represented in the Bundestag: the station feared that the Communists' utterances might violate the station's duty to uphold the democratic order. In 1957 the League of Germans appealed against the decision of the North German Radio to give it no time on the air and finally took its case to the Federal Constitutional Court, which decided:

> Article 3 of the Basic Law is violated if public radio stations which allow political parties broadcasting time for election propaganda exclude some parties from these arrangements although list nominations have been accepted from these parties in the areas covered by the station in question. . . . It seems admissible to allocate different amounts of time to parties in accordance with their importance. Their existing parliamentary strengths can be taken into consideration in this calculation, but new parties must also be allowed appropriate time.[1]

As a result of this decision all the small parties were allowed five or ten minutes each in the last week of the campaign.

Judging by their performance in other media, one might have expected the German campaign managers to make the most of their opportunities on the air. In fact they failed to do so. In almost paradoxical contrast to British and American electioneering, they attached surprisingly little importance to political broadcasting, hardly troubled to experiment with any but the most pedestrian techniques, and barely grasped, let alone exploited, the potentialities of the medium.

The content and manner of almost all the broadcasts were indifferent, with no particular contrast of styles between parties. The five-minute period did not of course lend itself to the development of any very telling argumentation by politicians inexperienced in the medium but accustomed to distinctly long-suffering live audiences, and they sometimes attempted to say more by speaking faster. (In order not to hurt too many feelings the party managers had themselves opted for the frequent short broadcasts which allowed them to put before the microphone the maximum of politicians for the minimum of time.) These broadcasts were distinctly regional in character, few politicians appeared before the microphone more than once, even the Chancellor was little in evidence, and not only the better-known Bundestag members but also Land ministers, Land party chairmen, and obscurer people (often not candidates for the Bundestag at all) were allowed their say. The speakers tended to repeat stock arguments in favour of their own party, rarely attempted to conduct any debate or reply to an opponent, and

[1] Bundesverfassungsgericht, 2 BvR Y/57 of 3 Sept. 1957.

seldom took any stand on questions of the day of delivery: some of the tapes arrived at the broadcasting stations a fortnight or more before they were to be put on the air. The one element of variety was the attempt by the CDU to use a fanfare said to have been reminiscent of announcements of victory during the war. When the West German Radio deleted this from the tape before broadcasting, protests were received both from the CDU and also from the Opposition, which had hoped to make capital out of the National Socialist associations of this music.

No figures of the audience for these broadcasts are available, but the radio stations were not surprised to receive an unambiguous number of highly unfavourable comments. While Bundestag debates often aroused tense interest, listeners did not seem to wish to hear political monologues in their homes. Only the half-hour 'Press Conference' organized on Sunday nights by the North and West German stations themselves scored a certain success through its spontaneity: each of the five main parties in turn nominated a spokesman to give an unscripted interview to five journalists, one representing each party.

Some 900,000 television receivers were licensed at the time of the election. The German television service, a single non-commercial network shared by the various broadcasting stations, followed the political principles of sound broadcasting and allocated a time ration to each of the larger parties. (Parties could buy time only in the Saar, where a commercial television station had been set up before reunification with Germany.) Television programmes varied from a ludicrously wooden and over-rehearsed 'interview with young voters' by a Free Democrat to a programme of maps, charts, and pictures in which the compère was none other than the Federal Chancellor himself. Some of the men who had appeared on television found their personal campaigning easier thereafter. For the rest, it may be doubted whether even the television programmes had any influence on party votes. Though the professional broadcasters thought otherwise, some of the party managers regarded this as the fault of the medium, not their own. After the election the campaign manager of the CDU, whose party had had the largest share of radio and television time, wondered whether party broadcasts and television programmes should not be abandoned for the future by common consent.

The largest commercial entertainment medium, the cinema, attempted to stay aloof from the 1957 election. Several large cinema chains refused to show films or slides of party propaganda and the newsreels ignored the election even while it was at its height. Only a restricted number of cinemas showed a newsreel designed to favour the Chancellor's party; the CDU on the other hand complained that the social and internationalist message of some commercial films shown during the election tended to favour the SPD.

The Campaign in the Streets

While the campaign on the air and in visual entertainment was thus restricted, the citizen's daily surroundings, in particular the street scene for at least the last five weeks of the campaign, constituted an inescapable reminder that the election was at hand. In some cities local by-laws and usages kept poster display and loudspeaker activity within close limits: in the centre of industrial Hanover, for example, posters were hardly to be seen except on commercial sites and on a few specially sanctioned low triangular frames built round lamp-posts and trees. But in the majority of areas bill-stickers seemed to know no bounds; in the old university city of Heidelberg the parties vied with each other in erecting veritable castles of posters in the chief traffic square, and railings, walls, trees, and any other vertical surfaces were made to hold party propaganda. Even in the open countryside one would at times drive down avenues of Adenauer portraits stapled on the roadside trees, with ugly slogans stuck to the backs of traffic signs on the other side of the road.

The poster campaign was on the whole orderly and the number of defaced posters moderate. Portraits of Ollenhauer occasionally had his eyes cut out, and a number of Adenauer posters were decorated with the moustache and falling black forelock reminiscent of Hitler. There was some organized pasting over of SPD posters with printed slips bearing such elegant mottoes as 'Says you' or 'Says Moscow'. A fair number of poster hoardings were destroyed and in Bad Godesberg twenty-nine out of thirty special SPD hoardings were dismantled during five successive nights. The SPD publicized a few free fights where supporters of the CDU were armed with rubber tubing or an iron bar. A number of arrests were made, several fines were imposed, and one or two people who attempted to defend posters against hooliganism sustained serious injuries.

Such incidents must not, however, be regarded as typical of the campaign. In one constituency where the son of the CDU candidate had been caught tearing down SPD posters his father made him put up SPD posters thereafter. In Schleswig-Holstein, a Land which prided itself on its 'British fairness' and sported the Anglicism of a paid Leader of the Opposition, the Returning Officer published a gentlemen's agreement between the parties in the Land Gazette, and incidents between the FDP and the German Party ended in one party offering to pay for the replacement of the defaced posters of its rival.[1]

Meetings

All the parties reported—and all the observers agreed—that political meetings had never been so well attended in any previous post-war election. The large proportion of young people of both sexes to be found at them was regarded as a particularly encouraging sign. The public opinion polls suggest almost unbelievably high figures: 30 per cent. of men and 8 per cent. of women said that they had attended a political meeting during the campaign.[2] If it is unlikely that 6 million voters really attended an election meeting, it would seem that many of those who did not at least felt that they should have done.

Most of these meetings were held either in a public hall or in an inn or restaurant. In the latter case the hire of premises was cheap or they could be used free of charge, the drinks, sausages, and even suppers consumed before and during the meeting constituting a sufficient incentive for the owner to make his premises available. Up to 2,000 people or more would thus be drinking their beer while listening to political oratory in the summer heat.

The two big parties had slightly different techniques of organizing their larger rallies. The CDU felt that more people could be attracted and that order could more easily be kept in a factory

[1] On the whole problem of electioneering in the streets the FDP's pamphlet *Electioneering and Public Relations—A Guide for Organisers, Propagandists and Speakers of the Party*, though plainly a counsel of perfection, was a mine of intriguing suggestions and curious warnings born of bitter experience. 'Particularly younger voters are deeply impressed if FDP slogans or the FDP emblem appear where putting them up is unusual or difficult, such as on the arches of a bridge or the chimneys of a factory.' If a poster war once began, humour could be used: the example suggested was that the slogan 'Security for all' could be supplemented with a strip adding *Funktionäre*. In small villages the parish crier should be hired with his bell: 'But care must be taken that a hostile attitude on the part of the crier does not reduce or even nullify the success of this publicity.' In towns the FDP recommended propaganda squads ('large numbers are an advertisement in themselves') to give pamphlets to children for distribution into houses; there would be 'no particular difficulties if balloons, paper flags and sweets are distributed to the children at the same time'. If records were borrowed for a loudspeaker car 'they must be checked carefully before use in order to avoid unwelcome surprises' (FDP, *Wahlkampf und Werbung, Leitfaden für Wahlkampfleiter, Propagandisten und Redner der Partei*, pp. 18–19, 23, 25, 30–31, and 36–38).

[2] Institut für Demoskopie, *Rückblick auf die Bundestagswahl* (in the series *Die Stimmung im Bundesgebiet*), Allensbach, Jan. 1958.

hangar or in a specially erected circus tent than in the open air; marquees holding up to 15,000 people were used for Adenauer's meetings where no hall was available to hold the crowds. The SPD, not having the friends who could make a factory floor available and not having the money to put up special marquees, tended to hold open-air meetings where they could get no hall large enough for their purpose. In the late evenings they even staged a few torch-light rallies of a tame kind.

Formally election meetings fell into two broad categories: 'demonstrations' (*Kundgebungen*) addressed by a few or even only by one prominent speaker (often without any effective chairman) at which no one else was allowed to speak; and 'assemblies' (*Versammlungen*) at which the main party speakers were followed by 'discussion speakers' often representing the chief opponents of the party which had called the meeting. Such 'discussion speakers' were as a rule allowed five minutes each to deliver their counter-attack or develop their views. Their contributions were sometimes of a high level and usually the most interesting part of the evening.

Yet neither type of meeting was entirely satisfactory. There was no tradition of question-time in Germany; even the parliamentary question was an innovation that had not yet fully developed in the Bundestag. As a result the parties faced a dilemma. If they handed over the microphone to the opposition they risked weakening the impression created by their own star performer: it was often difficult to shift a discussion speaker once he had warmed to his subject, particularly if he had brought his own *claque*, and occasionally parties watched helplessly as their own meeting was turned into a show of strength by the other side. Yet if they held a 'demonstration' it was natural that their opponents in the hall, having no other opportunity to make themselves heard, did so by noisy interruptions —and these in turn called forth the zeal of the stewards put there for the express purpose of keeping order.[1] Most of the meetings were

[1] The FDP's same electioneering guide gave the following instructions on the subject: 'It has been observed at the rallies of other parties that individual members had the task of carrying the rest of the audience with them by ostentatious applause at pointed passages in the speech. . . . Keep open the exits in order to facilitate the removal of disturbing elements from the meeting. . . . Stewards must be men ready to act, of physical strength, and of superior calm. . . . The chief steward must retain a reserve force of particularly tough men at his own disposal. While the other stewards, even without special instructions from their chief, where necessary remove those causing local disturbances from the hall, the reserve force is deployed only on the chief steward's instructions at points of crisis. . . . Do not start fights yourselves! If the opponents start fighting, retaliate with such emphasis that the objective (removal from the hall) is achieved. Beating up in retaliation exceeds the rights of self-defence and puts us in the wrong' (FDP, op. cit., pp. 30, 36–38).

quiet and orderly; those that became noisy did so sometimes for this procedural rather than for any deeper reason.

The CDU's larger meetings suffered from little organized interference. Admission was by ticket, and order was kept by contingents of up to 300 stewards drawn from the Catholic young men's organizations and from the *Junge Union*. In Munich a group of socialist students sought to distinguish themselves by heckling, but only succeeded in reducing one large meeting to chaos when a strong Communist contingent set up a less intelligent but more effective barrage of sheer noise. In general the CDU's audiences were well under control; where there was heckling, even of a reasonable kind, it was quickly suppressed. Adenauer's meetings in particular tended to be social events for the local Establishment where its members appeared with their carefully dressed wives for an evening of being seen by their acquaintances as much as of seeing and listening to their Chancellor.

The SPD's meetings in comparison were less efficiently organized. Particularly at outdoor meetings the party sometimes fared badly at the hands of its opponents. Ollenhauer was repeatedly insulted and involved in shouting matches with groups of hooligans, and even at indoor meetings SPD speakers occasionally found themselves in difficulties when groups of youths struck up various forms of chorus. It should not be assumed that the occasional barracking from which the SPD suffered was entirely the work of the *Junge Union* or the Catholic organizations; there was no doubt a good deal of private enterprise from youths out for a lark whose enjoyment of baiting the Social Democrats in the name of established authority much exceeded their enthusiasm for the CDU itself.[1] The SPD was obviously attempting to make political capital out of rowdyism. But, as a radio commentator reported from Munich, no one was killed and few

CDU stewards were occasionally paid up to seventeen shillings for their services and incidental expenses; as the CDU's corresponding instructions suggested: 'A few bars of chocolate, a few packets of cigarettes and here and there a 5-mark piece reinforce the willingness to help.'

[1] The *Süddeutsche Zeitung*, describing 'systematic interference' with Ollenhauer's campaign trip, which included attacks on his car, remarked on 29 Aug.: 'They are in the main youths below voting age from so-called good families, who conceitedly display their anti-socialist class snobbery and who simply enjoy putting themselves at the disposal of the wire-pullers of the "*Junge Union*" for a brawl. They behave with as much impertinence and immaturity as did the Hitler Youth in its day'. And *Die Welt* wrote on 12 Sept.: 'The *Junge Union* is particularly active in a negative sense. . . . They felt that they must demonstrate their political strength armed with marmalade pots, sirens, tin whistles and cow bells.' The SPD lost its sense of humour about such scenes of interference when they became less infrequent and when pitchforks were reported in dangerous proximity to one of its film cars.

people were beaten up seriously. Even the number of incidents publicized by the SPD may have compared favourably with those reported in pre-war British campaigns; it was certainly insignificant when measured against the German elections of the Weimar period. Manners were rougher than those current in British campaigns since 1945; but they were not such as to disturb seriously anyone not rather sensitive already on the subject of democracy in Western Germany today.

The Night of the Poll

Sunday, 15 September dawned as a bright but only moderately warm day, welcomed probably with a sense of relief by a good many voters. There was no mounting excitement, none of the feverish activity of 'knockers-up', and no rosettes or other paraphernalia of a British polling day. Voters began to arrive early, and in many places queues formed in front of the polling booths after each church service and before lunch. There was no last-minute rush such as so often occurs on the week-days on which British elections are held. Voters presented their poll-cards when they had remembered to bring them, retired to a booth or behind a schoolroom map to mark their two crosses, watched the polling officers stamp the envelopes, placed them in the locked metal urns, and then, with a sense of civic duty done, returned to their private lives.

After the quiet election day tension only began to rise in the evening as radio and television sets were tuned to hear the results. In Bonn hundreds of journalists, party politicians, and Government officials gathered in the Bundeshaus restaurant or in the party headquarters. Few politicians spent the evening in their constituencies, for there was no formal declaration of poll with laudatory sportsmen's speeches on the British model. (Two of the constituency returning officers, having calculated their results, went quietly home to bed and had to be woken up by the police for their results to be transmitted to the Land Returning Officers.)

As leader of the Free Democrats, Reinhold Maier had declared some days before the poll that the CDU could be expected to obtain an absolute majority of votes, but that it had kept the latest figures a secret in order to guard against an 'underdog effect' among the electorate. On the day before the poll, the Allensbach Institute published its figures: it predicted 50 per cent. of votes for the CDU, 32 per cent. for the SPD, and 7 per cent. for the Free Democrats. Few observers doubted that the Chancellor would emerge from the election as triumphantly as he had done in 1953, and the stock exchange had evidently been of much the same opinion for several days. Nevertheless no one could take the precise results for granted, and both the Free Democrats and the Refugees' Party were still nursing hopes that they might at least maintain their 1953 poll.

The radio stations were quick in announcing results as they came in, first by polling booth, then by aggregates of polling booths, and finally by constituencies, though they gave insufficient comparative data for the more casual listener to gain an immediate impression of the extent of the CDU's victory. The television programme was an hour or more behind the wireless in its publication of results. It was geared to the official declarations of the Federal Returning Officer in the Bundeshaus, whose staff checked and rechecked the figures as they arrived in coded form before they were officially declared. In return, however, the television camera set up in the Bundeshaus picked out one politician or commentator after another and presented scores of interviews while the results were coming in.

In the CDU election headquarters a representative of Vatican circles was among the first to offer congratulations, the champagne was brought in in large baskets, there was talk of using a majority to reform the electoral law, and mocking laughter greeted the declarations of one SPD politician on the television screen. In his office in the Free Democratic headquarters Döring leant against a bookcase watching the television set and prophesied a third wave of emigration from yet another authoritarian régime. The SPD's vast bungalow was filled with beer and sandwich parties. Heine explained the result in terms of the Germans' desire to follow their leader and re-emphasized the help given to the Chancellor by the West and the East, the clergy and the business world. At his press conference in the morning, Ollenhauer called on all democrats to join hands to prevent a new totalitarian system being set up in Western Germany, and painted his party's score in the brightest colours still available: the SPD had failed to prevent a single-party majority, but it had polled 1½ million more votes than ever before, and for the first time it occupied one-third of Bundestag seats. Any amendment of the Basic Law would thus be impossible without the SPD's consent—'an important factor in view of the CDU's long-term intentions'.

The victor of the battle, in the meantime, had gone to bed. He was not to be heard or seen till the morning, when loudspeaker vans playing martial music invited the population to line the road from his village home in Rhöndorf to the Chancellory in Bonn and to provide him with a triumphant reception. In the Chancellory gardens he reviewed thirty-four *Mobilwerbung* vans drawn up in a fitting guard of honour and presented their crews with commemorative medals. Beaming in the tempest of flashlights before a battery of microphones he stressed one phenomenon above all: that the CDU had won over so many workers to its side. He called on his party not to rest on its laurels, but to prepare forthwith for similar successes in the next round of Landtag elections (see Plate I *c*).

It was not until six weeks later that Adenauer was able to conclude the elaborate negotiations, conducted in a blaze of publicity, by which the new cabinet was formed. Even when the main issues were known to have been settled, days were spent in finding a combination of second-rank personalities and portfolios which would result in exact denominational equality within the cabinet. Lübke remained Minister of Agriculture despite all the attacks on him; but one more prominent man was less lucky. The Bavarian CSU—which now occupied one-fifth of CDU/CSU seats—succeeded in obtaining a fourth cabinet minister; but it had to accept the relegation of Schäffer, the *bête noire* of industrial interests, from the Ministry of Finance to that of Justice. The one clear victor of the struggle that broke loose within the party on the morning after the election was Erhard. The support he had enjoyed from the business community and the popularity mobilized not least by his private public relations campaign made him the first minister ever to be singled out as the most influential man in the cabinet after the Chancellor himself. The problem of Adenauer's succession was certainly not thereby resolved: but Schäffer had dropped out of the race, and if Etzel was now in the Cabinet it was symbolic that Erhard, as the political architect of that West German prosperity on which the new national consciousness was so largely based, became both chairman of the Economic Cabinet and Vice-Chancellor of the Federal Republic.

XIV

ELECTION RESULTS AND VOTING BEHAVIOUR

WE have so far explored the uncharted country of public opinion mainly by studying the calibre and direction of the guns trained on it. The voter himself has appeared on the stage only as an arbitral *deus ex machina* in the last scene. It is time to turn from the agitated electioneers to the calmer electorate. This final chapter must seek to sketch answers to a few at least of the questions that may be asked about the significance of the election results and the behaviour of the ordinary voters. How did the electorate react to the weight of propaganda directed against it? How far did the campaign affect the outcome of the vote? How far did the voters understand the electoral system? How did Land react on federal politics? How did different groups of the population —men and women, young people and old people, Catholics and Protestants, villagers and city-dwellers, native West Germans and refugees—cast their votes? The questions cannot all be conclusively answered: but at least the attempt must be made.

The Campaign and the Public

Commercial advertising may to some extent have inoculated the German public against any too easy 'rape of the masses'. But there is strong evidence that the campaigns for the Government were making an impact, and that at least the more politically indifferent were responsive to their wooing. It is often said that campaigns make little difference to the outcome of elections, and in Western Germany, too, opinion has often seemed static, at least through Landtag campaigns. But in the Bundestag election of 1957 —as probably also in that of 1953—matters were different. The polling institutions at any rate cited the 1957 campaign as one in which the electioneering appreciably affected the result of the poll.

Fig. 3 outlines the main shifts in party support as reflected in the series of soundings published by the three chief institutes of public opinion. Though some of their findings differ sufficiently to call attention to the dangers of drawing any too detailed conclusions without a closer analysis, all three institutes are agreed on three strongly marked phenomena: until spring the two big parties were more or less evenly balanced in public favour; in the summer the CDU tended to pull ahead of the SPD; but it was not until the last few weeks before polling day that the final spurt took place which

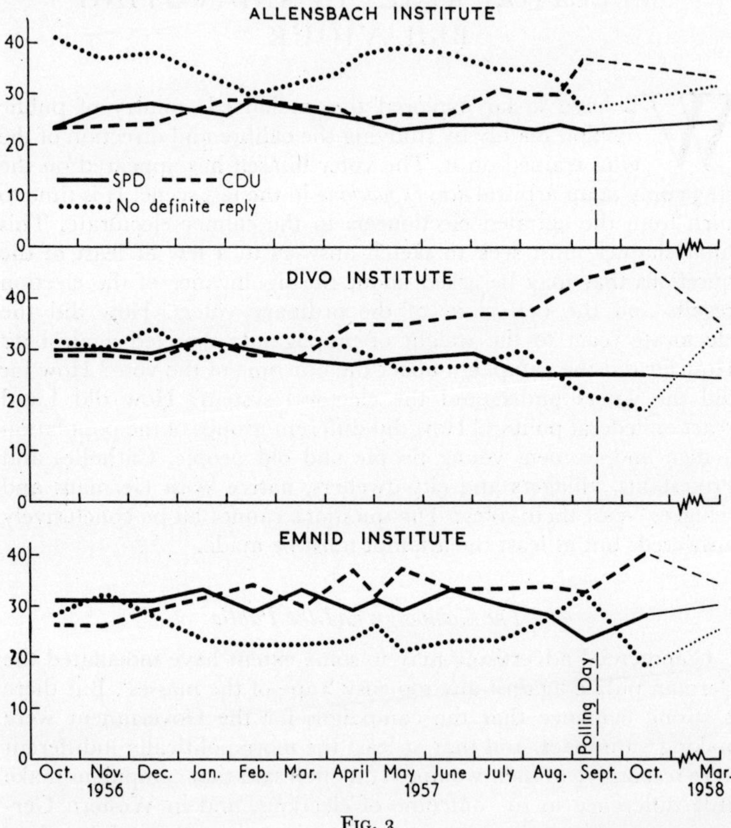

Fig. 3

made the CDU the first German party ever to win an absolute majority in the country. It was in these weeks that the CDU and the parallel organizations turned from their intensive cultivation of the 'pre-political field' to the deployment of all their resources in one massive onslaught, while no other events were taking place either in Germany or elsewhere in the world which could readily explain this dramatic development in voting intentions.

When one looks not merely at the CDU's lead over the SPD, but compares CDU support also with the percentage of respondents who gave no definite reply, two at least of the polling series strongly suggest a further conclusion. The two curves for the CDU and for the percentage of those who offered no definite reply form a mirror-image to each other: CDU support increased by as much as indefinite replies fell and indefinite replies rose by as much as CDU support fell. The popularity of the SPD shows far greater stability. The extent to which the CDU vote was drawn from those who tend between elections to regard themselves as politically uncommitted is borne out also by the results of opinion polls taken immediately after the election and those published six months later: after an initial 'bandwagon effect' just after the poll, the subsequent ebbing of political interest left support for the SPD virtually unaffected, while CDU losses made up the bulk of the increase in those who had given no definite reply to the polling institutions. It was thus no accident that the largest turnout in West German history was accompanied by the largest percentage vote ever cast for the CDU or indeed for any other German party.[1]

Of course absolute shifts in public opinion must not be exaggerated. Structural and historical patterns of voting are not swept away in ordinary times by even the most efficient publicity techniques. Nor should one place excessive reliance on every detail of such statistics. All three polls predicted the election result with sufficient accuracy.[2] Yet even the curves of party support depicted in Fig. 3 are not easy to handle. Some of the main shifts recorded by different polling institutions are parallel, and those are the ones we have so far used. But others appear at first sight to differ more

[1] The *Emnid* series mostly suggests the same conclusion. Only in one case, between July and August, do the two curves of CDU supporters and of indefinite replies rise simultaneously. If the rise in indefinite replies at the beginning of September appears at first sight to contradict the other two institutions, it is worth noting that, basing itself on these figures (which were gathered ten or more days before the poll), *Emnid* predicted 3 per cent. too few votes for the CDU and 1 per cent. too many for the SPD, an error which would suggest that a quite disproportionate share of those whom *Emnid* recorded as having given no definite replies at the time of the survey decided in fact to vote CDU.

[2] The forecasts published immediately before the election (which reveal a rapid rise in expected CDU support with the date on which the surveys were concluded) were the following as a percentage of votes cast:

	CDU	*SPD*	*FDP*
Emnid (concluded 5 Sept.)	47	33	9
Allensbach (concluded 9 Sept.)	50	32	7
Divo (concluded 14 Sept.)	53·5	33·5	6·5
Election result	50	32	8

fundamentally. It may be that different filtering techniques account for the different proportions of the population that gave no definite reply to questions about their party preferences: in May it was 39 per cent. in the case of *Allensbach* and 21 per cent. in the case of *Emnid*; but it is less easy to suggest reasons why between March and September the *Divo* figure should have dropped from 33 to 21 per cent. while the *Emnid* figure showed an almost converse rise from 22 to 32 per cent. Again, while *Divo* already noted a significant CDU lead over the SPD in April, *Allensbach* and *Emnid* still showed the parties neck and neck until June. A more precise description of the state of public opinion during the campaign must thus be given by those who dispose of a more elaborate empirical apparatus to carry through the job and who have experience of the different methods used by different polling institutions. It is fortunate that at least one such institute, *Divo*, has promised such a study. Pending its appearance, it seems wisest not to draw too heavily on the opinion polls in the present account.

The Consolidation of Both Large Parties

Fortunately the opinion polls are no substitute for an election, and it is with the elector's vote rather than his moods that we are above all concerned. In so far as the Bundestag election was designed as a plebiscite for or against a Chancellor it proved a triumph for Adenauer. But in so far as it was meant to produce a new legislature, the most striking fact to notice is that though the strength of the two Government parties in the country had risen from 48 to 53 per cent., there was no increase in their Bundestag majority. On the contrary: the net result of the election on the balance of parties within the Bundestag was a gain of one seat by the Opposition, the loss of one seat by the Government parties. During the life of the second Bundestag the CDU and the German Party had absorbed 24 members of the FDP, the BHE, and the Centre; this shift in party affiliations had almost exactly discounted the election result in advance.

But within both the Government and the Opposition camps a significant concentration took place compared with the situation before the election: while the loss of 16 seats halved the German Party's representation, the CDU won 15 seats; and while the whole BHE and the remaining independent (formerly Centre Party) member had been eliminated, the FDP regained 5 and the SPD won 16 additional seats.

The two biggest parties thus both had more seats in the Bundestag than ever before, as was natural since their combined poll had risen from 60 per cent. of votes in 1949 and 74 per cent. in 1953 to 82 per cent. Moreover, whereas the first Bundestag had contained ten parties and the second still six, the third contained only four—one of them again only by the grace of the CDU. One aim of the electoral system—to reduce the importance of splinter parties—thus made substantial progress both where votes in the country and where seats in the Bundestag were concerned.

TABLE VII

Bundestag Seats, October 1953, August 1957, and October 1957

	Government parties			*Opposition parties*		
	Oct. 1953	*Aug. 1957*	*Oct. 1957*	*Oct. 1953*	*Aug. 1957*	*Oct. 1957*
CDU/CSU .	244	255*	270	..	..	..
SPD . .	..	..	..	151	153†	169
FDP . .	48	..	..	..	36‡	41
BHE . .	27	..	..	..	19	..
DP . .	15	33	17	..	..	..
Others§ .	2	..	..	..	1	..
	336	288	287	151	209	210

* Including 5 Saar members.
† Including 2 Saar members.
‡ Including 3 Saar members.
§ The Centre Party supported the Government in 1953 though it was not represented in it.

Such figures have on occasion been used to argue that the German electorate favours a two-party system or that it is well on the way to achieving it. The two propositions are of course quite distinct. The first of them seems as flimsy as the animistic fallacy that the British electorate somehow 'wills' the size of the majority. Such 'collective decisions' are more realistically viewed as the net outcome of a parallelogram of forces; voters each decide on their own party preferences and do not 'pair' by establishing a tacit understanding on those who should vote for one party and those who should vote for the other to bring about the desired distribution of seats.[1] If the

[1] In so far as a public opinion poll taken in 1956 can be considered as any guide on the subject, it may be worth recalling that only 36 per cent. of a sample of the German electorate wanted the SPD and CDU to be the only parties, 40 per cent. preferred to see more parties, while 24 per cent. offered no opinion on the subject at all (Noelle and Neumann, op. cit., p. 260). The number of those who wished to see only one party in the State declined from 22 per cent. in 1951 to 11 per cent. in 1956 (ibid., p. 259).

German electorate really wanted a two-party system of the British type it is also strange that Adenauer should have gone out of his way never to form a single-party cabinet and that both FDP and SPD should have thought 'no single-party government' a good election cry.

It is, of course, true that whatever the system desired by the electorate, party preferences, above all among the youngest generation of voters, did tend to concentrate increasingly on the two biggest parties. But such a phenomenon is not most happily described as a trend towards a two-party system—a term that might contain misleading or hitherto unproven implications. So far there is little evidence that in federal elections votes lost by the one big party go to the other; in 1957 at any rate both chief parties increased their share of the poll simultaneously, each by one-tenth. Nor does it so far seem probable that a single-party government by one big party might replace a single-party government by the other. If we compare the 1957 results with those of 1949, then, while the SPD's poll has remained relatively stable, the votes of the anti-socialist camp, originally far more scattered between various parties, have concentrated increasingly on that of the Chancellor. What looks like a conscious move towards a two-party system since 1949 is in fact due above all to the intensified attraction of the CDU. This is not to dispute that all but the two biggest parties may be expected to decline further in the future: but to insist that an alternation in power between a Government and an Opposition party seems less likely after 1957 than after 1949.

Land Politics and Regional Differences in the Poll

What types of electors then were attracted by the CDU and by each of the other parties? The answer may be approached first of all in a very rough way through an examination of the election results separately for each Land. For just as the initial political situation and then the campaign itself differed in greater or less measure from one Land to another, so the decisions of the electorate were far from completely uniform in different parts of the country.

A glance at Table VIII is a reminder that the SPD's votes were the ones most evenly distributed through the Federal Republic. For sociological reasons its poll was naturally high in the two city-states of the Protestant North, and particularly low in the Catholic areas of the rural South. (It was 'unnaturally' low in the Saar, where Schneider's brand of national sentiment still retained the loyalty of an appreciable share of working-class voters.) The CDU, on the other hand, polled over half or nearly half the votes everywhere except in

TABLE VIII

Election Results by Länder

	*CDU**		*SPD*		*FDP*		*BHE*		*DP*		*KPD and GVP*		*Others*	
	A	*B*	*A*	*B*	*A*	*B*	*A*	*B*	*A*	*B*	*A*	*B*	*A*	*B*
Schleswig-Holstein . .	43	+1·0	31	+4·4	6	+1·1	8	−3·3	4	−0·2	..	−1·6	3	−1·0
Hamburg	37	+0·7	46	+7·7	9	−0·9	2	−1·0	5	−1·2	..	−5·0	1	+1·0
Lower Saxony . . .	39	+3·8	33	+2·7	6	−1·0	8	−3·2	11	−0·5	..	−1·7	3	+0·2
Bremen	30	+5·6	46	+7·1	6	−1·7	2	−1·3	14	−3·2	..	−5·5	2	−1·3
North Rhine–Westphalia .	54	+5·5	34	+1·6	6	−2·2	3	−0·2	2	+0·6	..	−4·4	2	−0·8
Hesse	41	+7·8	38	+4·3	9	−11·2	7	−0·8	6	+2·7	..	−4·2	1	+1·4
Rhineland-Palatinate . .	54	+2·6	30	+3·2	10	−2·3	2	−0·0	2	+0·5	..	−3·5	3	+0·7
Baden-Württemberg . .	53	+0·3	26	+2·8	14	+1·7	5	−0·7	1	−0·3	..	−3·8	1	−0·1
Bavaria	57	+9·4	26	+3·2	5	−1·6	7	−1·4	1	−0·2	..	−2·2	4	−7·0
Saar	54	..	25	..	18	..	0	..	1	..	..	..	1	..
Federal Republic														
including Saar . .	50	..	32	..	8	..	5	..	3	..	..	..	2	..
excluding Saar . .	50	+4·9	32	+3·1	8	−2·0	5	−1·2	3	+0·1	..	−3·2	2	−1·8

A, Percentage of valid votes polled 1957. *B*, Rise compared with 1953 as percentage of total valid votes.

* In Bavaria, CSU; in the Saar, CDU and CSU combined.

four predominantly Protestant Länder: in the cities of Hamburg and Bremen, in Hesse with its largely industrial character and its FDP tradition, and in Lower Saxony, where a poll of 11 per cent. for its ally the German Party brought the votes for the Government up to 50 per cent.

These figures of the 1957 poll taken by themselves must be seen chiefly in connexion with the economic and social structures and the historical traditions of the Länder concerned. Comparisons of the 1957 with the 1953 poll, on the other hand, bear out several points made about the 'conjunctural' factors in this particular election. The Länder which showed the most untypical changes were undoubtedly Hamburg and Bremen, where the SPD made exceptional advances, Baden-Württemberg, where the FDP gained votes while the CDU suffered an almost complete check, and Hesse, where the FDP lost more than half its voters and both the CDU and the German Party scored gains well above the average. These deviations from the average are useful touchstones against which to test our general rules.

In Hamburg the SPD increased its poll by 8 per cent. in a city in which the Communists had polled less than 4 per cent. in 1953 and would certainly have polled less than that in 1957.[1] This disproportionate SPD gain was not spread over the rest of the parties, but took place at the expense above all of the CDU, which failed to increase its poll by even 1 per cent. of votes. The reasons must thus be sought on both sides. The CDU had entered a 'Hamburg Block' coalition with the FDP and the German Party: its government of the city had been undistinguished and the administration was defeated heavily in the city elections two months later. On the other hand the Social Democrats enjoyed a high reputation in the city: Max Brauer had been an extremely popular mayor from 1946 until 1953 and the party leadership could claim solid administrative achievements when in office in the city which made it very difficult to represent them as a miscellany of inexperienced malcontents; the resulting image of the local Social Democrats naturally cast reflected credit also on the national party. Moreover, the SPD's Hamburg machine was well organized, amply financed, and led with imagina-

[1] The inclusion of the KPD and GVP polls of 1953 in the table under one heading, and their comparison with the gain in SPD votes, is not intended to reflect on any of these three parties with suggestions of 'guilt by association'. When two parties of the 'left' cease to exist and their leaders publicly ask their followers to vote for a third, the gain in votes of the third must be viewed against that background. Given a slightly smaller total increase in the SPD's poll than the total 1953 poll of the KPD and the GVP combined, a larger increase in any Land than these two parties' votes combined is worthy of remark, particularly when it is also larger than the average increase of one-tenth of the SPD's poll.

tion; it may well have outdone the CDU in its material election effort. Much the same factors were at work in Bremen, where the SPD's poll rose by 7 per cent.; but here the SPD was still in power, and the Bremen Christian Democrats did not suffer from the same handicaps as their Hamburg colleagues: their poll rose by 6 per cent.

In Baden-Württemburg the CDU barely held its share of the vote. In this south-western area with its healthy balance of agriculture and industry and its old traditions of liberal peasant democracy the campaign had been quiet, and no other Land showed results as similar to those of 1953. The SPD's advance was no higher than the federal average. But the Free Democrats, starting from a broader base than anywhere else, in a Land accustomed to a tripartite system and whose former Minister-President was now their federal leader, not only held their ground, but achieved a quite untypical rise in votes. They polled nearly a quarter of their federal total in this one Land.

The Free Democrats sustained by far their worst defeat in Hesse. They lost 270,000 votes largely owing to the defection of half their organization via the Free People's to the German Party. Hesse was accordingly the only Land in which the German Party had any substantial successes to record and they were sufficient to offset its losses elsewhere; but compared with the losses of the Free Democrats, DP gains in Hesse were slight. In net terms less than a quarter of the votes lost by the FDP went to the German Party: the bulk or the whole of the rest benefited the CDU, which here scored its second highest increase. The CDU won its greatest triumph in Bavaria, where it crushed the Bavarian Party. Thus in the two Länder in which the CDU made most progress the SPD also increased its poll by at least the federal average: both were Länder in which a smaller party suffered a heavy loss.

Schleswig-Holstein and Lower Saxony also offered some points of interest. They were the Länder in which the BHE had carried off its most spectacular successes in the past, and they were now the Länder in which it lost most votes. Refugees had been transferred from the rural areas of these Länder to the industrial towns of the West and South. Almost the smallest losses of the party were recorded in North Rhine–Westphalia: many who had voted BHE in 1953 probably voted for some other party in 1957, but their ranks were made up by reinforcements from among refugees more recently arrived from the rural areas of other Länder.

The Free Democrats did well both in Schleswig-Holstein and in a part of Lower Saxony. Their gains in Schleswig-Holstein—where the CDU's advance was remarkably small—were attributed largely to their special appeal to the farmers against Lübke, delivered with particular force by Otto Köhler, a former National Socialist farmers' leader, who headed the FDP list. The rise of the FDP vote in the urban areas may also have been due to the exertions of Leverenz, the Land Minister of Justice, and the Free Democrats felt that their steady participation in Land government had been an asset to them in the campaign. Their gains on and around the Lüneburg Heath in Lower Saxony the Free Democrats attributed to the intense efforts they had made there to attract the votes of former National Socialists: in seven constituencies in which the Free Democrats—in contrast to the trend in the rest of the Land—gained 10,000 votes, the German Reich Party (which increased its poll in the Land as a whole) found that it had lost 15,000.

Apart from the Rhineland-Palatinate (which saw no appreciable fall in BHE votes, and only a small gain for the CDU) it only remains for us to discuss North Rhine–Westphalia. This Land, containing nearly a third of the total electorate, naturally had the greatest influence on the federal average. The Free Democrats here lost another 130,000 votes: in the view of one of their organizers the 'Düsseldorf revolt' had been 'practically suicidal'. More important was the fact that in this Catholic industrial area the CDU was able to achieve a success not only well above the average, but also more than proportionate to its previous already dominant position. The SPD, on the other hand, suffered a severe reverse: it increased its vote by only half the average proportionate increase, and by only two-fifths of the percentage which the Communists and the GVP had polled in 1953. North Rhine–Westphalia contained a higher percentage of industrial workers than any Land except the Hanseatic cities, yet it was here that the SPD made its smallest advance of all. Rightly or wrongly the CDU claimed that after the break-through of 1953 to the Protestant areas, it had now scored a victory over the Social Democrats in the battle over the working-class vote as well.

The Postal Vote

Land election results usually still involve millions of votes and a more elaborate defence of the interpretations put upon them in the previous section demands a more detailed break-down of the poll. In a British election, in which all ballot papers cast in a constituency are mixed together before the count, only constituency results would be available to buttress the argument. In Germany, however, the study of electoral behaviour is helped by further break-downs. Even the separate counting of postal votes yields a significant differentiation.

The postal ballot was generally considered a great success; of some 1·7 million postal voting envelopes issued, more than 1·6 million were returned and over 1·5 million were accepted as containing all the requisite documents; and of these accepted ballot papers, only 1·5 per cent. were invalid. The postal vote thus accounted for at least a substantial part of the rise in turnout compared with the 1953 election; owing to the exclusion of insufficiently validated ballot papers from the ballot box it also lowered the average percentage of invalid votes.

More important for the present purpose is the fact that postal voting was loosely associated with certain income, occupational, and perhaps educational characteristics: people who were away from their homes on holidays or business trips in mid-September and went to the trouble of asking for postal ballot papers did not constitute a cross-section of the population. As might have been expected, the postal ballot therefore yielded materially different results from the personal votes. Whereas 6 per cent. of FDP and CDU votes arrived by mail, only 3 per cent. of SPD votes did so; and while the CDU had a lead of 16 per cent. in personal votes, its lead lengthened to 39 per cent. in the postal ballot. As Table IX shows, the CDU's absolute majority of votes was won only with the help of the postal voters; though only one-twentieth of the total, they increased the CDU's final lead over the SPD by 1 per cent. and they also, incidentally, turned the scales between candidates in one or two constituencies.

TABLE IX[1]

Postal and Personal Votes, 1957

	Personal votes	*Postal votes*	*All votes*
CDU . . .	49·6	60·3	50·2
SPD . . .	32·3	21·0	31·8
FDP . . .	7·6	9·7	7·7
Others . . .	10·5	9·0	10·4
	100·0	100·0	100·0

The Sample Survey of Marked Ballot Papers

We have seen in the chapter on the electoral law that the count was carried out separately in each ballot booth. The sociologist with access to an electronic computer can thus analyse some 50,000

[1] *Wirtschaft und Statistik*, Dec. 1957, pp. 681 and 628*.

separate voting results for areas with on average about 1,000 inhabitants and only 600 voters. The CDU carried out such an analysis of the 1953 election in preparation for its 1957 campaign. Various Land Statistical Offices have also correlated parts of these data with the social structure of the polling districts concerned. The present account of the election can dispense with a description of votes by individual localities, and it would tax the reader's patience to discuss the varying correlations between different sociological characteristics and voting behaviour as found in different Länder. Fortunately there are in addition extremely good federal figures which go into great detail: they were obtained by making a large representative sample of the electorate vote on ballot papers marked with the sex and age-group of the voter.

This sample survey of half a million marked ballot papers is one of the most valuable aids to the study of electoral behaviour to be found in any country. First carried out under an Order in 1953, it was given legislative sanction by paragraph 52 of the third electoral law:

> (1) The results of the elections to the German Bundestag are to be statistically examined.
>
> (2) In polling districts determined by the Federal Returning Officer in agreement with the Land Returning Officers and the Land Statistical Offices, statistics are also to be drawn up on the sex and age distribution of electors and voters with reference to the votes cast for the different nominations. Separate voting according to age-group and sex may only be carried out if the votes of individual voters do not thereby become identifiable.

These results by age and sex can easily be divided further according to other known data, particularly the size of the community in which the polling district is situated, the percentage of Protestants in that community, and its percentage of refugees.

In 1953 1 per cent. of voters cast ballot papers marked with their sex and age-group, and in 1957 that percentage was raised to 1½ per cent. in most Länder, and to 4 per cent. in four Länder in which the smaller parties were most active. The 1,007 polling districts in which ballot papers were marked were selected according to complicated statistical procedures and the results obtained in each category weighted in order to obtain as representative a federal result as possible. In 1953 Bavaria and the Rhineland-Palatinate had not fully participated in the operation, and the Saar of course was not then a part of the Federal Republic. The 1953 figures may for that reason have been slightly less accurate than those of 1957: but for most general purposes a comparison between the two years can safely be attempted within a margin of error of 1 or 2 per cent. of total votes. A comparison of the 1957 sample count with that of 1953 thus presents a dynamic picture of sex, age, and religious differentiations in voting behaviour.[1]

The 1953 sample survey already afforded statistical proof of the views commonly accepted about the voting behaviour of different sections of the population. It largely confirmed both common-sense views and the evidence of public opinion polls. 68 per cent. of women in overwhelmingly Catholic villages, for example, voted for the Chancellor's party, while only 28 per cent. of women in overwhelmingly Protestant villages did so.[2] A comparison of the 1953 with the 1957 sample survey shows a remarkable stability in the voting behaviour of most of these groups: in general the swing of 5 per cent. towards the CDU, of 3 per cent. towards the SPD, and of 2 per cent. away from the FDP was spread fairly evenly, men and women, Protestants and Catholics, city and village dwellers all shifting slightly in these directions.

Size of Community and Shifts in Voting Behaviour

The overall results of the election showed that 250,000 more votes were cast for constituency candidates than for party lists, the percentage of invalid list votes being 3·8 per cent. as against 3·0 per cent. for constituency votes. According to the sample survey, just over a third of those who cast invalid list votes also cast invalid constituency votes: we may thus presume that 2·5 per cent. cast an invalid list but a valid constituency vote, that 1·7 per cent. cast an invalid constituency but a valid list vote, and that 1·3 per cent. cast no valid vote at all, making 5·5 per cent. of the electorate who failed to cast two valid votes.

This figure is less disquieting than it might seem at first sight. In a number of constituencies the voters, even of the big parties, had no constituency candidate of their own party to vote for, and they often preferred not to follow their party's advice to support the

[1] For the results of the sample count in 1953 see Folio 2 of *Die Wahl zum 2. Deutschen Bundestag am 6.9.53*, published by the Federal Statistical Office as vol. 100 of *Statistik der Bundesrepublik Deutschland*, Kohlhammer, Stuttgart and Cologne, 1955. I am greatly indebted to Dr. Kurt Horstmann and his staff at the Federal Statistical Office for a photostatic copy of the manuscript tables on which their analysis of the 1957 sample count will be based. They are to be published as Folio 2 of vol. 200 of *Statistik der Bundesrepublik Deutschland*.

[2] To avoid clumsiness, communities of less than 3,000 inhabitants are referred to in the text as villages, communities with over 50,000 inhabitants as cities, and those with an intermediate number of inhabitants as towns; communities with less than 20 per cent. of Protestants are described as overwhelmingly Catholic, and those with 20–40 per cent. of Protestants as predominantly so.

constituency candidate of its ally.[1] Many voters may also have felt able to decide between the two big parties and their national leaders and programmes, but less competent to choose between local personalities, who were often unknown to them. The percentage of those who cast a valid list vote but no valid constituency vote thus seems low; and the majority of them no doubt deliberately allowed the left-hand side of their ballot paper to remain a blank.

On the other hand most voters who cast a valid constituency vote must also have wished to affect the distribution of seats in the Bundestag. A large proportion of those who failed to mark a cross on the right-hand side of the ballot paper must therefore have done so through negligence or through ignorance of the electoral system. They probably thought that once they had made their cross opposite the name of a candidate marked with a party label, their electoral duty was fulfilled. It was therefore suggested to the Federal Returning Committee that at future elections a higher poll at least of the more important list votes might be obtained by transposing the list votes from the right-hand to the left-hand side of the ballot paper.

The selective count gives a valuable indication of the extent to which the electoral system was in fact understood and its opportunities used by the electorate. Eighty-eight per cent. of voters cast their constituency and their list vote for the same party. A constituency candidate's personality can thus have played only a very minor role in the elector's choice compared with his party label—and that although (in contrast to the British system) the party composition of the legislature could hardly be affected by the votes cast for the constituency candidates. The highest 'party loyalty' of this kind was that shown by SPD adherents, of whom 95 per cent. gave both their votes for the party. (In 1953 this 'index of loyalty' had been as high as 97 per cent.) In the case of the CDU, on the other hand, the figure rose from 87 to 93 per cent.—a further small sign that what had begun as a party of *notables* was strengthening not only its organization but also its hold on the voters. 85 and 83 per cent. of the FDP and BHE list voters also cast their constituency votes for the candidate of the same party. In so far as the constituency vote represented almost a 'second preference' between parties as well as individuals, it is worth noting that of those who cast their list vote for the FDP, twice as many gave their constituency vote to a CDU as gave it to an SPD candidate; those at least whose loyalty to the party did not take them as far as to waste their constituency vote thus presumably saw the Free Democrats more often as an anti-socialist than as an anti-Government party.

[1] See Local Study B, esp. p. 339.

The most intensive cross-voting between two parties was that between the CDU and the German Party. By far the largest number of CDU voters who cast their constituency vote for a non-CDU candidate gave it to the nominee of the German Party: this fact was no doubt due above all to the electoral alliances made in several constituencies between the two parties, and to the voters' comprehension of these arrangements. But the fact that 19 per cent. of German Party voters cast their constituency vote for the CDU candidate (usually without being advised to do so by their parties) shows more: a good understanding of the electoral system, and also a realistic estimate of the chances of German Party candidates in most constituencies. Some of the voters of other small parties showed the same canny reluctance to waste a constituency vote on the hopeless candidature of one of their own party. But then it is perhaps wrong to express surprise that those who successfully complete highly complicated football pool and lottery coupons every week should be able to take the technique of the German electoral law in their stride.

Age and Sex Differentiation of the Voters

The majority of the electorate consisted of women, only 45 per cent. of men: only in the youngest age-group of twenty-one to thirty years was there a slight majority of men, while among those aged between sixty and seventy the losses of the first world war and the longer lifespan of women combined to put women in a majority of 58 per cent. The predominance of women among the electorate was such that even their lower turnout (87 per cent. as against the men's 90 per cent.) left them in a majority among voters, and even their higher percentage of invalid votes (4 per cent. as against the men's 3 per cent. for both constituency and list votes) left them in a majority of 54 per cent. among valid voters.[1]

As in 1953 the CDU was the favourite party with both sexes; it was in a minority of 45 per cent. among men but gained its absolute majority thanks to the excess of women over men and the fact that 54 per cent. of women voted for the Chancellor's party. The Social Democrats came second in order of preference among both men and women: 35 per cent. of men, but only 29 per cent. of women voted SPD. (The slight predominance of men among SPD voters had in

[1] Of the valid votes 9 per cent. were cast by men and 8 per cent. by women under thirty, 28 per cent. by men and 33 per cent. by women between thirty and sixty, and 10 per cent. by men and 12 per cent. by women at least sixty years of age.

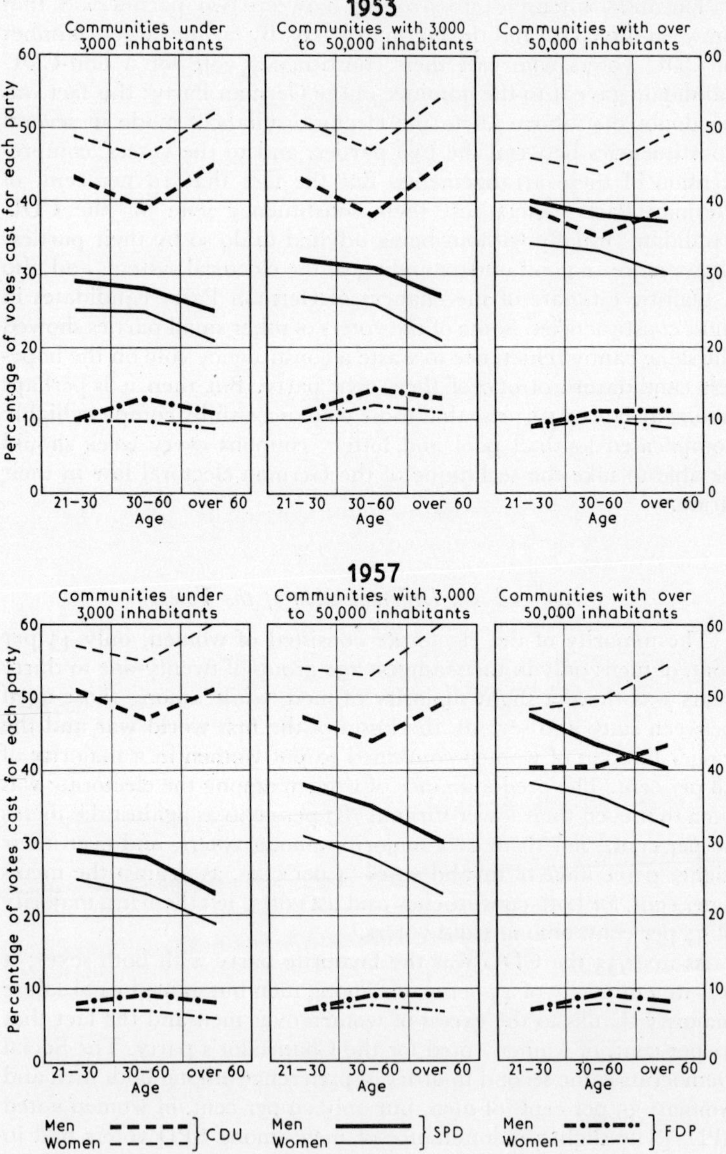

FIG. 4. Sex, age, size of community, and voting behaviour.

fact increased since 1953: six-sevenths of the SPD's gains came from men, only one-seventh from women.) The other parties also felt the attractions of the CDU for women; only the Refugees' Party remained about equally popular with both sexes.

The differentiation of voting behaviour according to age-groups was also clearly marked. Fig. 4 shows how the pattern to be found in each age-group was repeated in each sex and in each size of community. The CDU scored its greatest successes among the old (particularly among old women) and was least successful in the middle age-group from thirty to sixty. The SPD, on the other hand, polled its largest share of votes among the young and fared most badly among the old. The public opinion polls revealed that conscription was least popular among the young, and advancing age may perhaps also turn voters more conservative; but in so far as the SPD can contrive to keep its hold on its voters as they age, the party might draw some courage from the strength of the young among its voters.

In distinction to these two parties the Free Democrats were most popular in the middle age-group. We have already noted that, from the nature of the organization, the BHE may be expected to die out in due course. The sample survey confirms this view: no party had fewer young people and only the German Party had as many old people among its voters. Since also a quarter of the voters of the German Party were over sixty years old, neither of these small parties can expect demographic factors to work in its favour. The young in fact more than any other group opted for the two biggest parties.

Size of Community and Shifts in Voting Behaviour

Fig. 4 has shown the constancy between 1953 and 1957 of the differences in voting behaviour between the two sexes and between different age-groups. No less important than the differences in voting behaviour between age-groups and between sexes are the differences between various sizes of community. The three size-groups into which communities have been divided each contain roughly a third of the total electorate. The size of community naturally goes with a number of other social characteristics of the population[1] and, as Fig. 4 shows, the curves relating age and sex

[1] It would, however, be wrong to identify communities of less than 3,000 inhabitants with agricultural villages, since in several parts of Germany, notably in Baden-Württemberg and the Saar, an appreciable proportion of village-dwellers work in industry or mining; but it may, of course, safely be assumed that the proportion of farmers in the cities can be ignored.

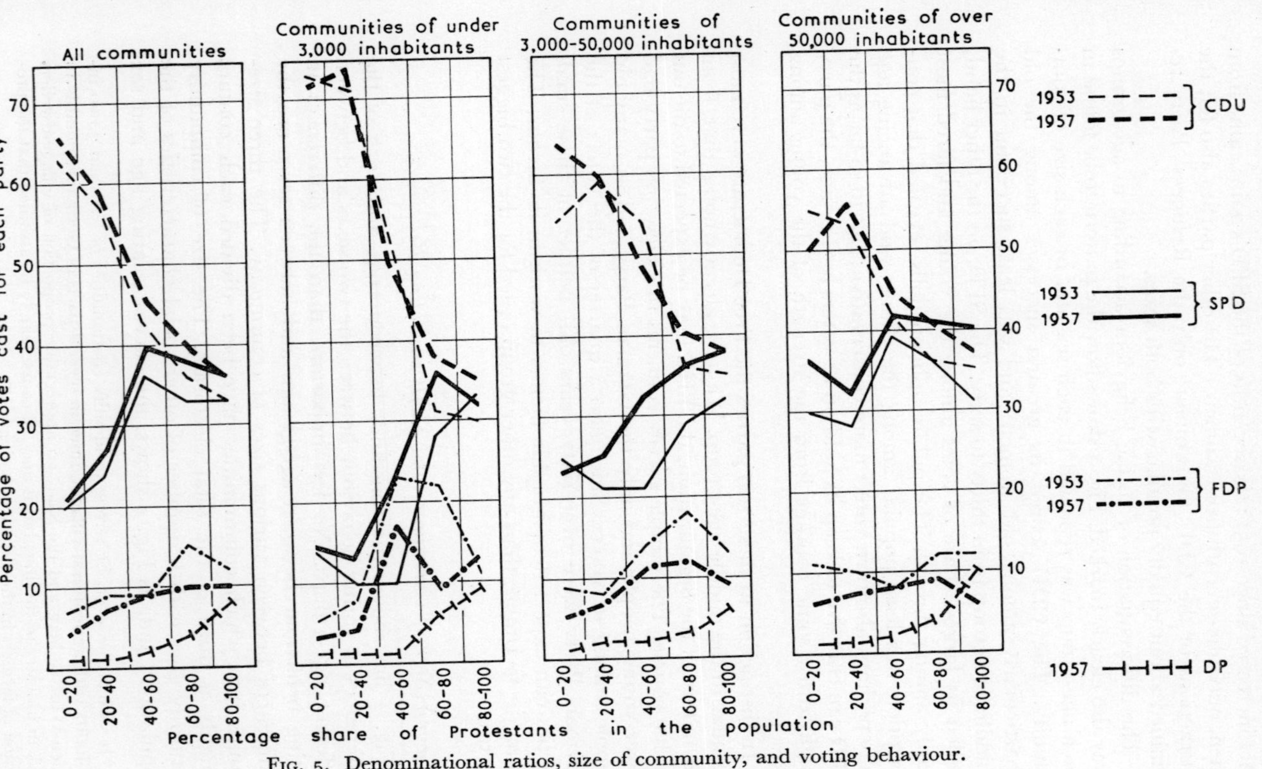

FIG. 5. Denominational ratios, size of community, and voting behaviour.

to voting behaviour, while keeping their shapes, shift appreciably as one turns from one size of community to another.

In 1953 CDU votes were lower while SPD votes were higher in the cities than in the rest of the country. In 1957 this difference was further accentuated. While in 1953 the CDU's poll in the villages lay close to that in the cities, its village poll rose far above its city vote in 1957; and SPD votes, though they rose elsewhere in the country, actually fell in the villages. A more detailed inspection of these curves shows that the CDU made its greatest progress between 1953 and 1957 in the villages, where the SPD's share of votes fell (except among young voters). In the cities, on the other hand, the Social Democrats' gains were as great as those of the CDU: while the CDU made little progress (except in the middle age-groups) the SPD scored its biggest successes of all among young city-dwellers, greatly increasing its bare lead over the CDU among young men. FDP votes fell somewhat between the two elections among both men and women of all three age-groups and in all three sizes of community.

Denominational Factors and Community Size

More interesting still are the associations between the relative strength of the two chief denominations in a community and its voting behaviour. These relationships are illustrated for the three different sizes of community in Fig. 5. Several phenomena emerge with great clarity from the survey.

In the first place the CDU vote tends to fall sharply as the percentage of Protestants in the community increases, while SPD, FDP, and German Party votes tend to rise. If one compares the percentage of votes cast for each party in overwhelmingly Catholic and in overwhelmingly Protestant areas, the CDU's figure falls from 66 to 36 per cent., the SPD's rises from 21 to 36 per cent., while those of the Free Democrats and the German Party rise from 4 and 1 per cent. to 10 and 8 per cent. respectively.

These figures take all sizes of community together. But there are highly significant differences in this respect between villages, towns, and cities. The religious factor is most strongly at work in the villages: in predominantly Catholic villages, for example, the CDU's lead over the SPD is one of 61 per cent. of the total poll. This lead falls to 41 per cent. in the predominantly Catholic towns. In the cities the degree to which differences in denominational balance are associated with differences in voting behaviour becomes rather less dramatic, though even here the CDU's lead over the SPD where the population is predominantly Catholic remains one of 24 per cent. In the case of cities with Protestant majorities the SPD vote in fact ceases to rise altogether as the percentage of Protestants increases, and the continued fall in CDU votes is almost entirely the obverse of a sharp rise in the votes cast for the German Party.

The explanation of this second phenomenon is not particularly difficult. The denominational balance of the statistics refers to nominal church membership, and we have seen that in cities and among Protestants religious observance was less prevalent than in villages and among Catholics. Moreover, the CDU was far from being considered a Catholic party or being rejected as such in cities with strong Protestant majorities: the party's most prominent men in such areas were often themselves leading Protestants, and the SPD could expect little gain as a result of denominational or anti-clerical feelings.

A third phenomenon has perhaps a less obvious explanation. The trends we have just noted are most clearly displayed in communities with a fair mixture of denominations; they seem to be attenuated or even broken as one approaches denominational homogeneity. In overwhelmingly Catholic villages the CDU vote is lower and the SPD vote higher than in only predominantly Catholic villages. In overwhelmingly Protestant villages the SPD vote is lower than in only predominantly Protestant villages, and while the CDU vote does not actually rise again as the proportion of Protestants exceeds 80 per cent. it does not continue to fall at the same rate as in the more mixed communities. (These facts are illustrated pictorially by the various kinks in our curves as they approach the edges in Fig. 5.) Similar breaks in the general pattern of voting behaviour may be found in the towns and the cities in the 1953 as well as in the 1957 results, and they are even more conspicuous if the votes for men and for women are segregated from each other.

The reasons for this third phenomenon must perhaps be sought along lines not dissimilar to those pursued in explaining the failure of the SPD's vote in cities to rise with rising Protestant majorities. In completely homogeneous communities, denominational influences on voting behaviour may be less active than in those where a minority of the other denomination is distinguishable. The lack of a consciousness of religious differentiation may allow slightly more Protestants to vote CDU, slightly more Catholics to vote SPD, than would do so if a denominational 'antibody' provoked some degree of political solidarity along denominational lines. To describe the situation in terms of residual traces of a *Kulturkampf* would be a caricature. But it is a curious fact that both in 1953 and in 1957 the

SPD polled its highest share of votes not in the cities with sizeable Protestant majorities, but in those which were most evenly divided. A tinge of anti-clerical sentiment or tradition among the electorate may well have been one of the factors which allowed the Social Democrats to reach these peaks in their vote.

The Refugees and the BHE

The BHE has been omitted from this discussion of denominational factors: on the whole the BHE vote rises as a Protestant majority in the population rises also. But the BHE vote, not unexpectedly, shows a far more striking correlation with a different demographic factor: the percentage of refugees in the community. (This correlation is illustrated in Fig. 6, in which the curves relating the percentage of refugees and the percentage of BHE votes in a community prove to be practically straight lines passing through the origin.)[1] In 1953, 4 refugees in 10 in the villages, only slightly less in the towns, but less than 1 in 4 of those in the cities voted BHE. In 1957 the proportions in the villages and cities still lay very close below those of 1953, but in the medium towns with less than 40 per cent. of refugees no longer over a third but less than a quarter of them voted for the party that claimed to speak for their interests: only in the towns with more than 40 per cent. of refugees did the BHE's share of the vote rise.[2] Between 1953 and 1957 the process of social and economic absorption, already far advanced in the cities by 1953, had spread more intensively to the smaller and medium-sized towns—except perhaps where refugees were about as numerous as the native population. More unfortunately still for the BHE, voting patterns in the villages had come to be of far less importance to it than those in the towns. Refugees had moved in large numbers from the villages (where they had often lived in camps on the outskirts of the community) to find better homes and work in the towns and cities. As a result of this transfer it was in fact in the villages that the party sustained its heaviest losses.

Federal and Land Elections

The structural stability of voting patterns at least between 1953 and 1957 which is revealed by this sample count stands at first sight

[1] In 1953 no adequate sample of cities with over 40 per cent. of refugees was available; as a result the lowest dotted line on Fig. 6 stops short of the others.

[2] In Fig. 6 the last point on the curve for medium-sized towns is based on two polling booths only; if the average percentage of refugees in these two areas was rather higher than in the corresponding area in 1953 (a not unlikely hypothesis) the 1957 line would not cross that for 1953, but still lie below it.

in striking contrast to the violently oscillatory pattern of Land and federal elections. Since the beginning of the Federal Republic the CDU has in every Land polled a smaller percentage of votes in each of the two Land elections than in the succeeding Bundestag election,

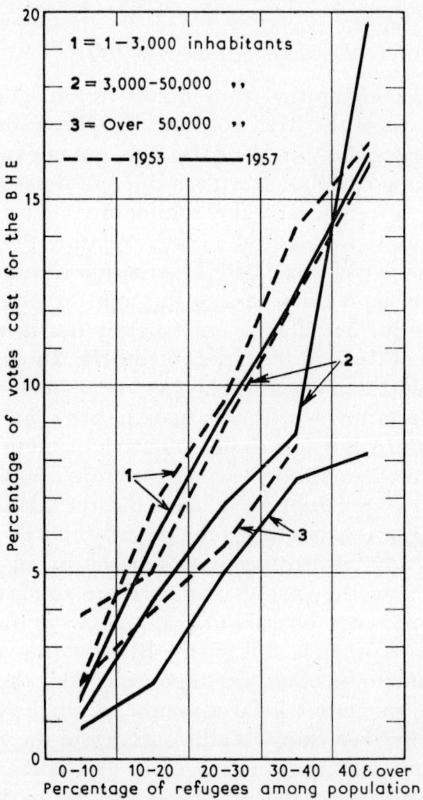

FIG. 6. Percentage of refugees and of BHE votes.

and the SPD has everywhere polled a larger percentage of votes in each Landtag election than in the succeeding Bundestag election.

The theoretical question why this happened is also of great practical importance. If the Christian Democrats have merely been lucky in that the two federal elections of 1953 and 1957 were held near the peaks of their ascendancy with the public, the appearance of a 'pattern' is accidental, and there is little guarantee that such a remarkable divergence of Land and federal election results will recur.[1] If, on the other hand, the regularity is more than fortuitous, the reasons underlying it will affect both political predictions and also policy and propaganda recommendations to the parties. If the CDU excels the SPD in electioneering efforts during federal campaigns more than during Land campaigns, or if the SPD, partly owing to its very structure, outdoes the CDU's campaigns in Landtag elections, a change in the balance of financial resources or propaganda efficiency could alter the pattern in favour or to the detriment of either party. If large portions of the electorate systematically distinguish between different types of election and vote for the Social Democrats on Land and for the Christian Democrats on federal issues, this conclusion should affect both the policy of the parties and also the quality rather than the quantity of their public relations work. And if it is Adenauer's personality which wins federal elections while the personalities of SPD Land politicians attract more votes at Land elections, then a time may come when the 'pattern' may become less relevant even if the SPD, for reasons which we have discussed, may find it more difficult to find a leader of equivalent charismatic appeal.

All these factors may be at work to a greater or less extent, but some at least are clearly subordinate. It has often been maintained that large sections of the electorate really oscillate between the parties. But Figs. 7 and 8 suggest a different picture. These diagrams depart from the more usual presentation by expressing party polls not in terms of valid votes cast, but as a percentage of the total number of electors.[2] Fig. 7 A confirms the existence of a regularity: it shows that there is a uniformly oscillatory pattern not only in the percentage of voters, but also—indeed even more so—in that of electors who vote for the CDU. Three rules in fact hold good for every Land throughout the diagram: firstly, the CDU's share of the electorate rose in each Bundestag election compared with the last; secondly, the CDU's share of the electorate rose in each Land election held since the establishment of the Federal Republic compared with the last; but, thirdly, in each Land election the CDU polled a smaller percentage of electors than at either the preceding or the following Bundestag election.

[1] The public opinion polls show that the CDU was more popular than ever before in the autumn of 1953 and reached a new peak of popularity in the autumn of 1957, the highest figures being obtained on both occasions immediately after the election.

[2] This is the method used by Schütz, op. cit., pp. 149–88. Hamburg and Lower Saxony have partly been omitted from the diagrams: where the CDU formed electoral alliances with other parties no CDU vote can be recorded for the Land elections concerned.

Fig. 7 B, however, demonstrates that this pattern cannot be explained simply by the 'swing of the pendulum' between the two main parties. It is here that the calculation of votes in terms of electors yields the most striking result: it eliminates the oscillation in the SPD's percentage between comparative success in Land and comparative failure in Bundestag elections. In three Länder in which the SPD led

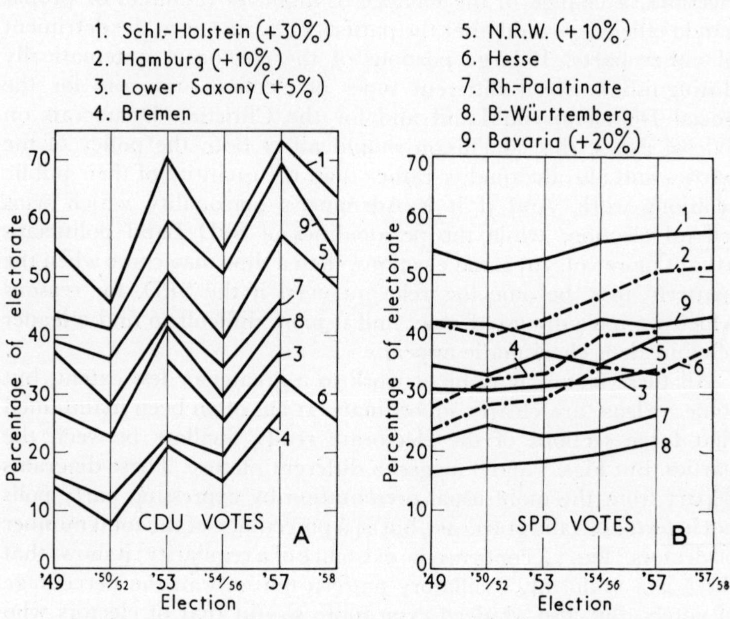

FIG. 7. CDU and SPD votes in Land and in federal elections.

the Government for longer than in any other and where it won the confidence of the electorate as a Government party—Bremen, Hamburg, and Hesse—the SPD's poll even shows a distinct upward trend; the rest of the curves are more or less horizontal. The SPD thus brings out a remarkably constant proportion of the electorate in Land as well as in federal elections: its comparative successes in Land elections, its comparative failures in Bundestag elections, are not primarily due to special efforts or to defections on the part of its own faithful voters: both phenomena depend on the voting behaviour of the remainder of the electorate.

A more precise picture of this non-socialist voting is presented by Fig. 8, which divides the electorate of each Land into four categories: CDU voters, SPD voters, those who voted for other parties, and

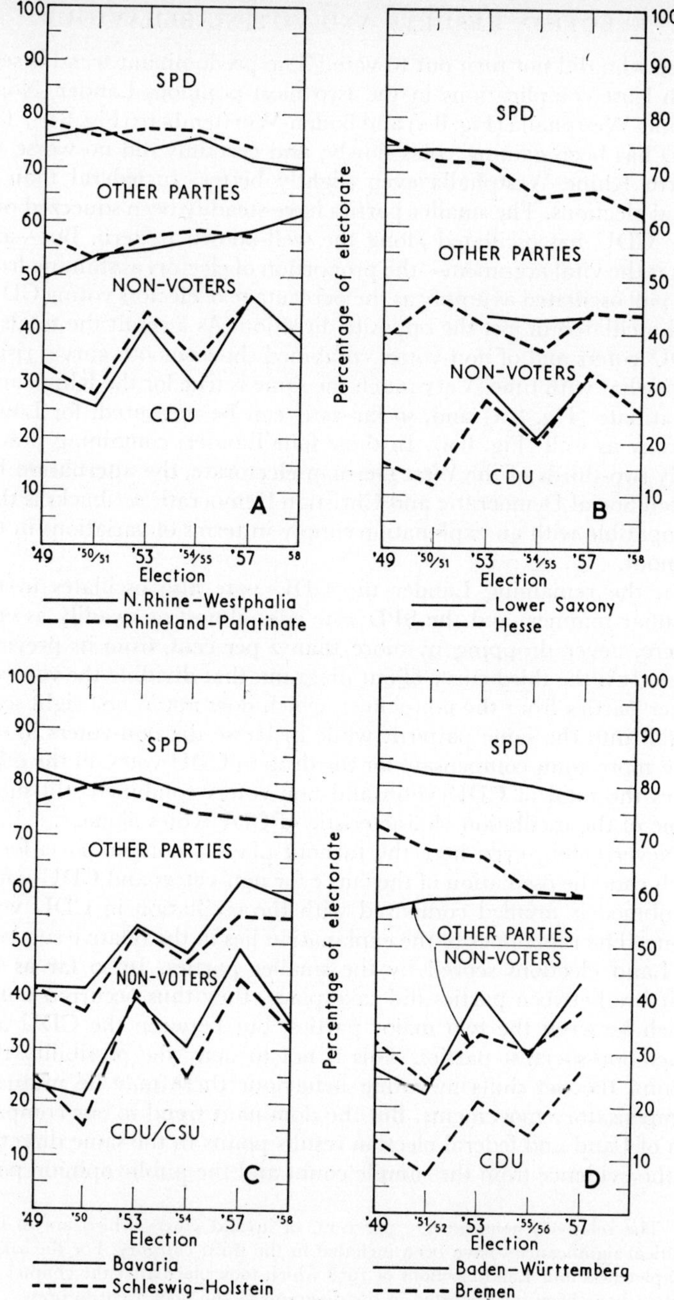

FIG. 8. Voting results in Land and in federal elections.

those who did not turn out to vote.[1] The predominant trend is seen with least complications in the two most populous Länder, North Rhine–Westphalia (Fig. 8 A) and Baden-Württemberg (Fig. 8 D). The SPD has been gaining votes slowly, and certainly did no worse (in North Rhine–Westphalia even slightly better) in federal than in Land elections. The smaller parties have steadily been squeezed out. The CDU has oscillated along the well-known pattern. But—and this is the vital argument—the proportion of electors abstaining from the poll oscillated as amply as the percentage of electors voting CDU, and oscillated in just the opposite direction. As a result the totals of CDU voters and of non-voters combined show smooth curves rising somewhat with time. Very much the same is true for the Rhineland-Palatinate (Fig. 8 A) and, so far as it can be measured, for Lower Saxony as well (Fig. 8 B). In these four Länder, containing practically two-thirds of the West German electorate, the alternation between Social Democratic and Christian Democratic set-backs is thus compatible with an explanation simply in terms of variations in the turnout.

In the remaining Länder the CDU vote also oscillates in the familiar manner, and the SPD vote rises almost as steadily as elsewhere, never dropping by more than 2 per cent. from its previous peak. It is the third curve of our diagram, that dividing the voters of other parties from the non-voters, which does not at first sight seem to fall into the same pattern: while in Hesse the non-voters in one case more than compensate for the drop in CDU votes, in the other cases the total of CDU votes and non-voters combined still shows some of the oscillation characteristic of CDU votes alone.

Nevertheless, even here the turnout plays a notable part: for in each case the oscillation of the curve for non-voters and CDU-voters combined is muffled compared with the oscillation in CDU votes alone. The remainder of the explanation lies in the relative successes in Land elections scored by the smaller parties. In so far as net switches between parties did take place, they thus occurred not so much between the two major parties, but between the CDU and other non-socialist parties. This is not to deny the possibility that behind the net shifts in voting behaviour there may lie mutually compensatory movements. But the dominant trend in our comparison of Land and federal election results points in the same direction as the evidence from the sample count and the public opinion polls,

[1] The relatively constant 2–3 per cent. of invalid votes—which are of little political significance—have been included in the third category. For the sake of completeness four Land elections of 1958 which took place after the chapter was written have been incorporated in the diagrams as the book went to press.

and would not lead us to attach any prime causal role to such unprovable mutually compensatary movements.

Conclusion[1]

These different sources of evidence thus all point to much the same picture. The Social Democrats have yet to poll a third of the electorate; the Christian Democrats have reasserted their hold on the *bourgeoisie* and on the Catholic workers; and the CDU's intensive propaganda was required not merely to convince the interested voters hesitating between CDU and SPD, but even more to mobilize the marginal electors symbolized by those 'little old mothers' at whom the CDU was consciously beaming Adenauer's political sex-appeal. The campaign brought to the polls a large number of those who do not vote at every election: and it was their votes which gave the Government its resounding victory.

The reasons why these marginal electors turned out and cast their votes for the CDU are not difficult to summarize. Continued and intensified political and economic success was the essential basis of Adenauer's renewed triumph: with the important exception of reunification, the Government appeared to have achieved (or even, as in the Saar issue, surpassed) every one of its aims. The whole apparatus of public relations skilfully paraded these successes before the electorate. Adenauer's own personality and the projection of 'Adenauer and his team', the moral support of the Catholic Church and the financial backing of the business community, the favour of the Western powers, events in Hungary and the attacks from the Kremlin all helped the CDU campaign. Against all this the Social Democrats could pit little but their opposition to atomic rearmament, a foreign policy unintelligible to much of the electorate, a variety of social demands, and the loyalty of their stalwart membership. As an alternative government, the Social Democrats never really captured the imagination of the people.

The West hailed Adenauer's victory as a ratification of its policy towards Germany and as a guarantee of the continued loyalty of one part of a divided Germany to the North Atlantic alliance. Western foreign offices were happy to continue their co-operation with the good European they had learnt to respect and to trust. The West had a stake in a strong and stable government in Bonn, and any change would have involved them in uncertainties. Whether an Opposition victory would really have entailed any very long-

[1] I am indebted to the Editor of *The Spectator* for permission to use as my conclusion the substance of an article which appeared in his columns on 20 Sept. 1957.

term dangers is another matter: perhaps after a period of experiment needing patience and imagination a change of government would ultimately have led to a bipartisan foreign policy and even greater clarity in central European affairs.

But whatever advantages Adenauer's victory had abroad, his party's absolute majority was hardly likely to prove an unqualified benefit to the young Republic itself. There is nothing wrong in a government being re-elected for a third term of office: nothing wrong perhaps even if its leading party increases its lead at each poll. Democracy—particularly in North America—is not dependent on constant alternation. But there are dangers if one party first has the largest influence in building up a new State and controls it for at any rate the first twelve years of its existence, fills it with personnel consisting to a great extent of its own supporters, and uses it to maintain itself in power. The federal system against which the Social and Free Democrats fought during the drafting of the Basic Law has given them certain countervailing preserves in Land and local government: without these the dangers of an abuse of power would have been considerably more acute—but even so the new democracy still has serious structural problems to face.

We have seen how votes have tended to concentrate on the two major parties—above all on the CDU—and how the Free Democrats have steadily tended to lose votes. One of the problems before German parliamentary democracy, if this trend were to continue, is how the Social Democrats could ever come to power by themselves; the survival of the Free Democrats and the SPD's capacity to compromise and ally with them thus seem presupposed in any attempt to give the CDU a vacation from Government responsibility.

If the Communists hoped for a splintering of the SPD or a radical swing to the left after this third federal defeat their hopes were doomed to disappointment. The SPD has faced worse rebuffs and emerged basically undivided. The 'monolithic' party officialdom that was a liability in the campaign proved an asset in defeat. Nor could the party turn to the left. It cannot win an ideological election, and if the issue is Christianity versus socialism it will for years to come stay cooped up within its own third of the electorate. Only with a more empirical approach, loyal, detailed constructive opposition, with new and attractive personalities of the type of Willy Brandt (who was elected Mayor of Berlin immediately after the election), with quiet persistent public relations work and a concentration on a 'changing of the guard' between the Ins and the Outs, can the Social Democrats expect to make any headway in the new social context of post-war Western Germany.

Nor are the problems all on one side. The unequivocal election result has placed an even greater responsibility squarely with the CDU. It gives the Christian Democrats the unchallenged strength and the respite from domestic political pressure to rethink their position within the State they have so largely created: their personal and financial links with various ramifications of the public service, their personal and financial links with the trade associations and with big and medium enterprise, and their political connexion with the Catholic Church all merit detailed appraisal as does Adenauer's own position within or above the party. Moreover, during election night there was talk of constitutional reforms that the SPD might have been unable to veto, and an electoral reform such as that attempted in 1955 could now be voted by the CDU alone. No such reform may be needed: it is remarkable enough that proportional representation allowed such a clear single-party majority to emerge in the Bundestag. But other temptations of absolute victory will remain.

The Christian Democrats have faced many problems in the post-war years. They have had the largest single share in constructing the prosperous and democratic Western Germany we know today. They took the lead in binding it to a European and a Western community, and now Western Germany's economic strength has allowed them (or forced them) also to assume much of the political leadership of continental Europe. Yet perhaps the acid test of their statesmanship is still to come. The Federal Republic regards itself as a Western shop-window to the East and as a model for other countries in Europe to follow. The CDU will no doubt use its absolute majority with due scruple even if public opinion is not on its guard. Should it fail, the nemesis would not be immediately apparent: but it might not be confined to Christian Democracy, nor for that matter to Germany alone.

APPENDIX

An Estimate of Campaign Expenditure

THE general principles along which one might attempt to assess the sums spent in the 1957 Bundestag election were indicated in Chapter X: where no evidence is available from a party organization, a quantitative estimate of its campaign multiplied by market prices must serve as a guide. The chief problem in this connexion is the expenditure of the CDU. We have seen that the party refused to publish any figures, and the 6·7 or 7 million DM mentioned at various times are quite obviously not a guide to the total.[1] It is no wonder if, therefore, one is driven to seeking evidence from the CDU's opponents.

In the heat of the battle, the SPD attempted a comprehensive calculation, and concluded: 'We have evidence on the extent of the avalanche of propaganda from the government, the government parties and industry. This evidence suggests that the resources expended by that side in the election campaign are of the order of between 90 and 120 million DM.'[2] This of course was a campaign declaration. But it was stated in such unparalleled detail that it would be cavalier to dismiss it as being no more than propaganda. The fact that it also represents the maximum reasoned claim staked out on the size of pro-Government expenditure makes it a natural starting-point from which to examine the question. If in the event our calculation results in a lower total, this is not surprising: the Social Democrats could hardly be expected to underestimate the funds deployed against them, and it must be stressed that the argument also leads us to a multiple of the only total ever mentioned during the campaign on the CDU side. The purpose of the present Appendix is thus not to expose the over-estimates of the SPD but to penetrate the veil of secrecy maintained in public by the CDU; and if in order to justify the conclusions reached in the present Appendix one is forced to compare them constantly with those of the Social Democrats, the resulting appearance of partisanship is due above all to the public silence of the CDU, and to the fact that only a close examination of the Social Democrats' methods of calculating the total can do justice to their pioneer argumentation in this interesting and difficult field.

According to the SPD's calculation 46 million DM were deployed between them by the CDU and the German Party; 40 million DM were used for direct and indirect influence on the election by the Federal Government and its ancillary public relations organizations; and 30 million DM were spent by 'The Balance', the 'Action Committee for a Social Market Economy',

[1] For greater accuracy and ease of comparison the argument of this Appendix is stated in Deutschmark terms. (11·75 DM = £1; 4·20 DM = $1.)

[2] *SPD Pressemitteilungen und Informationen*, 13 Sept. 1957.

and similar public relations campaigns carried on by single firms, trade and industrial organizations, and public relations institutes.

The cost of the German Party's campaign can be eliminated from this estimate and valuable hints gained for the calculation of the expenses of other parties as a result of the courtesy of the German Party in discussing its expenditure in detail. Immediately after the poll its campaign manager estimated the total cost of the party's campaign at 3·5 million DM—3.50 DM (or six shillings) per vote obtained. Some of his opponents put the figure nearer 5 million DM, but they were probably misled by being insufficiently familiar with conditions in the South of the country, where the German Party ran no substantial Land or local campaigns.

The central headquarters of the German Party organized its poster campaign in three successive waves:

1. The 'Dice' poster, printed in 58,00 copies, was exhibited for ten days on all ordinary sites in the North and West and on every second site in the South at a cost of 146,000 DM.
2. The 'Happy holidays' poster, printed in 34,000 copies, was exhibited for fourteen days particularly in summer resorts and near railway stations at a cost of 65,000 DM.
3. In order to guard against the destruction of posters expected in the heat of the last days of the campaign the 'Stop' poster was printed in 160,000 copies. Its printing cost 17,000 DM, its exhibition for fourteen days on all ordinary sites in the Federal Republic cost 190,000 DM.

The total cost of the central poster campaign was thus 400,000 DM for the exhibition of the posters, and perhaps another 30,000 DM for their printing.

In addition the German Party placed four successive advertisements of an eighth of a page at a time in 497 dailies with a total circulation of 10 or 11 million copies at a cost of 387,000 DM. Through a commercial address firm in Darmstadt it sent off nearly 3 million personal letters to farmers, professional and middle-class people at a cost of another 400,000 DM. The use of sixteen *Mobilwerbung* film vans in the campaign cost 148,000 DM, and we may reckon another 250,000 DM for federal brochures, bringing the central campaign expenditure up to 1·7 million DM. The estimate of 3·5 million DM made immediately after the election presumably represents a doubling of the figure for central expenditure.

If the German Party thus spent around 4 million DM on its campaign, that would leave an SPD estimate of just over 40 million DM for the CDU itself—not an over-estimate if funds were distributed between the two parties in proportion to the German Party's 3 per cent. and the CDU's 50 per cent. share of the poll.

No period of time was mentioned over which the CDU was alleged to have spent this money. But it is clear that one item at least—the preparatory polling of public opinion—even if incurred for the purposes of the campaign, had been disbursed over the previous years. As presented by the SPD the figure still contained a number of items which a stricter system of accounting would attribute not to the CDU itself, but to bodies such as those which carried on the parallel campaign in favour of Erhard's 'Social Market Economy'. The SPD's more widely framed estimate (reclassified and summarized in column (1) of Table X) attributed an expenditure of 41.9 million DM to the CDU headquarters and went on to state: 'To these costs must be added the expenditure of the intermediate and local levels of the CDU organisation, which require at least the same sum again, if not a higher one still.'

The present purpose of estimating the CDU's own expenditure incurred specifically for the election is, of course, quite distinct from the wider aim of

TABLE XI

The SPD's Estimate of the CDU's Central Expenditure

Reclassified according to the definitions set out in the text.
(millions of DM)

Column 1: Estimates published in *SPD Pressemitteilungen und Informationen* of 13 September 1957.

Column 2: Portions of these estimates that should be attributed to parallel campaigns (including the Erhard campaign).

Column 3: Items attributable to the Land and local organizations of the CDU.

Column 4: Remaining items attributable to the federal CDU (including the Adenauer campaign), reckoned at the SPD's estimate of prices and quantities.

The author's own estimates of CDU expenditure will be found in the text on pp. 309–10.

	(1)	(2)	(3)	(4)
(*a*) The illustrated magazine of the Erhard campaign	4·3	4·3	..	..
(*b*) The illustrated magazine of the Adenauer campaign and Adenauer's letter to the electorate	5·7	..	..	5·7*
(*c*) Posters	6·0	1·0	..	5·0
(*d*) Press advertising	6·0	3·0	..	3·0
(*e*) Film production costs	3·0	1·5	..	1·5
(*f*) Use of film vans	1·5	0·8	0·7	..
(*g*) Meetings	5·0	..	5·0	..
(*h*) Adenauer's train	1·5	..	..	1·5*
(*i*) *Ad hoc* publications	2·5	1·0	..	1·5
(*j*) Current publications	1·5†	..	..	..
(*k*) Direct camouflage propaganda instigated by the CDU	1·0	1·0	..	..
(*l*) Miscellaneous expenditure, including temporary staff and opinion polling since 1955	3·9	1·5	..	2·4
(*m*) Total	41·9	13·1	5·7	20·6

* Attributable to the Adenauer campaign.

† To be excluded altogether from campaign expenditure.

the SPD's publication. Certain of these items must therefore be excluded from the calculation. Item (*j*) should be excluded altogether as not arising specifically from the election—otherwise the cost of the SPD's party newspaper *Vorwärts* would need to be charged against the SPD's campaign. Item (*a*) and portions of a number of other items should also be segregated from the calculation for the CDU and reserved for later consideration along with other forms of parallel propaganda. As a result of such a tightening of definitions the SPD's estimate of the CDU's central expenditure would be reduced by between 10 and 15 million DM to between 25 million and 30 million DM. (More precise figures are given simply for the sake of argument in column (2) of our table.) How near to the truth is this redefined estimate, based on that of the CDU's opponents?

The Cost of the CDU Campaign

The easiest figures to check are those of press advertising. After the election was over the SPD was able to obtain figures prepared by one of the two leading firms of advertising analysts in Germany. From June until September—i.e. for the last three and a half months of the campaign—the CDU itself took up advertising space valued according to published advertising rates at 2,622,073 DM, and the two organizations of the Erhard campaign bought space valued at 1,943,622 DM, making a total of 4,563,695 DM in all. This sum, which neglects certain types of advertisements such as those in specialist periodicals, is somewhat below the 6 million DM of the SPD's pre-election estimate—but then that figure referred to a rather longer period.

Given their wider definition of all pro-Government propaganda over a longer period, the Social Democrats' figure was thus fairly accurate in giving an idea of the newspaper space involved. But this revised and narrowed figure of about 2·6 million DM spent on CDU advertisements was substantially accurate only as a result of two mutually compensating flaws: on the one hand it did not make due allowance for the very substantial sums paid by the CDU for advertisements in specialist periodicals carefully aimed at a specialist public, and, on the other hand, it neglected the quantity discounts, which could rise to more than a third of the nominal cost of an advertising campaign. In fact the CDU's central advertisements cost it about 1·5 million DM, and another million DM was spent at the Land and local levels.

A second check may be made in the case of the open air exhibition of films, which was estimated by the SPD to have cost 1·5 million DM. In accordance with the present purpose one must neglect the campaign in favour of NATO carried out in the early summer and presumably financed by the Ministry of Defence. There remain at most three months of such activity on the part of the CDU. The firm which hired out film vans, *Mobilwerbung* of Bonn, cannot have placed more than about 45 trucks at the CDU's disposal, for it owned less than 80, and 30 of these were hired to other parties. Even if *Mobilwerbung* charged the CDU full commercial rates without quantity discounts (about 150 DM per day all inclusive), the exhibition of films from *Mobilwerbung* vans would still have cost only about 600,000 DM. Most of the other CDU film vans were operated by volunteers or by the party's employees, whose wages, if temporary, were included in the SPD's estimate under the miscellaneous expenditure of item (*l*). Only about a third or a half of the sum suggested by the SPD for the total cost of all film exhibitions over a longer period can therefore be imputed to the CDU's election campaign. The production of the CDU's own films—as distinct from those of the Government and its various agencies—apparently cost about half the sum cited by the SPD. This figure seems all the more reasonable in view of the fact that, apart from three cartoon films, the party tended to use existing newsreel and documentary material.

The main distinction with which we have so far operated has been that between party and parallel campaigns; but that between central party expenditure and Land and local party expenditure is even more relevant when one considers the sums spent on posters. Here three types of expenditure must be distinguished: the development of the poster including the capital cost of the matrices for its printing, the paper and printing cost per poster, and the costs of exhibition. According to the SPD one double-sized poster exhibited on all the ordinary sites of the Federal Republic cost 55,000 DM per day.[1] Even on this calculation the CDU's forty-one-day campaign of two posters on all ordinary sites should not have cost more than 2·2 million DM. In fact it would seem that this price is too high, that quantity discounts were substantial, and that the cost of developing the posters and the large special sites hired for the last ten days could largely be fitted into the error thus introduced. The CDU's federal headquarters would not appear to have spent much more than 2·5 million DM on its poster campaign. How much more was spent by the Land and local organizations on the printing of posters for their own requirements, and how much they may have spent on distribution and exhibition, was a secret kept by each organization as against the federal headquarters and the rest. The 5 million DM of the SPD's estimate would thus seem to be adequate to cover both central and other poster expenses.

The other large items listed in the SPD's estimate of the CDU's central expenditure are the illustrated magazine *This is the Place at Stake* and the Adenauer letter (both distributed to every household), the cost of Adenauer's campaign train, and the central programme of meetings. The meetings, however—like the mobile film displays—were paid for not by the federal party, but by its Land and local organizations. Odd as it may seem, Adenauer's train, Adenauer's letter to the voters, and the magazine which took as its theme his chair in the Chancellory must also be distinguished from the federal party's election expenses: although some of the cheques involved were signed by the same party official as the CDU's own payments, this Adenauer campaign was not formally paid for out of the party budget, but

[1] The SPD's press release in fact referred to the curious concept of '*daily* costs of exhibition and printing' (SPD's italics). Standard size is roughly 46 × 32 in.

out of funds raised by the Chancellor himself or on his behalf. Pedantically defined, the CDU's own central budget appears to have comprised only 2·5 million DM on posters, 1·5 million DM on advertisements, 1·5 million DM on films, and perhaps 1·2 or 1·5 million DM on *ad hoc* publications and miscellaneous expenditure, making a total of perhaps 6·7 or 7 million DM in all. (This would seem to be the figure referred to by the CDU itself.) To this total must, however, be added the costs of the Adenauer campaign and other federal expenditure incurred to all intents and purposes on behalf of the party; they bring central expenditure into the region of 13–16 million DM.

The SPD wished to double the figure it had calculated for the CDU's central costs in order to take account of Land and local expenditure. Such a rule of thumb has a certain validity in the case of the SPD, which relied heavily on the local initiative of its members. It may also be applicable to the CDU if central expenditure is carefully defined. But it is inadmissible to double the original figure of 41·9 million as the SPD tried to do; for that figure charged to headquarters the cost of the larger meetings, of 'several hundred extra employees in the country at large', and a good deal of other Land and local expenditure, which a doubled estimate would then be counting twice.[1]

Nevertheless it is certain that heavy expenditure was incurred at the Land and constituency levels; its scale at times surprised even the CDU's own headquarters. Either the Land organizations in their reports to the headquarters minimized the money they had available, or else they must have found that at a late stage more money came into their coffers than they had expected. In Baden-Württemberg, for example, the Land office ran a sizeable if not very successful advertising campaign of its own prior and parallel to the federal one, and a good many similar Land initiatives were developed elsewhere.

But it was at the constituency level above all that candidates, their business associates, and their trade organizations were able to expend funds that never passed through the CDU's Land or even constituency accounts. In one perfectly safe seat in Baden-Württemberg the local candidate spent some 110,000 DM over and above the resources deployed in his constituency by the federal and Land campaigns. (He was a director of a large industrial concern which wished to take no risks about his election to the Bundestag.) 30,000–40,000 DM were spent by a good many candidates in their local campaigns, though others may not have spent much more than 10,000 20,000 DM. Given some 240 CDU candidates, perhaps a figure of 6 million DM would seem to be on the conservative side for expenditure at the local level, and expenditure at the Land level may have carried the total of non-federal spending well beyond 12 million DM.

[1] It is also difficult to reconcile a doubled figure of over 80 million DM for the CDU alone with the overall figure of 90–120 million DM unless some of the Government and private parallel campaigns are already included in the CDU figure. This does in fact seem to be one of the errors in the SPD's reasoning, as witness col. (2) of Table X.

As far as general impressions go, the SPD explained that it spent about 4 million DM at the centre, and we shall argue that it spent the same amount again on the regional and local level. It is true that a further amount might have to be added to obtain the market price of all the pro-SPD material distributed. It is also true that the CDU tended to choose expensive methods of propaganda whereas the SPD concentrated on the cheaper ones. But it is hardly conceivable that the CDU should have spent eight or ten times as much as the SPD, particularly when it is remembered that while the SPD began the campaign early, the CDU largely held its fire until August; it incurred, for example, three-quarters of its newspaper advertising costs in the last fourteen days of the campaign. The CDU may in the final stages of the battle have spent three or four times as much as the SPD: but even then we may reckon that its total expenditure in the last three or four months of the campaign was only in the region of 25–30 million DM.

The Cost of Parallel Campaigns

One of the main reasons why this narrow and temporally limited estimate comes out so far below the wider one of the SPD is, as we have seen, the inclusion of a part of the Erhard campaign and similar parallel activities in the Social Democrats' estimate of CDU expenditure. In col. (2) of Table X we segregated 13·1 million DM from the SPD's estimate of CDU expenditure. This part of the problem has thus so far simply been carried over by our redefinitions, and the level of expenditure on these parallel campaigns remains to be discussed.

The Social Democrats suggested that 40 million DM were being spent by the Government and 30 million more by private funds, and appended to their calculation of CDU expenditure a list of forty-one other organizations which had issued open or camouflaged pro-Government propaganda during the campaign. The SPD estimated the cost of the Erhard campaign at 20·3 million DM over several years. An institute of advertising analysis valued the space bought during the last three and a half months before polling day by the two organizations which carried through this campaign at 1,943,622 DM. Quantity discounts presumably reduced this figure to below 1·5 million DM. It is hardly likely that the two posters cost more than 500,000 DM in all. This leaves only the magazine *All of Us* to be considered. The Social Democrats estimated the cost of *All of Us* at 4·3 million DM—but their figure evidently disregards the revenue derived from the substantial commercial advertising which the publication carried; this revenue certainly helped pay for *All of Us* but must be deducted from its money cost to the Erhard campaign.[1] As a result, even a figure of 5·8 million DM may be

[1] Thus the cigarette firm Reemtsma, which gave substantial financial support to the FDP and also advertised in SPD publications, bought three-quarters of a page of *All of Us* for the display of its usual commercial advertisement, arguing (in a letter to the author): 'Since the consumption of our brands (like that of those at higher prices) is widely scattered, our smokers are to be found in all classes of the population. . . . We therefore cannot support any political tendency or any denomination, but must consider solely one thing: the development of the brand in question.'

2 million DM or more above what the Erhard campaign actually cost its promoters during the crucial four months before the election. On the other hand, the total cost of materials, printing, and distribution calculated without deduction of the advertising revenue might yield a rather higher figure.

The SPD's list of parallel campaigns went on to cite several larger initiatives: a poster on reunification at 2·5 million DM, a poster on Hungary at 1·8 million DM, the commercially unsuccessful illustrated paper *Bleib im Bild* with 2 million DM, and the ADK's exhibition train with 1 million DM. To this category of expenditure no doubt should be added the 2·3 million DM on the production and exhibition of films which figure in col. (2) of Table XI and refer in the main to the NATO campaign of the Ministry of Defence during the early summer. This makes a total of 10·3 million DM spent on a few campaigns which directly impinged on the election, and the SPD would no doubt ascribe this expenditure to Government funds.[1] A detailed revaluation of these figures would run largely parallel to the arguments already developed in the case of the CDU itself and might result in the reduction of the total by something like half, although in this case, of course, it is not the precise sum spent but rather the principle at stake that is of interest.

It was generally admitted that Government funds were used on a large scale before and during the election to propagate the Government's foreign, military, and domestic policies among the electorate. The Chancellor's fund of 11 million DM per annum was one of the chief sources of finance for such activity, the Press and Information Office with its annual budget of 20 million DM used a certain proportion of its funds in a similar direction, and the information budgets of the various ministries, particularly that of the Ministry of Defence, which amounted to 6 million DM per annum, were also used in part for overt and indirect activity of this kind. But no useful purpose would be served by attempting to calculate a wholly arbitrary figure of Government expenditure incurred more or less directly to return the Government parties to power. The line between propaganda for a government and its policies and for the Government parties and their personalities is not easy to draw in a State where the Opposition rejects such important parts of Government policy as was the case in the Federal Republic. This undoubted fact was used (even perhaps abused) by supporters of the Government to defend its information policy; but it is also a source of very real difficulty for any attempt at a break-down of information accounts for the purposes of political studies.

The remaining thirty-odd items on the SPD's list of other parallel propaganda added up to only 4,295,000 DM. They included such dubious ones as *Mann in der Zeit*, a Catholic monthly newspaper edited on behalf of the

[1] The SPD stated that the Federal Government had accumulated 40 million DM out of various budgetary items for direct and indirect influence in the election, the evidence cited being the statement of Professor Wilhelm Gülich, an SPD member in the Bundestag, during the debate on information funds on 20 June 1956 (150th sitting of the second Bundestag, p. 7998).

German bishops and sold at church doors on economic terms in an edition of over half a million copies. Certainly the SPD was right in claiming that its list was not exhaustive, even if its criteria of inclusion were loose. But on the whole one may assume that where publications were not noticed by the SPD, they were not noticed by the ordinary voter either.

On our definitions, therefore, it would not seem preposterous to suggest that the whole prime cost of the CDU's own campaign, of the Erhard and of similar private campaigns (though not of such governmental propaganda expenditure as was incurred during the first nine months of 1957 in addition to the normal public relations work) might still be fitted into a combined overall budget for the campaign itself of some 30–35 million DM. The inclusion of the cost of Government public relations for any length of time before the election would obviously result in a total that lay nearer the SPD's estimate and even farther away from the only figure ever mentioned during the campaign by the CDU.

Even after the monetary estimates of the SPD have been scaled down in accordance with tighter definitions and more realistic price schedules, the main point which the SPD sought to establish thus still emerges more or less intact. The sums spent by pro-Government campaigns were very large by any but American standards of comparison: they were a multiple of the sums spent in British elections,[1] and they were a multiple of the sums available to the SPD.

The Expenditure of Other Parties

In notable contrast to most other parties, the Social Democrats prided themselves on the publicity of their own financial arrangements. The Federal Treasurer of the party—in whose interest it was to put in a high claim against the campaign manager—assessed the cost of the federal headquarters' campaign as 4,116,696·8 DM, though unfortunately no breakdown according to campaign media is available.

To this federal expenditure must be added that of the party regions (and in some cases the sub-regions) and that of the local party organizations. The SPD regarded it as an established rule that campaign expenditure at the federal level represents only half of total spending. It was, therefore, not overstating its efforts when it declared after the election: 'Such information as we have already received shows that the local parties and the party regions spent much more than 2 million DM . . . so that the total spending of the party at all levels exceeded the sum of 6 million DM.'[2]

A number of party regions have kindly made available information on

[1] In 1955 the Conservative candidates spent some £458,000, the Labour candidates £379,000, and the Liberal candidates and other candidates £66,000 (see D. E. Butler, *The British General Election of 1955*, p. 114). Since these figures are declared on a constituency basis, certain central expenses—perhaps in the region of £100,000 but hardly more than £200,000—should be added to the figures for the two chief parties to allow for an international comparison.

[2] SPD, *Jahrbuch 1956/7*, p. 250.

their election spending, and these figures indicate a highly unequal distribution of funds varying from 4,356 DM to 24,011 DM per constituency, and from 21 to 53 pfennigs per vote obtained.[1]

TABLE XI

Expenditure in SPD Regions

	Constituencies	*SPD votes ('000)*	*Expenditure*		*Total of both*
			Regional	*Local*	
Rheinhessen	2	97	37,176	..	..
Hessen–Nord	6	271	41,999	102,070	144,069
Ostwestfalen–Lippe	8	334	120,325	54,550	174,875
Weser–Ems	10	298	31,095	'about same'	..
Niederbayern–Oberphalz	11	225	32,619	15,300	47,919
Mittelrhein	13	357	47,875	45,576	93,451
Franken	17	573	105,839	114,039	219,878
Five Regions	55	1,760	348,658	331,535	680,190
Seven Regions	67	2,155	416,928	..	..
Nineteen Regions	247	9,491	..	..	..

An extrapolation of these figures suggests that expenditure on the regional level lay between 1·5 and 2 million DM (the first figure being based on the number of constituencies, the second on that of SPD votes) and that total regional and local expenditure taken together lay between 3 and 3·8 million DM. Where the local expenditure is concerned, this may well neglect expenditure financed by the candidate personally and certainly omits the cost of meetings and other activities occasionally financed by friendly organizations such as trade unions. A certain clue to the ways in which this money was spent may be gained from the accounts of Rheinhessen, a region of only two constituencies, where constituency expenditure probably came out of regional rather than local funds. According to this break-down, one-third of the money was spent on posters and pamphlets, another third on newspaper advertisements and poster display, and the remainder on meetings, films, postage, and administrative expenses.[2]

[1] Although usually communicated exact to the pfennig, the figures in the third and fourth columns have been rounded to the nearest Deutschmark and their totals based on this approximation.

[2] The various items of election expenditure by the Rheinhessen region of the SPD were presented to its ninth regional party congress as follows:

Posters, leaflets, election newspapers, brochures	12,512 DM
Advertisements	8,744 DM
Poster display (through agencies, and purchase of temporary hoardings)	4,634 DM
Travel and transport	2,375 DM
Loudspeaker and film vans, films, slides, records and tape-recordings	2,366 DM

Note continued on p. 314

The region of Hamburg North-West, which had sixteen constituencies and polled 1,149,049 votes, occupied a rather special position. The regional organization there spent 35,364 DM on elections in 1957, while the local organizations (including the two very strong ones of Hamburg and of Bremen) spent 569,537 DM; but the latter figure includes the cost of the Hamburg city election of November 1957. Even if 200,000 DM were spent on that city election, the remaining 400,000 DM would suggest a higher rather than a lower estimate of the SPD's total campaign expenditure. Altogether a figure of 8 million DM would seem to be a reasonable estimate.

It must, however, be remembered that this figure also reflects only monetary cost. It does not reckon costs at market prices, for much of the printing was done by works under party control at rates appropriate to a vertically integrated concern; it does not (any more than the CDU figure) include all the many hours of patient effort put in by voluntary workers all over the country, who sometimes used up their annual holiday for the purpose; and it does not include the overhead costs of a large permanent staff which was scarcely supplemented by temporary employees during the campaign. For the purpose of a strict comparison at market prices, the figure should thus be upvalued a little—but hardly by more than a quarter.

The Free Democrats declared before polling day that they were spending 3 million DM 'but really no more than that'—half of it on the federal and the rest on the Land and local level. This figure was less than that which the German Party was declaring for its own expenditure, and could not be regarded as final. In fact when the reckoning was made after the election was over, the Free Democrats had spent a little over twice that amount. If the Refugees' Party spent a further 2 million DM, the total for the five bigger parties comes to around 55 million DM, and the seven small parties can hardly have spent more than 2 million between them at the outside. The total cost of the election to parties and private parallel campaigns, exclusive of expenditure by the Government and by such primarily non-political organizations as trade unions and Churches, must thus have come to an overall figure in the region of 55–60 million DM.

Note continued from p. 313

Meetings and demonstrations	2,212 DM
Postal distribution	2,048 DM
Postage, telephones, telegrams, and other expenditure . . .	2,283 DM
	37,176 DM

(Congress document SPD Rheinhessen, *9. Bezirks-Parteitag*, Budenheim, 22 and 23 Mar. 1958, p. 23.)

LOCAL STUDIES

LOCAL STUDY A

DIEPHOLZ-MELLE-WITTLAGE

BY ALFRED MILATZ

The Character of the Constituency

THE constituency of Diepholz–Melle–Wittlage lies in the predominantly Protestant agricultural area in the south of Lower Saxony. Of its nearly 180,000 inhabitants in 1950, 80 per cent. described themselves as Protestant, 18 per cent. as Catholic; 31 per cent. were engaged in agriculture and forestry, 26 per cent. in industry and the artisan trades, 19 per cent. in other sectors such as commerce, transport, and public and private services, and 19 per cent. were independent without a profession—mainly pensioners. The same census revealed that the population of the constituency had risen by 60 per cent. since 1939, and that 39 per cent. of the inhabitants were refugees and their children, mainly from the territories beyond the Oder–Neisse line.

A glance at the map reveals the curious horseshoe shape of the constituency, which results from the protruberance of North Rhine–Westphalia towards the centre of Lower Saxony at this point. Administratively the constituency consists of the three *Landkreise* (rural districts) of Melle, Wittlage, and Diepholz, and of the area around Uchte which is part of the *Landkreis* Nienburg.

These four sections of the constituency vary considerably in character, the most striking differences occurring between Melle and Wittlage on the one hand, and Diepholz and Uchte on the other. Although Melle and Wittlage take up only one-quarter of the area of the constituency, they hold two-fifths of its population. Both Melle and Wittlage contain an appreciable percentage of Catholics, 32 and 28 per cent. respectively, while in Diepholz only 9 per cent. of the population is Catholic. (Figures for Uchte as distinct from the whole *Landkreis* Nienburg are more difficult to obtain.) Both Melle and Wittlage have fertile soils, and large farms are rare in both: by contrast the soil of Diepholz and Uchte is only of medium quality, and nearly two-thirds of the 7,000 farms have more than 12 acres of land. It is thus worth asking how far the different geological, social, and religious traits of these various parts of the constituency, whose halves are joined only by a narrow strip of land, are reflected in their political life and in their voting behaviour.

Elections before 1918

By a rare piece of good fortune the area of this constituency coincides exactly with that of the fifth Hanoverian constituency which sent one member to the German Reichstag from 1867 until 1918. Even in this period of the Prusso-German Empire the constituency was always hotly contested between National Liberals on the one hand and Guelphs on the other, run-off ballots being the rule between

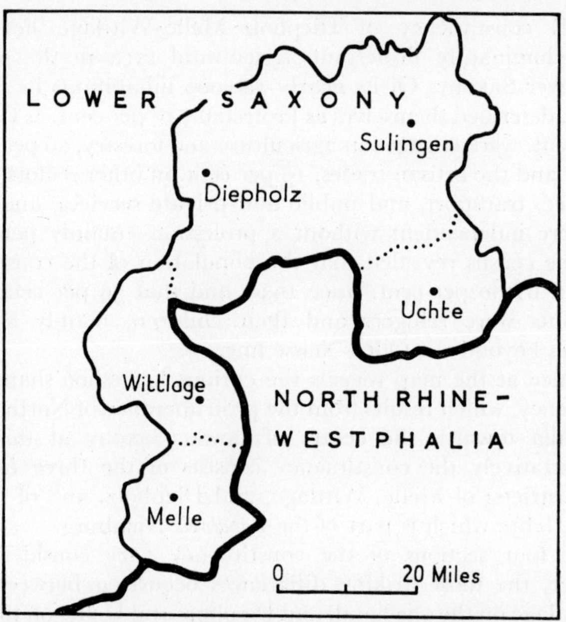

FIG. 9. The Constituency of Diepholz–Melle–Wittlage.

the candidates of these two parties. Neither Prussian Conservatives nor progressive Liberals polled any significant number of votes in any election.

The horseshoe shape of the constituency did not allow the population ever to feel that it really belonged together during the time of the German Empire. Melle and Wittlage with their important Catholic minority were always opposed to Diepholz and Sulingen. Since the Centre did not here figure as an independent political party, the Catholic quarter of the population of Melle and Wittlage allied with the strict Lutherans and voted for the Guelph candidate, if only because the elected Guelph members sat with the Centre Party in the Reichstag as their 'guests'. The Protestant holders of small and medium farms in the plain, who mostly kept livestock and therefore approved of the programme of the German Farmers' League, were, however, friendly to the Government, and joined forces with the National Liberal majority of the electorate of the districts of Diepholz and Sulingen. Thus the victory or defeat of the National Liberals depended principally on the turnout of their own supporters. This situation in fact constituted an inversion of the pattern more usually found in the province of Hanover: for here the old Hanoverian districts voted predominantly for the National Liberals while the new Hanoverian part of the constituency, on the other hand, voted Guelph.

Thus neither the political left nor progressive liberalism were able to make any mark in the fifth Hanoverian Reichstag constituency at any time; in the second (1874), third, sixth, seventh, tenth, and twelfth elections to the imperial Reichstag the National Liberal candidate was elected; and in the fourth, fifth, seventh (by-election), eighth, ninth, eleventh, and thirteenth (1912) the Guelph candidate won the day.

The Social Democrats, who lacked an adequate sociological basis, remained an insignificant political group in the constituency throughout the imperial era. It was not until the last Reichstag election of 1912 that they were able to poll 11 per cent. of valid votes (as against 29 per cent. in the Empire as a whole); the political battle was thus not fought, as elsewhere, between the right and the left, but between two groups of the right with a different social and denominational structure.

The Inter-War Years

The election to the constituent National Assembly in January 1919, a few weeks after the November revolution, only brought about minor modifications in the political structure of the constituency. It is true that, in accordance with the general trend, the majority Socialists became the strongest party; but their 22 per cent. share in the poll remained well below the Reich average and the Independent Social Democrats made no impression on the constituency. On the other hand a joint candidate of the Christian People's Party (a name adopted by the Centre Party) and the German-Hanoverians (the former Guelphs) also polled nearly 22 per cent., and a further candidate of the Christian People's Party alone polled 11 per cent.; thus the old Catholic-Guelph group together still polled 33 per cent. of all votes and had a relative majority. Despite the revolution, and perhaps precisely because of the extension of the franchise to women, the electorate had shown itself largely immune to change.

In 1920 electoral boundaries were redrawn to create larger constituencies in the interests of the system of proportional representation and the constituency was divided. Melle and Wittlage joined the larger constituency 14 (Weser–Ems); Diepholz and Sulingen, whose administrations were merged in 1932, and also the Nienburg country around Uchte, joined the larger constituency 16 (Hanover–South-Brunswick).

In Melle the Centre and the SPD maintained themselves as constant factors without major change and together were able to obtain a narrow majority of votes until 1930. The real political right, the German-Hanoverian Party with its federalist tendencies and strong roots in tradition, was able to attract many voters until 1929/30. It was not until relatively late that the National Socialists penetrated the district; and even their 33 per cent. poll in 1933, gained at the expense of the bourgeois parties (especially the German-Hanoverians), was not nearly as great as in most other areas of Lower Saxony: the National Socialists were unable to break into the block formed by the Centre and the SPD.

In Wittlage, too, the Centre Party was able to maintain its position, while the SPD, which here at first achieved a considerable expansion after 1918, was unable to do so. The more agrarian character of the district deprived the party of any regular following. Until 1928/9 the German-Hanoverian Party remained the real political right. But then it, too, was considerably reduced by the attack of the National Socialists. They had already won about 10 per cent. of votes by 1928, became the strongest party in the district in 1930, and with 47 per cent. of votes in 1932 nearly secured an absolute majority.

How different Melle and Wittlage were from Diepholz–Sulingen! The Social Democrats were unable to make any impact on this purely agrarian area, and until the plebiscite of 1929 the clear hegemony of German Nationals and German-Hanoverians was secure. Thereafter the National Socialists took the whole district by storm, completely broke up the German-Hanoverian and the German People's Parties, and decimated the German National Party. As early as 1930 Diepholz–Sulingen was one of the National Socialist strongholds of Lower Saxony and in 1932 an overwhelming majority of 69 per cent. of the voters of the district chose Hitler and his programme.

Earlier Post-War Elections

As in the rest of Germany, the democratic basic order was put out of operation when the National Socialists seized power in 1933. The political parties dissolved themselves or were prohibited, National Socialist totalitarianism took their place and increasingly imposed its order on all public life. The ensuing catastrophe of the second world war engulfed Germany, but it left the districts Diepholz, Melle, and Wittlage almost untouched. While the big cities fell in ruins, the agricultural areas were largely spared. But they were then obliged to take a particularly high number of refugees from the eastern territories after the collapse of 1945, and later from Middle Germany. This led to a drastic change in the former sociological structure; but on the other hand it also gave many a new impulse to economic development.

The election to the first Bundestag in 1949 showed fairly clearly that an overwhelming majority of the population of the constituency had again chosen the bourgeois camp. The German Party (DP) with its 34 per cent. had a clear lead, while the Social Democrats polled only 27 per cent. and the CDU 25 per cent. of valid votes. Moreover, the subsequent elections—the Landtag elections in 1951, the second federal election of 1953, and the Landtag election of 1955—showed losses for the SPD and gains, though alternating, for the two big bourgeois parties.

Three details characteristic of the situation in the constituency emerge clearly from Table XII. In the Landtag election of 1951, the right-radical 'Socialist Reich Party' (SRP) with its tendencies towards National Socialism under the demagogic leadership of Dorls and Remer polled roughly one-fifth of valid votes in the constituency, while in the same election the Lower German Union (an alliance of CDU and DP) suffered a remarkable set-back. Secondly, in the federal election of 1953 considerably fewer electors voted for the DP Land list than for the party's constituency candidate, while CDU votes revealed the obverse of this phenomenon. Thirdly, in marked contrast to the federal election of 1953, the DP emerged from the Landtag election of 1955 as once more the strongest party.

The results in the four administrative units of the constituency show these three phenomena in greater detail. The SRP's extraordinarily skilful agitation found a strong echo above all among the agricultural population in Diepholz: roughly one-third of the Diepholz electorate chose this successor organization of the National Socialist Party. On the other hand the SRP polled few votes in Melle and in Uchte. The party gained votes exclusively at the expense of the DP and the CDU; a year later—after the prohibition of the SRP—these two parties regained their votes apart from a portion which migrated to the FDP. The bourgeois camp in this district (above all the DP and the FDP, but also the CDU) remained prone to contagion from right-wing radicalism, and electoral tactics therefore had to pay more attention to extreme than to moderate tendencies.

In Diepholz, where the DP candidate lived, the discrepancy between constituency and list votes in 1953 was especially noticeable.

TABLE XII

Election Results in Diepholz–Melle–Wittlage

Election		*Electors*	*Valid votes**	*CDU†*	*DP*	*SPD*	*BHE*	*FDP*	*DRP*	*Z*	*SRP*	*Others*
Bundestag 1949 .		116,872	70	25	34	27	..	1	3	6	..	3
Uchte . .		14,877	63	18	51	23	..	2	3	2	..	2
Diepholz .		52,691	67	23	42	27	..	1	3	1	..	3
Wittlage .		20,240	75	24	27	28	..	1	3	15	..	2
Melle . .		29,064	75	32	20	30	..	2	2	10	..	4
Landtag 1951 .		115,085	72	32		20	18	3	1	5	20	1
Uchte . .		14,439	69	49		13	28	2	1	1	6	1
Diepholz .		51,970	71	27		16	19	3	1	1	33	1
Wittlage .		19,724	76	28		20	18	6	2	13	13	1
Melle . .		28,952	74	37		30	12	4	1	8	8	2
Bundestag 1953	‡	..	83	26	27	21	14	11	..	..	..	1
	§	110,187	84	32	21	21	13	7	6	..	..	1
Uchte .	‡	13,248	*80*	*19*	*44*	*16*	*15*	*4*	..	..	..	*1*
	§		80	22	40	16	15	3	3	..	..	1
Diepholz	‡	49,683	*81*	*18*	*31*	*18*	*16*	*18*	..	..	..	*1*
	§		83	27	23	17	14	11	9	..	..	1
Wittlage	‡	19,285	*85*	*35*	*21*	*24*	*12*	*7*	..	..	..	*1*
	§		86	37	17	23	12	6	4	..	..	1
Melle .	‡	27,971	*86*	*37*	*17*	*28*	*13*	*4*	..	..	..	*1*
	§		87	40	12	27	13	4	3	..	..	1
Landtag 1955 .		108,391	71	21	26	22	14	7	8	1	..	1
Uchte . .		12,799	66	11	38	18	15	13	4	0	..	1
Diepholz .		48,867	67	10	35	19	15	8	11	0	..	1
Wittlage .		18,892	75	30	17	23	11	8	6	3	..	1
Melle . .		27,833	78	33	14	29	13	3	4	2	..	1
Bundestag 1957	‡	106,241	*84*	*31*	*26*	*22*	*10*	*8*	*4*	0	..	..
	§		83	32	23	22	10	8	4	0	..	0
Uchte .	‡	11,984	*71*	*21*	*38*	*19*	*11*	*8*	*4*	..	..	..
	§		76	21	36	19	11	9	4	0	..	0
Diepholz	‡	47,280	*82*	*25*	*31*	*18*	*10*	*11*	*5*	..	..	..
	§		81	27	29	19	11	10	5	0	..	0
Wittlage	‡	17,892	*86*	*36*	*21*	*26*	*9*	*5*	*3*	..	..	..
	§		85	37	19	25	9	5	4	0	..	0
Melle .	‡	26,164	*88*	*37*	*17*	*29*	*11*	*3*	*3*	..	..	..
	§		87	39	13	29	11	4	3	0	..	0
Postal vote	‡	[2,921]‖	*99*‖	*46*	*19*	*16*	*10*	*8*	*3*	..	..	..
	§		99	46	16	16	10	8	3	0	..	0

* As percentage of electors.

† Party figures all as a percentage of valid votes (*in italics*).

‡ Constituency votes.

§ List votes.

‖ These postal voters are already included in the number of electors given for each part of the constituency. The valid votes are expressed as a percentage of total postal votes cast.

Eickhoff, the first Bundestag member of the constituency, here received 8 per cent. more votes than his party; the CDU candidate, on the other hand, polled 9 per cent. fewer votes than the CDU. The other three administrative areas showed similar relations: the overwhelming majority of the bourgeois camp quite correctly saw the 1953 election as a decision on Adenauer's policies, but once more expressed their confidence in their sitting member although he belonged to the weaker partner in the coalition. The 'Adenauer candidate' was not even accepted by all CDU voters: in Diepholz he polled only two-thirds of their constituency votes.

The same picture emerged even more clearly in the Landtag elections of 1955. The votes given to the Bonn coalition fell compared with 1953. But it was the CDU which suffered by far the greatest losses, while the DP, especially in Diepholz, even made some progress. Again the voters in the bourgeois camp made a deliberate attempt to differentiate between Land and federal politics and between the CDU and the German Party.

The SPD never regained anything like the 27 per cent. it polled in 1949, attracting roughly one-fifth of the electorate—and that only by virtue of the 27–30 per cent. it polled in Melle, while in Diepholz and Uchte it often remained in places considerably under 20 per cent.

The Refugees' Party, which made its first appearance in the Landtag election of 1951, was equally unable to repeat its initial success of 18 per cent.: in the 1953 and 1955 elections only about one-half of refugees (13–14 per cent. of votes) opted for the BHE.

The FDP, which until the federal election of 1953 had only been a splinter party, was thus able to achieve a comparative success and to double its share of votes. By taking over some of the slogans previously used by the radical right wing the FDP succeeded in attracting many of the adherents of the dissolved SRP; in Diepholz, for instance, a former stronghold of the SRP, it reached percentages far above the average in the constituency (11 per cent. of list votes and 18 per cent. of constituency votes), while in Melle, on which the SRP had made hardly any impact, it recorded no increase at all. Buttressed by a few quite strong local positions in the districts of Uchte, Diepholz, and Wittlage the FDP polled 7 per cent. But it was forced to make further tactical concessions to latent radicalism of the right and to champion not a moderate but a 'radical' liberalism of an oppositional stamp.

On the whole the Centre Party, the German Reich Party, and the Communist Party (prohibited in 1955) remained insignificant in the political life of the constituency. The Centre was still relatively successful in Melle and Wittlage until 1951; thereafter it was almost totally swallowed up by the CDU. But in 1955 the German Reich Party, part-heir of the SRP, once more drew attention to the dangers of right-wing radicalism by attracting 11 per cent. of votes in Diepholz.

There remain the DP and the CDU, the two biggest parties in the constituency. Based on County Diepholz and the district of Uchte, the DP was able to maintain its political leadership in the constituency in 1953, though this was by no means easy. The CDU, on the other hand, remained clearly superior in Melle and Wittlage, not least thanks to their strong Catholic minority. It would be going too far to declare (paradoxically) that the DP was carrying on the heritage of National Liberalism and the CDU that of the Guelphs. But one can recognize clearly not only in the voting figures but above all in the attitudes of the population even in minor political questions that the people do not see the constituency as an electoral whole: Melle and Wittlage still fight Diepholz and Uchte for ascendancy.

The Selection of Candidates

In April 1957 the parties began the selection of their candidates. They seem to have encountered few difficulties, the one exception being the CDU, where the date fixed for nomination was postponed for a week though the public learned nothing concrete about the reasons for this delay.

The SPD renominated its candidate of 1953, Heinz Zeese, the party's district chairman in Wittlage, head of the local office of the Ministry of Labour in Bohmte, and a trade union official. The CDU agreed on Dr. *jur et rer pol.* Karl Gossel, *Oberkreisdirektor* since 1948 in Melle, and *Landrat* of the district before 1934. The DP renominated the master baker Rudolf Eickhoff, mayor of Sulingen and head of the tradesmen's organization of Diepholz. The delegates of the BHE nominated the party's district chairman in Melle, a secondary school master who was deputy mayor of the town of Melle. The FDP nominated its district chairman, the mayor of Barver; and the DRP nominated a farmer who was mayor of Hustädte in the district of Melle.

The candidates put up by the FDP, the BHE and the DRP must have known from the beginning that they had no chance of victory. They were above all concerned to capture from the two Government parties not only list votes but also as many constituency votes as possible in order to reinforce the demands of their parties on the regional level.

The Campaign

The campaign began in the course of the summer, at first rather hesitantly. It was almost exclusively devoted to the general topics of German politics. There is no need to go into the details of this debate since it has already been described elsewhere in this book and the constituency followed the general lines. We need only look more closely at the specifically regional differences due to the economic structure, the mentality of the population, and their distribution over the area.

The parties presented their candidates to the population in numerous meetings held in even the most remote villages. These small meetings, attended often by only six or ten participants meeting in a village inn over a glass of beer, can be regarded as characteristic of electioneering in this region. Mostly they were the candidates' own affair, who devoted evening after evening to them. Only in the larger communes and in the towns were they supported by better-known campaign speakers, usually Landtag and Bundestag members. The population took a comparatively lively part, although—in accordance with its customs—those who came were mostly men. The discussions were always objective and calm. The DP, CDU, FDP, and DRP were especially active, while the SPD and BHE did little in the small villages and concentrated more on the towns and larger communes.

Over and above the little discussions which the candidates held at evening meetings in the local inn they also attempted to canvass farmers at home. This was an electioneering technique which seems to have contributed decisively to the success of the SRP in the Landtag election of 1951. In the 1957 campaign the DRP candidate was fairly active in this way.

Mass meetings with prominent speakers remained the exception in this rural area. Anton Storch, the federal Minister of Labour, spoke in a larger meeting in Diepholz and Würmeling, the federal Minister of Family Affairs, spoke at a meeting in Melle which took place immediately after the Catholic Mass on a Sunday. There were good audiences for Land ministers and the better-known Bundestag members of the various parties. Party officials were only very rarely put up as speakers even by the SPD. The DP introduced a special note with its 'German Day' held at the height of summer on the shore of one of the great lakes in the constituency: more than 2,000 people came to hear Hellwege at what friends and opponents rightly characterized as a 'family reunion'.

An important part in the electoral propaganda of the parties was played by the six newspapers published in the area of the constituency: they were partly local papers, partly local editions of larger papers published in Osnabrück or Bielefeld. With the exception of a local edition of the SPD's *Freie Presse* in Bielefeld these newspapers could, of course, make no special propaganda for any one party. But the agricultural population of the rural areas reads its local papers with intense interest, and their reports greatly increased the public's awareness of the election. They were careful to give equal treatment to all parties and shortly before polling day they allowed the candidates themselves to present their programme, a photograph, and a short biography. The FDP and the DP also made particular use of letters to the editor.

Election meetings were announced in the advertising columns and as polling day approached purely propaganda advertisements became more frequent. The FDP invested most in this kind of propaganda and was followed by the DP, DRP, CDU, and BHE in that order; the SPD, on the other hand, apparently expected small results from such advertising and, moreover, had inhibitions about advertising in bourgeois papers.

All parties conducted an intensive poster campaign, but almost exclusively with posters issued by the central campaign offices which paid no attention to local particularities. These were pasted up even in the smallest villages not only on communal hoardings but also on houses, fences, and trees. They were only rarely destroyed or defaced.

The parties also published large numbers of letters to the voters and election addresses to which many observers in the constituency ascribed considerable propaganda value. That of the CDU candidate, Dr. Gossel, was generally regarded as particularly successful owing to its objectivity and its virtual freedom from partisan argument.

Propaganda by word of mouth is especially important in a rural area whose inhabitants feel very closely connected and who discuss political questions and their attitudes to the parties with each other. Two examples may illustrate its efficacy. When the FDP candidate Freitag suffered a heart attack a few days before the poll and thus dropped out of the final round of the campaign this fact was widely known in the district of Diepholz in a matter of hours, and in the opinion of local observers it robbed the FDP of votes in favour of the DRP. The CDU used this bush telegraph quite deliberately with particular intensity just before polling day to spread the clever formula that Sulingen must at last give way to Melle (i.e. that Gossel must take the place of Eickhoff). Apart from the personal issue, this formula contained a sentimental allusion to the lasting opposition of the two parts of the constituency and a further reminder of the opposition between the two parts of County Diepholz—Diepholz and Sulingen—which had been merged only in 1932.

Since it had now been the CDU's coalition partner for eight years the German Party had far greater difficulties in 1957 than in 1953 in maintaining some form of independence in its argumentation on the hustings. In all major political questions it naturally felt forced to demonstrate its agreement with its senior partner. Only in agricultural policy did it try to maintain a standpoint of its own. The Free Democrats also tried to aim their blow precisely, knowing that they could only attract voters away from the DP. They narrowed down their propaganda quite consciously to questions of agricultural policy: it was clear that the bulk of the rural population of the constituency was in agreement with the general and above all with the foreign policy of the Bonn coalition, but felt a number of grievances where agricultural policy was concerned. The 1957 campaign in the constituency Diepholz–Melle–Wittlage thus differed from the general one in that the hottest fighting here took place not between the strongest parties, but between the DP and the FDP: the point at issue was the agricultural policy of the Federal Government on which even the DP was not united with the CDU and therefore had to attack the CDU itself. The Free Democrats charged the DP with having supported the Federal Minister of Food and Agriculture, Lübke, and the DP was thus forced to formulate a few vigorous agricultural demands against the CDU in order to prevent a loss of disgruntled agricultural voters to the FDP. Now that a Government as well as an Opposition party opposed Lübke's agricultural policy, the hands of the German Farmers' Union, which had been attacking Lübke for some time, were tied. It was no longer able to back one of these parties but forced to remain neutral between them and give benevolent support to both. The FDP proved to be the loser in this tug of war. The DP had to thank its candidate Fritz Logemann, an agricultural expert with a farm near Sulingen, for the fact that the Free Democrats' very skilful attack was beaten off. Logemann, who was elected to the Bundestag on the Land list, could take more credit for this operation than the DP's constituency candidate.

The Results

The CDU emerged as the clear victor on 15 September both as regards list and constituency votes, and the seat for the first time went to the CDU candidate. Even more clearly than in 1953 the electorate had cast a vote of confidence in Adenauer's policy. The CDU and the DP between them polled an absolute majority in each of the four administrative units of the constituency. The discrepancy between constituency and list votes which had turned the scales in 1953 was reduced: only Eickhoff polled 3 per cent. more votes than his party. The DP again led in Diepholz and Uchte. But in the old district of Diepholz (though not in Eickhoff's old district of Sulingen) it lost many votes to the CDU. As before, the CDU was far ahead of the DP in Melle and Wittlage, which distinguished themselves by a particularly heavy poll. Moreover, the postal vote clearly favoured the CDU. The electoral difference between the two parts, Melle–Wittlage on the one hand and Diepholz–Uchte on the other, thus survived.

The radicalism of the right, which had shown itself especially in Diepholz in the Landtag election of 1951, found no very clear expression in the 1957 poll, but there can be no doubt that part of the rural population still feels itself drawn in this direction today and that this latent inclination is only camouflaged by the democratic parties. The relatively high DRP poll in the district of Diepholz is a very convincing proof of this; moreover the electoral campaign showed that the FDP and the DP were able to attract the remnants of the former SRP electorate only by swinging vigorously to the right. Thus the former National Socialist stronghold of Diepholz still has its dregs of right-wing radicalism which can only be absorbed or eliminated by very skilful tactics on the part of the democratic parties of the right.

The constituency seat was won not by a party politician, but by a civil servant. The CDU thus reaped the benefit of the tendency immanent in large parts of the German *bourgeoisie* to value administration more highly than politics or the free interplay of the parties, a tendency which can intensify itself to become a faith in authority and which was considerably reinforced by the personality and tactics of Adenauer himself. The DP candidate Eickhoff, on the other hand, had to learn that years of parliamentary work do not increase but can, on the contrary, decrease the number of one's adherents.

The general trend towards the two main parties was also at work in the constituency and was a contributory factor in the victory of the CDU. But the aim of a two-party system, envisaged by many, still lies out of reach: the fight for the seat did not take place between the strongest Government party and the strongest Opposition party. The voter was not directly confronted with a choice on policy; and the followers of the German Party saw their party largely as an expression of regional loyalty and solidarity, and voted DP not least out of an emotional federalism.

If we disregard the FDP and the BHE, we are left with the SPD as the real loser of the election. It was unable to break out of the tower in which it had immured itself, not so much because its electoral tactics were bad, but because it remained hidebound by its old way of thinking. Rigid and immobile, its regional leadership did nothing to destroy the attitude of the rural and small town population which saw it still as a 'class party' for which one could not vote—if only for social reasons. If it wants to emerge from this tower and the 20 per cent. limit in the constituency it will need to present itself as a 'people's party' including all strata of the population. Politics after all consists, beside all else, in the ability to detect and to utilize the emotions of the electors. And this is a task which in 1957 was accomplished in Diepholz–Melle–Wittlage, as elsewhere, not by the Social but by the Christian Democrats.

LOCAL STUDY B

MUNICH-LAND

BY KEITH PANTER-BRICK

THE election in and around Munich was primarily a contest between the CDU and the SPD, with the FU(BP), as a rival to the CSU, playing an important subsidiary role. Munich itself is divided into four constituencies, all held by the CSU in 1953; the outer suburbs and part of the surrounding countryside form a fifth constituency, Munich-Land. This fifth constituency had also been easily won by the CSU in 1953; but in 1957 it had been chosen as one of the four constituencies where the SPD withdrew in favour of the FU(BP) candidate. The outcome in this constituency was thus very much in the balance; the struggle formed a small and, as it seemed at the time, possibly crucial part of the wider contest between the Government parties and the Opposition parties, and it also formed part of the FU(BP)'s own struggle for survival.

In fact of all the four FU(BP) candidates standing with socialist support, Weinhuber in Munich-Land was considered to stand the best chance of success. In 1953 the combined SPD and BP vote had not fallen far short of the CSU vote (39 per cent. compared with 44 per cent.) and had greatly exceeded it in the 1954 Land elections (49 per cent. compared with only 32 per cent.). The arrangement risked, however, being self-defeating. The two parties drew their main support from groups whose interests tended to conflict, farmers on the one hand and industrial workers on the other. Moreover, many of the SPD voters were refugees to whom the BP had in the past not shown itself very hospitable. Refugees had in any case very little sympathy for a purely Bavarian party. Thus a candidate well chosen for the purpose of getting out the BP vote was unlikely to prove very attractive to SPD voters; at the same time socialist support was bound to weaken any such candidate's appeal to the BP voters, many of whom confused the SPD with atheistic Communism. The arrangement was thus largely self-contradictory in terms of 'party image'. Neither side entered into it with any great enthusiasm. It was concluded simply as a marriage of convenience and it was to be understood as such. SPD voters, so it was hoped, would realize the importance of preventing a CDU/CSU majority.

FU(BP) voters, for their part, would know that it was the party's only chance of winning any seats in the Federal Parliament.

Even as a marriage of convenience it had its defects, at least from the FU(BP)'s point of view. This was made very evident in the course of the campaign. FU(BP) supporters, however much they might have wished to secure the party's representation in the Federal Parliament, had to ask themselves what other effects it would have. The SPD itself supplied the answer in a pamphlet designed to guide SPD voters how to vote. This showed the CSU being hauled down from its pedestal by the combined forces of the SPD and the FU(BP), with the caption 'Two votes bring the majority down'. The consequences of supporting the FU(BP) were made quite plain. No matter how much time Weinhuber spent explaining that the downfall of the Adenauer Government was not a necessary nor in any way a pre-arranged part of the electoral agreement with the SPD, no matter how often the electorate was told that it was being asked to vote for a Parliament and not a government, the impression remained that in this matter the FU(BP) was the SPD's accomplice. This impression was, of course, reinforced every time FU(BP) spokesmen referred to compulsory military service, defence expenditure, and the danger of government by a single party, for on these questions their voices were scarcely distinguishable from those of the Socialists. This marriage of convenience was thus one which resulted in identifying the FU(BP) with the Opposition. This made a large FU(BP) vote conditional upon a strong and widespread desire among the non-socialist electorate to cast an anti-Adenauer vote. This undoubtedly proved to be the FU(BP)'s greatest handicap.

With so much depending upon the outcome, public interest was concentrated upon the contest for first votes between Weinhuber and Seidl, the CSU candidate, a local notary. Seidl's own re-election also lay in the balance, for he had no place on the party list, but he had the advantage of having represented the constituency since 1953. He had worked hard defending the interests of his constituents in matters such as roads, water supply, taxation, compensation payments for the building of an airfield near Erding, a local authority's right to levy rates upon an American broadcasting station near Moosburg, and the plight of the refugees. He had held regular monthly meetings to deal with personal problems raised by constituents. Weinhuber was no less well known and just as respected, especially in the Erding district, where he ran a model farm on which he was still to be found threshing only a month before polling day and presided over the local Dairy Farmers' Association with a membership of over 2,000. His father had been a member of the Bavarian People's Party and he himself was a founding member of the BP. He sat in the Bavarian Parliament and had headed the poll in the Erding district in the 1954 Land elections. He had clearly won the confidence of his fellow farmers and many expected him to have their support, even if his party as such lost ground.

The other candidates were: Ertl (FDP), son of a farmer, holder of a diploma in agriculture from the Agricultural College in Freising and an official in the Bavarian Ministry of Agriculture; Reitinger (BHE), a leading member of the Hungarian-German refugee organization and a county councillor; Dettweiler (DP), a Munich lawyer nominated at the last minute; and Priebe (DRP), a commercial traveller from Munich.

The constituency itself is a mixed one. It includes most of Munich's outer suburbs and two areas of farmland, one lying to the north and the other to the east of the city but separated from it, and also from each other, by a fairly extensive stretch of moorland. The towns of Freising, Moosburg, and Erding stand at the edges of the farmland where it joins the moorland. The main lines of communication nearly all flow into these towns and along the edge of the moor into Munich. This layout is of some importance. The movement of population from off the land, and especially the departure of the refugees, left the farming areas with a shrinking but relatively homogeneous electorate, whereas in the Munich suburbs, in the villages with good train and bus services into Munich, and in or around the two towns of Erding and Moosburg, the electorate tended to be on the increase and more varied in character. The nature of the campaign and the distribution of the vote varied in these different parts.

In the farming areas to the north and east, comprising roughly 25 per cent. of the electorate, between 80 per cent. and 90 per cent. of the voters could be expected to vote for one or other of the more specifically Bavarian, Christian, and Conservative parties, the CSU or the FU(BP). The only question in doubt was the preference these village folk would have for the one party rather than the other. Thus almost the only campaigning to be observed in these villages was that done on behalf of these two parties, and votes turned to a considerable extent upon which was thought to offer the best guarantee for Bavarian interests, the Christian religion, and the farming community as an indispensable part of the social order. In just a few villages there was some small local industry, transplanted in most cases from the East, providing isolated pockets of SPD and BHE votes.

The most effective form of campaigning in these villages was still the traditional one of holding a meeting in the local inn over a litre of beer, preferably on a Sunday morning when the church drew the people in from the surrounding farms. Women rarely attended, for this is contrary to local custom, but as many as half the male electorate might be present. These meetings thus provided good opportunity for influencing votes and both candidates were fully occupied in delivering hour-long speeches in village after village. The men sat packed round the wooden tables, young and old, seldom expressing approval or disapproval and only rarely venturing to ask a question. As a rule they heard the speaker out in courteous and attentive silence. Some of Weinhuber's meetings were enlivened with statements of opposing views, but this was usually the work of younger CSU members organized from Freising.

It was very different in that part of the constituency which encircles Munich, an area of industrial and residential suburbs, housing not only those who have been drawn in from the surrounding countryside by the offers of employment but also those who have moved out of the city to enjoy the amenities of a villa in the green belt lying to the south. Here the social structure and political outlook was much more varied. Furthermore the campaign in this part of the constituency intermingled with that of Munich itself, and in two different ways. First, many of the people living in these industrial and residential suburbs went into Munich for various purposes and will have seen something of what was going on there. Secondly, the campaign in the outer suburbs was on similar lines and indeed in many cases organized from Munich itself. For instance, the SPD cabaret gave several performances in the outer suburbs; all the FU(BP) meetings were addressed by the Munich team of speakers, with Weinhuber putting in a brief appearance: the FDP had included Ertl in the leaflet which portrayed Dehler and the other Munich candidates, and this was distributed in a few of the outer suburbs. These outer suburbs thus formed quite a separate part of the constituency, subjected to quite different influences.

Between the two extremes of the farming villages and the Munich suburbs stood the country towns and the larger villages strung out along the main lines of communication. They shared to a considerable extent the interests and the preoccupation of the surrounding countryside but contained many groups of people more strictly comparable to the suburban areas—refugee workers, transport workers, administrators, and commutors. The activities of the SPD, BHE, and FDP reached out into these parts but varied greatly from place to place. In the small country town of Dorfen, for instance, where in 1953 the SPD won 400 of the 2,500 votes (rising to 500 out of 2,800 in 1957), there was practically no sign of socialist activity. Because the rural atmosphere was so strong and the commutors so tired by their day's journey into Munich, the SPD did not consider the effort worth while. In such places the SPD tended to rely, as in the farming villages, upon the radio, Ollenhauer's letter, the leaflet illustrating how one should vote, and, somewhat hopefully, upon voting habits. The contrast to Dorfen was supplied by Freising, an administrative, educational, and ecclesiastical centre enjoying the status of a county borough. Its larger and more highly organized electorate, totalling 30,000, a good proportion of whom were well educated and highly influential, invited the attention of all parties. Several party leaders held well-attended meetings which were generously reported in the local newspaper, the *Freisinger Tageblatt*. The electoral campaign in Freising was, however, very much overshadowed in the final week by the annual fair, a solid week of festivities taking up most people's spare time. Almost the only opportunity offered for electioneering was the distribution of leaflets among the crowds (the FDP candidate distributed 3,000 in this way, out of a total of 10,000 for the whole constituency). But one occasion was thought to provide too good an opportunity—the official address due to be given on 'Farmers' Day' by Dr. Baumgartner, in his capacity as Bavaria's State Secretary of Agriculture. It was suspected —not without reason—that this would be turned into an electoral address on behalf of the FU(BP). A notice of cancellation appeared in the local press but alongside it appeared a FU(BP) notice saying that the meeting would none the less be held. About 250 were present, a relative success, for this was almost half the number attending each of the main CSU and SPD meetings. Weinhuber, dressed in Bavarian costume, also addressed the meeting.

Thus the constituency as a whole was covered in very uneven fashion by the parties and their candidates. Seidl conducted the most intensive campaign. With more than a dozen people occasionally speaking on his behalf he was able to hold over a hundred meetings. Four prominent party leaders gave him their support. Strauss and Kiesinger each held a meeting in the outer suburbs of Munich; Schäffer spoke in Freising; and the chairman of the CSU held a meeting at Moosburg. No great use was made of posters, but a leaflet, presented in the form of a newspaper, was given wide distribution. A cartoon showed a car labelled FU hired from the SPD for electoral purposes: approaching from the left in breach of traffic regulations, it was hoping to move out in front of the CSU. Seidl's election address portrayed him in conversation with Adenauer and carried the slogan 'Again Seidl for Adenauer'. It listed Seidl's qualifications and his activities as a member of the Federal Parliament. First among the qualifications came the fact that he was a local notary who therefore knew better than anyone else the affairs of the people he was to represent. In meetings Seidl often said that farmers are not always best represented by farmers.

Weinhuber carried his campaign into most parts of the constituency, but he was short of supporting speakers and especially of big names.[1] He also made a late start compared with Seidl, who had held some meetings the previous Easter, long before Weinhuber knew that he would be a candidate. Nor was he able to issue any leaflets of his own.

The other candidates limited themselves to a few meetings, newspaper advertisements, a sparse display of posters, and a very patchy distribution of leaflets. The SPD did not stir itself unduly. The leaflet already referred to explained the reasons why the party's candidate, Reitzner, had withdrawn. Reitzner himself paid the constituency very little attention. He held very few meetings other than in the outer suburbs of Munich and the three towns Freising, Erding, and Moosburg. Lacking his support, the local party officials in the Erding district made no attempt to hold meetings and those in the Freising district found the experience discouraging.[2] These local party officials often found themselves inactive because the campaign material sent out from Munich was useless for the rural areas: for instance, posters and leaflets urging lower prices. Good use could have been made of loudspeaker vans had any been regularly available. The zeal and the difficulties of these local party officials can be illustrated by their work in Freising. Having insufficient funds to hire very much space on the town's own official hoardings they made nine of their own and erected them in various parts of the town.[3]

None of the organized groups of importance to the locality, such as the Catholic Church, the farmers' organizations, or the refugee organizations, came out openly in support of a particular party or candidate. The guidance which the Catholics had received from their bishops left them with a choice, at least as between Seidl and

[1] Baumgartner spoke in Freising, Erding, and Dorfen. He was also due to speak in Moosburg but on arrival was told that the audience numbered only a handful, whereupon he refused to enter the meeting. Moosburg was not a good place for meetings. The CSU chairman attracted a bare 200 and the FDP candidate scarcely 10.

[2] On one occasion there was no audience at all, everyone being at a local football match. On another occasion nine out of fourteen played cards. Learning from experience the party cancelled a third meeting when it became known that the local football club had arranged a meeting for the same time.

[3] A large-sized poster on the town's official hoarding would have cost 50 DM a week. The nine home-made hoardings cost the party 250 DM. As much again was spent on the main meeting when the chairman of the Bavarian Party came to speak. These two items were said to take up two-thirds of the available funds.

Weinhuber, which was of course for most people the really important choice. But although the church hierarchy itself expressed no clear preference a good part of the local clergy may be considered to have done so by putting in an appearance at Seidl's meetings—a discreet, but none the less public, mark of support. Moreover, the leaders of Catholic Action in Bavaria came out very plainly on the side of the CSU, declaring themselves against political experiments and any dissolution of existing defence treaties. The FU(BP) had in fact put itself in a difficult position. It claimed to show just as much respect for the demands of the church authorities as did the CSU but found itself bracketed with the SPD. The FU(BP) compared its relations to the Mother Church to that of an unloved son, blackened in his mother's eyes by the favourite son and consequently loved less and less. To convince the electorate that it provided better protection for the Church's interests attention was drawn to the higher church subsidies paid by the existing Bavarian Government compared with those paid when the CSU was in power: it was also contended that the CSU was ready to compromise with the SPD over teacher training as part of an agreement to form a CSU-SPD government in Bavaria. Yet those likely to be influenced in their political opinions by the clergy and Catholic organizations had in all probability already considered Weinhuber's association with the SPD a decisive reason for not giving him their support. It is therefore very doubtful whether they exercised a decisive influence.

The most important of the agricultural organizations, the Bavarian Farmers' Union, was in no position to take sides even had it wanted to do so. Its chairman, von Feury, occupied fifth place on the CSU list and spoke on Seidl's behalf. But Ernst, the regional chairman in Upper Bavaria, campaigned actively in support of Weinhuber, speaking at close on twenty meetings in the Freising area. The Bavarian Farmers' Union was associated with yet a third candidate: Ertl (FDP) held his job at the Bavarian Ministry of Agriculture on the Union's recommendation. It was impossible, therefore, for any one candidate or party to claim its definite support. Weinhuber's position as chairman of the Dairy Farmers' Association in the Erding district and the great debt it owed to him have already been mentioned. Its annual general meeting, attended by about 1,500 farmers, was held early in September, providing Weinhuber with a good occasion for reminding the members of what had been done under his direction on their behalf.[1] Baumgartner, as State Secretary of

[1] Except that during the reading of his report many of the farmers were busy eating, drinking, and talking, and that five waves of jet airplanes took off from the neighbouring airfield to pass directly overhead.

Agriculture, had been invited to address the meeting. There was some criticism afterwards that he had chosen to make a political speech, but he was listened to with considerable attention and frequently applauded.

The refugees were another group pulled by its leaders in several directions. The Sudeten-Germans, the most numerous group, could choose between Reitzner (SPD), who edited their paper *Die Brücke*, or Becker (BHE), who spoke several times in the Munich suburbs on Reitinger's behalf. Reitinger himself was a leading spokesman of the Hungarian-Germans, but some of his countrymen spoke on behalf of the CSU.

There was, however, a very close link between the FU(BP) and the *Bund der Flieger- und Kriegsgeschädigten und Evakuierten*, an association for those whose homes had suffered damage during the war. Its honorary president, Brentano-Hommeyer (who was the FU(BP) candidate in Munich West), held a meeting in Freising, and it was obvious that in some parts of Munich-Land the FU(BP) appeal was directed to these evacuees. Indeed, speaking for the association, Brentano-Hommeyer more or less identified its aims with those of the party.

The local press provided a good guide to the election. The Munich papers did not campaign very ardently for either Government or Opposition parties. The *Süddeutsche Zeitung* (read in the city rather than in the country areas) displayed more concern for democracy as such than for any change of Government policy, but, on those grounds, looked forward to the end of the Adenauer régime. Ollenhauer would not make a good Chancellor but would be better than Adenauer. The *Münchener Merkur* supported the CDU/CSU a little more enthusiastically and, with a circulation in the constituency of 17,000, was the most widely read. It issued regular supplements for both the Erding and Freising districts in which the local campaign was fully reported. Both these papers gave all the parties, except the smaller radical parties, an opportunity to state their case, and carried extensive advertisements from all the main parties.

In addition there were two more distinctly local papers, the *Freisinger Tageblatt*, with a circulation of 6,000 in the Freising area, and the *Moosburger Zeitung*, of which about 3,000 copies were sold in and around Moosburg. These also gave copious reports of local meetings, &c. Thus a good part of the electorate was kept fully informed, not only of the campaign at the federal and Land level, but also at the local level. The *Freisinger Tageblatt* stood close to the right wing of the FDP (one could say the DP except that the DP hardly exists in Bavaria). The *Moosburger Zeitung* was an outspoken supporter of the CSU, and did not in fact carry an advertisement for the FU(BP). The local press was therefore weighted in favour of the CSU, although it should be added that the *Münchener Merkur*'s comments on the FU(BP) were rarely very hostile.

The count showed that Weinhuber never really had much of a chance to win the seat. He secured only one-third of the votes given to Seidl, 24,000 against 75,000. The reasons are quite plain. First, the FU(BP) was itself not supported. Despite a higher turnout the party list secured a bare 10,000 votes against 22,000 in 1953. Clearly its association with the SPD had proved too great a handicap. A contradiction in terms of party image and, more decisive still, opposition to the Government of the day had lost the party much of the support which it might otherwise still have enjoyed. Seidl's arguments clearly carried greater weight. Although Weinhuber was in a good position to exploit the farmers' grievances over food imports which reduced prices and compulsory social insurance which raised costs, Seidl was able to remind the farmers of their relative prosperity, a state of affairs which might easily be jeopardized by a change of government. Foreign affairs and defence policy tended to be judged more in terms of resisting Communist expansion than in terms of securing German reunification. Seidl's emphasis upon a strong NATO as the only safe alternative to controlled disarmament, which the Russians refused to accept, made better sense than Weinhuber's opposition to compulsory military service and his reliance upon a small professional army, which was in any case to be denied the use of nuclear weapons. Weinhuber's contention that not armaments but education and the small farmers provide the best defence against Communism was flattering, but not apparently taken very seriously. Finally, Seidl was able to argue that a vote for the FU(BP) risked being to Bavaria's disadvantage since the final distribution of seats among the Länder had yet to be determined and in calculating Bavaria's quota all votes cast for the FU(BP) would be disregarded unless it won three constituency seats or 5 per cent. of the vote. To show that this was extremely unlikely Seidl told of how the FU(BP) had had great difficulty in finding candidates and speakers, of prominent BP supporters preferring to go on holiday rather than participate in a campaign as allies of the Socialists, and of how Baumgartner turned up to a meeting in Moosburg only to find no audience. One incident which occurred shortly before election day and received considerable publicity may also have had its effect. Baumgartner, campaigning in Altötting, was nettled by having his meetings constantly interrupted by members of the Catholic Young Farmers. Baumgartner retaliated by cutting off their share of money which all the Young Farmers' Organizations receive from the

Bavarian Government. This was sharply criticized in the *Münchener Merkur*. Seidl was not slow to point out that Baumgartner's criticism of Adenauer as a dictator could more properly be applied to Baumgartner himself.

The second reason why Weinhuber received so few votes compared with Seidl was the reluctance of SPD voters to give him their support. Only about 40 per cent. of those who voted for the SPD list gave Weinhuber their constituency vote. Of the rest, half abstained and the other half supported one of the other candidates.[1]

Where the distribution of list votes between parties is concerned the CSU's share of the poll rose from 44 to 54 per cent., that of the SPD from 21 to 25 per cent. The poll of the FU(BP), on the other hand, fell from 19 to 8 per cent., that of the BHE from 9 to 7 per cent., the Free Democrats' dropped from just above to just below 4 per cent., and all other parties put together polled 2 per cent.—as they had done in 1953.

But the distribution of party votes varied from one part of the constituency to another. The SPD was at its strongest in the towns and the Munich suburbs, polling around 30 per cent. in the three towns and over 40 per cent. in several of the suburbs. The CSU was strongest in the farming areas to the north and east, polling around 63 per cent. The FU(BP) managed to retain 16 per cent. in the farming areas around Erding—a measure of Weinhuber's local influence.

The effect of population movements on the distribution of the vote was also very evident. In the thirty farming villages where the voting population had declined the BHE's share of the vote was halved and the SPD's share of the vote also fell slightly, but where

[1] It is interesting to compare Munich-Land with the other three constituencies where the SPD agreed to support the FU(BP) candidate.

Constituency	*Excess of constituency votes over list votes expressed as a percentage of SPD votes*						
	Invalid	*FU(BP)*	*CSU*	*BHE*	*FDP*	*DP*	*DRP*
Munich-Land	29	42	11	9	8	2	1
Pfarrkirchen	30	41	12	13	5	3	..
Altötting	17	70	(−3)	14	2	2	1
Traunstein	17	68	(−9)	11	9	2	1

The reasons for this variation in the distribution of SPD votes is not entirely clear. The greater support in Altötting was probably due to (*a*) the CSU candidate's hostility to trade unions, (*b*) Baumgartner, who was himself the FU(BP) candidate, (*c*) the larger proportion of SPD voters who worked in factories and were, therefore, more accustomed to follow the recommendations of party leaders, (*d*) the hard work put in by the local SPD leaders.

the electorate had increased (in nearly every case a town, suburb, or village served by a railway line) the BHE maintained its share of the vote and the SPD was able to improve its position.

The election in Munich-Land thus left the CSU very much the dominant party. It had not only triumphed over the SPD but also crushed its closer rival, the BP. The electoral arrangement between the SPD and the FU(BP) had proved a disaster for the BP. The SPD could at least reflect that it had taken a few votes away from the CSU and helped to prevent the CDU/CSU from securing a two-thirds majority in the Federal Parliament. But the BP had failed to win any seats and worse was to follow, for the BP soon found itself out of office in Bavaria itself and was forced to accompany the SPD into opposition. The SPD lives to fight another day: it is doubtful whether the BP can entertain any such thought.

LOCAL STUDY C

COLOGNE

BY KLAUS SCHÜTZ

THE results in Cologne were awaited with particular interest. The city is the seat of Cardinal Frings, a prince of the Church extremely active in politics. Cologne had seen the beginnings of Konrad Adenauer's career: he had been the city's mayor from 1917 until 1933. Three-quarters of the city's population is Roman Catholic, and basing itself on the tradition of the Centre Party the CDU had until 1956 emerged as the strongest party in every election. It held all three city seats in both the first and the second Bundestag, polling 52 per cent. of votes in 1953. Nevertheless the Social Democrats entered the campaign with confidence: in the municipal elections of October 1956 they had scored a remarkable success, polling 46 per cent. as against the CDU's 42 per cent. The City Statistical Office called this 'a clear victory' unequalled even in 1919, and in a cautious commentary gave the SPD a chance of winning at least one of the seats.

The city is divided into three constituencies, Cologne I and II on the left and Cologne III on the right bank of the Rhine. No separate statistics of the social structure of the individual constituencies are available, but in the city as a whole 73 per cent. of inhabitants were Catholic, 21 per cent. Protestant; just 17 per cent. of the total population consisted of post-war immigrants, 10 per cent. being expellees from the territories east of the Oder–Neisse line. In 1950 over 40 per cent. of the inhabitants were workers, nearly 30 per cent. employees and civil servants, and nearly 20 per cent. were described as 'independent without employment'—largely no doubt pensioners of one kind or another.

The Candidates

The parties began their preparations early in the summer and the big parties had already put up their candidates before the summer holidays began. The Federalist Union, the Centre Party, the League of Germans, and the Union of the Middle Class (who would all have needed to collect signatures to put up constituency candidates) only competed for list votes: the nomination papers of two prospective FU candidates on the left bank were rejected since some of the signatures were too illegible to be checked in the electoral register.

The CDU candidate in Cologne I was Aenne Brauksiepe, a housewife aged forty-five. She did not live in Cologne, but had represented the constituency in the second Bundestag and the neighbouring constituency, Cologne II, in the first. Vice-chairman of the German Catholic Women's League and a member of the Federal Executive of the CDU, she took a particular interest in housing, had been a member of the relevant committees in past parliaments, and promised to do everything in her power to prevent Cologne 'losing its character as a result of soul-less dwelling-machines'.

In Cologne II the CDU put up the head of the Institute of German Industry, Dr. Fritz Hellwig. A native of the Saar, now aged forty-five, he had represented the constituency of Remscheid–Solingen in the second Bundestag. He had been chairman of the Bundestag Economic Committee, a member of the Federal Executive of the CDU, and was regarded as one of the economic experts of the party. He was the first Protestant to be put up as Bundestag candidate by the Cologne CDU. He succeeded the constituency member Dr. Hermann Pünder, who declared in letters to the press that he was standing down voluntarily on the grounds of his age.

On the right bank, in Cologne III, the CDU candidate was the federal manager of the Christian Democratic Employees' Association, Hans Katzer. He was thirty-eight years old, born in Cologne, and a member of the Public Services Trade Union. Since 1950 he had been a member of the City Council. He now stood for the Bundestag for the first time, thus taking over the constituency of another CDU trade unionist who had represented it since 1949 and gave no reason for not standing again.

For the city as a whole the CDU had thus obtained a well-balanced team: one woman and one representative each of employers and employees; two Catholics and one Protestant.

In Aenne Brauksiepe's constituency the Social Democrats put up a native of Cologne, Heinrich Hamacher. Aged fifty-eight, he was the party secretary in the Middle Rhine region, had sustained severe wounds in the first world war, and had spent many years after 1933 in prisons and concentration camps. He had been a city councillor since 1946. The SPD's 1953 candidate in the constituency had entered the second Bundestag via the Land list but did not stand again in 1957: this decision seems to have been demanded by the Trade Union Federation, of whose executive he had in the meantime become a member.

The SPD candidate in Cologne II was Hans-Jürgen Wischnewski, aged thirty-five, secretary of the Metal Workers' Union in Cologne. He was born in East Prussia, twice wounded in the war, had worked in the metal industry in South Germany, joined the trade union in Cologne in 1952, and was the chairman of the Cologne SPD.

The SPD's candidate in the third constituency was Heinz Kühn, a journalist born in the city forty-five years earlier, who had worked in the socialist youth organization before 1933. Forced to emigrate soon after Hitler's advent to power, he became editor-in-chief of the *Rheinische Zeitung* in Cologne after the war and was elected to the Landtag of North Rhine–Westphalia in 1948: there he was the party's whip until 1953, when he entered the Bundestag via the Land list. He was vice-chairman of the Press, Radio, and Film Committee of the Bundestag, and later served on the Foreign Affairs Committee. He was the only candidate of any party who was fighting his constituency for the third time.

Thus one of the SPD candidates was a journalist, the others trade union or party secretaries. Obviously the SPD was not guided by the sociological structure of the electorate in the choice of its candidates.

None of the other candidates could have any reasonable hope of election in a constituency, and they may thus be described more briefly. The nominal nature of their candidatures is borne out, for example, by the FDP's selection of the veteran chairman of the city party, a business consultant aged seventy, and the BHE's nomination of a corn-merchant aged seventy-two. The FDP's two other candidates were a lawyer and a woman expellee from Danzig who was a member of the Landtag; the BHE's other two candidates were the local secretary of a non-party society for the promotion of German reunification and a native of Posen (Poznan); the German Party put up its federal Secretary-General, a refugee, and a civil servant in the Federal Press Office, while the DRP nominated another refugee, another civil servant, and a thirty-year-old builder's labourer. Two of the FDP candidates were given places on the Land list, while the other smaller parties gave their constituency candidates in Cologne no such second nomination.

The Campaign

There are three main papers in Cologne. The *Kölner Stadt-Anzeiger* is the biggest, with a circulation of 131,000. It tried with some success to be neutral and to give information about the main meetings of all parties. The *Kölnische Rundschau* (90,000) and the *Neue Rhein-Zeitung* (30,000), on the other hand, made no bones about working for the CDU and for the SPD respectively. Both practically confined themselves to reporting meetings of their own party.

The Cologne campaign started with a vow from all parties to fight a fair campaign. The chairman of the Cologne SPD, Wischnewski, had suggested that the parties should meet and so the chairmen of the Cologne SPD, FDP, DP, and BHE signed a declaration that they would see to it that there was no personal or political defamation of character on posters, leaflets, or in speeches, and undertook to utter or admit no propaganda implying that one of the parties had a monopoly of national, Christian, or social conscience. The Christian Democrats refused to sign this agreement and issued a separate statement that their candidates would conduct the campaign fairly and objectively—but that while the CDU did not claim the monopoly of a national, Christian, or social conscience they felt obliged to stress that the CDU was the only party consciously subordinating its programme and its practical policy to Christian principles.

Candidates and speakers observed these undertakings fairly well and there were no serious incidents in the campaign. Only Kühn had to appear in court for one of his pointed remarks against the Federal Chancellor. Adenauer maintained that Kühn had told an audience that the Chancellor prayed for a CDU victory every evening, promising God a sacrifice of 15,000 soldiers—'we have already made a beginning at the Iller'. Kühn obtained a court injunction forbidding the Chancellor to repeat this report, but the injunction was lifted on 23 August, the court deciding that the Chancellor had 'not acted frivolously or in bad faith'. Occasionally posters were defaced or destroyed, but there were no serious incidents in the campaign. Meetings were orderly with the exception of a few FDP meetings at the outset of the campaign which were disturbed by DRP rowdies. There were hardly any hecklers and few opposition speakers in discussions.

The candidates did not meet during the campaign, and most of them did not even know each other. There were no joint discussions and no personal canvassing. For their election meetings the smaller parties had hired rooms in public houses. These were small—and yet rarely full. The bigger parties, too, complained of bad attendance at their neighbourhood meetings. But they were pleased with the good attendance at party rallies, saying that popular interest and attendance had never been so high.

As elsewhere, the street scene in Cologne was dominated by the

CDU's national posters. The CDU's loudspeaker and film vans appeared in fifty public squares in the city. 'Candidates talked to people at works gates', said the CDU's campaign organizer, 'and they talked to pre-political assemblies which had invited them, even in the laundry of a housing estate.' Apart from these 'pre-political' meetings—which in Cologne meant largely meetings of Catholic organizations—the CDU was the most active of Cologne parties with more than 120 meetings, forty-five of them for women. Katzer made some eighty speeches in Cologne. The other two candidates, being more prominent in the party, had to travel all over the Federal Republic and made only fifty and thirty respectively. Most meetings were addressed by party leaders as well as by candidates, but none of the speakers did more than produce variations on the main themes of the Christian Democratic campaign. Foreign policy was in the foreground: local problems were rarely mentioned.

On 2 September the Middle-Class Committee of the Cologne CDU called a meeting at which a first-rate team, including five members of the Bundestag and three candidates, appeared and spoke of their faith in a liberal economy, personal responsibility, and a social policy of the middle road. Seventeen speakers declared that the middle class had found its political home in the CDU. They appealed specifically to retail traders, artisans, house-owners, doctors, people engaged in trade, farmers, civil servants, and East Germans. The meeting, though somewhat exhausting, was thought a great success.

'The greatest political rally of the CDU since 1945', announced the loudspeaker van in front of the congress hall in the Trade Fair grounds on 7 September. Dr. Adenauer was to speak. The hall could hold 4,000; roughly 10,000 further attenders who had no tickets were accommodated in adjacent rooms or in tents. In the hall there was a brass band, a little loud for some tastes, but in keeping with the mood of expectancy and the Chancellor's later remark that electoral campaigns could not be conducted by academic discussions but needed simpler and harder weapons. The front rows were thronged with important people, guests of honour and clergy. The interior decoration was in good taste. There were flowers on the rostrum and federal, Land, and city crests and colours in the hall. There were no streamers, no posters, no badges, eagles or any of the other current electoral paraphernalia. Adenauer first greeted the visitors outside the hall. Inside he was received with loud applause. He spoke for two hours, occasionally letting himself go in Cologne dialect, and sharply attacked the Social Democrats and the FDP. A few quotations may illustrate the tenor of the speech:

> My heart is in Cologne and beats for Cologne. . . . [Loud and long applause.] Why do we consider a Christian party necessary? Firstly because . . . we are fanatical defenders of the freedom and dignity of the individual, secondly because we are accountable to God for all our political actions. . . . [Applause.] We, and many others, really owe our existence to the United States. . . . The United States are stronger than the Soviet Union and will remain so as long as the free world preserves its unity. . . . [Assent and applause.]

No dissenting voices were raised during the speech and the meeting ended with the whole audience rising to sing the national anthem.

The SPD opened its campaign with a large meeting on 26 June at which Erich Ollenhauer spoke. He described the home and foreign policy aims of his party and attacked the 'misuse of Christianity in the election campaign':

> One can think of every possible coalition without the CDU which would not endanger Christianity. The SPD has proved in its local and Land policy that it is ready and willing to render unto the churches what is their due, and not only to respect, but to protect the basic rights of the churches.

He called on the Adenauer Government to resign and was tempestuously applauded for his statement that the SPD's chief aim was the abolition of CDU/CSU hegemony in the Bundestag.

The Cologne SPD only used federal posters. They were not as numerous as those of the CDU, but there was a sufficient spread of them. There were a few unorthodox publicity ventures such as three pretty girls who were sent through the town carrying parasols with the slogans 'Vote for the SPD' and 'Youth votes SPD'. (Compare Plate IV*b*, which shows a similar stunt organized in Saarbrücken.)

One of the SPD candidates sent postcards to all householders in his constituency asking them to put their questions on them and to post them to him. Four hundred of these postcards were used and showed a multiplicity of problems: pension reform, housing, tax reform, European unity, older employees, the difficulties of owners of old houses, shop closing hours, capital punishment, the taxation of married couples, equal rights for women, rents, the civil service, support for the retail trade, conscription, and so on. In most cases the candidate himself called on those who had asked to see him, and wrote to the rest.

The SPD did more than other parties to advertise its meetings in the press. It also conducted meetings for special groups of the population such as women and the middle classes. Heinz Kühn held a joint meeting with a Protestant Professor of Theology on 'The atom bomb and Christian responsibility', and the Young Socialists of Cologne held a protest meeting against atomic armament.

Prominent SPD speakers, apart from Erich Ollenhauer, included the Minister-President of North Rhine–Westphalia, Fritz Steinhoff, and Carlo Schmid, who addressed an audience of a few thousand in the square in front of the town hall on 9 September. This meeting was the climax and, in a sense, the end of the SPD campaign in Cologne. Schmid put the alternatives facing the electorate as follows:

> The voter must now decide whether to endorse further rearmament, the continuation of a cold war policy, the atom bomb, and increased tension in the world. Whoever is against these dangers will have to give his vote to the SPD on 15th September even if he disagrees with that party in many other respects.

By contrast, the methods of the FDP's campaign showed more local initiative. The Cologne party supplemented the federal poster programme with a poster of their own which symbolized the FDP as a third force between the black and red party blocks. There were also match containers with the party insignia and the inscription: 'And they saw the light—and voted FDP' and cakes of soap bearing the slogan 'For cleanliness in politics—FDP.' A week before the poll the party sent a cavalcade of cars decorated with posters through the city, for the last fortnight a dinghy with the admonition to vote FDP cruised on the Rhine, and on the eve of the election three aircraft trailed party streamers across the sky. In the city centre the party erected a small tower representing the *Juliusturm*.[1] 'Away with the tax screw' and 'Down with the *Juliusturm*' were the slogans, and the party's eve-of-poll meeting was held beside this tower. The finance required for these stunts was raised locally.

The FDP held a number of small meetings, all of them badly attended, and six big ones at which attendance was regarded as very satisfactory. At one of these the doyenne of the Bundestag, Dr. Marie-Elisabeth Lüders, appealed to the women of Cologne to throw aside their political apathy, fulfil their civic duty, and make their numerical preponderance felt also in politics. Speaking before about a thousand people at another such meeting, Reinhold Maier declared, 'The train of state is about to enter a dark tunnel, and the Federal Chancellor's election train is its vanguard.'

The other parties attracted no attention either by their propaganda or by their meetings, and voluntary associations and the Churches do not seem to have played any very noticeable part in the campaign. The Catholic organizations put their meetings at the disposal of candidates and speakers of the CDU, and all parties tried to

[1] The *Juliusturm* in Berlin, in which the Prussian State had hoarded its war reserve of gold, had come to symbolize the surplus of tax and other receipts over expenditure hoarded by Fritz Schäffer as Federal Minister of Finance.

address a number of special meetings arranged by other organizations. The chairman of the Diocesan Committee of Catholic Organizations in Cologne wrote in the paper of the archdiocese that the Church did not identify itself with any party and was not infusing religion with party politics. It was rather the other way round: the parties could not help 'being subordinated and judged by God's order'. As particular criteria of voting decision he enumerated the salient points of the appeal of the Central Committee of German Catholics: 'Scrutinise works, not words!' He asked all Catholics to exercise the virtues of justice and prudence in the election. Thus a quiet campaign was followed by a quiet election.

The Results

At no election since 1919 had there been such a high turnout as 84 per cent.—an achievement for a city which earlier commentaries had described as electorally lazy. The CDU scored its greatest victory since its foundation, nearly doubling its vote since 1949 and winning an absolute majority even on the right bank of the river. Its voters had risen by 50,000 compared with 1953 and by 100,000 compared with the city elections of 1956.[1] The SPD had admittedly gained 16,000 votes since 1953, but it had lost 19,000 compared with the city elections, and as a result of the higher turnout its percentage of the poll dropped from 46 to 32 per cent.—an obvious defeat. The Free Democrats' vote had remained more or less constant, but its share of the poll was the lowest ever, and the other parties only accounted for 4 per cent. of votes between them.

There were more valid constituency than valid list votes, and this fact partly explains why all the CDU and SPD candidates received more votes than their respective parties. But in addition the voters of the Centre, the League of Germans, and the Union of the Middle Class had no candidate of their own to vote for, and a number of adherents of other smaller parties did not wish to waste their constituency vote on a hopeless candidature: they gave it to the candidate of a party not too far removed from their own—a choice of the lesser evil. Thus in the constituency where the CDU had put up its economic expert Hellwig, 23 per cent. of those who cast their list vote for the German Party did not vote for the German Party's candidate, while in the constituency where the CDU had nominated a trade unionist, the difference between the German Party's list and constituency votes was only 13 per cent. It is worth noting that the voters of some parties showed rather greater 'discipline' in this respect: the difference between the BHE's list and constituency votes amounted only to between 6 and 8 per cent., and in the case of the DRP to between less than 1 and 4 per cent. But then these minor parties—BHE, German Party, and DRP put together—only polled 3 per cent. of list votes.

TABLE XIII

Election Results in the City of Cologne

Election	Electors '000	Turnout %	Valid votes '000	CDU Votes '000	CDU %	SPD Votes '000	SPD %	FDP Votes '000	FDP %	Others Votes '000	Others %
Bundestag 1949	412	72	293	127	31	98	33	34	12	34	12
Bundestag 1953	477	80	372	194	52	121	33	32	9	22	6
Landtag 1954 .	*489*	*60*	*288*	*134*	*46*	*98*	*34*	*35*	*12*	*21*	*8*
Municipal 1956 .	*522*	*65*	*338*	*142*	*42*	*155*	*46*	*25*	*7*	*16*	*5*
Bundestag 1957	537	84	431	249	58	137	32	28	7	17	4

Although the election had gone clearly in favour of the CDU in each of the three constituencies, the three defeated SPD candidates also entered the Bundestag: all three were elected via the Land list. Nor were these six the only representatives of Cologne in its 'southern suburb' Bonn: though none of the FDP candidates were so fortunate, two further members of the Cologne SPD and six additional Cologne Christian Democrats were elected on the North Rhine–Westphalian Land list. Cologne can thus boast of the respectable contingent of fourteen members of the third Bundestag all closely associated with the city.

INDEX

PRINTED IN GREAT BRITAIN
AT THE UNIVERSITY PRESS, OXFORD
BY VIVIAN RIDLER
PRINTER TO THE UNIVERSITY